FASCISM
IN BRITAIN
A History, 1918–1985

For Hazel, Kevin and Sally

FASCISM
IN BRITAIN
A History, 1918–1985

Richard Thurlow

Basil Blackwell

Copyright © Richard Thurlow 1987

First published 1987

Basil Blackwell Ltd
108 Cowley Road, Oxford OX4 1JF, UK

Basil Blackwell Inc.
432 Park Avenue South, Suite 1503,
New York, NY 10016, USA

British Library Cataloguing in Publication Data
Thurlow, Richard
  Fascism in Britain: a history, 1918–1985
  1. Fascism—Great Britain—History
  I. Title
  320.5′33′0941   DA566.7
  ISBN 0-631-13618-5

Library of Congress Cataloging in Publication Data
Thurlow, Richard
  Fascism in Britain

  Bibliography: p.
  Includes index.
  1. Fascism—Great Britain—History. 2. Great Britain
—Politics and government—20th century. I. Title.
DA578.T48   1986   320.5′33′0941   86–17543

ISBN 0-631-13618-5

Typeset by Alan Sutton Publishing, Gloucester
Printed in Great Britain by Butler & Tanner Ltd, Frome and London

Contents

Illustrations

The publishers and author are grateful to the following for permission to reproduce photographs: Barnaby's Picture Library (2); BBC Hulton Picture Library (9, 14, 18, 19); Camera Press (23, 24); The Photo Source (6, 7, 10, 11, 12, 17); Popperfoto (1, 3, 4, 5, 8, 13, 15, 16, 20, 21, 22); Rex Features (25).

The plates appear between pages 142 and 143.

Acknowledgements

I would like to thank the following individuals for helping me at various stages of my research into British fascism: Caesar Aronsfeld, David Ashton, David Bland, Hilary Blume, Alan Booth, Neil Forsand, Gerry Gable, Richard Griffiths, Jeffrey Hamm, Kenny Lunn, Anthony Masters, Nicholas Mosley, Robert Row, Richard Russell, Robert Skidelsky, Robert Stanton, Gerry Webber and Nigel West. Special thanks are due to Dave Baker, Tony Kushner and Stuart Rawnsley for allowing me access to their completed research and some of their primary material. In addition, I would like to express my gratitude for Dave Baker's comments on the manuscript and Colin Holmes's sound advice, help and encouragement over many years.

I would also like to thank the Board of Deputies of British Jews, the British Museum, the Home Office, the Imperial War Museum, the London School of Economics Library, the National Council for Civil Liberties Archive, the National Maritime Museum, the Newspaper Library of the British Museum, the Public Record Office, *Searchlight*, the University of Sheffield Library and the Wiener Library for their assistance. I acknowledge gratefully the financial assistance received from the University of Sheffield Research Fund.

Grateful thanks too are due to the secretarial help given by Irene Thurlow, Connie Goodwin and Pam Smith, who valiantly struggled to decipher my near illegible handwriting. Last but not least I would like to thank my parents, wife and children for their support, encouragement, love and affection over the years.

Abbreviations

Introduction

This book was planned as an attempt to connect in a political tradition the history of inter-war British fascism with the emergence of racial populist and neo-fascist movements in post-1945 society. This has not been presented in any systematic or convincing manner before, although of course there have been a variety of works published on many aspects of inter-war and post-1945 developments, ranging from the excellent to little more than pro- or anti-fascist propaganda.

I have already published several articles on British fascist ideology covering the historical development of this theme from 1918 to the present day. Yet it quickly became apparent to me that to write the history of British fascism from the perspective of its ideology was in some ways misleading or false. Fascism was and is an action-orientated movement where the function of ideas is to explain behaviour more in terms of instinct than of rationality. Sorting out the various, often contradictory, strands in such thought and the emphasis placed on aspects of them by different groups would help to explain the variety of British fascism and the reasons for Mosley's revolt against the establishment; yet it would be of only relative importance in assessing the phenomenon. Other historical, sociological and political factors would have to be given a larger explanatory role.

The original intention of the book was, however, overtaken by events. During the course of its completion the Home Office released a significant proportion of its intelligence material on inter-war British fascism and other activities and organizations associated with it. This has been declassified in four separate batches and I have been informed that there are no specific plans to make more papers available. Indeed, it has been made abundantly clear that all the closed files will remain securely under lock and key until the twenty-first century unless there is a change of policy. Some new material may surface as resources permit the declassification of more general files but much of the most significant material has now been assessed. I have now analysed this material and looked at fresh sources to fill in missing links. Thanks to luck, the generosity of several researchers in the field who have allowed me access to their primary material, and the use of already published work, significant progress has been made towards shedding light on some of the unanswered questions about British fascism.

When I started writing this book, I had no idea that the use of intelligence material as a new source for contemporary historians was about to be proclaimed by Christopher Andrew. Although his magisterial *Secret Service* deals only briefly with some of the material covered in this volume, and he misses some of the most important aspects of the surveillance of fascist and related activities by the Security Service, *Fascism in Britain* can be seen and judged as a case study of the assessment of intelligence material and its use in conjunction with more orthodox sources. Indeed, this volume not only analyses declassified material from the Home Office and Cabinet Papers but also assesses some of the material from other intelligence sources on British fascism, most notably the Board of Deputies of British Jews, *Searchlight* magazine, and some FBI files.

Although much has been written about inter-war fascism, many aspects of it remain a mystery. Previous literature on the British Union of Fascists (BUF), by far the most significant organization, had neglected one of the most intriguing problems. Little of substance had been written on the decision to outlaw the British Union in 1940 and the reasons for the mass internment of many British fascists without trial for varying lengths of time after that date. The autobiographies of Sir Oswald and Lady Mosley, Robert Skidelsky's *Oswald Mosley*, and Nicholas Mosley's two volumes on his relationship with his father shed more darkness than light on this matter. I was convinced there had been a cover-up; 'Mosleygate' comprised of more than Mussolini's significant funding of the BUF in its early years and the negotiations with Hitler, via his wife, to establish a commercial radio station in

Germany which would give Mosley a virtual monopoly of such franchises, and whose profits were to be channelled into British fascism. These things have been written about before; I intended that this volume should highlight the events of 1939–40 and their significance. The material unearthed in the so-called Mosley Papers at the Public Record Office, the Cabinet Papers and other sources has enabled a proper evaluation of these events in chapters 8 and 9. New sources also suggest secretive contact between Mosley and the German nazi underground after 1945.

The new material at the PRO is at first reading rather disappointing. It comprises four separate batches. The first relates to Special Branch and Chief Constables' reports on the BUF between 1934 and 1939 and the evaluation of this material and agents' reports by MI5 officers. The second is mainly concerned with the internment of Sir Oswald and Lady Mosley. The third relates to material from other files on the BUF, to separate organizations such as the Nordic League (NL) and the Imperial Fascist League (IFL), jew-baiting, issues relating to public order posed by fascist and anti-fascist political violence, and the interrogation of Commandant Mary Allen. The fourth deals with the internment of members of the BUF and other organizations under DR 18b. The general impression gained from a superficial glance is that the Security Service was able to penetrate the IFL and NL to a much greater extent than was the case with the BUF. Indeed, it quickly became apparent that Mosley was so security-conscious that he appeared to be more concerned with limiting and controlling the information the authorities received about his activities than with running an efficient organization. However, the material did bring to light an important organization called the Nordic League, which had been curiously neglected in previous literature on fascism and anti-semitism in the inter-war years, despite the significant attention paid to it by both the Security Service and the Board of Deputies of British Jews in 1939.

Taken as a whole, it initially seemed that the Mosley Papers told us little that was new or could not be gleaned from other sources. There was valuable material on the attitude of the state and of the police to the fascists and anti-semitism, on the internal history and finance of the BUF, on the debate over public order in the middle 1930s and the attitude of the Advisory Commission on Internment, but little that was fresh on such key themes as political violence and anti-semitism. However, when this material was re-assessed in the light of other sources, the Mosley Papers were seen to be far more valuable than they first appeared.

Several key examples illustrate the importance of the Mosley Papers. Crucial intelligence reports about secret meetings of the fascist political fringe in 1939–40, whose implications contradicted all that has been released about such matters from sources close to the BUF, could be partly confirmed from the diary of Sir Barry Domvile which put the Security Service reports on such matters in an entirely different light; they could no longer be dismissed as a conspiracy or plot on the part of the authorities to frame Mosley. It may well be that such events were misinterpreted by MI5 in the light of the crisis of May 1940, but they could not be disregarded. Similarly, the Special Branch and the Board of Deputies agents' reports on Nordic League meetings and the antics of Maule Ramsay MP complemented neatly the impression gained by MI5 infiltration into the Right Club, which is already known from American sources. By juxtaposing parts of the Cabinet Papers, the Mosley Papers, the Domvile diaries and material about the Right Club, I discovered that a plausible account of the most secretive and sensitive aspects of fascist history in 1939–40 could be written for the first time.

This discovery led to further questions about the Mosley Papers: what they did and did not contain. The Home Office papers on fascism mainly comprise reports from Special Branch and MI5. In essence, the files reflect the information released to the Home Office by MI5. The actual files of MI5 are never made public and, to judge from information made available to Mosley's internment hearing, there was much significant material in MI5 files on the BUF which was not available in the Home Office papers. These have also been 'weeded' of all classified material.

A less deliberate screening is provided by the mere process of survival. Given the vast quantities of paper generated in the state bureaucracy, it is not surprising that a significant proportion of it has been lost. What survives is to be found in the General or Subject files, and the Personal files of the Home Office; and this material can be released after a thirty-year period under the amended terms of the Public Records Act. However, as there is no Freedom of Information Act, such material is released upon the discretion of government departments and the resources they have at their disposal. With regard to the release of papers on British fascism, pressure from a most unlikely alliance of Lady Mosley and left-wing Labour MPs has been responsible for the release of the Mosley internment files.

The fact that the Public Records Act has prevented the release of sub-files within the material that has been made available has further complicated the problem. This relates to material which infringes national security, which discloses the names and operations of agents, or would cause embarrassment or worse to individuals or their descendants. In essence it allows the authorities plenty of excuse to prevent the release of significant material if they see fit. Where Mosley and the BUF are concerned, the most significant retained material appears to relate to the somewhat dubious methods MI5 used to obtain information about the BUF and possibly material compromised by Anthony Blunt when he was Guy Liddell's assistant at MI5 in 1940.

But there are more serious omissions occasioned by the Public Records Act than just sub-files within series. Although the Home Office is extremely helpful, given limited resources and the restrictions of the Public Records Act, it imparts as little information as possible about what has been retained. Nevertheless, it is known that with regard to British fascism and associated activities the most significant material not yet released or assessed are those files pertaining to the Right Club, the Link, the Tyler Kent affair, and most of the administrative files relating to internment and DR18b and Mosley's activities between 1945 and 1955. Among personal files, the most significant to be withheld include Archibald Maule Ramsay MP, Sir Barry Domvile, Bertie Mills, Alexander Raven Thomson, Anna Wolkoff and Arnold Leese. Nothing has been released on the wartime activities of important fascist renegades like William Joyce and Theodore Schurch. American sources and the revelations of Joan Miller, an ex-MI5 agent, have told us much about the Right Club, the Tyler Kent affair and Maule Ramsay, and the material in the Home Office and Cabinet Papers and the Domvile diary show how they were linked to British fascism. What is still in doubt, however, is the significance of the Link. There have been few leaks about what was discovered about this organization, although it is known that it was viewed as an important vehicle for German propaganda in Britain by Goebbels, and that the Security Service was very interested in the activities of its Central London branch. (The branch was chaired by H.T. (Bertie) Mills, who was connected with most of the fascist organizations in 1939–40.) But the fact that so much material has been retained, and under present policy it will never be released, makes it necessary to ask why these files are so sensitive. This question will be tackled in chapter 9.

Since the Second World War intelligence material on British fascism has been obtained from *Searchlight* magazine and the Board of Deputies of British Jews. *Searchlight* in particular has become a significant intelligence agency, using highly reliable moles to infiltrate the various fascist organizations, and has been the willing recipient of information emanating from factional in-fighting within different groups. It is also associated with various anti-fascist and anti-racist groups and has combated both racism and fascism on a broad front. Its agents, particularly Ray Hill, have been responsible for significant damage to such groups and *Searchlight* has played a key role in the decline of the National Front and even more extreme neo-fascist organizations.

Other sources apart from intelligence operations have been relied on for information. Both fascist and anti-fascist viewpoints provide useful perspectives in assessing the cause and nature of conflict and political violence. However, it should be stressed that although fascist, anti-fascist, MI5 and other intelligence operations views have to be borne in mind, I have used my own judgement in interpreting the information at my disposal. I am critical of the sophisticated cover-up of several BUF activities, MI5's interpretation of the BUF and fascist activity during the Second World War, and several aspects of *Searchlight's* analysis of the contemporary neo-fascist fringe, for example, even while understanding the reasons for each of these. I am more in sympathy with the interpretation of fascist activities by the Security Service between 1934 and 1939 – and can accept at face value the genuine political idealism, even if it was naive, of some who supported Mosley in the 1930s. Most fascists were also patriotic Englishmen, although there were some who would have been potential collaborators had there been a nazi invasion in 1940.

The operational definition of fascism adopted by this book is relatively straightforward. It deals with those movements which in terms of members and activity were significant in the inter-war period and which advertised their allegiance to the creed by calling themselves fascist. This means the British Fascists, the Imperial Fascist League and, of course by far the most significant, the British Union of Fascists. However, I have also examined other groups which were partly fascist or were immediate precursors of elements in the tradition. This includes the Britons and the Nordic League. Aspects of other movements which were not specifically fascist have been assessed because they were involved in crucial episodes of the story, most notably the Right Club, the Link and the British People's Party in 1939–40.

After 1945 the definition of 'fascist' became less obvious. Whereas in the 1930s British fascism was generally perceived as an eccentric pursuit best ignored, the events of 1939–45 turned it into a political pariah. Almost universally detested, those who wished to appeal to the tradition had to do so in revisionist guise. Only Arnold Leese's racial nationalism appeared to be intransigent and even he no longer called himself a fascist. Survivors of the tradition like Mosley and Chesterton started new movements apparently more in tune with political reality than inter-war fascism, and these represented a synthesis of some of their pre-war beliefs and their different perceptions of the changed geo-political realities of the post-war world. Both Mosley's Union Movement and Chesterton's League of Empire Loyalists can be seen partly as different revisionist forms of the fascist movement. In terms of their connections to the tradition, the former led nowhere, while the latter became one of the foundation stones of the National Front.

Second- and third-generation British fascists were to appeal to various aspects of the fascist tradition, usually hidden behind a coded smokescreen which used the more respectable language of a conservative fascism or conspiracy theory to hide extremist sentiments. The abysmal failure of the National Socialist Movement, which tried to resurrect the Leese racial nationalist tradition in pure form with all the paraphernalia of Hitler worship and a jackboot mentality, gave way to a barely disguised form of nazi propaganda in *Spearhead* in the National Front. Although not all elements in the coalition which was the Front were nazi – in fact some elements openly opposed the fascist mentality – racial populism and anti-New Commonwealth immigrant policies papered over the cracks between reactionary conservatives and die-hard nazis. This façade broke down periodically in bitter leadership struggles. Meanwhile, some hard-line nazis went underground and were implicated in racial attacks and sporadic violence.

If the definition of British fascism can be seen mainly in terms of the historical development of the phenomenon then its theoretical content and political appeal also need some consideration. The doctrine of fascism implies charismatic leadership or dictatorship, the role of an elite in transforming society, a belief in dynamic political action, the nationalist orientation of the state, a corporate structure of government and industry, and hostility to internationalist doctrines and forces like communism and liberalism. Nazism was a radical form of fascism which imposed upon the basic assumptions of fascism, nordic racism, anti-semitism, imperialist doctrines of *Lebensraum* and a social Darwinian philosophy. Fascists looked more to Italy while nazis revered national socialist Germany as their mentor.

In Britain the Mosley form of fascism was closest to Mussolini's Italy in its inspiration. Leese's racial nationalism was the British equivalent of nazism in its philosophy, even if Leese himself was no Hitler and was quite critical of him during the war. However, both forms were too closely modelled on their foreign inspiration and, although perfectly genuine, the British traditions to which they appealed provoked little cultural response. Only when linked to the issue of anti-immigrant racial populism did British fascism make any headway, and even then its impact was Janus-faced. Suspicion of fascist influence eventually led to significant defections and the severe weakening of the impact of the National Front in the late 1970s.

1

The Twilight of the Gods, 1890–1914

Bitish fascism, like its European counterparts, had its roots deep in the social tensions and ideas fostered by an age of modernization and change. Its emergence was, however, mainly based on native political tradition and a belief that a new type of man with fresh ideas was needed to break the mould of politics, so that Britain could meet the problems of the twentieth century. Some fascists found their utopia in idealized versions of various parts of British history; others looked to the future, expecting fascist struggle and power to create this new man with new values who would revolutionize British society. British fascism was to be a strange blend of these pre-existent modernizing and anti-modernizing elements.

Some theorists in the British Union of Fascists (BUF) saw the origins of British fascism in an idealized view of Tudor government and the reign of Elizabeth I, but its roots are actually to be found in reactions to the political, economic and social problems of late Victorian and Edwardian Britain, and to the disillusion created by the First World War.[1] Together these influences were sufficient to create the various peculiar amalgamations of ideas and personnel from right across – and in some cases from outside – the conventional political spectrum, which were to be the

[1] A.L. Glasfurd, 'Fascism and the English tradition', *Fascist Quarterly*, 1, 3 (July 1935), p. 363; J. Drennan (W.E.D. Allen), *BUF, Oswald Mosley and British Fascism* (London, 1934), p. 30; B.L. Farr, 'The development and impact of right wing politics in Great Britain, 1903–32', PhD thesis, University of Illinois, 1976, pp. xi, 305.

hallmarks of British fascism. The failure of the political elite adequately to manipulate and incorporate emerging populist mass forces in this period also proved crucial to the activism and conflict associated with British fascism. This chapter examines these developments in the period before 1914.

The radical right

In general, Britain has not been thought to conform to any European pattern of economic, political or social crisis in this period, despite recent work which has suggested that this picture needs modifying.[2] Many historians still view the Edwardian era as a period of relative social stability, if not a 'golden age'.[3] Yet just beneath the surface of Edwardian society the differences between groups and classes in the nation widened as the century progressed, the growth of single-issue pressure groups only partly under the control of the political establishment increased, and the principles of liberalism as providing the basic consensus values of politics were increasingly challenged. The growth of populist radicalism, particularly in the 1911–14 period, with the development of labour unrest, syndicalism, the suffragette movement and the Ulster Volunteer Force, certainly gives more than a semblance of credibility to the gloomy analysis of George Dangerfield's classic interpretation of the period, *The Strange Death of Liberal England*.[4]

Recent work has suggested that there was a European revolt of the right in the early twentieth century representing a rebellion of traditionalist forces who were determined to preserve their status and position in society despite a modernization process that was making them economically redundant.[5] The crisis was spearheaded and orchestrated by agrarian elites and supported by

[2] G. Searle, 'The revolt from the right in Edwardian Britain', in *Nationalist and Racialist Movements in Britain before 1914*, ed. P. Kennedy and A. Nicholls (Oxford, 1981), p. 21.

[3] D. Reed, 'Introduction. Crisis age or golden age?', in *Edwardian England*, ed. D. Reed, (London, 1982), pp. 14–39. See also *The Edwardian Age. Conflict and Stability*, ed. A. O'Day, (London, 1979).

[4] G. Dangerfield, *The Strange Death of Liberal England* (London, 1935).

[5] A.J. Mayer, 'Internal Crisis and War since 1870', in *Revolutionary Situations in Europe 1917–22*, ed. C.L. Bertrand (Montreal, 1977), pp. 206–11; F.L. Carsten, *The Rise of Fascism* (London, 1970), p. 10.

middle-class, *petit bourgeois* and peasant strata who felt threatened by that process. However, the emergence of radical right in British politics in the Edwardian era only partially confirms this thesis.[6] Its most important elements were the so-called 'Die-hards', the Unionist peers who defied the party whip by voting against the Parliament Act in the House of Lords in 1911; and the Round Table group organized around the Imperial ideas and national efficiency programme of Milner and his collaborators. The political views of these two groups were broadly supported by Leo Maxse's *National Review* and the *Eye Witness* (later the *New Witness*) of Hilaire Belloc, G.K. and Cecil Chesterton.[7] There were also several left-wing supporters of the Campaign for National Efficiency and a programme of imperialism and social reform, including Robert Blatchford and the *Clarion* newspaper with its emphasis on national socialism, and elitist Fabians such as the Webbs, George Bernard Shaw and H.G. Wells.[8]

Yet despite the similarity of ideas, this group never really represented a coherent alternative to the dominant liberal ethos of the age. The Die-hard peers were suspicious of Milner's conspiratorial methods and his attempts to encourage the formation of a governmental and administrative meritocracy, and of his interest in Lloyd George's proposal of a coalition government at the constitutional conference in 1910. The Chestertons' *Eye Witness* with its distributionist arguments was fundamentally opposed to the landed interest which so many of the Die-hard peers personified. Indeed, in 1911, Belloc and Cecil Chesterton wrote *The Party System*, whose basic argument was that British politics had been corrupted by the social and institutional ties between the two front benches in the House of Commons.[9] They were thus opposed to any coalition of separate parts of the existing political establishment.

If the emerging radical right was split over tactics in the Edwardian era, it also lacked unified leadership and direction. The stroke which incapacitated Joseph Chamberlain in 1906, and the

[6] Searle, 'Revolt from the right', p. 21f.

[7] Idem, 'Critics of Edwardian society: the case of the radical right', in O'Day, *The Edwardian Age*, pp. 79–96.

[8] G. Searle, *The Quest for National Efficiency* (Oxford, 1971), and B. Semmel, *Imperialism and Social Reform* (London, 1960), pp. 53–82, 216–33.

[9] K. Lunn, 'The Marconi scandal and related aspects of British anti-semitism, 1911–14', PhD thesis, University of Sheffield, 1978, p. 79.

temperamental disinclination of Milner to soil his hands in party political arguments, seriously weakened its position. It was therefore relatively easy for Lloyd George to deride the opposition in the House of Lords to the 1909 budget and the 1911 Parliament Act as emanating from 'backwoodsmen'. In fact the Die-hard opposition in the Lords was at least in part one of political principle deriving from the belief that the Liberal government was undermining the national interest.[10] The Die-hards were not simply a declining agrarian elite reacting against modernity. In fact, most of the landed aristocracy had successfully diversified their agricultural interests out of the sorely pressed cereal sector, and had also invested profitably in developing new industrial projects. Similarly, Die-hard peers had lost neither status nor influence in local politics with the decline of the role of Justices of the Peace and the rise of elected local government after 1888.[11] The Die-hards did also include political reactionaries such as the Halsbury circle, but in general their arguments were rationally expressed in terms of reasoned opposition to what they saw as the aims and objectives of political liberalism.

The beliefs of the Die-hards and most of the Edwardian radical right were based upon a particular interpretation of the national interest. Broadly speaking, most of them supported tariff reform, compulsory military service, an expansion of the army and navy, the development of social welfare, the introduction of the political referendum, an end to 'alien' immigration and armed resistance to Home Rule in Ireland. Many had ambiguous attitudes towards Germany. As nationalists, they were fearful of Germany's rapidly developing military and industrial power and the challenge this posed the British Empire; yet they admired many aspects of Wilhelmine Germany, particularly its administrative efficiency, social welfare programme and the leading role of the state in national development. Most of the Edwardian radical right demanded a similar modernization of British society and called for the state to play a more active role in national life. For these reasons most of them had supported the Campaign for National Efficiency since 1902.[12] However, for the Die-hards in particular

[10] G.D. Phillips, 'The Diehards and the myth of the backwoodsmen', *Journal of British Studies*, 16 (Spring 1977), pp. 105–20.

[11] Idem, *The Diehards* (London, 1979), p. 56 and p. 81.

[12] Searle, *The Quest for National Efficiency*.

this radicalism was also based on a belief in the need to preserve aristocratic dominance and to strengthen British imperial power. Their opposition was not only to the actions of the Liberal government after 1906, but also to the leadership of the Unionist party, which in the view of most Die-hards had either colluded with, or failed adequately to oppose, the new liberalism which threatened the traditional social basis of British society.[13]

The Die-hards' revolt against the cosy traditions of high politics shared some of the same assumptions as the later Mosley fascism.[14] However, the influence survived in a more direct form in the patriotic press and the links they had with the British Fascists (BF) in the 1920s. In particular, the eighth Duke of Northumberland took up the Die-hard beliefs of his father and extended the tradition in journalistic form long after the First World War with the publication of a newspaper, *The Patriot*, from 1922 to 1950. Nesta Webster, a leading figure for a time in the BF, contributed several series of articles upholding the principles of 'true conservatism' as emanating from aristocratic paternalism.[15] Sir Oswald Mosley similarly saw the social origins of his beliefs in his roots in the landed gentry.[16] Continuity between Edwardian values and inter-war fascism can also be found in the person of A.K. Chesterton, second cousin of G.K. Chesterton, who was a leading member of the BUF, although family connection was of relatively minor importance in the complex origins of his fascist beliefs.[17]

However, many of the national issues around which the Edwardian radical right mounted their forlorn challenge were to provide of equal significance with personal connections. Although the BUF were to show opposition to the remaining privileges of landed society in the anti-tithe campaign in the 1930s, and Mosley had a much more favourable view of Irish nationalism and Germany than had the Edwardian radical right, there was a distinct and discernible continuity of ideas in their interpretation

---

[13] Phillips, *The Diehards*, p. 158.

[14] J.R. Jones, 'England', in *The European Right*, ed. H. Rogger and E. Weber (London, 1965), pp. 29–70.

[15] *The Patriot*, 9 Feb. 1922.

[16] O. Mosley, *My Life* (London, 1968), and R. Skidelsky, *Oswald Mosley* (1975), pp. 23–44.

[17] D. Baker, 'A.K. Chesterton. The making of a British fascist', PhD thesis, University of Sheffield, 1982, pp. 268–77, 331–4.

of the national interest, how it should be maintained, and some of the assumptions on which the concept was based. Many fascists also linked the threat of Carson and the Ulster Volunteer Force in 1914 to revolt against Home Rule in Ireland with the spirit of the BUF challenge to the National Government in the 1930s.[18]

Yet neither the rebel peers in the House of Lords nor the permeation strategy of the Milner circle managed to break out of the charmed circle of high politics. The galvanizing and educating of the masses became the function of the political leagues and pressure groups, given the fissures within the party and the lack of leadership shown by Balfour and the Unionists before 1911.[19] It was, therefore, the general Edwardian crisis of British Conservatism which gave birth to the modern radical right in British political history. The BUF were later to attempt the fusion of part of the anti-liberalism of the Edwardian radical right with the educational strategy of the political leagues and the oratorical tradition of mass politics as developed by Gladstone and Chamberlain, among other elements. British fascist political style and content was to owe much to these native traditions and consequently appeared somewhat old-fashioned by the inter-war period.

The political leagues of Edwardian England were mainly radical right pressure groups designed to encourage the electorate and the masses to agitate for the interest that they represented. Of particular significance for the later development of fascism was the Tariff Reform League formed in 1903 by Joseph Chamberlain. This struck at the heart of economic liberalism, attacking one of the basic consensus values of Victorian politics, free trade. It operated both in the sphere of high politics, where its influence dominated Unionist party strategy between 1905 and 1910, and in wider terms by trying to break the allegiance of the electorate and the masses from free trade through a campaign of political education.[20] Its twin policies of protection for British industry, and the establishment of Imperial Preference, were to be precursors of Mosley's plans for an autarchic British Empire and

[18] Drennan, BUF, Mosley and British Fascism, pp. 290–1; R. Benewick, The Fascist Movement in Britain (London, 1972), p. 24; Farr, 'Right wing politics', p. 113.

[19] R.A. Rempel, Unionists Divided (Newton Abbott, 1972).

[20] A. Summers, 'The character of Edwardian nationalism: three popular leagues', in Kennedy and Nicholls, Nationalist and Racialist Movements in Britain, pp. 70–87; A. Sykes, Tariff Reform in British Politics 1903–13 (Oxford, 1979).

also survived in slightly altered form as the basic nationalist platform of the National Front in the 1960s and 1970s.

Indeed, the activities and personality of Joseph Chamberlain were to influence British fascism in a number of ways. It is no accident that Mosley's base in the 1920s, Birmingham, was the political stronghold of Chamberlain and his family. Chamberlain, like Mosley, was arrogant and contemptuous of the lesser intellectual skills of his political colleagues. Both failed to play the rules of the parliamentary game and put principle above loyalty to party. Chamberlain split the Liberals in 1886 over Home Rule in Ireland, thus sending them into the political wilderness for much of the next twenty years. His turn to Protectionism in 1903 and the resulting divisions it created among the Unionists seriously weakened them before the First World War, and the issue was to lose Baldwin the election in 1923.[21] Chamberlain, like Mosley, was not averse to allowing mass populism to degenerate into street conflict and violence, as Lloyd George discovered when he was forced to dress up as a policeman to avoid being lynched in a riot in Birmingham in 1901.[22] Some of his other ideas were also to find an echo in British fascist politics. For instance, his proposal in 1899 of an Anglo-Saxon alliance of Britain, Germany and the United States based on race, has been resurrected by John Tyndall in the New National Front in the 1980s.[23]

Other leagues dominated by the radical right were designed to promote various sections of Britain's national defences. The Navy League and its rival, the National Maritime League, both successfully promoted the necessity to maintain Britain's lead in the new naval deterrent, the Dreadnought battleship, and the National Service League under Lord Roberts agitated for army reform and introduction of conscription.[24] The emphasis of the Edwardian radical right was to preserve Britain's defences to enable her to resist rival imperialist aggression without the need for compromising alliances. Splendid isolation was preferable to the Entente Cordiale. Feeling threatened by the rise of Germany

[21] J. Amery, *Joseph Chamberlain and the Tariff Reform Campaign* (London, 1969).

[22] R. Rhodes James, *The British Revolution*, vol. I, 1880–1914 (London, 1976), p. 205.

[23] W. Mock, 'The function of race, in Imperialist Ideology. The example of Joseph Chamberlain', in Kennedy and Nicholls, *Nationalist and Racialist Movements in Britain*, p. 193. John Tyndall, 'Tyndall speaks. Our Anglo-Saxon heritage' (Cape, New National Front, 1981).

[24] Summers, 'Edwardian nationalism', pp. 70–87.

and the gradual deterioration in relations between the two countries, the radical right thought the best solution was to have powerful and numerous defences – the line developed by Mosley in the 1930s. However, far from seeing Germany as the potential enemy by 1933, Mosley saw her foreign policy as not being directed against British interests, and this represented a marked shift in emphasis away from the arguments of earlier British patriotic and fascist movements in the 1920s, who still saw 'the Huns' as one of the chief threats to the Empire's security.

The liberal consensus and Britain's decline

The most basic shared assumption among the Edwardian radical right was that the existing political system had been unable to check the sharp decline in British power in the late Victorian and Edwardian eras. (British fascists were later to argue that this process had become intensified by the effects of the First World War). This concern took a number of forms. In the economic sphere, Britain's position as the leading industrial nation had clearly been superseded by the United States and Germany by 1914. In 1870 Britain had 31.8 per cent share of world manu-facturing production compared with the United States 23.3 per cent and Germany's 13.2 per cent, but by 1913 the USA had 35.8 per cent, Germany 15 per cent and the United Kingdom 14 per cent. Britain's share in the output of pig iron and steel had dropped even more calamitously from 46 per cent to 13.9 per cent and from 35.9 per cent to 10.3 per cent of world production in the same period.[25] Perhaps of even greater significance was that the British economy had been slow to develop the new chemical and electrical products of a second industrial revolution, and since 1870 her economic growth had been relatively sluggish compared with both the mid-Victorian period and her rapidly developing rivals.[26] In the words of one historian, British industry in 1914 was like 'a working museum of industrial archaeology'.[27]

---

[25] P. Cain, 'Political economy in Edwardian England: the tariff reform controversy', in O'Day, *The Edwardian Age*, pp. 36–7.
[26] P. Kennedy, *The Rise of the Anglo-German Antagonism* (London, 1980), pp. 291–305.
[27] C. Barnett, *The Collapse of British Power* (London, 1972), p. 88.

Although the relevant statistics were not available to contemporaries, popular opinion was inflamed by such journalistic propaganda as E.E. Williams's *Made in Germany*, published in 1896.

Britain's economic base was thought to be especially significant by the radical right, for on it depended the resources that could be spent on national defence. The issue became of paramount importance to many when it was shown that the leadership of the armed forces, the quality of its recruits and indeed the human capital of the nation as a whole was also defective – points highlighted by the Boer War. The fact that it took five times the number of British troops, armed with the most modern equipment, to subdue the Boer farmers showed the rest of the world that Britain was no longer a significant factor in power politics. Just as worrying was the fact that only one in three who volunteered for the armed forces was fit enough to be sent to South Africa, thus confirming the empirical surveys of Booth and Rowntree on the extent and effect of poverty in urban areas.[28] The Edwardian radical right came to argue that the reforms of the Conservative government from 1902–5, and of the Liberal government after 1906, either did not go far enough, or were financed in such a way as to be detrimental to the national interest.

In particular, the radical right was concerned that Britain was no longer the world's foremost power and had lost her pre-eminence in Europe to Germany.[29] Although in general they supported the reforms in the army, the establishment of the Committee of Imperial Defence in 1904, and the Selborne-Fisher naval programme beginning in 1902, they wished them to be extended to include universal male conscription and the building of yet more battleships. The radical right had dreaded the possibility that the reforms would be put into reverse after the comprehensive victory of the Liberals in the general election of 1906. The growth of Germanophobia on the radical right was orchestrated by *The Times* and a plethora of literary outpourings of the genre of George Chesney's *Battle of Dorking* (1871), prophesying a German invasion.[30] From such propaganda a

[28] Searle, *The Quest for National Efficiency*, p. 34; J.R. Hay, *The Origins of the Liberal Welfare Reforms 1906–14* (London, 1975), p. 31.
[29] Kennedy, *Rise of Anglo-German Antagonism*, pp. 306–20.
[30] I.F. Clarke, 'The Battle of Dorking 1871–1914', *Victorian Studies*, 8 (1965), pp. 309–27.

veritable spy mania developed, aimed chiefly at wealthy German Jews. Indeed, it was the campaigns of the radical right and the Unionist party in Parliament which persuaded the Liberals to increase the Dreadnought building programme, thus precipitating a major fiscal and constitutional crisis between 1909–11.

The radical right saw their chief enemy as the all-pervading liberal consensus which underpinned the values of high politics in Victorian and Edwardian Britain, and tainted the Unionists almost as much as the Liberal party. They were opposed to many aspects of its influence, excepting the moral attributes of justice and good government. For them, it was the political programme which stemmed from most of its assumptions, rather than any objective economic factors, that had led to Britain's weakness and decline. The feeble policies of government dominated by the woolly, moralistic and humanitarian assumptions of liberalism thus accounted for the collapse of British power.[31] Gladstonian moralism and Cobdenite internationalism between them were blamed in great part for the crisis of empire which the radical right perceived. The British Empire had been created, they argued, by men who had courageously planted the flag in all the corners of the globe. These men showed initiative, resource and qualities of leadership. They had been betrayed by the flaccid, small-minded and puritanical elements in government who were more concerned with playing the party game and maintaining their own privilege than with ensuring the future security of the Empire.[32] Of contemporary politicians only Joseph Chamberlain was credited with the necessary will, resolve and vision to pursue an active policy which would strengthen national power, and he was physically incapacitated after 1906.

Specific objections to liberalism as a doctrine raised by the radical right were centred on two aspects in particular: economic and foreign policy. In the economic sphere, the doctrine of *laissez-faire* and the sanctity of the market place had led to Britain becoming the victim of unfair foreign competition. Free trade in a world of rival capitalist economies had forced Britain to become the dumping ground for the excess production of these rivals hiding behind protected markets. Just as serious in the view of the

---

[31] Kennedy, *Rise of Anglo-German Antagonism*, pp. 306–21.
[32] Barnett, *Collapse of British Power*, p. 59.

radical right, the liberal state had only a night-watchman role to play in the activities of the economy. Positive direction and greater state involvement in guiding the economy would merely lead to a misallocation of resources according to liberal economics. The Edwardian radical right demanded that the government pursue a national policy based on the realities of state power, as in Bismarckian and Wilhelmine Germany, rather than relying upon the theoretical dogma of classical liberalism.[33] Similarly in foreign policy it was the *realpolitik* of Bismarck and not the vapid moralizing of the Gladstonian Nonconformist conscience which should determine policy. This meant that strategy had to be determined by a new conservatism, based on Social imperialism and a Social Darwinian view of the world, where survival of the fittest was determined by the military and economic power of the state, not by liberal good intentions. Peace was to be attained by economic and military strength, not by the weakness inherent in liberal internationalist doctrine, whose free trade and *laissez-faire* dogma meant cuts in government and military expenditure.

In the real world, however, the options open to the British government in the Edwardian era were rather different. The greatest weakness in the radical right view of British society was that the possibility of a national consensus of values and attitudes was a utopian delusion, given the fundamental divisions over policy between the Liberal and Conservative parties, and the lack of unity within both organizations.[34] Similarly, its caricature view of the nature of liberalism and the Liberal government bore little relation to reality, for liberalism was never a unified ideology. The Liberal party in Edwardian England represented an alliance of disparate and often contradictory interests of old Whigs, Gladstonians, Cobdenites, Liberal imperialists, Nonconformists, land reformers and new liberals amongst other elements.[35] Of particular importance was the increasingly pronounced influence of ideas stemming from T.H. Green, stressing the need for the state to provide assistance for those who were unable to benefit from the market mechanism. In his welfare policies of 1906–15, Lloyd

[33] Kennedy, *Rise of Anglo-German Antagonism*, pp. 308–15.
[34] Rempel, *Unionists Divided*; K.O. Morgan, *The Age of Lloyd George* (London, 1971), pp. 17–37; K.W.W. Aikin, *The Last Years of Liberal England, 1900–1914* (London, 1972), pp. 9–31.
[35] Kennedy, *Rise of Anglo-German Antagonism*, p. 332.

George was to blend the traditional assumptions of the old liberalism with the positive social programme of the new liberalism.[36] This included the establishment of old age pensions and the tentative introduction of a degree of health and unemployment insurance. Yet, like the radical right, his actions were deeply influenced by the social welfare programme of the German government.

Nor was it reasonable to accuse the Liberal government of neglecting the national defences. Although expenditure on the armed services was reduced from £66 million in 1905–6, to £59.2 million two years later, it then consistently rose sharply to reach £77 million on the eve of war. In that great totem of Edwardian national virility, the number of Dreadnoughts possessed by Britian and Germany respectively, the British were comfortably ahead in 1912 by fifteen to nine.[37] The real complaint the radical right had against political liberalism was how such expenditure was to be financed, given that it was not prepared to sacrifice its social welfare programme. The Lloyd George budget of 1909 was designed to finance the payment of old age pensions for those over seventy, as well as the Dreadnought programme. The proposed land tax and increases in direct personal taxation of the wealthy, by however modest an amount, was wrongly seen as a revolutionary attempt to attack the social basis of power in British society.[38] Here all elements of the political right united in the belief that the financing of such necessary expenditure should be met by import duties and the revenue raised from tariff protection. Yet even here Chamberlain's and the radical right's views were misguided, for many of the newly emerging white dominions were extremely suspicious of the concept of Imperial Preference, and in particular were concerned about the effect it would have on their manufacturing industries, which they were anxious to protect.[39]

Viewed in total, the Edwardian radical right's chief contribution to British fascism was to bequeath many of the assumptions and the nationalist politics in which it was rooted. However, Mosley

[36] Morgan, Age of Lloyd George, pp. 38–57; S. Collini, Liberalism and Sociology. L.T. Hobhouse and political argument in England 1880–1914 (Cambridge, 1979); M. Freeden, The New Liberalism: an ideology of social reform (Oxford, 1978).

[37] M. Howard, 'The Edwardian arms race', in Reed, Edwardian England, pp. 146, 156–7.

[38] B. Murray, The People's Budget (Oxford, 1978).

[39] Cain, 'Tariff reform', pp. 40–1; Farr, 'Right wing politics', p. 12.

was far more ready to break completely with the parliamentary system than was any section of the Edwardian radical right. Even Milner, although he hated party politics, saw the permeation of government as the only practical solution to implementing national policies. Mosley's fascism was based in part on similar nationalist assumptions to those of the Edwardian radical right, which were unrealistic and utopian in the pre-1914 era, and even more so by 1933. However, this was not the only source of Mosley's fascist revolt. Of at least equal importance was the programme of fiscal reform and the Keynesian economic programme which originated in mainly left-wing sources[40] – ideas which derived mainly from the experience of the First World War and its aftermath.

Race, culture and evolution

It is, of course, clear that the origins of Mosley fascism must be seen in his criticism of the 'old gang' game of conventional party politics. Yet after his failure to convince popular opinion of the existence of a crisis of British government he unleashed a campaign which had deep roots in late Victorian and Edwardian politics, namely his highly controversial use of political anti-semitism after 1934. The connections between the radical right in Edwardian Britain and political anti-semitism were almost as close as Mosley's later orchestration of the theme, although for the most part BUF criticism of Jews was far more specific than either the Edwardian British Brothers League anti-alien campaign or the innuendo of the conspiracy accusations of the National League for Clean Government in 1913–14. Anti-semitism had not been as serious a problem in England as in Russia, France and Germany in the period before the First World War, but there was a strong link between various anti-alien groups like the Parliamentary Alien Immigration Committee, the British Brothers League, the London League and the Immigration Reform Association, in the campaign against Jewish immigration between 1901 and 1906.[41] Both this

---

[40] R. Thurlow, 'The return of Jeremiah. The rejected knowledge of Sir Oswald Mosley in the 1930's', in *British Fascism*, ed. K. Lunn and R. Thurlow (London, 1980), pp. 100–13.
[41] C. Holmes, *Anti-Semitism in British Society 1876–1939* (London, 1979), p. 91; S. Wilson, *Ideology and Experience. Antisemitism in France at the Time of the Dreyfus Case* (London, 1982); P. Pulzer, *The Rise of Political Anti-Semitism in Germany and Austria* (New York, 1964); N. Cohn, *Warrant for Genocide* (London, 1970), pp. 118–37.

movement and Mosley's use of this theme were directed mainly at the East End of London where a strong cultural tradition of anti-Jewish hostility could be called upon for political purposes. The function of anti-semitism was to mobilize a populist movement in support of an anti-alien campaign and thus to incorporate the non-political masses in a protest movement against both the Jewish immigrant and, more importantly, the liberal values of the political establishment.

Another Edwardian form of anti-semitism bequeathed to the British fascist tradition was the conspiracy theory of history. This in its anti-semitic form derived from nativist traditions, even if it was the arrival after the First World War of *The Protocols of the Elders of Zion* that gave it such notoriety.[42] The British variant of anti-semitic conspiracy theory was developed from both the political left and right. J.A. Hobson, for example, drawing on British and South African experiences, was highly critical of the activities of Jewish capitalism, whilst the Tariff Reform League differentiated between beneficial home investment and 'alien' capital being invested abroad.[43] More direct was the attempt to set up a 'radical plutocrat' enquiry, mainly aimed against German and Jewish capitalists, as a response to the alleged connections between alien finance and the British Liberal government, which was loudly endorsed by Maxse's *National Review* and the 'Chesterbelloc' circle. Indeed, the campaign of Cecil Chesterton's *New Witness* during the Marconi scandal was to be the driving force behind the National League for Clean Government in 1913.[44] The Edwardian radical right was to equate the attempts of German-born Jewish capitalists like Sir Alfred Mond to improve relations between Germany and Britain with treasonable activity, a belief which had distinct echoes in the more virulent anti-semitism of the Britons Society after the First World War.

The late Victorian and Edwardian eras were also to be crucial for the formation of beliefs which were to be of great importance to British fascism. As with the continental forms of fascism, the

[42] Lunn, 'The Marconi scandal', p. 381; idem, 'Political anti-semitism before 1914: fascism's heritage?', in Lunn and Thurlow, *British Fascism*, pp. 20–40, and G.C. Lebzelter, 'Anti-semitism. A focal point for the British radical right', in Kennedy and Nicholls, *Nationalist and Racialist Movements in Britain*, pp. 80–103.

[43] C. Holmes, 'J.A. Hobson and the Jews', in *Immigrants and Minorities in British Society*, ed. C. Holmes (London, 1978), pp. 136–40; Lebzelter, 'Anti-semitism', p. 82.

[44] Lunn, 'The Marconi scandal'; idem, 'Fascism's heritage?', pp. 20–40.

years 1880–1914 were to be of fundamental significance to the emergence of British fascist ideology.[45] Some of these ideas were to derive from similar sources to those in Europe, but usually through native propagandists who interpreted the influence in terms more directly applicable to British political culture. However, the intellectual traffic was a two-way process. British intellectual ideas from this period, particularly with regard to contemporary scientific attitudes towards race and the impact of Social Darwinism on society, were to play an important role in the formation of fascist ideas in general, and nazi views in particular.[46] With regard to British fascism this cross-fertilization of ideas was to be particularly significant with regard to the linked issues of race, culture and evolution on the one hand, and the influence of heroic vitalism on the other.

Such ideas were also to play a key role in shaping the varieties of British fascism. Although the principal difference between the racial nationalism of Arnold Leese's tiny Imperial Fascist League (IFL), the militant conservatism of the British Fascists, and the radical planning of the BUF, can be seen as related to the role anti-semitism initially played in their respective movements, at root there was a significant divergence between their respective attitudes towards race and culture, and the evolutionary implications therein. Thus although a more extremist view was expressed by William Joyce in the BUF, in general Mosley's fascism, like the British Fascists, inherited the jingoism and the ideology of British imperialism from the Edwardian era.[47] In particular this tradition viewed the British as possessing innate governing qualities which justified their rule over other indigenous groups in the Empire.[48] However, the mainly liberal assumptions of Edwardian imperial attitudes also survived, as did the belief that good government and sound administration demanded the rule of law and relative even-handedness between groups in the

[45] Z. Sternhell, 'Fascist ideology', in Fascism. A Reader's Guide, ed. W. Laqueur (London, 1979), pp. 325–406.

[46] P. Hayes, 'The contribution of British intellectuals to fascism', in Lunn and Thurlow, British Fascism, pp. 168–86.

[47] W. Fest, 'Jingoism and xenophobia in the electioneering strategies of the British ruling elites before 1914', in Kennedy and Nicholls, Nationalist and Racialist Movements in Britain, pp. 171–89.

[48] Mock, 'The function of race', pp. 190–201; C. Bolt, Victorian Attitudes towards Race (London, 1971); V. Kiernan, The Lords of Human Kind (London, 1972), p. 325ff.

Empire. This relatively mild racism, then, was not too far removed from official attitudes towards the colonies in the inter-war period, and was used as the chief plank in the argument that the BUF was not a racist organization.

The historical legacy of British imperialism was not the only source of British fascist ideas on race, however. For nazism, Arnold Leese's racial nationalism, and the more pretentious materialist tradition which underlay the National Front theory of race, derived many of their racial beliefs from nineteenth- and early twentieth-century British scientific attitudes. This racism contained both cultural traditions developed in the distant past and the ethnocentric middle-class moralism and aesthetic ideas of beauty which had been an implicit part of post-Enlightenment science, and whose assumptions remained unchallenged until the twentieth century.[49] Amongst such views was the alleged superiority of so-called Aryan or Anglo-Saxon stock. Also of particular importance was the ascription of corporate character values and the psychological behaviour of groups to external physical differences of race, an idea with its roots in the anthropological theory of polygenesis or separate creation of different racial groups.[50]

Post-Darwinian biology contributed three more crucial elements to this potent brew of value judgement and scientific endeavour when applied to human society. These were the theory of the survival of the fittest, the emergence of neo-Lamarckian ideas in social thought, and the merging of the Darwinian theory of natural selection with Mendelian genetics to form the 'modern synthesis'.[51] The development of the understanding of the principle of heredity and the laws of genetics led to frighteningly utopian ideas of scientific breeding and pure racial types achieved

[49] G.L. Mosse, *Toward the Final Solution* (London, 1979), pp. 1–34; G. Jones, *Social Darwinism and English Thought* (Brighton, 1980), pp. 103–4; R. Hofstadter, *Social Darwinism in American Thought* (Boston, 1955), pp. 170–200, and L. Poliakov, *The Aryan Myth* (New York, 1974), pp. 11–128.

[50] M.D. Biddiss, 'The politics of anatomy: Dr. Robert Knox and Victorian racism', *Proceedings of the Royal Society of Medicine*, 6, 9 (April 1976), pp. 247–8; D.A. Lorimer, *Colour, Class and the Victorians* (Leicester and New York, 1978), p. 137; N. Stephan, *The Idea of Race in Science* (London, 1982), pp. 20–46.

[51] R.J. Halliday, 'Social Darwinism: a definition', *Victorian Studies*, 14 (1971), pp. 389–405; Jones, 'Social Darwinism and English thought'; G.W. Stocking Jr., 'Lamarckianism in American social science 1890–1915', in *Race, Culture and Evolution*, ed. G.W. Stocking Jr. (New York, 1968), pp. 234–69.

through eugenic experiments.[52] These beliefs formed part of what might loosely be called the ideology of Social Darwinism, which received much of its intellectual stimulus from British scientists and social scientists in late Victorian and Edwardian England.

For example, the concept of the survival of the fittest, when applied without modification to the human rather than the natural world, implied that the most technically advanced groups and races were the fittest and hence superior to others. Furthermore, the neo-Lamarckian idea that groups or races could inherit learned acquired characteristics, or 'social heredity' as Benjamin Kidd called it,[53] was later used by fascists to imply that leadership changes in the state could induce more rapid changes in society in a short period. Finally, the racist interpretation of genetics implied a rather less optimistic creed; Galton's stirp theory and Weissmann's experiments arguably showed that there was no link between cells involved in reproduction and those in the rest of the body. Lamarckian theories of evolution, therefore, were merely figments of the imagination. Alleged racial characteristics were determined by what came to be called the 'genetic code' and, according to racists, any unsuitable 'outcrossing' from the parent stock would weaken the 'gene pool'. The fact that evolutionary theory and Mendelian genetics implied no such conclusion was, not surprisingly, to escape the attention of most fascists.[54]

The distinction between Lamarckian and Darwinian theories of evolution was to play a big part in the differences in outlook between various British fascist groups. The question as to whether culture created race, as neo-Lamarckian fascists in the Mosley tradition mainly argued, or whether race determined culture, as racial nationalists stated, explains some of the heated ideological debate within British fascism. However, this divergence over the significance of race meant a difference of emphasis rather than outright contradiction. In theory, Lamarckian ideas implied an anti-racist perspective, since new values and psychological attributes could be acquired by all. In practice, the nineteenth-

[52] R. Schwartz Cowan, 'Nature and nurture: the interplay of biology and politics in the work of Sir Francis Galton', *Studies in the History of Biology* (Baltimore, 1977), pp. 133–208.

[53] Hayes, 'The contribution of British intellectuals', p. 178.

[54] A. Chase, *The Legacy of Malthus* (Illinois, 1980), pp. 466–92; J.J. Gould, *The Mismeasure of Man* (New York, 1981), pp. 321–34, and M. Barker, *The New Racism* (London, 1982), pp. 100–64.

century neo-Lamarckians limited their theory of use inheritance to those of European stock, by arguing conveniently that evolution had come to an end among the 'lower races' since they could no longer respond to the challenge of the environment.[55]

This was the tradition Mosley was to follow, rationalizing it by neo-Spenglerian cultural morphology and the restless spirit of 'Faustian man'.[56] Ethnic groups with allegedly or actual non-European origins such as the Jews or the later so-called 'coloured' immigrants could be stigmatized as culturally different rather than racially inferior, as in the racial nationalist view.[57]

The debate about positive racial values also developed out of nineteenth- and early twentieth-century attitudes. Mosleyites, following Spengler, believed there was a common European cultural heritage. Racial nationalists were divided about whether European supremacy was determined by the blend of races within Europe, or could be accounted for by the alleged attributes of the Nordic/Aryan or 'Anglo-Saxon' race.[58]

Equally significant for the new society that fascists wished to create was the influence of vitalism and its links to the evolution controversy. In particular, Mosley's fascism developed a mixture of heroic vitalism and creative evolutionism as its philosophical basis.[59] Although these idealist voluntarist philosophies were to have a much greater influence on the continent, they nevertheless provide an interesting contrast to the materialist determinist base of racial nationalism. The link of vitalism and creative evolutionism into British fascist thought was also provided by ideas that germinated in the pre-1914 era. Yet while Mosley developed his own interpretations of the ideas of heroic vitalists like Carlyle, Nietzsche, Wagner and Spengler, his particular interest in the subject derived principally from the work of George Bernard Shaw.[60] It was the message contained in Shaw's didactic work,

[55] J.S. Haller Jr., *Outcasts from Evolution* (London, 1971), p. ix.

[56] R.C. Thurlow, 'Destiny and doom. Spengler, Hitler and British fascism', *Patterns of Prejudice*, 15, 4 (October 1981), pp. 17–33.

[57] Barker, *The New Racism*, pp. 12–29; M. Banton, 'What do we mean by racism?', *New Society*, 10 Apr. 1969, pp. 551–4; J. Rex, *Race Relations in Sociological Theory* (London, 1970), pp. 159–60.

[58] A.J. Gregor, 'National socialism and race', *The European* (1958), pp. 273–91; R.E. Herzstein, *When Nazi Dreams come True* (London, 1982), pp. 1–12; G.G. Field, 'Nordic racism', *Journal of the History of Ideas*, 38 (1978), pp. 523–40.

[59] E. Bentley, *The Cult of the Superman* (Gloucester, Mass., 1969; first published 1944), pp. 233–5.

[60] Skidelsky, *Oswald Mosley*, pp. 476–7.

rather than the metaphysical truths to be derived from his aesthetic appreciation, which was to be of crucial importance for Mosley. In particular the message contained in *The Perfect Wagnerite* (1898), *Man and Superman* (1902) and *Back to Methuselah* (1921) was to be seminal.

The Perfect Wagnerite was Shaw's interpretation of the allegory in Wagner's Ring Cycle of operas. Behind the plot, which Shaw viewed somewhat improbably as an argument for socialist revolution, was a belief that the dwarves, giants and gods were a stage in evolution prior to the emergence of man.[61] At another level Siegfried was the new type of man, with his courage and the amoral attitude to life that was needed to supersede the main types of present humanity; the materialist money-obsessed capitalists (dwarves), the dull plodding workers (giants), and the clever intellectuals and politicians who could rationalize and organize present society (the gods), but who lacked the dynamic will to action either to prevent its decay or to develop it to a higher level.

The dream sequence in *Man and Superman* was also significant. Here Nietzsche's concept of the superman was discussed. Mosley always saw Nietzsche's message in Shaw's terms. The function of the Superman was viewed as much in terms of domination over others as in the will to power leading to self-control.[62]. Thus Nietzsche's vitalism was interpreted in political rather than ethical terms.

Back to Methuselah was Shaw's attack on Darwin's theory of evolution. In it he argued that man had the power and the will to evolve a higher humanity. Mind and will-power, rather than the chance mechanisms of natural selection, were to be the means by which society was to progress; the higher types evolved partly by eugenic breeding. The contemporary politicians, with their meaningless party political games, were to be superseded and the extension of life expectancy to 300 years was to be the chief aim of man. Bergson's concept of the *élan vital*, the life force, and creative evolutionism, were to be 'the religion of the twentieth century'.[63] The idea that a new type of man with new values could

[61] G.B. Shaw, *The Perfect Wagnerite* (London, 1932), pp. 170–85; N. Mosley, *Rules of the Game* (London, 1982), p. 59.

[62] Idem, *Beyond the Pale* (London, 1983), p. 38.

[63] G.B. Shaw, *Back to Methuselah* (London, 1931), p. 79; G.R. Searle, 'Eugenics and politics in the 1930's', *Annals of Science*, 36 (1979), p. 167; O. Mosley, *The Alternative* (London, 1947), p. 223.

be evolved, and that man could act as God, was anathema to some British fascists, however. For instance, Nesta Webster based her conspiracy theory on opposition to the gnostic heresy. For her the values of British society needed only to return to the tradition of aristocratic paternalism and the values of Christian civilization for health to be restored.[64]

Thus the years prior to the First World War were to be crucial to the emergence of British fascism. In politics, criticism of the party system and Britain's decline as a world power were to lead to the growth of right-wing nationalist sentiment, whose main concern was a perceived crisis of empire. Parallel to this was the development of ideas which outlined two ways in which British society could be regenerated, either through the racist materialist solution of eugenic breeding, or the vitalist conception of the will to power and the new man evolving through planned effort. The First World War was to deepen the sense of crisis for many who felt threatened by the continued decline of British pre-eminence. It was also to provide a stimulus for more 'socialist' origins of British fascism: the increased sense of community engendered by the need for co-ordinated national effort, the move towards directed national planning, and the revulsion against the slaughter in the trenches. The impact of these phenomena will form the next chapter of this analysis.

However, compared with the European experience there were no developments in British politics before 1914 comparable to the formation of the Action Française in France, or the emergence of volkish nationalism and the ideology of cultural despair in Wilhelmine Germany.[65] The Action Française was an integral nationalist mass movement whose adherence to absolutist monarchism, anti-liberalism, anti-parliamentarianism, rabid anti-semitism, and collaboration with syndicalism after 1910, totally alienated it from the political cultures of the Third Republic. Although volkish nationalism did not erupt into a serious political challenge before 1914 in Germany it did create a romantic nationalist subculture which provided a base from which nazism could build in the post-war era. The fact that Britain had neither a

---

[64] N. Webster, *Secret Societies and Subversive Movements* (London, 1928), p. 30.
[65] E. Weber, 'France', in Rogger and Weber, *The European Right*, pp. 71–127; F. Stern, *The Politics of Cultural Despair* (London 1961), and G.L. Mosse, *The Crisis of German Ideology* (London, 1966).

co-ordinated integral nationalist populist movement, nor was influenced significantly by romantic nationalism before 1914, helps explain the uphill task which British fascists faced in their later attempts to revolutionize society.

2

The Lost Generation, 1914–1932

It's all right, Mrs Feeney. 'The slums have died in Flanders' as my friend 'Spectre' West once wrote to me. I told you about him remember. Eight wound stripes, one eye, one hand Mrs. Feeney. His face a black patch, his body a map of scars! Come on, lets drink his health!

Henry Williamson, *A Test to Destruction*

The First World War and its impact on British society was to have a profound significance for the emergence of British fascism. Yet this relationship was deeply problematic, which helps to explain the diversity of opinion and the contradictions within the phenomenon. The influence of the war was to affect social classes, groups and individuals in Britain in a variety of ways and many came to support fascism for disparate political, economic and social reasons. Some saw fascism as a means to restore an alleged utopian past of harmonious political, economic and social relationships which had been swept away by the war and replaced by the degenerative effects of the extension of the franchise in 1918 and the emergence of political democracy. Other fascists interpreted it as a locomotive of history: an opportunity to create a new society where the major political consequence of the war, the greater direction and control of economic activity by the government, could be harnessed for social reform in peacetime. This too would necessitate a new political system where traditional party politics would need to be subordinate to a national will for reform and the consequent reduction of democratic rights.

The attraction of fascism after the First World War

It must, however, be stressed from the outset that even among the most alienated fascism was far from being the only political response to the continued decline of Britain and the mounting economic problems after the First World War. For some who, given European experience, seemed to be the most prone to the appeal of fascism in the lower middle classes, it proved to have only marginal importance in the 1930s in Britain.[1] Indeed, apart from a few regionally isolated areas like the north-west of England before 1934 and the East End of London after 1935, fascism was not of major political significance.[2] Among the small minority of combatants who found it difficult to adjust to civilian life after the war, who were anti-semitic, militantly anti-communist and concerned about the continued decline of Britain, individuals were almost as likely to be anti-fascist as supporters of fascism. Douglas Reed, for example, who resigned as Central European Correspondent of *The Times* in 1938 over his newspaper's support for appeasement politics, and whose background and life history read like the classic facsimile of the alleged fascist, proved in practice to be a crusading anti-fascist.[3]

The fact that Britain was a victorious power in the First World War also helps to explain fascism's limited impact on the country. For after the war, national resentment could neither fester on an unrequited national grievance as in Italy, nor on a stab-in-the-back myth to explain defeat as in Germany. Several consequences of the war ultimately did lead some in British society towards fascism, however. In the immediate post-war period the problems created by the Russian Revolution, the emergence of a socialist Labour party as the major opposition party in Britain, and the extension of the franchise in 1918 to reward the working class and women for their role in the war, frightened some elements among the middle classes. In the longer term the failure of the National Coalition, and the Conservative and Labour governments in the 1920s, to create the 'home fit for heroes', turned some towards

---

[1] N. Killingback, 'The BUF and the petite bourgeoisie', conference paper, n.d.

[2] S. Rawnsley, 'Fascism and fascists in Britain in the 1930s', PhD thesis, University of Bradford, 1981; J. Brewer, *Mosley's Men* (Aldershot, 1984).

[3] R. Thurlow, 'Anti-nazi anti-semite: the case of Douglas Reed', *Patterns of Prejudice*, 18, 1 (Jan. 1984), pp. 23–34.

more radical solutions for Britain's problems than the return to normalcy and safety-first politics of what Mosley was to call the old gangs of British politics.

In consequence, fascism was to emerge in Britain in the 1920s as a supposed imitation of Mussolini's example in Italy, although in reality it was little more than 'Conservatism with knobs on', in Arnold Leese's graphic definition of the British Fascists.[4] Its immediate origins have to be seen mainly as an ultra-conservative response to the social consequences of the First World War. In general it was almost exclusively extreme right-wing elements who were first involved, but they tended to be of two distinct types. The first were supporters of the Die-hard Conservatives, an unofficial parliamentary group who admired their aristocratic pre-war namesakes, opposed the continued survival of Lloyd George's coalition after the Coupon Election of 1918,[5] and wished for the restoration of what they termed 'true conservatism'.[6] The Die-hards were opposed to the rise of a socialist Labour party and militant trade unionism, which they saw as a revolutionary threat to property and the stability of British society. In particular, they saw the function of the British Fascists as providing stewards for Conservative party meetings to help maintain free speech and law and order. An unarmed paramilitary group, their role in practice proved to be a cross between an adult boy scout movement and a slightly more sinister defence force and strike-breaking organization.

Rather more ideologically committed to a new form of politics were those for whom anti-semitism was seen as the reason for the changes in British and European society engendered by the First World War. Of particular importance here was the formation of the Britons Society in 1918 which was to be the immediate precursor of British racial fascism. This reactivated the pre-war nativist tradition in more virulent form and combined it with the dissemination of the emergent bible of European anti-semitism, the *Protocols of the Elders of Zion*.[7] This more sophisticated and rationally expressed conspiracy theory of anti-semitism was combined with gutter racist anti-semitic abuse in its publications.

---

[4] A. Leese, *Out of Step* (Hollywood, n.d.), p. 49.
[5] M. Cowling, *The Impact of Labour* (London, 1971), pp. 70–90.
[6] *The Patriot*, 9 Feb. 1922.
[7] V. Marsden, *World Conquest through World Government* (London, 1921).

The miniscule middle-class membership was insignificant as a group, but the survival of the publishing arm of the organization and the influence of the society on Arnold Leese were to be of crucial significance to the development of racial fascism in Britain. Other groups with links to the pre-war Die-hards also used their influence to help advertise the *Protocols of the Elders of Zion* through newspaper publications. The Duke of Northumberland purchased the *Morning Post* and established a new weekly, the *Patriot*, to popularize the idea of a conspiracy.[8] Even *The Times* for a while in the aftermath of the Russian Revolution suggested that there was more than a grain of truth in the concept of a Jewish world plot.[9]

The immediate roots of British fascism thus grew from those who tried to ignore the real consequences of the First World War. The mixture of reactionary conservatism and political anti-semitism in the main represented a response of those who asked for a stable hierarchical society based on paternalistic deference. What small political influence it possessed was confined to the immediate post-war years of social tension, inflation and unemployment. Its survival after the early 1920s was a part of the more eccentric sections of the political underground.

Of far greater significance for the inter-war period were those who saw fascism mainly as a positive force which would create a new society deriving directly from the war experience. The anaesthetizing shock of the trenches was to bring about a delayed-action reflex for many who had fought in them. The failure of the politicians to create a society which adequately compensated for the horror and trauma of the war produced a mood of frustrated anger which tinted the utopian cravings of many attracted to fascism. British fascism in the 1930s was to represent the mood of the trenches bitterly coloured by the disillusion of fifteen years' hindsight. Clearly, of course, it was far from being the only political response to the war. As in France, communism, pacifism or religion were just as likely to mark the outlook of those who had experienced the camaraderie, fear and gore of trench warfare.[10] Yet in the 1930s, British fascism was to represent a distinctive consequence of the same phenomenon. It was the

---

[8] Cowling, *Impact of Labour*, pp. 85–90.
[9] *The Times*, 8 May 1920.
[10] F. Field, *Three French Writers and the First World War* (London, 1976).

peculiar mixture of alienation and reformism which created the most enduring legacy of British fascism, the tradition of political violence and anti-democratic values co-existing uneasily and with some contradiction with a pragmatic modernizing economic programme. After 1934 this was to be combined with the anti-semitic obsession of both ultra-conservative reactionary fascism and racial nationalist traditions in the BUF, despite the fact that it was expressed in slightly less virulent form and appeared to have more social roots.

Mosley and post-war radicalism

Of those connected with the BUF the experience of three individuals stands out in connection with the impact of the First World War. The founder and leader of the BUF, Sir Oswald Mosley, was a self-conscious political spokesman for the 'lost generation' and the survivors of the First World War. A.K. Chesterton, an important member of the leadership of the BUF and later first chairman of the Directorate of the National Front, was another for whom the war had profound significance. Chesterton's experience was more exacting than Mosley's, which helps to explain his more irrational and emotional form of fascism. The third individual was the writer and novelist Henry Williamson, author of *Tarka the Otter* and other nature books. He was a non-active member of the movement, but an analysis of his heavily autobiographical books and novels, in which the First World War is of crucial significance, throws considerable light on the origins of fascism. Indeed it is his support for Mosley, expressed on many occasions, which goes some way to account for the continuing neglect of his work by much of the literary establishment. Even the most perceptive of critics of the literature of the First World War, Paul Fussell, has totally ignored Williamson's most important work on this theme. This is indeed unfortunate, for Williamson, perhaps more than any other writer, accurately described the experience of the common man in the trenches and the lingering and traumatic effects it had on the survivors of the experience.[11] Although character and aesthetic

---

[11] H. Cecil, 'Henry Williamson: witness of the Great War', in *Henry Williamson: The Man, The Writings*, ed. B. Sewell, (Padstow, 1980), p. 70.

ideals differentiated Williamson from post-war society more radically than the large majority of the participants in the conflict, an analysis of his work helps to explain why other idealists and embittered individuals at all levels of the movement should turn to fascism as a solution to the problems of British society in the inter-war years.

The principle significance of the First World War will be examined here through an analysis of these three individuals. Other examples of the influence of 'war socialism' on the emergence of British fascism, such as its impact on John Beckett, could have been chosen.[12] Wider sociological studies of the BUF have also emphasized the importance of direct and indirect consequences of the war, most particularly the impact of mass unemployment.[13] The examples developed here are heavily biased towards the leadership and intellectual rationalization for the movement. It has been estimated that 60 per cent of the fascist elite had been members of the armed forces and over 40 per cent saw active service in the First World War.[14] However, it should not be forgotten that the unofficial populist ideas of the rank and file, particularly with regard to anti-semitism, unemployment and political violence, were often significantly different from the formulations of the leadership.[15]

Many at all levels of the movement, who were too young to have had experience of the First World War, were nevertheless affected by its indirect effects. They saw the military discipline, anti-socialist politics, the threat of confrontation with left-wing elements, and anti-semitic baiting of immigrants and British citizens of Jewish religion, as a source of excitement which gave meaning to a dull existence. Even quarrelsome members of the leadership, like William Joyce, appear to have been attracted to the movement by such motives.[16] In the East End of London, some joined the BUF because it appeared to offer a kind of explanation for economic and social problems which had their roots in the

---

[12] C. Holmes, 'John Beckett', in *Dictionary of Labour Biography*, ed. J. Bellamy and J. Saville, vol. VI (London, 1982), pp. 24–9.

[13] Rawnsley, 'Fascism and fascists'.

[14] W.F. Mandle, 'The leadership of the British Union of Fascists', *Australian Journal of Politics and History*, Dec. 1966, pp. 362–80.

[15] N. Nugent, 'The ideas of the British Union of Fascists', in *The British Right*, ed. N. Nugent and R. King, (London, 1977), p. 146.

[16] W. Cole, *Lord Haw Haw – and William Joyce* (London, 1964).

interaction beetween a native working class and a stable Jewish minority.[17] Fascism appealed both to the classically prejudiced and to those who thought objective social factors a justification for projecting antipathy towards an outgroup. However, it should be emphasized that even in the East End a large majority of the native host population were anti-fascist. Perhaps of greater importance than those who were attracted to fascism for irrational or emotive reasons were those who were ideologically committed to the form of radicalism which BUF doctrine and propaganda promulgated. Many such individuals, from Alexander Raven Thomson in the leadership to fascist rank-and-file like Jeffrey Hamm and Robert Row, were deeply committed entrants into the movement who were to stand by Mosley through all his trials and tribulations. Such individuals were often attracted to the BUF because they felt that Mosley had a practical solution to the problem of unemployment and would create a more just society.

At the other extreme, many short-term members in the 1930s saw the BUF as little more than a social organization in which political activity was very much a secondary phenomenon. Numerous purges in the regions were designed to root out less than committed fascists, which helps to account for the high turnover of membership in the 1930s;[18] A.K. Chesterton in particular was notorious for the war he waged against literal social fascists, being responsible for expelling over 300 members in Stoke in 1935 who used the local headquarters as a drinking club.[19] Others joined for even more dubious reasons. Several cases of serious criminal activity, including burglary and fraudulent use of BUF funds, have been commented upon both by academic studies and by more sympathetic observers like Henry Williamson.[20]

Nevertheless, despite the wide variety of motives which led individuals to become fascists, it remains true that the hierarchical and authoritarian structure of the movement gave additional weight to the official ideology and explanation of events. As the

[17] C. Holmes, *Anti-Semitism in British Society 1876–1939* (London, 1979), pp. 175–90.

[18] S. Rawnsley, 'The membership of the British Union of Fascists', in *British Fascism*, ed. K. Lunn and R. Thurlow (London, 1980), pp. 158–60.

[19] D. Baker, 'A.K. Chesterton. The making of a British fascist', PhD thesis, University of Sheffield, 1982, p. 231.

[20] Rawnsley, 'Fascism and fascists', p. 105; H. Williamson, *The Phoenix Generation* (London, 1965), p. 319.

movement and the significance of British fascism owed so much to
Sir Oswald Mosley, and as he increasingly came to see himself as
the political spokesman for the lost generation and the survivors of
the First World War, it is the impact of that event I want to
examine first.

Mosley's own experience of the First World War was less
traumatic than either Chesterton's or Williamson's. Although he
performed valiantly as a navigator in that most dangerous of all
the branches of the armed forces, the Royal Flying Corps, in 1915,
and during his service sustained a serious leg injury, there is little
evidence that he experienced the full horrors of trench warfare.[21]
Nevertheless the legacy of the war did determine his career
choices. His limited experience of the nature of modern warfare
convinced him that those who sacrificed themselves for their
country should not die in vain. The war turned an immature,
irresponsible aristocrat into a man who combined the frivolity of
his youthful lifestyle with the dedicated, passionate, highly articu-
late and rational exponential qualities of the reforming
politician.[22] Mosley came increasingly to see himself as the
spokesman of the war generation, who refused to compromise his
idealistic principles with the political realities of the post-war
world.

For Mosley the lesson of the First World War was simply the
necessity to keep faith with those who had paid the ultimate price.
He devoted his life to politics for a twofold purpose: to ensure that
the useless slaughter of the First World War was not repeated, and
that the survivors of that horrific experience should live in a better
world. These were far from ignoble aims. Some considered it to
Mosley's credit that a man who had the ability to attain the
highest office in government should have ignored the rules of the
political game because of his devotion to principle. Others interpreted it as Mosley's attempt to change the conventions of British
politics by iconoclastic disregard of the traditional forms of
political discourse.[23] Utopian reformism was to replace the art of
the possible in Mosley's new political game.

Mosley's political odyssey in the inter-war period ultimately led
him and some who admired him to fascism, the most radical

[21] N. Mosley, *Rules of the Game* (London, 1982), p. 7.
[22] O. Mosley, *My Life* (London, 1968), pp. 44–71.
[23] N. Mosley, *Rules of the Game*.

rejection of the cosy nature of the high politics of British tradition. Fascism resulted from the frustration with, and alienation from, a system in which politicians were obsessed with the conventions of party politics to the detriment of the need for radical change (highlighted by the First World War); and radical change was vital if Britain's accelerated economic and political decline was to be reversed.[24] Mosley, the rebel with a cause, first tried to reform the system from within during the 1920s. Failure led him to mass manipulation and an attempt to revolutionize British politics from outside the system. The failure of this attempt, first in the New Party in 1931, and then in the BUF between 1932 and 1934, led to the degeneration of Mosley's rationalistic pleas for reform to the gutter politics of the later 1930s. The collapse of Mosley's challenge as a reforming force, and the close connection this had with political violence, was to represent an ironic commentary on the nature of British politics. Mosley revolted over the wrong crisis, for he failed to see that considerable social and economic reform would result from a Second World War, a conflagration which he bitterly opposed and which led to his internment in 1940.

The fact that Mosley was turned into a reforming politician by the First World War highlighted his dilemma. He became the youngest beneficiary in the coupon election of 1918, fighting on a programme of 'socialistic imperialism' in his Harrow constituency. From the outset he was at odds with the Conservatives, nominally his own party, who increasingly saw the return to normalcy, along with the need to return to the governmental conventions of party politics of the pre-war era, as the top priority. The Coalition government under Lloyd George became more and more constrained by the demands of Conservative retrenchment. Mosley himself admired Lloyd George's qualities of leadership and had been impressed by his energy and administrative skills at the Ministry of Munitions from 1915 to 1916. He liked his personal style of government, and his establishment of a Cabinet Secretariat and his own personal advisers or brains trust in the 'garden suburbs'. In particular Mosley was influenced by Lloyd George's ability to bypass bureaucratic red tape and through dynamic activism attempt to tackle head-on the mounting prob-

[24] R. Skidelsky, *Oswald Mosley* (1975), p. 72.

lems of British society. Mosley's later fascist ideas on government owed much to Lloyd George's wartime reforms of the administrative structure, even if they had been devised in a democratic framework. His point was that a war in peacetime would have to be fought against unemployment, as it persistently remained above one million in the 1920s, and rose towards three million during the severe cyclical depression between 1929 and 1932. Lloyd George's later ideas in the green and yellow books of the Liberal party in the 1920s were to play crucial roles in BUF policies on agriculture and unemployment in the 1930s.[25]

Yet if Mosley came to see Lloyd George as a fellow economic radical, objections to the management of Irish policy divided them in the early 1920s. Mosley was opposed to the reprisals of the Black and Tans in Ireland and began to identify himself more and more with Lord Robert Cecil's League of Nations Union. By 1923 he had fallen out with Lloyd George, the Conservatives and Lord Robert Cecil over Ireland, economic policy and Mussolini's invasion of Corfu respectively.[26] Increasingly, Mosley came to see unemployment and economic policy were the key issues in British politics. In 1923 he began to study economic theory and became convinced that government objectives, far from ensuring a return to prosperity, were actively discouraging it through deflationary policies and obsession with the return to the gold standard at pre-war parity. Mosley consciously educated himself through the writings of Keynes, Hobson and other Independent Labour Party (ILP) theorists to become the most perceptive of all government critics actively opposing the consensus of economic policy-making in the 1920s. His mistake was to assume that the Labour party would provide a more receptive political vehicle for his ideas than the Conservatives. The fundamental divide in British politics in the inter-war period proved to be not the differences between the rapidly growing and supposedly socialist Labour party and the long tradition of high politics, encapsulated in the party divisions between the Conservatives and the steadily decaying Liberal party, but between the economic conservatives and economic radicals across the political spectrum.[27]

In the inter-war period the radicals made little headway. In

[25] J. Campbell, *The Goat in the Wilderness* (London, 1977), pp. 121–3, 219–24.
[26] Skidelsky, *Oswald Mosley*, pp. 109–27.
[27] Idem, *Politicians and the Slump* (London, 1970), p. 11.

government both the Conservatives and the Labour party followed vigorously orthodox economic policies. The radicals, such as Harold Macmillan in the Conservative party, the Independent Labour Party group and maverick individuals like Mosley and Ernest Bevin in the Labour movement, were effectively isolated and had little impact on policy. Only in the rapidly declining Liberal party did the radicals have any significant influence on policy. Lloyd George spent large sums of his private fortune (acquired in rather dubious circumstances as a treasure chest for the Coalition Liberals between 1917 and 1922), in research activity which recommended radical policies for the Liberals in areas such as land reform and unemployment policy in the 1920s.[28] Yet even Lloyd George's influence was reduced to a family group of four followers in the 1930s, as the rest of the divided Liberals, although in two distinct factions, supported the coalition government. The goat, as he was jocularly known, was to end his political life in the wilderness.

The parallel experience in the inter-war period of this fellow economic radical Lloyd George is also instructive in another sense. His period of power from 1917–22 as prime minister of the coalition Liberal and Conservative government showed that the limits of economic and social radicalism were constrained by the realities of contemporary politics. Whilst the extension of the franchise and Christopher Addison's hopes for building the 'homes fit for heroes' showed a genuine desire for the radical elements in government to reform British society, the fact that Britain needed to export nearly one-third of her output to pay for essential imports necessitated the re-establishment of settled trading patterns and the development of new markets. However, the growth of economic nationalism on a world-wide scale during the war, the re-drawing of the political map of Europe, the effect of the Versailles Treaty, and the large debt due to the Americans to help pay for the war, all ensured that the freedom of action to expand welfare was strictly limited.

Domestic economic factors further complicated this gloomy picture. The rapid inflation which resulted directly from the cost of financing the war raised the cost of British industry significantly, and made much more difficult the attempt to restore financial

[28] K.O. Morgan, *The Age of Lloyd George* (London, 1975).

stability. Similarly, the fact that over 60 per cent of Britain's exports were dependent on the declining and low-productivity industries in coal, steel, shipbuilding and cotton, caused severe structural problems and rapidly increasing unemployment, when the new pattern of domestic and foreign demand became relatively stabilized in the 1920s.[29]

Thus even for governments with radical good intentions, which for the most part the Lloyd George government was, there were formidable obstacles to piecemeal reform. When increasing financial problems necessitated retrenchment, Addison's schemes for housing reform and other increased social benefits had to be jettisoned as a result of the harsh cuts of the Geddes Committee.[30] Radicals in the inter-war period became divided among themselves as to the degree to which social and economic reforms should be subordinated to financial constraints. The party divisons between leading reformers such as Lloyd George, Mosley and Macmillan also hindered co-operation, as did personal hostility within political parties (on all occasions between Mosley and Ernest Bevin in the Labour movement and intermittently between Lloyd George and Keynes in the Liberals). Outside the charmed circle of high politics, radicalism on the far left developed utopian socialist blueprints which neglected pragmatic considerations of how they were to be achieved. Financial reformers were divided between the monetarists and distributionists, and both were relegated to the economic underworld in terms of their influence on the political establishment.[31] On the political right the fourth estate busied itself in a revived version of the old Chamberlain protectionist pipedream of Empire Unity, as now expounded by the press lords Rothermere and Beaverbrook.[32] The fact that radicals both inside and outside parliament were often divided among themselves and had no uniform political views or remedies was emphasized by their ineffectiveness in the Economic Advisory Committee in the 1930s.

The essential disunity between the radicals made it easy for the inter-war period to be dominated by the conventional wisdom of

[29] S. Pollard, *The Development of the British Economy* (London, 1969), pp. 214–28.
[30] K.O. Morgan, *Consensus and Disunity* (Oxford, 1979), pp. 80–108.
[31] R. Thurlow, 'The return of Jeremiah', in Lunn and Thurlow, *British Fascism*, pp. 100–13.
[32] A.J.P. Taylor, *Beaverbrook* (London, 1972), pp. 246–328.

economic orthodoxy and sound finance. This was personified by the ascendancy in the political sphere of Stanley Baldwin and the rise in the economic sphere of Montagu Norman, the Governor of the Bank of England. Baldwin's rise to power as the Conservative leader and prime minister in 1923 and 1924–9 was ruled by two considerations: first, the need to tame the Labour party and to force it to accept the conventions of parliamentary politics; and second, to ensure that Lloyd George be kept out of office at all costs.[33] Safety First, the uninspiring motto of his 1929 election campaign, represented his policy in political and economic matters. The aim was to restore as far as was practically possible the conditions of the pre-First World War era. This was symbolized by the doomed attempt to restore the gold standard at pre-war parity as the basis of economic policy, which necessitated vigorous deflation to ensure financial rectitude in the altered conditions of the post-war world. It also meant the obligation to meet international debts, and for Baldwin to negotiate the $3\frac{1}{2}$ per cent interest repayment on the American war loan in 1922. The policy of Norman and the Cunliffe Committee succeeded in placing economic and financial policy in a straitjacket between 1918 and 1931, severely limiting all subsequent British governments in the 1920s.[34]

Paradoxically, then, despite the election defeats of 1923 and 1929, the success of Baldwin's political strategy was almost total. The Labour party in its two minority governments in 1924 and 1929–31, despite some minor foreign policy successes, failed to pass any much-needed radical social legislation and Ramsay Macdonald behaved in a constitutionally impeccable manner. What was more to the point was that socialism in power meant economic conservatism in practice. Philip Snowden, Chancellor of the Exchequer from 1929 to 1931, was as much obsessed with financial rectitude as any Conservative and proved to be Mosley's doughtiest opponent in the Labour party. The failure of the General Strike in 1926 marked the end of any possibility that extra-parliamentary forms of left-wing mass politics could alter effectively the economic policy of the government. Meanwhile Lloyd George's radical plans, although ensuring a partial revival of the Liberal corpse in the 1929 election, were effectively

---

[33] Cowling, *Impact of Labour*, pp. 15–44; Campbell, *The Goat in the Wilderness*.
[34] K. Middlemas and J. Barnes, *Baldwin* (London, 1969), pp. 64–87.

sidelined, and the accident of illness was to ensure that he played no part in the formation of the coalition government of 1931 either.

Mosley's political career in the 1920s has to be viewed in the context of the triumph of economic conservatism. He joined the Labour party in 1924 on the mistaken assumption that socialism in power would achieve economic and social reform. In practice, as his experience as Chancellor of the Duchy of Lancaster between 1929 and 1930 proved, it lacked the will to implement any radical reform. The Labour party possessed a utopian ethic of socialism but it failed to develop the pragmatic programme either to alter the capitalist state which it inherited or to reform it from within. Mosley did find kindred spirits in the Labour movement, some of whom followed him into the New Party and a smaller proportion into fascism, but although the party conference and the Labour movement in general were sympathetic to his practical suggestions, the Labour government rejected his proposals. Mosley's new success in the Labour party was to challenge effectively Chamberlain's political control of Birmingham and to turn the ILP into one of the most significant sources of radical ideas in the 1920s. However, neither of these achievements were to prove to Mosley's advantage in the 1930s. His undoubted personal success in the 1920s in Birmingham was not to be repeated in the 1930s, as fascism made less impact there than in the East End of London or the north-west. The ILP rapidly declined into a fundamentalist socialist sect which was soon expelled from the Labour party.

Mosley resigned from the Labour government in 1930 as a result of the Cabinet turning down his reflationary programme contained in the Mosley Memorandum. In political terms this represented, in Mosley's view, a viable synthesis of available radical ideas, which together would provide an effective attack on the immediate problem of mass unemployment and a longer-term beginning to the larger aim of reversing the decline of the British economy. After his narrow failure to convince the Labour party conference in 1930, he and six other MPs left the Labour party to form the New Party, which actively campaigned on the Mosley Manifesto, a rewritten version of the memorandum. Unfortunately for Mosley, although the economic crisis worsened in 1931, bringing about the fall of the deeply divided Labour government, it was replaced by a National Coalition made up of

Conservatives, the majority of the Liberals and a few Labour MPs under Macdonald, Snowdon and Thomas. This was virtually the Conservatives in disguise with Baldwin, rather than the prime minister, Macdonald, its chief architect. In the general election of 1931 the National government won a veritable landslide with a majority of 410 seats. The New Party was obliterated, losing all its members of parliament.[35]

The failure was to end Mosley's effective attempt to change the policies of British government from within the parliamentary party spectrum. He now had nowhere to go, despite overtures from all three political parties.[36] After a long, bitter process Mosley had discovered that the rules of the political game and the increasing conservatism of British government militated against effective action from within the political structure. Convinced of the rightness of his policies and fearful of the consequences of economic decline, Mosley became attracted to the forms of activist mass politics in an attempt to rejuvenate society. British fascism was born of the failure of economic conservatism to check the rapid decline of Britain in the inter-war years. In spite of its obvious imitation of continental movements it was to be a profoundly British variant, with social and political roots in domestic problems.

Chesterton, Williamson and the appeal of post-war fascism

If Mosley came to fascism as a result of the failure of the process of British parliamentary politics to create the new society, the same could not be said of others, like Chesterton and Williamson, who had little or no contact with high politics. Indeed, an important element in the BUF was provided by those who came to fascism from outside the traditional party spectrum and who had little or no previous political experience. Other values from different spheres of activity were transposed to the political sphere to justify the move. In the cases of both Chesterton and Williamson it was the combination of the lingering after-effects of the war and the transposition of supposed aesthetic values to the political sphere, together with personal traumas of varying intensity, which

---

[35] D. Marquand, *Ramsay Macdonald* (London, 1977), pp. 534–40.
[36] N. Mosley, *Beyond the Pale* (London, 1983), pp. 1–6.

accounted for the turn to fascism. An interesting difference between the two was that Chesterton was never able to escape the effects of this potent brew after he became a fascist, whereas Williamson managed to do so to a considerable degree, despite his continued personal support for Mosley until his death.

For both Chesterton and Williamson the First World War was a searing experience which provided lasting images of heroism, horror, comradeship, leadership and fear. It marked them off from other men and made it difficult for them to settle down to the dull conformity of civilian existence after the war. The war on the Western Front in 1917–18 had turned Chesterton into an alcoholic, a condition which he finally controlled in the later 1930s, thanks to the generosity of Mosley who financed his cure at a special clinic in Germany.[37] His most enduring memory, which haunted his imagination for much of the inter-war period, was of his time as a nineteen-year-old officer in 1918 when he led an action to capture enemy trenches at Epehy. His great courage at the time eventually earned him the Military Cross, but the harrowing experience was for a long while foremost in his mind and symbolized by the walk back to his commanding officer over a mass of dead German and British soldiers in which his feet scarcely touched the ground.[38]

Small wonder therefore that as a drama critic he grasped the significance of R. C. Sherriff's famous play, *Journey's End*, in 1929. Its hero, Stanhope, a young officer who survived three years on the Western Front imbibing increasing quantities of whisky, saw death, the escape into nothingness, as the only answer to the squalor of the trenches and the daily horror of seeing brave men victims of the slaughter and wastage.[39] Chesterton, a Stanhope who survived, found in fascism a positive political creed with which he could identify. He could now move from cultural idealism and aesthetic values to political commitment. Yet this was not to represent journey's end for Chesterton's political development. His growing disillusion with Mosley in the later 1930s led to his resignation from the movement and the collapse of his revolutionary faith. He became an alienated reactionary for

[37] Baker, 'A.K. Chesterton', p. 237.
[38] Ibid., p. 63.
[39] cf. R. Skidelsky, 'Reflections on Mosley and British fascism', in Lunn and Thurlow, *British Fascism*, p. 97.

whom the trauma of the First World War was reinforced by the memory of the fascist God that failed, and his thought became increasingly dominated by the negative obsession of the conspiracy theory of history.

Williamson's experiences of the war were just as deeply ingrained. He had been a survivor of many of the major actions of the war, firstly as a volunteer soldier and later as a commissioned officer. Two events in particular were graphically imprinted on his mind. The first was the Christmas truce of 1914, when after the horrendous fighting of the first Battle of Ypres, German and British troops fraternized and played football together on Christmas Day. This for him came to symbolize the futility of the war, which seemed to be fought for no discernible purpose, between opponents whose essential common humanity was denied by the mass slaughter.[40] Patriotism had been distorted by lying propaganda and the massacre of European civilization resulted from the dominance of corrupt political and industrial interests, which were the only ones to benefit from the war. For Williamson, only soldiers who had fought in the war, and who understood the horrors of modern conflict, could save Europe from further disaster. Hence his attempt to enlist T. E. Lawrence in a campaign to prevent war with Germany in the 1930s, which ended in Lawrence's tragic death,[41] and his naive belief that since Adolf Hitler had been a member of the German regiment with whom he had fraternized in 1914 he was basically a man like Williamson who wished to maintain peace at all costs, unless forced into war by the manipulation of others. Williamson felt he had a special bond with Hitler, and even at times imagined aloud that he had spoken to him on that fateful Christmas day.

The image of hope which had thus arisen in Williamson's mind was soured by the reality of his second obsession: the sheer horror of his experience on 1 July 1916, when 60,000 British soldiers were killed or wounded on the first day of the Battle of the Somme. This for him highlighted both the frightfulness of war and the ineptitude of the governing classes.[42]

The essential effect of such knowledge was to alienate

[40] J. Middleton Murry, 'The novels of Henry Williamson', in idem, *Katharine Mansfield and other Literary Studies* (London, 1959), pp. 125–6.
[41] H. Williamson, *Genius of Friendship* (London, 1941), p. 75.
[42] Idem, *The Golden Virgin* (London, 1956).

Chesterton and Williamson from the contemporary world. Both of them found it difficult to express their feelings on the war, except in the third person, so strong were their views. This was particularly the case with Williamson who used the vehicle of his vast epic *The Chronicle of Ancient Sunlight* to develop his most mature insights into the nature of the war. Chesterton also tended to express his own feelings in the mouths of alleged fictional characters. Both men's views in the inter-war period were highly subjective and embittered; both lacked the necessary detachment and sense of objective hindsight to bring the experience into proper perspective. Indeed, fascism was to appeal to many who, on whatever grounds (most of them rational), suffered from an inability to see problems of contemporary society except in an intensely alienated form. Chesterton's views were to become increasingly obsessional from the 1930s onwards; Williamson, as *The Chronicle of Ancient Sunlight* was to prove, particularly in its early volumes, regained a considerable measure of detachment and objectivity in his professional vocation as a novelist after the Second World War.

Yet in the inter-war period for both Chesterton and Williamson the myth of the trenches bred a contempt for civilian society and those without direct contact with the nature of modern warfare. It was almost as though such an experience gave the initiated a glimpse of a deeper level of reality than the allegedly shallow analysis of contemporary society by those who had not faced at first hand the traumas of modern warfare. Such views predicated the existence of higher forms and judgements than the empirical mode of reasoning and pragmatic values of British society. Both Chesterton and Williamson, and to an increasing extent Mosley, were to utilize such ideas to justify the fascist revolt. British fascism was to come close to being rationalized as the political revolt of the romantic imagination in the twentieth century.

Paul Fussell has developed the interesting point that the first world war was a peculiarly literary war. It occurred at a moment in time when reading represented the chief leisure activity, apart from sex and drinking, for the British population. For the upper class the belief in the educative values of classical English literature was still strong. The desire for popular education and self-improvement for the masses was at its peak.[43] In the context of

---

[43] P. Fussell, *The Great War and Modern Memory* (London, 1979).

British fascism Chesterton was to use the aristocratic upper-class literary conventions to justify the impact of the war on his espousal of fascism. Williamson, through his mainly autobiographical work, was to provide a panorama of views on the impact of the war on ordinary working people and the lower middle classes, and through the hero of *The Chronicle of Ancient Sunlight*, Phillip Maddison, was to show how the experience could lead to support for fascism; Mosley was to appear as Sir Hereward Birkin and the BUF as the Imperial Socialist party in the later volumes of the epic.

The move to nationalism

It was not, however, merely through political and artistic influences that the impact of the First World War was to provide such an important background influence for British fascism. The impact of the war and the dislocation of the British economy and society that it caused greatly expanded the variety and impact of ideas on the sources of fascism. Williamson was also attracted to Mosley because of his positive views on British agriculture.[44] For those who were dismayed by the threatened collapse of the ruling class in central and eastern Europe and the rise of the Labour party and extension of the franchise in Britain, anti-semitic conspiracy theories of history, particularly as outlined in the *Protocols of the Elders of Zion*, were to gain a momentary influence in polite society before returning to the political underworld.

More important, perhaps, was the confluence of stimuli which activated the revolt of Sir Oswald Mosley against the political establishment. Far more than any other fascist leader, Mosley's view of the post-war world was based on a rationally expressed intellectual critique. This contained two main elements: a reasoned attack on conventional economic policy in the 1920s, and a growing questioning of the philosophical basis of government and society. Together they were to form the essential background to the most important British variant of fascism. At the outset it should be stressed that Mosley's mode of reasoning owed far more

---

[44] D. Mosley, 'The politics of Henry Williamson', *The Henry Williamson Society Journal*, no. 3 (May 1981), pp. 21–2.

to continental than to British tradition, to a synthesis of ideas rather than empiricism. This was then applied to the native influences on his economic thought.

The development of Mosley's economic ideas in the 1920s showed a gradual transition from a socialist to a nationalist perspective. Mosley's socialist ideas, mainly worked out under the influence of the Birmingham Labour Party and the ILP, were basically a synthesis of Keynesian monetary theories and socialist concepts of planning, J.A. Hobson's under-consumptionism, C.H. Douglas's ideas of social credit and the war-time experience of government direction of industry.[45] These ideas were published in the pamphlet *Revolution by Reason* in 1925. In this document, Mosley had argued for a managed currency rather than the return to the gold standard at pre-war parity as the basis of economic policy, for nationalization of the banks, the establishment of consumer credits to supplement working-class purchasing power, the development of an Economic Council to plan production, and the setting up of a mechanism to check that money supply was equated to production potential.[46] The general aim was to ensure that the purchasing power of the population was equal to the vast expansion of industrial capacity in the war. Only if effective consumer demand was increased could the new productive powers of industry be used at their full potential and unemployment avoided.

Although this synthesis of ideas has been rightly praised by subsequent historians and political commentators,[47] Mosley came too realize during the later 1920s that such ideas could only partially solve Britain's economic problems. In particular he came to appreciate that Britain's reliance on decaying staple industries, whose production costs were making them increasingly uncompetitive in the post-war world, could only be saved by the abandonment of free trade and the adoption of more protectionist policies. His earlier work had convinced him of the importance of the home market in maintaining effective demand, so a new policy which emphasized its expansion was called for. Also the rapid growth of unemployment in the later 1920s convinced him that more vigorous short-term measures were appropriate. Schemes of

---

[45] Thurlow, 'The return of Jeremiah', *British Fascism*, pp. 103–4.
[46] O. Mosley, *Revolution by Reason* (Birmingham, 1925).
[47] A.J.P. Taylor, *English History 1914–45* (Harmondsworth, 1970), p. 359.

public works financed directly by central government owed much of their inspiration to Lloyd George's yellow book, *We Can Conquer Unemployment*, and his own work as Chancellor of the Duchy of Lancaster. Gradually the concept of a new integrated market based on the planned development of resources in the British Empire as a whole took place, as Mosley borrowed and integrated Joseph Chamberlain's imperial ideas and Rothermere and Beaverbrook's British Empire development schemes into his plan. Other ideas such as the problem posed by third world economic development and Douglas's fears of new technology destroying rather than creating employment were used to justify such policies.

In a remarkable series of speeches in the House of Commons and in the Memorandum and Manifesto in 1930 and 1931 Mosley developed his ideas. The growing nationalism of his schemes needed only the more autarchic economic plan and the authoritarian nature of political control to turn it into fully-fledged fascism. Since he was elected in 1918 on a platform of socialistic imperialism, complete rejection by the political establishment of his more sensible ideas turned the potential into a certainty.

But if Mosley's practical search for radical economic policies was to provide a meaningful response to solve the problems of inter-war Britain, both Chesterton and Williamson survived by developing the higher metaphysical values derived from aesthetic appreciation of literature. By adopting such beliefs and applying them to contemporary society both found sustenance in elitist moral and ethical beliefs which were far removed from contemporary reality. As a result both were prone to a disastrous application of metaphysical cultural values to political analysis – in the case of Chesterton and his role as a drama critic and provincial journalist in the 1920s, to a vision of cultural despair based on a parallel theory of criticism to that of his friend the Shakespearian scholar, G. Wilson Knight.[48] Williamson's romanticism and nature worship, on a rather lower level of theoretical conceptualisation, was to owe much to the books of Richard Jefferies, in particular the sunlight imagery of much of his work.[49] Both failed to see that there was an epistemological gap

[48] Baker, 'A.K. Chesterton', pp. 146–217.
[49] D. Hoyle, 'In the monkey house', *The Henry Williamson Society Journal*, no. 4 (Nov. 1981), pp. 6–16.

between metaphysical values as applied to culture and society. By arguing that such beliefs represented a higher appreciation of reality untroubled by empirical criteria both became prone to naive interpretations of political society, most notably Chesterton's virulent cultural anti-semitism and Williamson's curious views on Hitler. Such beliefs that society needed to be reconstructed with new cultural values implied the revolutionary transformation of individuals. The fascist concept of the new man fitted in well with such ideas.

Mosley too became increasingly prone to blur the distinction between art, philosophy and life. Although he was far more concerned with the didactic message of Shaw, Goethe and Wagner than with their artistic values, he transposed his interpretation of their meaning to the political sphere. This was particularly pronounced in his interpretation of Nietzsche, where the latter's ethical concerns were translated by Mosley into political equivalents.[50]

It was not only in the area of economic ideas and cultural criticism that the First World War was to be important to the roots of British fascist thought. The devastation and restructuring of European society gave credence to a whole variety of forebodings about the collapse of European civilization. The genre of apocalyptic historical prophecy reached its apotheosis in the writings of Oswald Spengler, whose *The Decline of the West* had been published coincidentally at the time of Germany's military defeat. The influence of Spengler's thought on the BUF was to be seminal, as Mosley and W.E.D. Allen were to signify.[51] In their view, Spengler diagnosed the main historical trends of human society and accurately predicted the fate of decaying bourgeois society. For fascists, however, Spengler's prophecies were too gloomy. Fascism would revive the corpse of Europe and prevent the final decline into barbarism.

In *The Decline of the West* Spengler argued that world history exhibited a cyclical pattern based on the organic growth and decay of separate cultures through time. He argued against the linear view and stated that the study of history could only be understood through an intuitive understanding of spiritual destiny, rather than

---

[50] O. Mosley, 'The philosophy of fascism', *The Fascist Quarterly*. 1, 1 (Jan. 1935), p. 39.
[51] O. Mosley, *My Life*, pp. 316–35; J. Drennan (W.E.D. Allen), *BUF, Oswald Mosley and British Fascism* (London, 1934), pp. 176–204.

the material cause and effect relationship of modern science. Metaphysical values should be used to interpret history correctly. The main cultures which Spengler analysed were the Apollinian (Classical), Magian (Eastern) and Faustian (Western). Following the organic method Spengler delineated what he considered to be the significant ideas and symbols of the spring, summer, autumn and winter phases of each culture. As each culture neared the end of its organic life cycle the creative stage was finished and the atrophying civilization stage began. For Spengler, this historical progression was a deterministic feature of all cultures, although heroic actions of individuals and peoples could delay the inevitable sequence of the next phase of development. Caesar figures could delay the collapse of civilization and the return to barbarism.[52]

It was the discussion of the contemporary civilization phase of Faustian Culture and his prophecies for the immediate future which gave Spengler his notoriety. For him the civilization stage of European culture had been ushered in by the French Revolution. The key symbol of European life, the nation, had been transformed from a dynastic culture-creating unit to a liberal democratic rationalist state. The nineteenth century was seen as the age of liberalism and democracy and of the victory of money values. For Spengler, democracy was a sham and parliament a front for external forces who ruled by other means. This form of alleged manipulative government could only be transformed by the values of the new caesars, the 'fact men' of history, who relied on blood, instinct and *realpolitik* and not on rationalistic ideology to influence masses and govern nations. Without them society would be swamped by new barbarians, both from inside and outside the civilization. Spengler was particularly worried by the threat of a Russian invasion of Europe.

Mosley, arguing that Spengler's understanding of caesarism was profound but that he had failed to see the potential in modern science to rejuvenate society, saw fascism as a 'mutiny against destiny'.[53] It was caesarism and science, fascism as a revolutionary corporate system of organization based on modern technology and a unified national purpose, which would renew the youth of European culture for Mosley. Yet apart from this acknowledged

[52] R. Thurlow, 'Destiny and doom, Spengler, Hitler and "British" fascism', *Patterns of Prejudice*, 15, 4 (Oct. 1981), pp. 24–6.
[53] Drennan, *BUF, Mosley and British Fascism*, pp. 176–204.

intellectual debt and critical reaction to Spengler Mosley developed other ideas from his work. Spengler's concept of the alleged unity of European culture and its primary Faustian symbols was to be the basis of his 'Europe a Nation' campaign after the Second World War. Similarly, his idea that contact between different cultures merely led to decay and that Magian Jews and Faustian Europeans were bound to live in friction with each other, was to be an important intellectual influence on Mosley's cultural anti-semitism and to re-inforce his later views on apartheid.

Thus the First World War was clearly of particular importance to the origins of British fascism for both its political and cultural roots. This was to be demonstrated by the significance given to Remembrance Day parades from the British Fascists through the BUF to the National Front and its splinter groups.[54] The emergence of fascism symbolized a reaction to the continuing decline of Britain and the developing economic and social problems which had been accelerated by the war. British fascism was to contain extremes from both political right and left as well as to incorporate large numbers with no previous political background. It was to be influenced by both native British sources and events on the continent, but the most distinctive features, like all continental fascisms, was to be its intensely nationalist roots.

[54] *British Lion*, Dec. 1927; *The Blackshirt*, 14 Nov. 1936; J. and V. Tyndall, 'The boys of the old Brigade', *Spearhead*, Nov. 1983.

3

The British Fascists and Conservative Fascism, 1918–1934

British fascism originated in several distinct and contradictory reactions to the long-term decline of Britain and the dislocation caused by the First World War. In the 1920s fascism represented mainly an extremist form of the Die-hard revolt which developed away from the concept of high politics. However, looked at from the perspective of the 1980s, it is not at all clear that groups which styled themselves upon Mussolini's movement in the 1920s were of greater significance than certain more obscure British nationalist organizations of the period, since these provided crucial financial and ideological legacies for later generations of British fascists, most notably anti-semitism. This chapter looks at the development of a conservative fascist tradition and the following one assesses racial nationalism. Both traditions were very marginal in their impact in the inter-war period; their practitioners were regarded as highly eccentric by the small minority who knew of their activities, and as a nuisance by the police.

Dissemination through publication

Indeed, the origins of both traditions lay more in publishing activity than in organizing mass political movements. The funding of a Die-hard journalistic empire centred on the *Morning Post*, the *Patriot* and the Boswell Publishing Company, by Alan Percy, the eight Duke of Northumberland, and Dame Lucy Houston, was non-fascist in inspiration, although the *Patriot* supported the

British Fascists (BF).[1] Similarly, the Britons Society and Publishing Company appeared to be nothing more than a minuscule middle-class organization with a bee in its bonnet about Jews. The BF on the other hand was named after the new Italian experiment in 1923, even though it had little direct knowledge of the aims and ideas of Mussolini. Its history was of minor significance in itself, although its activities did lead to a degree of confrontation which acted as a precursor to the political violence later to become associated with the BUF in the 1930s. Its importance as a fore-runner was due less to its political ideas than to its military discipline and its administrative personnel, who were later to help organize the day-to-day running of the BUF.

These groups had deep historical roots in the opening months of the First World War, which had seen the renewal of the sources of criticism of the radical right against the Liberal government. The continuing military stalemate, even after the advent of the coalition governments of 1915 and 1916, saw the emergence of both populist and radical right resentment, searching for an explanation of the impasse on the western front.[2] This became increasingly focused on the anti-Liberal, anti-Prussian and anti-semitic elements in the Die-hard tradition, which was elaborated in a simplistic conspiracy theory. Journals such as Cecil Chesterton's *The New Witness* and Leo Maxse's *National Review*, and right-wing political authors like Arnold White, argued that there was an alleged hidden hand in British government working against the national interest to secure the victory of Germany. This campaign was directed principally at naturalized Englishmen of German and Jewish extraction who were thought to have conflicting loyalties. The rise of Lloyd George to become prime minister in December 1916, and the close proximity of Rufus Isaacs, Edwin Montague and Sir Alfred Mond as his advisers, gave a spurious plausibility to such claims. Since the beginning of the war demands had been made for the internment of naturalized aliens, and a spy mania developed. Lord Haldane was forced to resign from government as a result of coalition, and eminent businessmen such as Sir Ernest Cassel and Sir Edgar Speyer withdrew from public life for the duration of the war.[3] Even the

---

[1] M. Cowling, *The Impact of Labour* (London, 1971), p. 83.
[2] C. Hazlehurst, *Politicians at War 1914–1915* (London, 1971), pp. 121–224.
[3] C. Holmes, *Anti-Semitism in British Society 1876–1939* (London, 1979), pp. 122–4.

royal family changed its name to Windsor and Prince Louis of Battenberg resigned from the Admiralty as a result of this climate of thought.

Yet the radical right was forced into an awkward position during the war. On the one hand its ultra-patriotism and Germanophobia made it an important driving force behind the campaign for no compromise and total victory; but against this was the undoubted fact that the most dynamic political leadership and organizing ability to ensure this outcome was provided by Lloyd George, the radical right's *bête noire*.

When Lloyd George became prime minister in December 1916 he was backed by the Unionists in a coalition government. With the continuing stalemate in 1917 and early 1918 it was not surprising that the radical right became restive and began to campaign both inside and outside the Unionist party for the removal of Lloyd George. An unofficial Die-hard faction of the Unionists tried to undermine the coalition from within, supporting the army in its battle with Lloyd George over military control on the western front during the Maurice debate.

Two Conservatives, Henry Page Croft and Sir Richard Cooper, stalwarts from the pre-war Chamberlain tariff reform campaign, founded the National Party in 1917 as a protest against the Coalition government. Its programme included the raising of the conscription age to fifty, the closing of German-owned businesses, the internment of enemy aliens, conscription for Ireland, a guaranteed price for home-grown cereals, protection for British industry and counter air raids against German towns. The party put up twenty-three candidates at the Coupon Election in 1918, but only Croft and Cooper were elected. The party rejoined the coalition in 1921 in order to work against it from the inside. Both Croft and Cooper assaulted the honours system and Lloyd George's use of patronage, but by 1922 they had joined forces with a wider Die-hard campaign of which the Duke of Northumberland was the figurehead and Maxse and Gwynne its main publicists.[4]

The radical right's anxieties had been further strengthened by the effects of the Bolshevik revolution of 1917. Not only had it removed Russia from the war, but its call for international

---

[4] Cowling, *Impact of Labour*, pp. 75–8; Farr, 'The development and impact of right wing politics in Great Britain, 1903–32', PhD thesis, University of Illinois, 1976, p. 112.

revolution and the threatened collapse of the ruling class in much of central and eastern Europe in 1918, combined with an increase in working-class militancy at home, frightened many in the middle classes even outside the radical right. A plethora of pressure groups and popular movements grew up to give vent to such feelings, including the British Empire Union and the National Citizens Union.

This fear found its most extreme expression in the activities of Alan Percy and his supporters, who can be seen as a connecting link between the pre-war Die-hards and a conservative fascist tradition. Although his death allegedly prevented the Duke of Northumberland from founding an anti-alien party,[5] there were distinct links between the more extreme fringes of the Die-hard revolt and the emergence of British fascism. The chief connections proved to be anti-semitism, anti-socialism and a patriotic espousal of the cause of the British Empire. This was expressed in a more rational and less extreme form than in the Britons Society, although individuals like Baron Sydenham of Coombe appeared to be connected with both. Die-hard conservatism represented a continuation of the fears and anxieties that had surfaced in those most respectable publications, *The Times* and the *Morning Post*, with their debates over the *Protocols of the Elders of Zion* and the *Cause of World Unrest*, at the end of the war.[6] Indeed, the Duke of Northumberland was to purchase the *Morning Post* as a mouthpiece for Die-hard conservatism in 1924. The general tone was to follow the case put forward by Maxse and the Chestertons. The basic argument was that traditional conservatism should re-establish itself by an uncompromising opposition to liberalism and socialism and by combating the supposed international Jewish conspiracy whose sole purpose was the undermining of the British Empire.

To these ends the Duke of Northumberland financed a publishing house, the Boswell Publishing Company, in 1921 and established a weekly newspaper, *The Patriot*, in 1922. With further injections of capital of £2,500 from Lady Houston and an anonymous bequest of £6,750, the cause of aristocratic Die-hard conservatism was to survive, at least in journalistic form, until

[5] Cowling, *Impact of Labour*, p. 85.
[6] G.C. Lebzelter, *Political Anti-Semitism in England 1918–1939* (London, 1979), pp. 13–28; Holmes, *Anti-Semitism in British Society*, pp. 147–56.

1950. The family connection linked the enterprise to the pre-war Die-hard revolt, and Nesta Webster – the principal author of the Boswell Publishing Company – linked it to both the National Citizens Union and the BF.[7]

Even with the addition of the *Morning Post* to the publishing empire in 1924, Die-hard journalism was fighting a losing battle. Aristocratic paternalism and Die-hardism had little place in Baldwin's Conservative party. Its evocation of an idealized pre-war era and its commitment to anti-semitism prevented it from joining forces with other maverick Conservative press barons like Rothermere and Beaverbrook. The dominance of orthodox economic policies, cautious pragmatism and consensus politics reflected the mood of the British electorate in the 1920s rather more than did the utopian assumptions of the Die-hard remnant.

Indeed, in political terms Die-hard conservatism proved to be even less relevant than its pre-war namesake. The Duke of Northumberland's political concerns had little or no significance for contemporary society, a fact acknowledged by Nesta Webster in her conspiracy theory novel, *The Secret of the Zodiac*. Here Parbury (Baldwin), the prime minister, was portrayed as supporting the League of Nations, recognizing Soviet Russia and encouraging self-government in India.[8] His benign indifference to the grave problems of the contemporary world was seen as one of the main causes of the threatened collapse of British civilization and of the total isolation of the Die-hards. Baldwin was to undermine the radical right as effectively as he disarmed the left in the inter-war period. The radical right mainly drifted back towards the Conservative party and only a small minority associated with the emerging fascist movement. The rump of Die-hard support around the Boswell publishing concerns was to survive as part of an underground tradition. In 1950 the company was wound up and its copyright taken over by the Britons Society, in a merger of racial nationalist and Die-hard conservative traditions – an ideological alliance of two of the major strands of political thought which later heavily influenced the ideas of the National Front.

[7] R. Griffiths, *Fellow Travellers of the Right* (London, 1983), p. 89.
[8] 'J. Sterne' (N. Webster), *The Secret of the Zodiac* (London, 1933), p. 61.

Rotha Lintorn Orman and the British Fascisti

Rather less ideological in its programme was the British Fascisti formed in 1923 by Rotha Lintorn Orman. Although there were links to other organizations, such as through Arnold Leese to the Britons and Nesta Webster to the extremist Die-hards, the organization's political roots had greater connections to the mainly middle-class pressure groups which evolved at the end of the war to protect property against the alleged socialist menace, the most important of which were the British Empire Union, the Middle Classes Union and the National Citizens Union.[9] These in turn were similar in political structure and function to pre-war pressure groups which had reflected popular anxiety against German competition.[10] There was some evidence, however, that for fascism to evolve in Britain, it needed to recruit new members from the lower middle and working classes, who had few, if any, previous political connections. Certainly many of the ordinary rank and file, like William Joyce in the early years, were of this nature; and it seems significant that J. Havelock Wilson of the Seaman's Union, a stalwart of working-class anti-socialist movements, spoke at an anti-Bolshevik meeting stewarded by 600 fascists at the Royal Albert Hall in 1926.[11]

Rotha Lintorn Orman was a spirited young middle-class woman who was concerned about the growing industrial unrest and threat to property posed by the emergence of a socialist Labour party and an alleged communist menace. She was born in 1895 to an army major and his wife and was granddaughter to a field marshal. Her independence and organizing ability had been displayed early when she joined the Girl Scouts in 1909 and formed the first Bournemouth troop of guides. During the First World War she volunteered for the Women's Reserve Ambulance and twice won the Croix de Charité for gallantry for heroic rescues in Salonica. Invalided home with malaria in 1917, her war experiences no doubt contributed to her indifferent health and drink problem, which were to be factors in the weakness of the BF

[9] Farr, 'Right wing politics', pp. 53–100.

[10] A. Summers, 'The character of Edwardian nationalism: three popular leagues', in *Nationalist and Racialist Movements in Britain before 1914*, ed. R. Kennedy and A. Nicholls (Oxford, 1981), pp. 70–87.

[11] *British Lion*, late July 1926.

before her death in 1935.[12] Her main concerns in the internal politics of the BF were to encourage independence and self-reliance in women, to combat socialist Sunday schools and the Kibbo Kift, to establish BF children's clubs, and to discourage takeovers by more militant authoritarian or anti-semitic rivals.

Rotha Lintorn Orman admired Mussolini as a man who had dealt firmly with the socialist menace. Apart from that fact she knew little of the nature or content of his fascist experiment. She borrowed the name and very little else from Italy. There was some connection between the British Fascisti and Italy, however, but no evidence of foreign funding. Several of the closed files on the BF seem to refer to their activity in Italy through their links with the International Centre of Fascist Studies, and the Foreign Office was aware that a British resident called Captain Strina was attempting to form a legion of the organization amongst expatriates in that country.[13] However, apart from that connection the British Fascisti reflected Rotha Lintorn Orman's own experience of the Girl Guides, public service and a military background rather than any emulation of continental examples or ideologies. As a result the BF was organized as a cross between a glorified boy scout movement and a paramilitary group.

The organization was run by an executive council who were responsible to a grand council, and was administered locally at the county level. Districts were created that were responsible for the basic unit structure of seven members. The movement was divided between the infantry (the small unit of seven men), the cavalry and motorized transport, the propaganda and publicity section and the intelligence department. The membership was further split between the active flying squads and the reserves. Active members paid six shillings a month whilst inactive ones paid one shilling.[14] Meeting platforms were festooned with a plethora of union jacks and members wore badges and gave the Italian fascist salute. In 1927 the blue shirt was adopted as the official uniform and in the 1930s a beret and dark trousers or skirt were added. Vastly inflated claims were made about the membership, which reached its peak in 1925–6 with several thousand active members. Accounts published during the bankruptcy proceedings in 1935

[12] Griffiths, *Fellow Travellers*, p. 92.
[13] PRO HO 144/19069/211–12.
[14] R. Benewick, *The Fascist Movement in Britain* (London, 1972), pp. 27–39.

suggested that the subscription income had been £6,848 in 1925, £604 in 1928 and afterwards less than £400 a year.[15]

The position of Rotha Lintorn Orman in the organization was explained in large part by her financial resources. Her mother had handed over most of her fortune of £50,000 to Rotha and this was used to fund the organization. She also received a monthly allowance from her mother. The grand council of the movement was dominated by retired military officers of the Colonel Blimp type, Die-hard conservatives, landed gentry and emancipated middle-class women. The first president was Lord Garvagh, who was succeeded by Brigadier-General Blakeney from 1924–6. Blakeney, who had been general manager of the Egyptian State Railway from 1919 to 1923, was responsible for organizing the tight-knit military discipline of the organization and for turning the BF into a limited company, the anglicized British Fascists Ltd, in 1924. He was also later to be connected with both the Imperial Fascist League (IFL) and the BUF.[16]

Other notable members who entered fascism through the BF, included Arnold Leese, later of the IFL, and William Joyce, Neil Francis Hawkins, E.G. Mandeville Roe and H.J. Donovan of the BUF. Arnold Leese was one of two fascist councillors elected at Stamford in Lincolnshire in 1924.[17] William Joyce's fanatical commitment to fascism was strengthened after receiving a razor slash on his cheek while helping steward a Conservative party meeting at Lambeth Baths in October 1924.[18] Neither found the BF a suitable vehicle for their increasingly anti-semitic views as the organization did not become hostile to Jews before 1932. Leese considered the initials of the organization to be unfortunate, and argued quite logically that it was misnamed, as its platform had little to do with fascism.[19] Nesta Webster, however, who was a member of the grand council for three months in 1926 and 1927, thought that the BF had done more for British patriotism than all the other middle-class organizations put together,[20] and soon after

[15] H. Blume, 'Anti-semitic groups in Britain 1918–1940', MPhil thesis, University of Sussex, 1971, p. 106.

[16] Griffiths, *Fellow Travellers*, p. 355.

[17] A. Leese, *Out of Step* (Guildford, 1947), p. 49.

[18] J.A. Cole, *Lord Haw Haw and William Joyce* (London, 1964), p. 30.

[19] Leese, *Out of Step*, p. 49.

[20] *British Lion*, 7 Jan. 1927.

leaving established a Patriots Enquiry Centre, a kind of Die-hard library where the ultra-right could study the socialist menace.[21]

The fact that such later fascist luminaries became rapidly dissatisfied with the BF was due mainly to its failure to become either an accepted ally of the state preparations against political extremism or a credible independent political movement in the 1920s. In spite of its activism, its military discipline, the stewarding of right-wing Conservative speakers, the attempted abduction of Harry Pollitt, and strikebreaking activities, the BF made little impact. The increasing eccentricity of its founder alienated many as well. Although there was no leadership cult, Rotha Linton Orman developed an increasing knack of instigating factional disagreement in the movement at periodic intervals, and as a result of the lack of initiative, leadership and purpose, there was a high turnover of membership.

The first serious split occurred in 1925 with the formation of the National Fascists, a group of about 100 which broke away from the parent organization on the grounds that the BF were neither sufficiently anti-semitic nor fascist. For a time it proved to be more militant than the BF. A meeting in Hyde Park in 1926 was attended by 1,000 people and ended with a fight with communist demonstrators.[22] Other stunts included the breaking up of Labour party meetings and vandalizing a *Daily Herald* van by driving it into the railings of a London church. The movement survived as the National Fascists for three years, with a black shirt uniform. However, it too suffered from factional splits and lack of finance. In the winter of 1926–7 a power struggle brought it to the attention of the police. Its leader, a Colonel Seymour, was charged with committing common assault on Charles Eyres, the leader of the Croydon branch of the organization, after a dispute in which Eyres claimed that Seymour had misappropriated funds and altered the constitution to turn himself into a virtual dictator;[23] this led to Seymour drawing a sword and pointing an unlicensed gun at Eyres. In terms of ideology, the National Fascists were more extreme than the BF. According to an article in the paper's journal, the *Fascist Gazette*, communists were 'wild beasts' whose 'hell's spawn' should be pushed into the sea.[24] Socialists and commun-

[21] *Daily Telegraph*, 19 Nov. 1927.
[22] PRO HO 144/19069/85.
[23] PRO HO 144/19069/107–9.
[24] PRO HO 144/19069/93; *Fascist Gazette*, no. 18.

ists would be drastically punished, and the present franchise system would be restricted in the National Fascist state.

An equally serious split occurred in 1926 over the issue of the General Strike. This posed the problem of the relationship between the BF, the government and the Conservative party. During the strike Rotha Lintorn Orman organized a fleet of cars from her mother's London address to transport strike-breakers to work. She offered the services of 200,000 members – a grossly inflated claim – to join with the National Citizens Union in the Organization for the Maintenance of Supplies. Sir William Joynson Hicks, the Home Secretary and vice-president of the National Citizens Union, threatened to resign from that organization if the proposal was accepted. He objected to the aims of the BF and its vague idea to introduce a corporate state. The proposal of help could only be accepted if the BF altered their constitution to make explicit their belief in parliamentary government. While Blakeney and five other members of the fascist grand council accepted these terms, Rotha Lintorn Orman dug her heels in and with other members narrowly defeated the proposals, which would have abolished the independent status of the BF.[25] Blakeney and several others then resigned.

These two internal rows greatly weakened the movement. After the General Strike it rapidly declined and Rotha Lintorn Orman's tenuous grasp of reality disintegrated still further. Several attempts to gain permission to publish a photograph of King George V in the BF journal, *The Lion*, were refused. Her request to hold a Remembrance Day parade two months early in 1927, when 15,000 BF members would salute the king at Buckingham Palace during a march to the Cenotaph, was turned down.[26] The police became irritated too with the need to check her unsubstantiated claim that there were communist arms dumps and Russian involvement in plans for revolutionary uprisings.[27] Such activities as there were led to sporadic violence with communists and communist front organizations, such as the disruption of the International Class War Prisoners Aid meeting at Trafalgar Square in January 1927.[28]

[25] PRO HO 144/19069/21–3.
[26] PRO HO 144/19069/26.
[27] PRO HO 45/25386/37–40.
[28] PRO HO 144/19069/79.

As the BF increasingly lacked purpose and credibility other emerging movements became interested in its assets. Rotha Lintorn Orman, who appeared to become steadily more dependent on alcohol, became increasingly intransigent. She split the organization again in 1931 when Francis Hawkins and Mandeville Roe accepted Mosley's merger terms with the New Party, whilst the women on the committee turned them down. However, in the 1930s, with her deteriorating health and the takeover of its most committed members by the BUF, the BF became practically moribund. There were plans to revive it and turn it into an Ulster Loyalist pressure group when a leading member, Archibald Whitmore, an ex-member of the Ulster Volunteer Force, announced to influential people at the Bath Club that he planned to develop the BF in Ireland along the same lines as the movement in 1914.[29] However, this plan and one for merger with the IFL failed to materialize.[30] Negotiations with another pocket Mussolini, Lt. Colonel Graham Seaton Hutchinson, and his National Worker Party, also fizzled out; his proposal to merge the two groups into the British Empire Fascist Party probably collapsed when the BF realized that the National Worker Party was aptly named. In spite of Hutchinson's claims that he had 20,000 members in the Mansfield district, and large numbers of followers in Lancashire and other industrial areas, and that he had printed hundreds of thousands of copies of the *National Worker*, there was no evidence that he had any members in his organization.[31]

Increasing financial difficulties became another problem when Rotha Lintorn Orman's mother cut her allowance, believing that the BF had been taken over by disreputable elements, who lived off her daughter's money and manipulated her by making her increasingly dependent on alcohol and drugs. Druken orgies and undesirable practices were alleged to have taken place at her London home.[32] Whatever the truth behind this accusation, it was noticeable that the BF became increasingly anti-semitic in its death throes. In 1933 its total membership was believed to be about 300, but the cost of a fund-raising appeal for £25,000 proved to be more than the sum collected and the movement went £800 into debt. When in 1934 a further loan of £500 from a Colonel Wilson

[29] PRO HO 45/25386/37–40.
[30] *British Fascism*, June 1934.
[31] PRO HO 144/19070/92.
[32] PRO HO 45/25386/37–40.

was not repaid, he forced the movement into bankruptcy after Rotha Lintorn Orman once more vetoed a merger with the BUF. She never recovered from the demise of Britain's first fascist organization and died a year later.

The decline of the BF, which ended in such inglorious circumstances in the bankruptcy court, was due to several factors. The organization lacked coherent leadership and purpose and was little more than a patriotic group with a foreign-sounding name. Although developed as a mass movement, it had no leadership cult, and despite William Joyce's scar, confrontation with socialists was small beer compared with the castor oil politics of Italy in the 1920s. Its importance for the development of fascism in Britain has to be seen in terms of the administration and discipline which the group who left to join Mosley in 1931 supplied to the BUF.

Nesta Webster and the conspiracy theory

The impact of the ideological inheritance of these conservative elements by later forms of British fascism was to be delayed. The BUF had little time for the reactionary tone of Die-hard conservatism, and its anti-semitism was derived from social and economic grievances rather than from an ideological tradition. Its significance was to be more for the racial nationalist tradition and the development of non-Mosley fascism after the Second World War. The contribution of the reactionary aristocratic conservative case and its pseudo-academic presentation was to provide an underground tradition which possessed a dual function, an appeal to patriotic nationalists and an ideal cover for died-in-the-wool fascists and nazis to re-emerge in more acceptable guise.

The contribution of the Duke of Northumberland's publishing ventures to the eventual emergence of conservative and racial fascism in Britain was to supply a seemingly rational conspiracy theory on which opposition to the British political system could be based. The *Protocols of the Elders of Zion* were proved to be a forgery by *The Times* in 1921 and this went some way to defuse the growth of anti-semitic tendencies within the wider political culture.[33] For those who wished to retain belief in the conspiracy

---

[33] Holmes, *Anti-Semitism in British Society*, pp. 151–6.

explanation of modern political events, an alternative version was supplied by the *Morning Post*, the *Patriot* and the publications of the Boswell Publishing Company. All these sources supported Die-hard conservatism and their conspiracy views were resurrected later by British fascist groups. Although the main contributors to this tradition, such as the Duke of Northumberland, Baron Sydenham of Combe, Catherine Stoddart and Nesta Webster, were implicit believers of the *Protocols*, a more historical explanation was offered. This was based on the research of Nesta Webster, the grand dame of British conspiracy theory, who saw Jews in alliance with other subversive forces, as being behind all the ills of the modern world, from the threats to the British Empire through to the nudity movement.[34]

The alternative to the *Protocols* as a base to the conspiracy theory was the revival of the French counter-revolutionary tradition, which had been developed in the first articles in the 'Cause of World Unrest' disclosures in the *Morning Post* in July 1920, and was handed down to posterity in more permanent form in Nesta Webster's version of world history. The basic argument of this tradition was that revolution was caused by the machinations of secret societies, who used their knowledge of occult forces to undermine authority and the stability of governments. Freemasons were seen to be the power behind the French Revolution, whose role in contemporary disturbances such as the Russian Revolution had been taken over by the Jews.

Nesta Webster had been deeply influenced by the occult revival of the late nineteenth century, although she was hostile to its basic humanist and evolutionary precepts.[35] Somewhat ironically, given the role bankers were to play in the conspiracy theory, she was the daughter of a director of Barclay's Bank. Her ideas can fairly be described as the intersection of personal and group fantasies.[36] Her personal delusion is described quite clearly in her autobiography. Whilst researching the material for her second book, the *Chevalier de Boufflers*, a romantic story about two French aristocrats on the eve of the French Revolution, she underwent a mystical experience. She became convinced that she had read the letters of the Chevalier de Boufflers to the Comtesse

---

[34] N. Webster, *The Socialist Network* (London, 1926), p. 121.
[35] Idem, *Spacious Days* (London, 1949), pp. 88–9.
[36] D.B. Davis (ed.), *The Fear of Conspiracy* (Ithaca, 1972), p. xii.

de Sabran in another life, and that she might be a reincarnation.[37] This belief so dominated her thoughts that she began to form a coherent political ideology based on what she imagined the *ancien régime* to have been like, and became convinced of the perfection of the aristocratic society of eighteenth-century France. For Nesta Webster the French Revolution came to represent the cause of all the problems of the modern world.

Although the Chevalier de Boufflers was highly successful, with fifteen editions published, her attempt to place it in context in *The French Revolution* was harshly treated by some historians. Her contention that this event was a result of a twofold plot of the Duc d'Orléans and the Illuminati, organized from Germany, was heavily criticized by several reviewers. In retrospect it is clear that the rejection of her work merely deepened her anxiety and revealed the beginnings of a persecution complex. Her literary concern about the doleful consequences of the French Revolution was turned into a political neurosis by the contemporary situation in 1918.[38]

Nesta Webster's fears had been reinforced by the collapse of the traditional social order in Europe in 1918. This led her to search for a continuous tradition which had been activated by occult means and linked the French and Russian Revolutions. With the transition from a basically personal hatred of the French Revolution to the more general threat to society posed by the Russian Revolution, continental freemasonry became insufficient as a causal explanation. The Jewish cabbala was introduced as the force which originally inspired the freemasons.[39] The Jews became the link which undermined both the English national state and the structure of society. It had been the Jews, together with Prussian militarism, that had been behind the Russian Revolution.[40] To this ethnocentric anti-semitism Webster added a belief in the sentiments, if not the authenticity, of the *Protocols of the Elders of Zion*. This, she argued, was very similar to the code of Weishaupt,

---

[37] N. Webster, *Spacious Days*, p. 173.

[38] Idem, *World Revolution* (London, 1919), p. viii; R. Gilman, *Behind World Revolution*, vol. I (Ann Arbor, 1982), pp. 13–37; R. Thurlow, 'The powers of darkness', *Patterns of Prejudice* 12, 6 (Nov.–Dec. 1978), pp. 10–12; J. Michell, *Eccentric Lives and Peculiar Notions* (London, 1984), pp. 62–74.

[39] N. Webster, *Secret Societies and Subversive Movements* (London, 1928), p. 166.

[40] Idem, *World Revolution*, p. 311.

the founder of the Illuminati, which in her view had caused the French Revolution.

This interpretation of the forces behind history in *The French Revolution* and *World Revolution* was taken to its logical conclusion in her most notorious work, *Secret Societies and Subversive Movements*. With meticulous footnoting, she now argued that all plots and revolutions against the social order in human history had been caused by secret societies, through the use of black magic, mass hypnotism and telepathy.[41] With eight editions published by 1964, this was to be the main connection linking Nesta Webster to the development of the fascist conspiracy theory.

Although a member of the BF grand council in 1926, her political roots and beliefs emanated from Die-hard conservatism. Of little significance in the inter-war period, her ideas developed a new lease of life, both in Britain and the USA, after the Second World War, because her rationally expressed anti-semitism and pseudo-academic version of world history proved influential in themselves, as well as providing a respectable cover for more extreme ideas.[42] Her work became an ideal basis for a revisionist fascist conspiracy theory. Those who wished to appeal more directly to fascist or nazi ideas would criticize her Christian and anti-German ideas, while stating that she was on the right track. Others argued that her theories lacked an understanding of financial power. (The channel for the survival of Webster's ideas in Britain within the fascist tradition was to be provided by the publications of Arnold Leese and the Britons Society.) Although her views are still regarded as highly eccentric outside reactionary conservative and fascist circles, it is interesting to note that some historians now argue that secret societies like the IRA and the Mafia have indeed played a significant role in world events, and that the Illuminati conspiracy in the 1780s was truly a model for future revolutionary organization.[43]

The BF, despite its short connection with Webster, was to have little relevance for the development of a native fascist ideological tradition. This was apparent in the BUF where the main administrative clique, who were recruited from the BF, were

---

[41] Idem, *Secret Societies*, p. 30.
[42] Gilman, *Behind World Revolution*, pp. 1–12.
[43] J. Billington, *Fire in the Minds of Men* (New York, 1980).

derided as totally lacking in ideas by the more ideologically committed.[44] Nevertheless Mandeville Roe, an ex-BF member, did write a book on the Corporate State in Italy, and together with Alexander Raven Thomson provided the chief source of such ideas in the BUF. Yet apart from this the BF policy was vague and generalized. Its main components included the upholding of the monarchy, promotion of class friendship, the elimination of the slums, the encouragement of Empire trade, the drastic restriction of immigration and hostility to Bolshevism and socialism.[45] There was no overt anti-semitism before 1932, although calls for the purification of race and criticism of moneylending no doubt could be interpreted as such by those who saw the hidden hand of the Jews everywhere. The significance of the BF therefore was to be in its administration and the fact that it was the first British organization to link itself specifically with Mussolini's new form of politics, in however diluted a form.

[44] PRO HO 144/21063/10–11.
[45] British Lion, late June 1926.

4

The Jew Wise,
1918–1939

M ore ideologically militant than the British Fascists, although even fewer in numbers, were the groups who could be seen as closest to the nazis in their thought and inspiration. These were the self-proclaimed 'Jew wise',[1] an odd mixture of reactionary conservatives and racial fascist enthusiasts whose obsession with political anti-semitism was to lead to an alternative tradition in British fascism to that provided by Mosley. The most important exponents of these beliefs in the inter-war period came from three organizations: the Britons Society, the Imperial Fascist League and the Nordic League. The common element in all such movements was a fanatical belief in the authenticity and argument of the notorious forgery, the *Protocols of the Elders of Zion*, an obsessional Jew hatred based on a gutter anti-semitism or an older Christian tradition, and a racial nationalist outlook.[2] Reliable intelligence reports from meetings of such groups refer to such audience comments as 'Kill the Jews', 'Perish Judea', 'We hate them' and 'Bastards'.[3] The conspiracy mentality of members of these organizations represented a mirror image of the alleged Jewish plot to subvert the world, and partly explained the secrecy with which they hid most of their activities, and the fact that so very few knew of their existence.

[1] PRO HO 45/24968/116. See also 'Memorandum on the Nordic League and other organisations', Nordic League File, Board of Deputies of British Jews, 1939, p. 14.
[2] N. Cohn, *Warrant for Genocide* (London, 1967), p. 169.
[3] Memorandum on Nordic League, p. 20; PRO HO 144/21379/237; HO 144/22454/136.

Extreme anti-semitism and its significance

Although parts of this tradition have been examined in great detail, some of the most important aspects of it for this theme have received little attention. The major historians of political anti-semitism in Britain in the inter-war period, Colin Holmes and Gisela Lebzelter, have produced fascinating accounts of the publication of the *Protocols* in England, the ideology of the belief system and the personalities of Arnold Leese and Henry Hamilton Beamish.[4] However, they have said very little about the membership or the nature of political argument within the Britons or the IFL, and almost nothing on the most important of the extreme anti-semitic organizations, the NL, and its guiding spirit, Archibald H. Maule Ramsay MP. Indeed, only one unpublished study has referred to the activities of this group and the concern with which the Board of Deputies of British Jews viewed it.[5] Yet in many ways recently released Home Office papers on the IFL and the NL, particularly when it is related to the information in the Board of Deputies Archives, gives us much-needed new information on these matters. This is as significant and interesting material as the recently released Mosley papers and helps to illuminate the divergent nature of British fascism and the very mixed and complex attitudes fascists and anti-semites had towards Hitler.

The relevance of these organizations certainly did not lie in the number of their supporters and activists. Although each of them gave greatly inflated estimates of their membership, reliable intelligence reports suggest that they were shoestring operations with minimal popular impact. The minute book of the Britons speaks of average attendance at meetings of between thirty and fifty members, and Special Branch officers discovered that the circulation of its newspaper *The Hidden Hand* was only 150 per month.[6] Even the most detailed study of Arnold Leese and the IFL

[4] C. Holmes, *Anti-Semitism in British Society 1876–1939* (London, 1979), pp. 49–85; idem 'New light on the "Protocols of Zion"', *Patterns of Prejudice*, 11, 6 (Nov.–Dec. 1977), pp. 13–20; G. Lebzelter, *Political Anti-Semitism in England 1918–1939* (London, 1979), pp. 49–85.

[5] H. Blume, 'A history of anti-semitic groups 1918–40', unpublished MPhil thesis, University of Sussex, 1971, pp. 248–50.

[6] The Britons Minute Book, PRO HO 144/21377/28.

has overestimated the size of membership;[7] intelligence reports
have suggested that IFL numbers, despite inflated claims of several
thousands, averaged only 150 during most of the 1930s. Its
activities were only kept going by fifty enthusiasts living in London
and the obsessional fanaticism of Leese, its guiding spirit.[8] The
print order for its main propaganda vehicle, *The Fascist*, published
between 1929 and 1939, was certainly more impressive than for
the journal of the Britons; but of the 3,000 produced, 1,000 were
purchased by a Mr Pope of Porthcawl and many of the remainder
were sent to South Africa.[9]

The Security Service reported in the war that the IFL was mainly
subsidised by Leese's private means and that the largest individual
contribution, by a Colonel Macdonald of Brussels in the period for
which cash books were found between September 1930 and
August 1933 and from June 1937 to November 1938, was only £5
per month with a special donation from him of £50 in November
1938.[10] The more popular meetings of the NL were attended by
between 200 and 400, although attendances fell rapidly in the
summer of 1939.[11]

The membership of such groups showed a marked bias towards
individuals of *petit bourgeois* or middle-class background who
had obsessions of varying intensity about the Jews. Otherwise
members seem to have exhibited a fairly normal range of
personality and most seem to have been socially well-adjusted
despite the extremism of their anti-semitic views. There was also a
small working-class and youth element attached to the IFL, some
of whom acted as a kind of precursor of the skinhead and football
hooligan types later attracted to the National Front and British
Movement.[12]

The true significance of these groups was fourfold. Firstly, the
Britons and the IFL, although unimportant in themselves, were to
provide crucial financial, publishing and ideological links to the
revival of British fascism after the Second World War. Second,
the activities of Maule Ramsay and the two secret societies he was

[7] J. Morell, 'The life and opinions of A.S. Leese. A study in extreme anti-semitism', MA
thesis, University of Sheffield, 1974, p. 25.
[8] PRO HO 45/24967/37.
[9] PRO HO 45/24967/37.
[10] PRO HO 45/24967/105.
[11] PRO HO 144/21381/244; Memorandum on Nordic League, p. 22.
[12] M. Billig, *Fascists* (London, 1978), pp. 235–95.

connected with, the Right Club and NL, and his links with Mosley in 1939–40, were to be responsible for the internment of many fascists without trial in the Second World War, and in part the mutual recriminations between Mosleyites and racial nationalists which fragmented the revival of the tradition after 1945. Third, the important *Rex* v. *Leese* case in 1936 as explained later nevertheless established reluctance by the authorities to prosecute obvious cases of seditious libel against Jews and other minorities if public order was not threatened, because publicity might create more harm than good and because of the fear that jury acquittals might be misunderstood. Fourth, the IFL was associated with secretive underground activities which implicated it as one of the originators of a tradition of direct action and racial violence against immigrants.

Whilst there were obvious similarities between this tradition and nazism, its inspiration and origins occur in a period before anybody in England had heard of Hitler. Prior to the First World War unrelieved hostility towards the Jews, which expressed both obsession with their alleged power and ascribed to them filthy moral and personal habits, was rare. Only Joseph Banister in his *England under the Jews* appeared to suggest a total pathological malice towards them.[13] He was a journalist who later edited the *British Guardian* in 1924.[14] Sir Richard Burton had also revived ill-informed prejudices in his accounts of alleged Jewish ritual murder, even if the Board of Deputies of British Jews forced drastic pruning of his original text.[15] Yet the same forces and influences on society which saw the emergence of the Die-hards as the main force of the radical right after the First World War also saw more extremist reactions from a small but significant group who thought like Banister, and who were prepared to use Burton's supposed evidence.

Beamish and the Britons

More plebeian than the Die-hards and entirely independent of Conservative control were the activities of populist organiza-

[13] Holmes, *Anti-Semitism in British Society*, pp. 42–5; J. Banister, *England under the Heel of the Jew* (London, 1907).

[14] 'The Britons' (London, 1952).

[15] Holmes, *Anti-Semitism in British Society*, pp. 52–3; R. Burton, *The Jew, the Gypsy and El Islam* (London, 1898).

tions who rose to challenge the Coalition government in by-elections at the end of the war. Fired by the oratory of such as Horatio Bottomley and Pemberton Billing, groups such as the Silver Badge Party of ex-Servicemen showed the degree of dissatisfaction with the management of the war. Standing as an Independent, Henry Hamilton Beamish came within 1181 votes of winning such a by-election in Clapham in June 1918. In December 1918 he came second in the same constituency in the Coupon election.[16] After a short association with Pemberton Billing's Silver Badge Party of ex-Servicemen, Beamish quarrelled with him and developed his own organization, which he called the Britons Society.

Of all the multiplicity of middle-class organizations which arose as a response to the dislocation of war and the perceived threat of socialism in Great Britain, the distinguishing feature of the Britons Society was its crude and obsessional anti-semitism. Formed by Beamish in 1918 as a patriotic organization dedicated to the eradication of what it termed alien influences in British life, the Britons campaigned for the forced expulsion of Jews from England and for the revoking of the Act of Settlement of 1700,[17] which would ensure that immigrants and their descendents would be ineligible to hold public office. The Britons claimed to discern a 'hidden hand' in British government which had delayed the victory against Germany in the war, and argued that Jews had organized an international conspiracy designed to promote anarchy and disorder in the world. With such beliefs the Society proved receptive to both the nativist anti-semitic tradition which had been focused on the anti-alien campaign in the East End of London between 1900 and 1905, to the Marconi scandal before the First World War, and to international influences such as the White Russian anti-semitic propaganda directed at the Bolsheviks after 1918. This latter influence became more pronounced when the Britons took over the George Shanks version of the *Protocols*, entitled *The Jewish Peril*, in 1920, and published the Victor Marsden version, *World Conquest through World Government*, in 1921.[18] Later the Britons showed an interest in the activities of

[16] G. Lebzelter, 'Henry Hamilton Beamish and the Britons. Champions of anti-semitism', in *British Fascism*, ed. K. Lunn and R. Thurlow (London, 1980), pp. 41–56.

[17] *The Jew's Who's Who*, ed. H. Beamish (London, 1920), pp. 258–9.

[18] C. Holmes, 'The Protocols of the Britons', *Patterns of Prejudice*, 12, 6, (Nov.–Dec.

the National Socialist Workers Party in Munich and Beamish spoke at a Hitler meeting.[19]

The Britons remained a small lecturing and debating society, with a minuscule middle-class membership.[20] The organization concentrated its activities on publishing anti-semitic literature, most notably the *Protocols* and Beamish's own concoction *The Jew's Who's Who* (1920). Beamish had formed the provocatively titled Judaic Publishing Company, which was renamed the Britons Publishing Company in August 1922. Apart from the minutes of the two meetings in 1932 and 1948 there is little evidence that the Britons Society survived longer than that of its regular monthly publication from 1920–5. This was the journal *Jewry Ueber Alles* which had just been published in February 1920, and had altered its name to *The Hidden Hand* in September 1920 and to the *British Guardian* in May 1924.

The Britons Publishing Society, however, had a much more lasting effect on British racist thought. Dedicated to printing anti-semitic material and to disseminating the *Protocols* and other variants of the conspiracy theory of history, it was formally separated from the parent society in 1932, and continued as a publishing and distribution business for extreme right-wing groups until the 1970s, producing eighty-five editions of the *Protocols* as well as becoming the main outlet for circulating American conspiracy theory works and racist material.[21] As a small clandestine organization the Britons Publishing Society was to become the main ideological source of an underworld whose principal themes were later to influence the racial nationalist tradition from the IFL through to the National Front.

The founder and president of the organization from 1918 to 1948 was the above-mentioned Henry Hamilton Beamish. Beamish was the son of an admiral who was *aide de camp* to Queen Victoria, and brother of the Conservative MP for Lewes. He fought in both the Boer and First World Wars. In South Africa he came to the conclusion that the Boer War had been fought for the benefit of Jewish gold and diamond financiers, who were

---

1978), pp. 13–18; G. Lebzelter, 'The Protocols in England', *Wiener Library Bulletin*, 31, 47–8 (1978), pp. 111–17.

[19] *The Hidden Hand*, 3, 2 (Feb. 1923).

[20] C.C. Aronsfeld, 'The Britons Publishing Society', *Wiener Library Bulletin*, 20 (Summer 1966), pp. 31–5.

[21] *Britons Library*, List no. 3, 1978.

exploiting British imperialism for their own international
purposes. This, combined with the presence of Jewish revolutionaries in the Bolshevik uprising, and the alleged Jewish capitalist funding of the communists from Wall Street, convinced him
that there was a plot to undermine civilization and the British
Empire.[22] The British government was seen as completely
dominated by Jewish interests since the Marconi scandal, with
Isaacs, Montagu and Mond allegedly pulling the strings behind
Lloyd George. With the rise of Lloyd George to become prime
minister in 1916 Britain was now ruled by the 'Jewalition'.[23] The
manifest disasters of the war could be quantified exactly in
anti-semitic terms. Jews were supposedly responsible for one-
quarter of the casualties of the war.[24]

Beamish decided to communicate such views to a wider public.
Together with H. McCleod Frazer of the Silver Badge Party for
ex-Servicemen, Beamish displayed a notice at Charing Cross in
1919 which alleged that Sir Alfred Mond was a traitor and that he
had allocated shares to Germans during the war. In substance this
merely repeated the libel levelled against Mond by the New
Witness in October 1918, where it was alleged that the Mond-
Nickel Company had distributed shares to enemy subjects without
government sanction.[25] This represented the end of a campaign
where patriotic English Jews of German extraction were
denounced as potential or actual traitors by the popular press and
the New Witness, National Review or John Bull. Whilst such
German immigrants earnestly desired peace, there is no evidence
of unpatriotic behaviour.[26] Beamish was sued by Mond and
judgement was found in the plaintiff's favour to the cost of
£5,000. In order to escape payment Beamish fled the country and
he only returned to Britain at irregular intervals from then on. His
later role as a kind of travelling salesman of international anti-
semitism is only tangentially related to the scope of this study,
although he was to be of considerable significance in his role as
vice-president of the IFL and the legacy he bequeathed to Arnold

[22] Lebzelter, 'Henry Hamilton Beamish and the Britons', p. 42.
[23] Jewry Ueber Alles, 1, 7 (Aug. 1920).
[24] The Hidden Hand, 1, 10 (Nov. 1920).
[25] Holmes, Anti-Semitism in British Society pp. 123–4.
[26] C.C. Aronsfeld, 'Jewish enemy aliens in England during the First World War', Jewish
Social Studies, 18, no. 4 (Oct. 1956), pp. 275–83.

Leese was to help him revive racial nationalism after the Second World War.

In Beamish's absence the Britons survived under the direction of Dr J.H. Clarke until his death in 1931. Although Clarke tried to maintain interest, the organization foundered after the *British Guardian* ceased publication in 1925. J.D. Dell, a solicitor, became honorary secretary of the Britons Publishing Society until his retirement in 1949. In the inter-war period, apart from publishing the *Protocols*, the Britons made little impact. Indeed, the authorities made no move against the organization during the Second World War and it continued its activities unmolested. This earned it black marks in the eyes of its founder, Beamish, who considered it a decrepit and defunct organization not worthy of his continuing support. Arnold Leese, who was to become the undisputed leader of the IFL in 1932, was highly critical of Dell's social credit views about Hitler as a supposed Jewish agent, but after Beamish's death in 1948 he used part of his inheritance to revive the Britons.

Membership of the Britons Society in the 1920s included more than ultra-conservative political reactionaries. Given the nature of its virulent anti-semitic propaganda, it was surprising that some fairly well-connected and distinguished individuals were associated with the organization. These included Dr J.H. Clarke, chairman from 1918–31, who was chief consulting physician to the Homeopathic Hospital in London, and was claimed to have some influence with the Conservative Die-hards in the 1920s; Walter Crick, the Northampton boot manufacturer, who was vice-president from 1925–36; and Arthur Kitson, the inventor, currency reformer and entrepreneur who provided another link with manufacturing industry. Other members included Lord Sydenham of Combe, an ex-Governor of Bombay and Victoria, Australia, as well as a secretary of the Imperial Defence Committee; George Mudge, Professor of Zoology at the University of London; Victor Marsden, Russian correspondent of the *Morning Post*; the Churchman Prebendary A.W. Gough; the explorer Bessie Pullen Burry; Lady Moore; Capel Pownall, the archery expert; and a bevy of military men including Lt-Colonel A.H. Lane, Brigadier-General Blakeney and Captain Howard.

There were some interesting connections between these individuals and others associated with the Britons, apart from the common commitment to the British Empire. The experiences of

Beamish, Lane and Joseph Banister linked them not only with the anti-alien campaign prior to 1914, but also with the anti-semitic critique of Jewish capitalists in South Africa by Sir William Butler.[27] Kitson, Crick and Clarke were all talented individuals who disagreed strongly with the prevailing establishment views in their field. The fact that their discoveries were either ignored or did not bring their just rewards was partially responsible for inducing a conspiracy mentality. The presence of such energetic ladies as Bessie Pullen Burry in the Britons, of Nesta Webster and Catherine Stoddart in the Duke of Northumberland's publishing concerns, as well as Rotha Lintorn Orman's role in the British Fascists and Mary Allen's, Mary Richardson's and Mrs Dacre-Fox's membership of the BUF, suggested a peculiar side-effect of the suffragette movement; political commitment and involvement could develop in very different directions from the dedicated socialism of Sylvia Pankhurst or the militant conservatism of her mother and sister. Indeed, the suffragette movement and its link to fascism represented one kind of genteel revolt by spirited upper-middle-class women against the stultifying effects of the Victorian ethic of limiting the role of respectable ladies to ornaments in the social round.[28]

Arnold Leese and the IFL

There were close ties between the Britons and the IFL. Beamish was a vice-president of this organization and spoke at several of its meetings on his infrequent visits from abroad in the 1930s. Arnold Leese, its leader, was a member of the Britons and had gained a strong belief in the *Protocols of the Elders of Zion* as a result of contact with Arthur Kitson in Stamford, Lincolnshire, where Leese had lived in the 1920s.[29] Anthony Gittens, secretary of the Britons from 1949 to 1973 and a member since 1924, was a prominent member of the IFL in the 1930s and opened a branch at Kentish Town in London.

The IFL originated in November 1928 as a patriotic anti-socialist organization. It acquired its fanatical anti-semitism only

---

[27] J. Webb, *The Occult Establishment* (La Salle, 1976), p. 253.
[28] N. Webster, *The Sheep Track* (London, 1914).
[29] A. Leese, *Out of Step* (Hollywood, n.d.), p. 48.

after Arnold Leese became its guiding spirit in 1930. The movement was originally formed by Brigadier-General D. Erskine Tulloch,[30] and was controlled by a directorate of three persons, Major J. Baillie, L.H. Sherrard and Arnold Leese. Baillie and Sherrard resigned in 1932 and Leese became the sole leader of the organization, assuming the title of director-general.[31]

Leese was a veterinary surgeon who had retired from his practice in Stamford in Lincolnshire in 1928. This had some claim to be the hotbed of British fascism in the 1920s owing to the fact that Leese and a colleague had successfully stood for the local council on a British fascist policy in 1924. However, Leese quarrelled with the 'BF's', as he called them, because he thought they lacked dynamism and credibility. Moving to Guildford, Leese's fanaticism and his willingness to devote all his time and resources to the new movement soon made him the fulcrum of racial nationalist activity in Britain. His ability to provide finance for publishing a newspaper, *The Fascist*, and a constant stream of pamphlets devoted to fascism, anti-semitism and racial nationalism, and his own editorial drive, made him a natural source of inspiration.

However, although Leese's virulent anti-semitism and racial fascist beliefs made him the nearest equivalent in outlook to an English Hitler, his personality and attitude to leadership were very different. Leese's lack of impact, of course, was also due to the very different cultural traditions and values of British society compared with those of Germany. Leese had a pronounced anti-authoritarian streak in his behaviour and a quarrelsome personality. His loneliness as a child had been reinforced by his years of solitary endeavour in the north-west frontier in India and Kenya, which made him the world's leading authority on the diseases of the camel.[32] He found it very difficult to work in collaboration with others. Although not untalented as a journalist, despite his venomous and eccentric views of Jews, he lacked any personal charisma. Racial nationalists and extreme anti-semites respected Leese's fanaticism and dedication to the cause, but were not prepared to obey his commands or views without question, nor were they able to get personally close to him. For his part

[30] PRO HO 45/24967/105.
[31] PRO HO 45/24967/37.
[32] Leese, *Out of Step*, pp. 1–37.

Leese accepted discussion and political argument in the IFL provided that official policy was not contravened.[33] In practice this meant a marked toleration of a variety of extremist ideas provided that the individual had proved himself to be 'Jew wise'. Leese's view was that the chief function of the IFL was a training organization for an élite of anti-semitic propagandists, not as a political party in its own right.

The organization of the IFL was divided into three separate hierarchical structures. The first was the Graduates Association, comprising the leading members who were designed to become the future governing aristocracy of the fascist corporate state. Beneath them were to be the fascist Legions, the militant branch of the League who were divided into active and passive sections of members. The Activist Confederations were to be associate members who were to disseminate the belief in corporatism throughout the community. In practice there were two types of member: the fifty or so of middle-class or *petit bourgeois* origin who formed the backbone of the appreciative audience at Leese's regular Wednesday night diatribes against the Jews at his London headquarters represented the core of the IFL; there were also working-class members who engaged in street meetings at intermittent intervals and who were involved in direct conflict and physical violence with members of the Jewish community. As well as central London headquarters, branches were known to exist at Hackney, Kentish Town, Bristol, Glasgow and Newcastle upon Tyne. The only paid official in 1936 was P.J. Ridout, who was paid £2 a week, mainly out of Leese's own funds.[34]

Amongst the coterie of fanatical enthusiasts around Leese, the most interesting were those who comprised the 'literary board' of *The Fascist*. This was a fluctuating group of four or five individuals who were responsible for the literary output of the organization. The Board of Deputies of British Jews managed to infiltrate a reliable agent into the IFL for a time in 1937 and his information provides a fascinating glimpse of its workings. The chief implication of his findings was that although Leese was the dominant personality of the movement, the literary output usually ascribed to him was in part a joint enterprise of the literary board. In particular, one of Leese's most notorious pamphlets, 'My

[33] PRO HO 45/24967/105.
[34] PRO HO 45/24967/37.

Irrelevant Defence', was co-written with Charles W. Gore. This outlined the basis of Leese's claim that the Jews were guilty of ritual murder, which had led to his being charged with seditious libel in 1936. Gore apparently did not want his name on the cover of the book and wished for it to be published by the Canadian fascist, Arcand, so that he could not be sued.[35]

Although not formally a member Gore had a profound influence on Leese. He thought that fascism was played out in England and that the IFL should merge into a new organization that he planned called the 'National Union of British Workmen'. His literary pretensions were further highlighted when he sent a copy of his unpublished manuscript 'The Island of Madagascar as a National State for the Jewish people and Why' to Lord Rothschild, who forwarded it to the Board of Deputies in 1938. By this time Gore had split with Leese and offered information on the IFL to the Board of Deputies, which was declined.[36]

Others prominent in the literary board were H.H. Lockwood, an insurance agent, who contributed regularly to *The Fascist*. He was considered to be one of the most dangerous of all the fascists and was interned until the end of the Second World War. S.H.E. Fox also attracted the attention of the Security Service. He was an editor in Shell Mex house and a frequent visitor to Germany, who entertained members of the nazi party when they visited this country in the 1930s.[37] However, the only person Leese was associated with in the 1930s who was later to become distinguished in his own field, was the popular medieval historian and expert on Gothic architecture, John Hooper Harvey.[38]

The kind of material which members of the Graduate Association enjoyed at their weekly meetings was best exemplified by a Jewish intelligence report of a lecture given by the IFL vice-president H.H. Beamish in 1937, entitled 'National Socialism (Racial Fascism) in Practice in Germany', which appeared to have been fairly typical of his beliefs. Members heard Beamish tell the audience that Germany was a great country today because Hitler had named the enemy and it was to be hoped that he would soon

[35] Intelligence Report, 27 Oct. 1937, IFL file, Board of Deputies of British Jews.
[36] Rogues Gallery File (C6/9/3/2), Board of Deputies of British Jews.
[37] Ibid.
[38] C. Holmes and A. Kushner, 'The charge is ritual murder', *Jewish Chronicle*, 29 Mar. 1985. IFL handbill, advertising the content and distribution costs of 'The Heritage of Britain' by J.H. Harvey, IFL file, Board of Deputies of British Jews.

call an international conference on the question. According to
Beamish, the IFL knew of three remedies to the Jewish question: to
kill them, sterilize them or segregate them. In answer to questions
after the lecture Beamish said that the Russian Revolution had
killed off the intelligentsia and that the country was now inhabited
by 'animal life people'. With a chilling prophecy he then stated
that it would be the task of a great leader, Hitler for preference, to
march into Russia in the next five years and place one half of the
population in the lethal chamber and the other half in the zoo.
After the applause had subsided Leese then spoke to the effect that
national socialism had been vilified in this country, and that
Germany was supposed to have nudist camps of unclean practices,
which was untrue, but the IFL's photographers had penetrated into
nudist camps in this country, which were perfectly foul and run by
Jews. The meeting was then closed with all present saluting with a
'Heil Hitler', much to the agent's embarrassment.[39]

If the more intellectual middle-class members were titillated by
such political discourse, the IFL had more mundane functions.
Clothed in full dress uniform, the members wore a black shirt
(blouse pattern), khaki breeches, puttees, black boots and black
beret. Black or grey trousers were worn on duties other than full
dress parades, and a brassard showing a Union Jack with a
swastika superimposed was worn on the left arm in conjunction
with the uniform. This was usually worn when selling *The Fascist*
and for other ceremonial duties. Some working-class members of
the Legions also held open air meetings in Hackney and other
locations in the East End of London at irregular intervals. After a
letter to the Home Secretary in 1934 complaining that the IFL
speakers had stated at these meetings that they would clear all
Jews out of the country, and if this was not possible they would
starve them and murder them, Special Branch reported that a Mr
Pipkin and a Mr Smith of the IFL, both about twenty-one years of
age, had made reckless and rash statements at such occasions.[40]

Although the IFL's extremism, lack of resources, and failure to
make any impact made it of marginal political significance, the
Jewish community were worried about its potential. The genocidal
language of its speakers and propaganda undoubtedly increased

[39] Intelligence Report, 15 April 1937, IFL file, Board of Deputies of British Jews.
[40] PRO HO 45/24967/11.

tension in areas of high Jewish concentration such as the East End of London. Equally significant was the secrecy with which the IFL operated. It appeared that within the organization was a secret group which was responsible for extra-legal anti-semitic 'excitement'. This appears to have been responsible for several stunts and was implicated in the general increase of physical violence against Jews in the East End in the middle 1930s. On Empire Day 1934 an IFL flag showing a Union Jack, in the centre of which was a swastika, was attached to the flagmast at London's County Hall as a protest against the alleged Jewish preponderance on the LCC and in its employ. In June 1935 an LCC plaque on the house where Karl Marx had lived was removed by the IFL and replaced by an anti-Jewish notice.[41] The Jewish agent reported in 1937 that a secret group known as the 'tough squad', under the direction of Gore and Ridout, operated with members of the BUF at night in the East End. While the leadership of the IFL was evidently opposed to Mosley, they were prepared to co-operate with the rank and file of his organization.[42] Leese distinguished between the 'Kosher Fascists' and the 'British Jewnion of Fascists' elements in the leadership of the BUF and possible allies within the membership of that organization who would be useful to his anti-semitic campaign.

With the increased growth of tension in the East End in 1936 the Security Service became interested in the activities of the IFL. In view of the complaints of the Board of Deputies of British Jews and the virulence of Leese's propaganda, the government tried to silence him through recourse to the law. As a result of the publication of the accusation that Jews practised ritual murder against Christians, Leese and his printer Whitehead were tried on charges of seditious libel and creating a public mischief on 18–21 September 1936. Using the argument that the Jews, not being a definite community, were not His Majesty's subjects and therefore not under the protection of his laws, and quoting the Gospel of St John that the Jews were descended from the devil, Leese's defence was partially successful. He was found not guilty of the serious charge of seditious libel but guilty of the lesser misdemeanour of creating a public mischief. In spite of this partial acquittal Leese

[41] PRO HO 45/24967/37.
[42] Intelligence Report, n.d., IFL file, Board of Deputies of British Jews.

still went to prison. He was given six months' hard labour after he refused on principle to pay the fine. Leese claimed that his 'martyrdom' had been achieved against the wishes of the Jury who had acquitted him on the serious charge.[43]

Thus although the authorities had their wish and Leese was effectively silenced for six months, during which time the IFL became a virtually moribund organization, the *Rex* v. *Leese* case had opened a Pandora's box of possibilities for the racial nationalists. The Attorney-General had been astonished at the verdict and came to the conclusion that the jury had viewed Leese as a stupid crank with honest convictions who should not be convicted of the serious charge of seditious libel.[44]

After his release from jail Leese decided to challenge the validity of his imprisonment by publishing *My Irrelevant Defence*, a lengthy justification of his charge that the Jews ritually murdered Christian children for their blood at Passover.[45] In spite of the fact that Leese's charges were much more blatant than in the original offence the authorities decided not to prosecute in case an acquittal might be misunderstood by the general public. Recently released Home Office papers in fact show that the authorities drew back from prosecuting even the most blatant cases of anti-semitic propaganda both before and during the Second World War despite the fact that it was ostensibly being fought to destroy Hitlerism. The comments of both ministers and civil servants also showed a critical attitude towards British Jews within wide sections of the establishment.

The government's reluctance to act in such cases was shown in relation to a further blatant abuse of the Jews at a Nordic League meeting on 20 May 1939. A.K. Chesterton, the ex-BUF propagandist, became so carried away by the effect of his anti-semitic diatribe that he ended his speech by advocating the use of lamp-posts to string up the Jews. Unfortunately the two verbatim reports of what was said slightly disagreed with each other. Whereas the report of an ex-police inspector highlighted the genocidal implications of Chesterton's speech, that of the Special Branch scribe merely stated that the whole of his discourse was

---

[43] PRO HO 45/24967/52, *Rex* v. *Leese* (London, 1937).
[44] PRO HO 45/24967/62.
[45] A. Leese, *My Irrelevant Defence* (London, 1938), pp. 1–12.

directed towards racial discrimination and hatred of the Jew.[46] The Home Secretary, Sir Samuel Hoare, noted that any influx of refugees from the continent might bring together the political extremes – the fascists who had been attacking the Jews for three years and the communists and other left-wing elements who might argue that Jewish refugees were taking away Gentile employment. Hoare also agreed that he had been advised by the Director of Public Prosecutions that charges of seditious libel against individuals attacking Jews as a group would in all probability fail.[47] A senior civil servant later corrected the Home Secretary's interpretation by arguing that offensive speeches against the Jews as a whole might be liable to prosecution if they were likely to occasion a breach of the peace under the Public Order Act.[48] As Chesterton was preaching to the converted there was no chance of this, so he avoided prosecution.

During the Second World War a similar problem arose with regard to the publication of Alexander Ratcliffe's *Truth about the Jews*, brought out by the British Protestant League. Here a different Home Secretary, Herbert Morrison of the Labour party, argued that legislation protecting a particular group of persons would set a most dangerous precedent, and that although Ratcliffe's pamphlet was deplorable, he could not prevent its publication. In Morrison's view, a law for the protection of the Jewish community might have an effect contrary to that intended.[49] Before he became Home Secretary Morrison had argued that the best way for Jews to prevent anti-semitism was to ensure that they could not be blamed for social injustices in areas where they lived.[50] Whereas fascists and anti-semites were free to libel Jews as a group in the most foul language in their publications, the Jews were supposed to be more English than the English according to Morrison. This kind of governmental double standard towards minorities survived until the passing of the Race Relations Act in 1965.

[46] PRO HO 144/21381/26.
[47] PRO HO 144/21381/186; J.A. Cross, *Sir Samuel Hoare* (London, 1977), pp. 284–5.
[48] PRO HO 144/21381/187.
[49] PRO HO 45/25398/278–9.
[50] C. Holmes, 'East End antisemitism 1936', *Bulletin of the Society for the Study of Labour History*, 32 (Spring 1976), pp. 26–32.

Maule Ramsay's secret societies

The IFL was not the only extreme anti-semitic organization in existence in the 1930s. Another small group of racial nationalists called 'The Nordics' amalgamated with the IFL in 1934; other organizations such as the Militant Christian Patriots, the White Knights of Britain and the National Socialist League were among the most conspicuous examples. Short-lived fascist organizations like the United Empire Fascist Party and the National Socialist Workers Movement appeared and disappeared in the 1930s. After 1937, when the international situation worsened, increasing numbers of militant fascists and anti-semites, disillusioned with Mosley and Leese, and encouraged by nazi success in Europe, saw the need for an umbrella organization which would co-ordinate anti-semitic activity. It appears that the Nordischer Gesellschaft in Germany sent representatives to this country in 1935 to encourage such a grouping and that their spokesman referred in 1937 to the NL as being the English branch of international nazism.[51]

The NL had managed successfully to screen its activities from the attention of historians and political commentators to this day, but it was not so lucky with the relevant authorities. Both MI5 and the Board of Deputies of British Jews were well aware of its significance. Its importance was highlighted by the fact that Britain's most notorious extreme anti-semite, Archibald H. Maule Ramsay, MP appeared to be its guiding spirit, which explains why there is now significant intelligence information on this secret society; the fact that Jewish sources, MI5 and the Council for Civil Liberties broadly confirm each other, suggests that the reports were reliable. Indeed, Ramsay's secret societies, the Nordic League and the Right Club, were so easily penetrated by intelligence agents, and the government has now released some of this material, that when this information is checked against independent sources it becomes possible to present a plausible account of what the British fascists were up to during 1939 and 1940.

While Special Branch sent along junior officers to transcribe proceedings at NL meetings in 1939, the most important information we have on its activities is that procured by an

---

[51] PRO HO 144/22454/6.

intelligence agent working for the Board of Deputies of British Jews. Disturbed by the evidence of an increase in organized hostility towards the Jews during 1938, Neville Laski used his contacts with Special Branch at Scotland Yard to employ a recently retired inspector to penetrate the NL for the Board of Deputies.[52] According to a letter in the files this man's name was Pavey.[53] His success in being accepted at the highest levels of the League enabled him to provide graphic accounts of their meetings and organization.[54] He was so successful in avoiding suspicion that he was sent to a nazi 'summer school' in Germany in August 1939 as a representative of the League. A photographic memory enabled him to avoid the obvious suspicions which Special Branch officers noting the proceedings obviously fell under at such meetings. His reports, which confirmed those of Special Branch, testified both to the reliability of his memory and to his obvious potential as an infiltrator. There is evidence too that E.R. Mandeville Roe, an ex-member of the British Fascists and the BUF, also submitted reports on the NL to the Board of Deputies in 1939.

Archibald Maule Ramsay was, with Mosley, the most significant figure on the fascist fringe of British politics. Although he vehemently denied being a fascist, merely wishing to purge the Conservatives of all Jewish influence,[55] his unparliamentary statements expressed to the NL and his connection with the Tyler Kent affair in 1940 left considerable room for doubt. The Security Service thought that Ramsay was unbalanced and suffered from persecution mania so far as the Jews were concerned.[56] In 1931 he was elected as Conservative MP for Peebles, as a supporter of the National Government. In 1938 he read *The Protocols of the Elders of Zion* and appeared to suffer the same 'road to Damascus' transformation of personality which afflicted Arnold Leese on reading that document. Henceforth he interpreted all political phenomena in terms of an anti-semitic conspiracy theory. While he was increasingly regarded as a wild eccentric on the fringes of the Conservative party in Parliament, his extra-parliamentary activities included becoming in 1938–9 the

[52] S. Saloman, *Now it can be told*, File C6/9/2/1, Board of Deputies of British Jews.
[53] Letter to Inspector Keeble, n.d., File C6/10/29, Board of Deputies of British Jews.
[54] Memorandum on the Nordic League, PRO HO 144/21381/270–93.
[55] A.H.M. Ramsay, *The Nameless War* (London, 1952), pp. 103–5.
[56] PRO HO 144/22454/87.

dominant personality in two secret societies, the NL and the Right Club. He was convenor of the fourteen-strong council of the NL and leader of the RC.

The NL, according to its constitution, was an association of race-conscious Britons. Its aim was to provide a convivial meeting place where the enlightened could help formulate a programme to teach the uninitiated the nature of the enemy which was undermining the country. It saw its role as co-ordinating the activities of extreme anti-semitic and racial nationalist bodies in fighting the so-called Jewish menace. To that end it eschewed a leadership cult and had a formless organization, although a council decided its policy. The Security Service and the Jewish agent noted its connections with practically all the fascist and anti-semitic bodies, such as the IFL, the National Socialist League, the White Knights of Britain, the Britons Society, the National Socialist Workers Party and the Militant Christian Patriots. There were also connections with more respectable organizations such as the Liberty Restoration League and the United Ratepayers Association. The only significant exception to Maule Ramsay's co-ordinated attempt to unify the fascist political fringe was Mosley's refusal to connect his organization to the movement. However, after the NL was disbanded at the outbreak of war, ex-members of this organization were to join the move towards a closer collaboration of anti-semitic, pro-nazi and peace movements.

The NL appears to have originated as a development of the White Knights of Britain. Like the NL this too was a secret society and had its headquarters at the same address in licensed premises in Lamb's Conduit Street, London. According to the *Memorandum*, the NL was the power behind the Militant Christian Patriots as well as having close connections with the IFL. In terms of individual connections, with the exception of Mosley and some of his personal lieutenants, the membership of the NL included a galaxy of anti-semitic and pro-nazi notables, a veritable who's who of the fascist political fringe. Apart from Maule Ramsay these included Brigadier-General R.B.D. Blakeney, Serocold Skeels (a known nazi agent), Major-General J.F.C. Fuller, H.H. Beamish, Arnold Leese, P.J. Ridout and Jock Houston. Membership of the League was through connections to accredited anti-semitic and pro-fascist organizations and showed a predominant middle-class bias with one-third of the audience being women.

The activities of the NL were primarily restricted to private meetings in 1938, although it was connected with the Militant Christian Patriots at the end of the Munich Crisis when it urged Chamberlain not to get Britain involved in Jewish designs for a world war. During 1939 it surfaced and held several public meetings in London of a pro-nazi or pro-appeasement character. It also had public viewings of nazi propaganda films of an anti-semitic nature, including one on the ritual slaughter of animals. Its notoriety and extremism, which was a principal reason why Mosley refused to get involved before the Second World War, was mainly due to the wild verbal excesses at its meetings. The toast at the bar was 'P.J.' or Perish Judah. This was a nazi form of greeting that had been popularized by P.J. Ridout of the IFL in 1936, presumably as a conscious pun on his own initials.[57] In the aftermath of Kristallnacht the NL had to be treated by the authorities as more than an eccentric lunatic fringe organization.

The secrecy of the League was primarily due to its connection with the White Knights of Britain, or the Hooded Men as they were sometimes called. This was a British 1930s version of the Ku Klux Klan which was active in 1936–7. With an elaborate initiation ritual modelled on the conventions of freemasonry, its aim was to 'rid the world of the merciless Jewish reign of terror'.[58] It was an occult body with secretive passwords and much mumbo jumbo. The meetings of the order, like those of the NL, took place among festoons of swastikas, and members had to swear blood-curdling oaths to its patron saint King Edward I, who had expelled the Jews from England. Death was the alleged penalty for those who divulged the secrets of the order. Commander E.H. Cole was the chancellor of the organization and T. Victor Rowe played the key role of the man on the door in the initiation ritual.[59] The order claimed over 7,000 members – but this was a wild exaggeration typical of this group.

At the beginning of the war the Security Service categorized the NL as a seditious body whose speakers did not hesitate to advocate methods of violence to achieve their ends, many referring to a coming revolution.[60] There was also a tendency towards the

[57] PRO HO 144/21379/237.
[58] 'The White Knights of Britain', Intelligence Report C6/10/29, Board of Deputies of British Jews.
[59] PRO HO 144/21381/250–1.
[60] PRO HO 144/22454/85–6.

advocacy of a genocidal solution to the so-called Jewish question and much anti-semitic abuse at their meetings. Amongst the most extreme speakers were Maule Ramsay, Captain Elwin Wright, Commander Cole, Seracold Skeels, A.K. Chesterton and William Joyce. Ramsay steered an erratic course between advocating the possible use of violence against Jews if other measures would not achieve their object, and milder comments. If Jewish control could not be challenged constitutionally it would have to be done by acts of Steel;[61] and he saw the time approaching when, like the mayor of Bethlehem, he would have to arm his son against the Jews.[62] On other occasions he drew back from the implications of this argument by not referring directly to the Jews and by arguing that the British army would always obey the orders of the cabinet even if there was a Jewish Minister for War such as Hore Belisha.[63]

Other members did not mince their words with regard to the British government. William Joyce attacked the 'Slobbering, bastardised mendacious triumvirate' of Churchill, Eden and Cooper and argued that conscription would bring into the army thousands of young fascists whose training should not be wasted.[64] Elwin Wright, who up until 1937 had been secretary of a respectable Anglo-German Fellowship, advocated the shooting of Jews, called Neville Chamberlain a liar and a traitor and stated that Parliament was a 'blackmailing corrupt body of bastards'.[65] For Commander Cole, the Palace of Westminster was full of dirty corrupt swine and the House of Commons was a 'house of bastardised Jews'.[66] Cole's extreme anti-semitism had developed as a result of his exposure to the *Protocols* when he had been involved with allied help to the White Russians in the Civil War in the 1920s.

While the attitude of British fascists and anti-semites to the nazis must be left to a separate chapter, the logic of 'Jew wise' anti-semitism implied a similar outcome to Hitler's genocidal programme. For NL members shooting the Jews was the favoured solution, although on one occasion Wright suggested they should

---

[61] Intelligence Report of Nordic League meeting, 10 July 1939, Box 41/1, National Council for Civil Liberties.
[62] Memorandum on Nordic League, p. 9.
[63] Ibid., p. 12.
[64] Ibid., p. 18.
[65] PRO HO 144/21381/237.
[66] PRO HO 144/21381/236.

be destroyed painlessly and Chesterton wanted them strung up on lamp-posts.[67] Serocold Skeels inverted the logic of genocide: as the Jews ritually slaughtered cattle and the Talmud viewed gentiles as animals, growing Jewish power threatened the security of the *goyim* everywhere; the Jews would soon have the legal power to murder whom they chose.

Such arguments naturally alerted the authorities to the possible threat posed by such an organization. However, although there were some well-connected members and the Security Service was conscious of the links with the German nazis, the very eccentricity and extremism of the NL made it totally alien to British political culture. It completely failed to influence public opinion when it emerged from its secret society chrysalis in 1939, and in spite of its extremism and the uncertainties of the law with regard to seditious libel where public order was not threatened, the authorities decided that any move against the group would give it unwanted publicity and might achieve more harm than good. Only on the outbreak of war were steps taken to discourage its members from any anti-war activity when two of its leading members, Oliver Gilbert and T. Victor-Rowe, were interned on 22 September 1939. The organization had already terminated its activities at the outbreak of war, although members still met unofficially in Gilbert's house. Most of its members then joined other anti-war organizations and many were interned in 1940.

Ramsay's other secret society, the Right Club, was also ostensibly closed down at the outbreak of war. However, Ramsay and some of his closest associates still met and its activities were in fact to provide the government with the excuse to intern many fascists without trial in 1940. It was formed in 1939 for the same purpose as the NL, to amalgamate and strengthen various extreme right-wing and pro-fascist movements. The RC was ostensibly less nazi than the NL and was aimed at infiltrating and influencing the establishment to further Ramsay's campaign to lessen the alleged Jewish influence on the Conservative party. It began life as a kind of January Club of the NL, but it rapidly became more significant. The RC concentrated its activities on contacting potential sympathizers, particularly in the armed forces. Ramsay signed up over 300 persons, whose membership was duly noted in the

---

[67] Memorandum on Nordic League, pp. 20, 22.

so-called 'red book'. The authorities were more worried about this group than about the NL and only one document about it has so far been released, despite the fact that it was successfully infiltrated by several agents. The story of the RC – which will be given in more detail in another chapter – has still not been fully told, mainly because the documentation on it has been treated like the Crown Jewels.

Racial nationalist ideology

Such generalized and unsystematic anti-semitic obsessions as were displayed by individuals in these groups would suggest that little could be learned from an attempt to study the belief systems of such movements. The crude and splenetic expression and presentation of such views suggested irrational pathological prejudice rather than a coherent ideology. No doubt personality problems played some part in the views of many of the individuals concerned, but perceived characteristics of Jews and their alleged behaviour provided a rationalization of such extremist views for most members of these organizations. Arnold Leese's anti-semitism owed much to his hatred of Jewish methods of slaughtering animals and the cruelty that he believed resulted. Arthur Kitson's views developed from a generalized critique of the banking system and the role Jews supposedly played in it. Several of the other known members of such groups had Arab connections or were opposed to Zionist ambitions in Palestine.

Whatever the origin of these views, the groups produced literature which fed such beliefs and this material found a wider readership through the NL. Much of the content of such literary activity was little more than political pornography. The Britons' newspaper regaled its limited readership with many of the anti-semitic slanders of White Russian propaganda from the Civil War, including tales of how Jewish Bolsheviks boiled deacons in water and drunk the resultant soup.[68] Leese fell foul of the authorities by publishing allegations that Jews indulged in ritual murder of Christian children for religious purposes.[69] Both the Britons' and the IFL literature contained lurid tales of alleged Jewish

[68] *Jewry Ueber Alles*, March 1920.
[69] *The Fascist*, July 1936.

responsibility for crime, the white slave traffic, for casualties in the First World War, for corrupting public life and for financial malpractices and banking irregularity. In much of this material there was little attempt to relate such antipathy and prejudice to a consistent and coherent theory of behaviour, but the assumption and arguments on which it was based can be seen as the origins of a racial nationalist ideology which was to be more rigorously formulated at a later date. In short, the obsession with blaming all the supposed ills of the modern world on to the Jews which common to these groups was so great that coherence and intellectual consistency were often disregarded. It was not until after the Second World War that a distinction between an exoteric display of prejudice and an esoteric anti-semitic ideology can be discerned in racial nationalist literature.[70] In the inter-war period the two were often mixed in a totally unco-ordinated manner. As a result the negative obsession of anti-semitism played a much greater role than the positive outline of racial nationalism and the Nordic, Aryan or Anglo-Saxon theme of such ideas. Yet an analysis of the ideology behind the antipathy and prejudice displayed in racial nationalism, despite the fact that so little of the expression of such ideas was coherent or systematic, is important for three reasons. First, the basic assumptions of such ideas in altered form were later developed into the ideology of the National Front. Second, the comparison with nazi ideas provides a guide to the influence of Hitler on British racial nationalism. Third, the comparison with Mosley's fascism shows quite conclusively that as well as the competition between potential British Führers, and the personal and political gulf between British fascist movements, there was an ideological divide which hindered closer co-operation. All these factors were to play an important role in the disaster of 1940. Racial nationalism, which played a minor role in British fascism in the inter-war period, was to become much more significant in the revival of the tradition after the Second World War.

The ideology of racial nationalism was nowhere coherently formulated in fascist literature in the inter-war period. Yet its inherent assumptions were implicit in most of the literary output of the Britons and the IFL and were disseminated through such

---

[70] M. Billig, *Fascists* (London, 1978), pp. 124–6.

groups as the NL. It was based on certain fundamental beliefs, which were expressed in extreme form, deriving ultimately from certain aspects of nineteenth-century scientific enquiry and social philosophy. It represented a synthesis of certain ideas, expressing as uncritical positivism which amalgamated certain propositions from anthropology, biology, psychology and sociology, which was presented as an hierarchy of race. This formulation mixed highly subjective behavioural views with the more objective criteria of nineteenth-century science to create a British variant of nazi ideology. Although there was little trace of the blood mysticism or metaphysical argument which so characterized Houston Stewart Chamberlain's and volkish ideas in general in Germany, some elements derived from romanticism.[71] The assumptions which derived from scientific sources were more heavily accentuated in English racial nationalism than in nazism and ultimately stemmed from an Anglo-American tradition rather than from continental sources.[72] As has been pointed out, several important nazi ideas come directly from English sources, and it was the use of such indigenous ideas rather than the copying of a successful foreign movement which accounted for the ideology of English racial nationalism.[73]

These ideas originated in the ethnocentrism of mainstream anthropological thought, which was strongly coloured by both the romantic movement and the Darwinian revolution in science. Anthropological ideas of the Great Chain of Being had traditionally placed those of European descent at the peak of that classification, and those of other origins at lower levels of development. At the apex of achievement was the Aryan or Nordic group, most notable in those of Anglo-Saxon lineage. According to anthropologists and linguists most heavily influenced by the romantic movement, they were the sole creators and carriers of culture even among European groups.[74] Early nineteenth-century science had indiscriminately merged physical criteria of classification with psychological characteristics to produce an

[71] H.A. Macdougall, *Racial Myth in English History* (Montreal, 1982), p. 119.

[72] R. Thurlow, 'Some more peculiarities of the English: the fascist views of evolution, race and national character', Conference Paper, History of Ideology of Anglo-Saxon Racial Attitudes 1870–1970 (1982), p. 16.

[73] P. Hayes, 'The contribution of British intellectuals to fascism', in Lunn and Thurlow, *British Fascism*, pp. 168–86.

[74] L. Poliakov, *The Aryan Myth* (New York, 1977), pp. 188–92.

ideal type classification of human groups; aesthetic ideals of beauty and heroic personality attributes had been ascribed to the Aryan or Nordic group, and all other races or ethnic groups were accorded inferior appearance and character references.[75] Whilst the inconclusive debate between monogenists and polygenists in anthropology, and the influence of Christianity and political liberalism, somewhat tempered the ethnocentrism of scientific and official attitudes, the Darwinian revolution swept away many of the restraints which checked the development of racist views, at least for those who could see no difference between evolution in the natural world and human achievements.

Although the influence of the Darwinian revolution on social and political thought in general is a highly complex one, and had several ambiguous or contradictory features, its impact on those prone to extremist ethnocentric or racist views was profound. In particular, the tendency to relate the supposed forces of natural selection and vigorous competition from the natural to the human world equated the different achievements of culture and technological development with variations in skin colour and other physical characteristics.[76] Social Darwinism, with its emphasis on the survival of the fittest and chance variation, denied the effects of will, conscious planning and human agency in evolution, and of altering the fixed characteristics of different groups or races. By the end of the nineteenth century, the Darwinian revolution appeared to offer scientific proof of the processes of evolution. Weismann's germ plasm theory, that inheritance of characteristics was genetically determined, Galton's stirp theory and work on hereditary genius, and the biometric work on population statistics, appeared to give empirical verification to the societal implications of Darwin's theories.[77] The rival Mendelian genetic discoveries were rather more problematic and complicated, although if certain assumptions were made then racial crossing inevitably led to the weakening of the inherited characteristics of the allegedly higher type.

For racial nationalists, all these influences led inexorably to one conclusion. The hierarchy of race with Aryans or Anglo-Saxons at

[75] G.L. Mosse, *Towards the Final Solution* (London, 1979), pp. 1–34.
[76] G. Jones, *Social Darwinism and English Thought* (Brighton, 1980), pp. 103–4.
[77] R.J. Halliday, 'Darwinism, biology and race', Conference Paper, History and Ideology of Anglo-Saxon Racial Attitudes 1870–1970 (1982), pp. 13–14.

its apex was under threat of contamination from the supposed lesser breeds. Implementation of eugenic control of alleged inferior groups, whether they be the urban proletariat, the Jews or coloured peoples, was seen as of vital importance. Racial nationalists saw the Jews in Manichean terms: they were the ultimate enemy, an anti-race derived from the mixing of incompatible elements and which had originated not in Palestine, but in the Khazar empire of southern Russia. Of mongrel breed themselves, the Jews were purportedly engaged in a conspiracy to bastardize the races of mankind and to bring the natural nation states of the world under the control of a one-world Jewish superstate.

The logic of such views naturally contained a number of contradictions. In terms of Darwinian theory, the most successful groups were those who had the highest reproduction rate. The fittest in British society should therefore have been the lower class and the immigrant, both of whom had higher birth rates than the upper classes. This fact obviously did not conform to the elitist views of 'fitness to rule' of most racial nationalists. The image of the Jew posed problems too. On the one hand he was supposedly an inferior being, with anti-social habits and disgusting personality traits; on the other hand he possessed a superior intelligence and sufficient group solidarity to leave him on the verge of world domination. But for individuals like Arnold Leese intellectual consistency mattered much less than his hatred of the Jews. At one NL meeting the self-confessed animal lover and Jew-hater suddenly adopted a full-blooded Lamarckian argument to explain the difference between Swedish and British cattle. Apparently Swedish cows, secure in the knowledge that they were going to be stunned by true Aryans before they were slaughtered, were happy and friendly towards man; British cows, who might be bled to death for kosher meat, had no such guarantee and were morose and sullen as a result.[78] Leese's ludicrous argument appeared even more bizarre, given his inflexible belief that acquired characteristics could not be inherited and that genetic endowment and not environment, culture or education determined behaviour; when applied to mankind these ideas led him to criticize Spengler and other nationalists for seeing culture rather than race as determining human action. For Leese, this

---

[78] PRO HO 144/22454/60.

explained why Spengler was national socialism's worst enemy.[79] This also strongly differentiated Leese's fascism from Mosley's since the latter explained his fascist revolt with reference to neo-Lamarckian arguments and Spengler's historical and cultural vision.[80]

In spite of such obvious inconsistencies the basis of racial nationalist beliefs were outlined in the literature of the Britons and the IFL. G.P. Mudge, in a series of articles in *The Hidden Hand* entitled 'Pride of Race', translated the arguments derived from traditions in nineteenth-century anthropology and biology into language racial nationalists could understand.[81] Today Mudge's views read like a classic case study of most elements of nineteenth-century racism. His mixture of Social Darwinism, categorization of national and racial types, the Manichean conflict between Aryan and Jew, reading of personality from physical attributes, primitive eugenics, the aesthetic ideal of beauty and the use of middle-class value judgements were all symptomatic of this. So too was the assumed superiority of Nordic men and Anglo-Saxon nations. Particularly significant was the fact that despite the Nordics' supposed love of liberty the more authoritarian qualities were emphasized, and there appeared to be a shift from traditional nineteenth-century assumptions of Anglo-Saxon authority over colonial peoples to an elitist anti-democratic control of 'Nordics' over 'Mediterraneans' within British society.

The transition from nineteenth-century Anglo-Saxonism to racial fascism was completed by Arnold Leese. The quality of the conceptualization of his thought was low, but the garrulous style of *The Fascist* and his pamphlets contained an implicit if dimly perceived racial philosophy which linked Leese to this tradition. Leese believed that race was the factor which determined history and cultural achievement and that different types of men had fixed and immutable types of character and personality, exactly as with dogs.[82] He also possessed a Manichean view of society, in which the future of civilization depended upon the outcome of the struggle between Nordic and Jew. For Leese, the Nordic or Aryan

---

[79] *Gothic Ripples*, no. 66 (15 July 1950); PRO HO 45/24968/124.
[80] O. Mosley, *Tomorrow we Live* (London, 1938), pp. 69–72.
[81] G.P. Mudge, 'Pride of Race', *The Hidden Hand or the Jewish Peril*, vol. 2 (Feb. 1924); ibid., vol. 3 (Mar. 1923; ibid., vol. 4 (Apr. 1924).
[82] A.S. Leese, 'Communism and race', *The Fascist*, Oct. 1931.

was the sole creator of culture and civilization. His noble and heroic qualities were diametrically opposed to the negative qualities of the Jew. The chivalrous, virtuous and humanitarian values of the Aryan contrasted with the assumed sadistic blood lust, ritual murder and hatred of the *goyim* allegedly typical of Jews. Whereas for Leese there were no pure races, 'race mixing' could be of two kinds. Where the parents were of radically different types this led to the degeneration of the qualities of the higher race, but if the racial outcrossing was between individuals whose characteristics were complementary or similar then it was beneficial. In practice this meant that Leese denounced the influence of Arabs, Negroes, Somalis and Chinamen whom he considered were defiling the race, particularly in seaports, as well as the alleged Jewish menace. To Leese immigration and race-mixing was a Jewish plot to undermine the British Empire, and to ensure that the 'poisoning of our Anglo-Saxon blood by this yellow negroid horde is proceeding a pace'.[83]

Leese's idiosyncratic views on race derived from his own experiences rationalized in terms of a particular intellectual tradition. Leese mentioned Hans Gunther, *The Racial Elements of European History*, L.A. Waddell, *The Makers of Civilisation in Race and History*, Madison Grant, *The Passing of the Great Race*, and Lothrop Stoddard's books, *The Revolt against Civilisation*, *The Rising Tide of Colour against White World Supremacy* and *Racial Realities in Europe*, as his main intellectual sources. This represented a merging of nazi Nordic influences with an Anglo-American anthropological tradition. It was also significant that J. Hooper Harvey's first book, *The Heritage of Britain*, was dedicated to Waddell. This book, which was advertised by the IFL, stressed the 'Gothic' origins of British culture where Goths were described as pure Aryans of the ancient royal caste.[84] Waddell, a Professor of Tibetan at the University of London, believed that the Aryans were the bearers of culture and had originated all the main civilizations in history.

Racial nationalism also included a critique of Jewish banking policies. Leese's own diatribes about the Jewish financial octopus

---

[83] Idem, 'The colour problem in Britain', *The Fascist*, June 1932.
[84] J.H. Harvey, *The Heritage of Britain* (Little Bookham, 1943), p. 8n (IFL handbill, advertising the content and distribution costs of the forthcoming 'The Heritage of Britain' by J.H. Harvey, IFL file, Board of Deputies of British Jews.

owed something to his links with Arthur Kitson, who had explained to him his belief in the quantity theory of money in Stamford. Kitson was a prolific inventor whose own difficulties in financing and manufacturing his patents had led him to a radical critique of the banking system. While in the United States in the 1890s he had been heavily influenced by the Populist and Democratic Parties' assault on the Gold Standard. Much of the rest of his life was dedicated to opposing British financial policy and the monetary straitjacket in which it placed British industry. For Kitson what was produced, and not the amount of gold bullion, defined the wealth of the nation, and financiers – particularly Jewish bankers – had hijacked the economy in a conscious conspiracy.[85] The state should plan the growth of the economy and not be constrained by artificial financial pressures.[86] Kitson's views were derided by the establishment but he had important influence in both radical and lunatic fringe circles.

Leese was not the only one in British fascism influenced by Kitson's arguments. Much of the ILP's important critique of Gold Standard policies in the 1920s was heavily influenced by Kitson, who had given several lectures to the organization.[87] Mosley's Birmingham Proposals in 1925 were a direct outcome of such ideas. Mosley's ideas and critique of the Gold Standard were better thought out than Kitson's and derived mainly from Keynes, but they nevertheless provide the one tangible link between the two main traditions of British fascism. In most other respects, in terms of personality, ideology, political credibility and intellectual coherence, Mosley's and Leese's fascism were about as far apart from each other as it was possible to be.

[85] A. Kitson, *The Bankers Conspiracy* (London, 1933), p. 52.
[86] Idem, *Trade Fallacies* (London, 1917), pp. 175–6.
[87] J.L. Finlay, *Social Credit: The English Origins* (London, 1972), pp. 23–6.

5

The BUF and British Society, 1932–1939

The British Union of Fascists represented the mature form of the fascist phenomenon in British society, being the only organization with any pretension to significance in inter-war Britain. Formed in October 1932 by Sir Oswald Mosley, it drew its inspiration from Mussolini's Italy and most of its initial impetus from the youth movement of the New Party (Nupa) and the membership files of the British Fascists. Mosley had decided during the 1931 general election campaign to form a fascist movement, after the devastating defeat in which the New Party lost all its parliamentary seats and twenty-two of its twenty-four candidates forfeited their deposits, and his visit to Mussolini in Rome and to nazi leaders in Munich in January 1932 merely strengthened his resolve.

The early years

Mosley's turn to fascism was a response to the failure of the British parliamentary system of government to adopt radical reform to cure unemployment, and to prevent the continued economic and political decline of Britain. This failure was symbolized by the crushing victory of the 'old gangs' as Mosley called them, in the general election of 1931. Ironically, given the severe limitations of freedom of speech planned in the future fascist state, Mosley deemed it necessary to protect that liberty by providing more rigorous stewarding of public meetings to prevent them being broken up by left-wing activists. Hence the somewhat incongruous background to the emergence of Britain's most important fascist organization: the publication of a reasoned pragmatic plan of action to attack unemployment in Mosley's *The Greater Britain*, combined with the creation of a uniformed defence force to ensure that those who wished to hear of such ideas at public meetings would be able to do so.

Thus from the beginning the BUF exhibited a Janus-faced appearance; it was a movement which was intellectually the most coherent and rational of all the fascist parties in Europe in its early years, yet whose aggressive style and vigorous self-defence attracted political violence. Paradoxically, the failure of the BUF was linked to both phenomena. It failed to convince the nation that authoritarian methods were necessary to solve Britain's economic crisis and prevent further political decline, and it was blamed for fomenting the violence and public disorder which became associated with its activities in the 1930s. Furthermore, the British economy staged a revival in that decade. New industries and housebuilding in the south and east of the country led to a growth rate which rivalled that of the mid-Victorian era, and apart from a minor dip in the statistics in 1937–8 the sustained restructuring and recovery of the economy created many new jobs and reduced rates of unemployment in all but the most depressed areas dependent on the declining staple industries.[1]

For a party whose purpose was to solve the unemployment problem the BUF was conspicuously unsuccessful in recruiting a mass following from its victims. Apart from the cotton campaign in Lancashire in 1934 the BUF made no headway in the areas of high regional unemployment. Apathy or the new loyalties to working-class politics, where both the Labour and Communist parties were militantly hostile to fascism, ensured that the BUF made no impact in such localities.[2] Neither increased living standards for the majority nor the despair of mass unemployment in the depressed areas proved conducive to the growth of fascism in Britain. The crisis of British society which Mosley saw as essential for the success of his movement, and which he predicted as having arrived in 1932, stubbornly failed to materialize.[3]

---

[1] D.H. Aldcroft, *The Inter War Economy: Britain 1930–39* (London, 1973); S. Pollard, *The Development of the British Economy* (London, 1969), pp. 92–174; B. Alford, *Depression and Recovery* (London, 1972).

[2] J. Stevenson and C. Cook, *The Slump* (London, 1977).

[3] J.D. Brewer, 'Fascism and crisis', *Patterns of Prejudice*, 13, 2–3 (Mar.–June 1979), pp. 1–7.

The political violence which became inextricably linked with the BUF proved to be the other great negative factor in its fortunes, despite some temporary gains amongst those who were frightened by working-class and Jewish militancy. Yet two facts must be stressed at the outset with relation to this problem in inter-war Britain. First, although it was a serious issue which eventually led to the introduction of the Public Order Act in 1936, such violence was only a pale reflection of the conflict which led to the growth of fascism in Italy and Germany in the inter-war period.[4] There was no British Horst Wessel, nor indeed any anti-fascist martyr, as a result of political disturbances in the 1930s, although claims were made that a Blackshirt died later from injuries inflicted at a meeting at Holbeck Moor in Leeds.[5] Second, political violence in England was not invented by the BUF, nor did it come about as a response to its activities. Throughout the 1930s Mosley stressed the propaganda theme that Blackshirt methods were necessary to prevent 'red terrorism'. Although his accusations on that score were greatly exaggerated, the police had experienced problems with increased disorder at meetings as a result of the depression. The deployment of police at the end of the National Unemployed Workers Movement hunger march in London in October 1932 saw the most intensive public order precautions since 1848.[6] In Bristol twenty-nine persons were arrested for assaulting the police, malicious damage and disorderly conduct with respect to the activities of the National Unemployed Workers Movement and the Communist party in 1931 and 1932.[7]

Certainly Mosley's constant harping on the theme of left-wing intimidation was a fairly effective recruiting ploy throughout the 1930s. The second MI5 report on the activities of the BUF argued that the Olympia meeting on 7 June 1934, which so alienated influential opinion, actually increased support amongst those who were concerned about political disruption by left-wing activists. For two days a representative cross-section of working-class men, ex-officers, and public schoolboys queued from morning to night

[4] F.L. Carsten, *The Rise of Fascism* (London, 1967), pp. 45–120.
[5] N. Driver, *From the Shadows of Exile* (n.d.), pp. 39–40.
[6] J. Stevenson, 'The politics of violence' in *The Politics of Re-appraisal 1918–39*, ed. G. Peele and C. Cook (London, 1975), pp. 146–65; Stevenson and Cook, *The Slump*, pp. 145–94.
[7] PRO HO 144/20140/267.

at the Black House to join an organization which they saw as being dedicated to preserving freedom of speech.[8] The Security Service, on the other hand, argued that violent demonstrations which threatened public order could only benefit political extremism in general, as it provided incentive for recruitment for both fascists and communists.

Mosley justified the turn to fascism as the result of the increased disruptive tactics used by opponents of the New Party. However, followers like Harold Nicolson noticed other fascist traits in 1931. Mosley's adoption of a more authoritarian manner and the increasing importance he gave to developing the youth organization as a relatively disciplined defence force led to the departure of many of his more important political collaborators like John Strachey. The immediate cause of the decision to adopt fascist methods was the attack on Mosley at a New Party meeting in Glasgow in September 1931 when he was hit on the head with a stone and attacked with a life preserver. Mosley then decided to expand his personal bodyguard, the so-called 'Biff Boys', to create a more disciplined and trained group. Nupa, the New Party youth movement, was rapidly enlarged to create a viable defence force which later became the basis of the elite I Squad, and Harold Nicolson suggested a uniform of grey flannel trousers and shirts.[9] Nupa emphasized physical fitness and organized discipline. However, the original 'Biff Boys', the hearty undergraduate types who had been trained by the Jewish boxer Ted 'Kid' Lewis, were now joined by others with more controversial opinions and methods; in August 1932 a nineteen-year-old member of the New Party was convicted of sticking labels on shop windows in London's Oxford Street urging the expulsion of the Jews from Britain.[10]

During 1932 Mosley approached the other fascist movements in Britain to see if co-operation was possible. He attempted a takeover bid of the major fascist groups, demanding their subordination and acceptance of him as their new leader. This determined the name of Mosley's fascist movement, the British Union of Fascists, when it was formed in October 1932. However,

---

[8] PRO HO 144/20142/115.

[9] H. Nicolson, *Diaries and Letters 1930–1939* (London, 1966), p. 89.

[10] S. Rawnsley, 'Fascism and fascists in Britain in the 1930s', PhD thesis, University of Bradford, 1981, pp. 75–6.

Mosley only had limited success in this endeavour. His deputy, Robert Forgan, had satisfactory talks with Neil Francis Hawkins about the amalgamation of the New Party with the British Fascists, but the grand council of the British Fascists voted against a merger by one vote in May 1932 after its founder Rotha Lintorn Orman, who was very suspicious of Mosley and regarded him as a near communist, vigorously opposed the change. The men on the Committee, led by Francis Hawkins and E.G. Mandeville Roe, then resigned from the British Fascists and joined Mosley, bringing with them a copy of its membership list.[11] Francis Hawkins was to rise to effective second-in-command of the BUF after 1936 and the impact of the ex-British Fascist members was to be significant in the organization and administration of the movement. Mosley contemptuously dismissed the remaining British Fascists as 'three old ladies and a couple of office boys',[12] and after the split Mosley ignored the existence of the British Fascists. During the Jewish protest demonstrations against the nazis in Hyde Park on 23 July 1933 a small lorry carrying British Fascists in a counter-demonstration shouted abuse at BUF headquarters. In retaliation for this, and fearful that they might be blamed for any fascist hostility towards the Jews, between fifty and sixty BUF members wrecked the BF's headquarters.[13]

Further negotiations with the remaining BF membership resumed in July 1934. Colonel Henry Wilson negotiated with Mosley in an attempt to merge the two organizations. He had lent £500 to the BFs to liquidate pressing debts, and in order to obtain repayment had either to bankrupt them or obtain financial backing from elsewhere. However, between Wilson's meeting with Mosley and that of the British Fascist grand council, Rotha Lintorn Orman changed her mind and, allegedly under the influence of drink, strenuously opposed the proposal. The merger plan was again abandoned, and Wilson began bankruptcy proceedings to wind up the BFs.[14]

The proposal to merge the IFL with the BUF completely failed. Mosley had chaired a meeting where Arnold Leese and Henry

[11] C. Cross, *The Fascists in Britain* (London, 1961), p. 65; A.K. Chesterton, *Oswald Mosley. Portrait of a Leader* (London, 1937), p. 17.
[12] R. Skidelsky, *Oswald Mosley* (London, 1975), p. 291.
[13] PRO HO 144/19069/197–8.
[14] PRO HO 144/20142/67–8 and 71.

Hamilton Beamish had addressed Nupa on 'The blindness of British Politics under the Jew Power' in April 1932, but from then on relations rapidly deteriorated. Leese saw Mosley as an unprincipled opportunist and argued that his fascism was not based on racial nationalism. He was also extremely suspicious of Mosley's first wife, Cynthia Curzon, accusing her of having Jewish blood in her veins. To Leese, Mosley was a 'kosher fascist',[15] a Jewish agent planted to discredit the whole concept of fascism in Britain; to Mosley, Leese was no more than an anti-semitic crank. However, the existence of a potential rival, no matter how eccentric, meant that there was an alternative fascist allegiance open to disgruntled members of the BUF. The effects of this personal hostility and rivalry led to unofficial direct actions being taken by members of the BUF in November 1933. A fight involving 150 people led to BUF members breaking up an IFL meeting, tearing up its banner and beating up Arnold Leese and Brigadier-General Blakeney, the ex-president of the BFs. Rubber truncheons, knuckledusters and chairs were used as weapons and there were many injuries. After this, according to MI5, the IFL became moribund and no longer ranked as a serious competitor to the BUF.[16] After this assault Mosley reputedly was forced to discipline his own followers in order to maintain order in the BUF, and to discourage further acts of violence which invited retaliatory action by the authorities.

Mosley repeatedly argued that his Blackshirt organization was a self-defence force and that although he could have disrupted other political meetings he never chose to do so. A policy of legality and the maintenance of public order was officially adopted by the BUF in its attempt to portray itself as a responsible organization. Indeed, the altered conditions of 1939 led to some co-operation between fascist, anti-semitic and pro-German groups, although Leese was excluded from the informal alliance. Before this, however, potential rivals had been either ignored or treated ruthlessly by the BUF. Conditions for co-operation included total subservience to Mosley's leadership, and for those like Leese who objected, unofficial violence often resulted. A group of Blackshirts vandalized the offices of the British United Fascists in Kensington

---

[15] A.S. Leese, *Out of Step* (Hollywood, n.d.), p. 52.
[16] PRO HO 144/20141/309.
[17] Cross, *The Fascists in Britain*, p. 82.

in 1933;[17] in 1936 Blackshirts in Liverpool assaulted the Social Credit Greenshirts with knuckledusters at their headquarters;[18] and William Joyce's Nationalist Socialist League was also subject to disruption by Blackshirts after he left the BUF in 1937.

The early history of the BUF saw a rapidly expanding movement becoming quickly embroiled in conflict with left-wing opponents. At first many of the new recruits were from Mosley's New Party; some were old followers from the ILP. Mosley tried to recruit from Conservatives and from those who were affiliated to no party. To the left he stressed the revolutionary aims of the BUF whilst to the right he emphasized authority and ordered government.[19] While several important recruits, such as Robert Forgan, and in 1934 John Beckett, were to join the movement from the left, and W.E.D. Allen was to play an important role in the story of the BUF, in general it was those who came to fascism from outside politics who were to prove the most important elements in the organization. During 1933 Ian Hope Dundas, Alexander Raven Thomson, A.K. Chesterton and William Joyce all joined either as a result of Mosley's charismatic personality or convinced by the fascist creed. Dundas, a martinet figure, was to be Mosley's chief of staff, Raven Thomson his leading intellectual, Chesterton his best polemicist and Joyce the leading speaker, who rivalled Mosley in the brilliance of his oratorial style, even if the content was often rabid nonsense.

It was the excitement and potential violence which the BUF seemed to offer which proved the biggest recruiting spur. From the outset the establishment of a uniformed and disciplined fascist defence force, the Blackshirts, was Mosley's first priority. Under the first commander, Eric Hamilton Piercy, and adjutant Neil Francis Hawkins, they were organized on paramilitary lines, particularly the elite I Squad at the Black House, Mosley's headquarters. Blackshirts were driven to meetings in armour-plated vans. Interrupters were warned that fascists did not tolerate hecklers, who if they continued where then ejected from the meeting. Knuckledusters and leaded hosepipes were sometimes used at early BUF meetings, though Mosley rapidly banned their use by Blackshirts.[20] A graphic example of early Blackshirt

[18] PRO HO 144/20146/136–8.
[19] *Blackshirt*, Feb. 1933.
[20] Cross, *The Fascists in Britain*, p. 70.

violence was provided by the principal of Ruskin College, Oxford, who took sworn affidavits from victims who had been roughly treated at Mosley's meeting in Oxford in November 1933. These included allegations of having been thrown downstairs, of fascists banging the heads of interrupters on the stone floor, and of protestors having fascist stewards' fingers rammed up their nostrils.[21]

However, it would be misleading to suggest that fascist violence was the sole cause of conflict. As with Hitler's nazis, Blackshirts argued that in using weapons they were merely copying the tactics of their opponents. The National Headquarters reputedly had a museum of offensive weapons used by anti-fascists which included knuckledusters, rubber piping, coshes of all sizes, razors set in potatoes and daggers.[22] Mosley, with his combative language and stormy oratory, proved later to be no sluggard at defending himself with the good old British fist. At a Prestwich meeting in 1936 he lost his temper at persistent heckling, jumped into his audience and knocked three of the ringleaders senseless.[23] When one of his own officials insulted him at a Leeds meeting Mosley knocked him unconscious.[24] Mosley was himself quite seriously hurt by a brick at a meeting in Liverpool in 1937. The violence associated with the BUF from the outset, and which continuing throughout its history, represented an interaction of mutually opposed and conflicting forces.

After a visit to see Mussolini's International Fascist exhibition in the spring, Mosley organized the first large BUF march in June 1933 when 1,000 Blackshirts marched through London. The anti-fascists largely ignored this demonstration. Soon afterwards, in the autumn of 1933, the BUF bought the lease of the Whitelands Teachers Training College, Chelsea, which was turned into fascist headquarters, the so-called Black House. This became the organizational, intellectual and social centre of the BUF. The movement's leading officials had offices there and between 50 and 200 Blackshirts were in residence at various times, living under military discipline. Opponents argued that the cellars were used for punishment purposes, and Special Branch alleged that a man

---

[21] PRO HO 144/20141/157.
[22] Driver, *Shadows of Exile*, p. 33.
[23] Ibid., p. 39.
[24] Ibid., pp. 31–2.

had been seriously wounded by a knife in the stomach after horseplay between fascists at Black House.[25]

The rapid growth of the BUF and the increased problems of public order associated with it led to the government showing an interest in BUF activities. At a conference in the Home Office in November 1933 attended by the Commissioner of the Metropolitan Police, two officers of MI5 and a superintendent from Special Branch, it was decided that information should be systematically collected on fascism in the United Kingdom.[26] From the spring of 1934 onwards in a series of reports MI5 evaluated the significance of this intelligence. Most of this material is now available for consultation and, interpreted with care, it illuminates many aspects of BUF activity, since the papers expand and complement other sources.

The drive for expansion received its greatest impetus from the support given to the movement by Lord Rothermere, who was persuaded by Mussolini to back Mosley. For six months his newspapers gave prominence to BUF activities, which was a splendid opportunity to increase propaganda, and produced a sharp boost in membership figures.

During the same period Mosley tried to increase the quality of his followers too. At the beginning of 1934 he attempted to gain more influential and financial support from establishment and entrepreneurial sources; hence the formation of the January Club, a dining group which although not specifically a front organization, nevertheless was designed to influence politicians, businessmen and members of the armed services towards the fascist case. The leading spirits behind the club were Major Yeats Brown, the Bengal Lancer, Dr Robert Forgan, deputy leader of the BUF, Sir Donald Makgill and Captain Luttman Johnson, all of whom where either members of the BUF or had close connections with Mosley. The function of the club was to allow leading fascists to discuss contemporary political issues with experts and some opponents in a convivial after-dinner atmosphere. As many as 350 attended such functions and amongst members and guests were Lord Middleton, Brigadier-General Spears, Sir John Squire, the Earl of Iddesleigh, Lord Russell of Liverpool and Sir Charles Petrie. MI5 was particularly interested in the contacts made with

[25] PRO HO 144/20140/289.
[26] PRO HO 45/25386/54–9.

the armed services,[27] but the Security Service could find little sign of important influential support for Mosley in Parliament, even at the peak of the BUF growth in 1934. Only three Conservative MPs had shown much interest in the movement,[28] and the political establishment in general thought the best policy was to ignore Mosley. A few radical spirits were interested but most sympathized with Baldwin's long-held view that Mosley was 'a cad and a wrong 'un'.[29]

Other areas of the establishment were infiltrated by fascists, and groups were set up in the Civil Service and in several educational centres and public schools, including the Universities of London and Birmingham, Stowe School, and Winchester, Beaumont and Worksop Colleges.[30] Mosley's and Rothermere's interest in aviation led to the formation of a fascist flying club in Gloucestershire in 1934.[31]

As Mosley tried to make the presence of the BUF felt in 1934, so popular opposition to the growth of fascism increased. This was particularly marked amongst the organized working class. At the grass roots level this was shown when John Beckett, the ex-MP for Gateshead and recent Mosley recruit, returned to his old constituency as part of a speaking tour in May 1934. Greeted with shouts of 'traitor', he had to run the gauntlet of 3,000 anti-fascists in Gateshead and 5,000 in Newcastle. At Leicester a hostile crowd several thousands strong prevented A.K. Chesterton who was then the Midlands organizer, from attending a meeting.[32]

It was, however, after Mosley's Olympia meeting on 7 June 1934 that public opinion in general began to harden significantly against the BUF. Although the meeting led to an immediate increase in recruitment, the BUF lost the propaganda war concerning responsibility for the violence associated with the occasion, and in retrospect it marked the turning-point in the fortunes of the movement. About 12,000 attended, including about 2,000 Blackshirts, half of whom acted as stewards. The police were not in attendance, although 762 officers were in

[27] PRO HO 144/20141/300–6.
[28] PRO HO 144/20140/117.
[29] T. Jones, *Whitehall Diary*, ed. K. Middlemas (London, 1969), vol. II, p. 195.
[30] PRO HO 144/20140/286; J.D. Brewer, *Mosley's Men* (Aldershot, 1984), p. 86.
[31] PRO HO 144/20142/118; P. Addison, 'Patriotism under pressure. Lord Rothermere and British foreign policy', in Peele and Cook, *The Politics of Reappraisal*, p. 200.
[32] PRO HO 144/20140/76, 96–8; Brewer, 'Fascism and crisis', p. 86.

reserve in case of trouble. Special Branch had warned that political violence was a possibility as the communists were planning to disrupt the meeting; they allegedly had plans to locate the main power switch so that the lights could be cut off at a favourable moment.[33] Mosley's speech was interrupted continuously by hecklers who were unceremoniously removed by the stewards. According to Mosley, the interruptions showed the necessity for the fascists to have a defence force and demonstrated that for many years past there had been no freedom of speech in the country. According to Special Branch, very violent treatment was meted out in the foyer to the men removed by the Blackshirts;[34] the police intervened just in time to prevent serious injury. As it was, in the fighting at the meeting and afterwards many sustained injuries. Five were detained in hospital, including two fascists, and one doctor saw between fifty and seventy victims. He suggested that, given the nature of the wounds, it seemed that knuckledusters and razors had been used on members of the public.[35]

With hindsight it is clear that left-wing opponents planned to disrupt the meeting, for over 1,000 anti-fascists were involved in a counter-demonstration and in the systematic attempts to wreck the occasion. However, it is also plain that the fascists deliberately over-reacted and that the indelible impression left on most uncommitted observers was one of Blackshirt violence which frightened and dismayed many neutrals. Also, given the political context, it was not surprising that the growth of fascism should meet with such hostility in Great Britain. Organized labour pointed out the obvious possible parallels between fascism in Britain and its German and Italian counterparts. The General Secretary of the Associated Society of Locomotive Engineers and Firemen wrote to the Home Secretary arguing that the growth of fascism created a threat to organized labour since it had led elsewhere to the suppression and murder of trade unionists.[36] The National Federation of Professional Workers had already objected to the proposed constitutional reforms of the BUF and what they saw as plans for the suppression of Parliament, the imprisonment of

---

[33] PRO HO 144/20140/58.
[34] PRO HO 144/20140/29–34.
[35] PRO HO 144/20141/366–7.
[36] PRO HO 144/20140/7–8.

opponents, and the establishment of a private army.[37] The National Joint Council of the Labour party, the parliamentary Labour party and the Trades Union Congress, in a deputation to the Home Secretary, argued that unless the government took action against the BUF the Labour movement would be unable to control the justified anger of extremists who were already forming anti-fascist organizations such as the Greyshirts.[38] Such actions were understandable, given that fascist speakers like William Joyce were already bluntly stating at public meetings that freedom of speech could not be tolerated in a fascist state.[39]

However, it was the loss of Lord Rothermere's support and the free publicity in the *Daily Mail* that contributed most to the decline of the BUF. In an exchange of letters Rothermere said he could no longer support a movement which was becoming increasingly to believe in dictatorship, anti-semitism and the corporate state.[40] Mosley argued that the loss of Rothermere's support was due to the threat of Jewish advertisers like Joe Lyons withdrawing their business from his newspapers.[41] But Rothermere's action was mainly caused by the unfavourable publicity for the BUF which followed the Olympia meeting, and the link in the public mind between its political creed and the far more sinister and violent events of the Night of the Long Knives of 30 June 1934 in Germany.

Growing confrontation with political opponents rapidly became a method of obtaining much-needed publicity, once Rothermere's support had evaporated. In the second half of 1934 and in 1935 the movement all but collapsed as a national force, and to revive its fortunes the fascist political programme was de-emphasized and instead more attention was paid to fomenting local and regional grievances in populist campaigns. Thus the 'tithe war' was supported in agricultural areas, a cotton campaign in Lancashire, and shipping policies were emphasized in Liverpool. Sectional groups like the Fascist Union of British Workers tried to organize strikes at the Firestone works in Brentford and on Birmingham buses. The movement also represented individuals

---

[37] PRO HO 144/20140/162–81.
[38] PRO HO 144/20141/51.
[39] PRO HO 144/20140/275–7.
[40] *Daily Mail*, 19 July 1934; *Blackshirt*, 20 July 1934.
[41] O. Mosley, *My Life* (London, 1968), pp. 346–7.

before the Public Assistance Boards, and collected information on the structure of British industry for the future fascist state, but its efforts soon petered out.[42]

The turn to anti-semitism

The use of political anti-semitism within the BUF has to be seen in the context of these efforts at revival. Following Rothermere's defection, radical voices within the movement suggested the use of open anti-semitism to stimulate popular response. Mosley, genuinely puzzled by growing Jewish hostility to the BUF, asked A.K. Chesterton who was now on the Headquarters staff to examine the influence of Jews in British Society. Whilst Chesterton's later justified reputation of being one of the most rabid anti-semites connected with British fascism would suggest that this was like asking a cat to drink a bowl of cream, there is little evidence to suggest that prior to his involvement in the BUF he viewed the world primarily through anti-semitic spectacles, despite being a second cousin to such notorious anti-semites as Cecil and G.K. Chesterton.[43] Although the report was not published, it convinced Mosley of Jewish dominance in British society and that over half the assaults committed on fascists had been by Jews. The interpretation given by Mosley and Chesterton to such findings would suggest that there was already a pronounced anti-semitic influence within the BUF which from the autumn of 1934 onwards was officially condoned by the leadership.

Indeed, anti-semitic behaviour had been incipient within the ranks of the BUF from the outset and included elements first recruited from the New Party. At the level of the official leadership anti-semitism was forbidden.[44] However, double standards were used and attacks on the 'alien menace' in the fascist press used many anti-semitic stereotypes long before it was accepted as an official weapon; for instance in *Blackshirt* in October 1933 those Jews who attacked fascism were likened to a cancer in the body politic.[45] But responsibility for the developing conflict with the

---

[42] PRO HO 144/20140/73; Brewer, 'Fascism and crisis', p. 77.

[43] D.L. Baker, 'A.K. Chesterton. The Making of a British Fascist', PhD thesis, University of Sheffield, 1982, p. 235.

[44] *Blackshirt*, 1 April 1933.

[45] Ibid., 30 Sept.–6 Oct. 1933.

Jewish community as with the hostility of the Labour movement, has to be seen as a matter of convergence. There was plenty of evidence to suggest a pronounced development of anti-semitic tendencies in the BUF ranks during 1933 and 1934;[46] but as the Metropolitan police records make clear, militant Jewish youth and communist elements were assaulting Blackshirts selling newspapers at this time.[47]

The ending of Rothermere's support and the turn to political anti-semitism were crucial to the future history of the BUF. Dropped by the one section of the establishment which supported it, and adopting policies that ensured that popular opinion would become increasingly hostile, Mosley destroyed whatever small likelihood the BUF had of becoming an effective force in British politics. It became increasingly a political pariah, relegated to a marginal position in society, which could be safely ignored by influential opinion. Thus a vicious circle of political impotence was set in motion by Mosley; in order to obtain much-needed publicity for the programme and political ideas of the BUF, which it was now denied in the national press, the techniques and methods of low politics leading to street conflict with political enemies were encouraged. The increasing switch to populist methods, and the threats to public order and the political anti-semitism with which this became associated in the public mind, meant that Mosley's movement went increasingly beyond the pale. His earlier refusal to play the party game had led the political establishment to ignore him, and their view was now reinforced by the problems for public order brought about by Mosley's street-corner politics.[48]

The rapid mushrooming of activity in 1934 and its equally spectacular decline led the Security Service to re-evaluate the development of the BUF. During 1935, as a result of intelligence information, they came to the conclusion that Mosley received most of his finance from Mussolini and that the national roots of the movement were weak and kept alive by artificial means.[49]

---

[46] Rawnsley, 'Fascism and fascists', p. 77.

[47] PRO Mepo 2/3069.

[48] N. Mosley, *Rules of the Game* (London, 1981), and idem, *Beyond the Pale* (London, 1983).

[49] PRO HO 45/25385/38–49.

Fascism in Britain was to be an irritant in society, not a serious threat to the establishment.

Mosley's turn to political anti-semitism was signalled by his Albert Hall meeting in October 1934 when he attacked both the 'big' Jews who were seen as a threat to the nation's economy and the 'little' Jews who allegedly swamped the cultural identity of localities where they settled.[50] The official attitude to British Jewry taken by the BUF saw Jews in terms of a national rather than a religious or racial issue. Jews were supposedly a nation within a nation who owed allegiance to an international community rather than to the British State. Unlike the role it played in the IFL, political anti-semitism never became a total ideological explanation of all the imagined ills of British society for most of the official leadership of the BUF, though there were obvious exceptions like William Joyce and some of the speakers he trained for the East End campaign of 1935–7. In general, however, the developments of BUF anti-semitism from a rather vague ideological formulation to a virulent political weapon has to be seen as part of the strategy of lining up fascist sentiments behind regional issues, which attracted popular attention in different localities.

The immediate trigger to the anti-semitic campaign was the reception of Jock Houston as a speaker in the East End of London in 1935. Houston mixed earthy Cockney presentation with a crude political anti-semitism which drew a positive response from many in his growing audiences.[51] Apart from the area around Manchester, all other regions were experiencing a steep decline in membership by 1935, and anti-semitism now showed itself to be a viable propaganda vehicle in a particular locality; from then on it was given special prominence. Elsewhere it proved a negative variable, even in areas with a sizeable Jewish presence such as Leeds or Manchester. In Birmingham there was a virtually total neglect of anti-semitism.[52]

These tactics were necessary because the major national political issues of 1935 had proved in practice to be disastrous flops for the BUF. In particular, the 'Mind Britain's Business' campaign against the League of Nations policy to boycott fascist

---

[50] PRO HO 144/20143/71–80.
[51] PRO HO 144/20145/14–17.
[52] J. Brewer, 'The British Union of Fascists and anti-semitism in Birmingham', *Midland History*, 9 (1984), p. 114.

Italy after her invasion of Abyssinia in 1935 cut little ice. The fact that Mosley had lost his main propaganda outlet meant that the British public for the most part paid little or no attention to beliefs which appeared to derive from ideological sympathy with Italian fascism or more sinister reasons.

The other major issue of 1935 was also a non-event for the BUF. The general election of that year was boycotted by Mosley, using the less than inspiring slogan of 'Fascism next time' as the rationale for his decision. The fact of the matter was that the BUF had neither the organization nor the quality of personnel necessary for a national political campaign. The comprehensive victory of the National government showed how little impact fascism in particular and political extremism in general had made on the British public by 1935. From a national movement designed to revolutionize the political structure of the nation, the BUF had degenerated into an organization which became increasingly dependent on a localized campaign playing on anti-immigrant racial populist themes, which was to be the main pattern of British fascism from then onwards. National campaigns, like the support for Edward VIII during the abdication crisis of 1936,[53] and the portrayal of the BUF as a peace movement in the later 1930s, either fell on deaf ears or were only partially successful in changing the focus of fascist politics from the parish pump and the anti-immigrant concerns of the East End of London to wider issues.

The move from anti-Jewish sentiments to full-scale political anti-semitism went through several stages. It took twelve months from the Albert Hall speech in October 1934 until anti-semitism was used as the main plank of a political campaign. Even then Mosley appeared at first to have some regard to public opinion and the image the BUF projected of itself. Thus when it was discovered that Jock Houston had a criminal record he was immediately moved from London to Manchester, and replaced in Shoreditch by Charles Wegg Prosser, a law student with an impeccable background.[54] However, this appointment was not approved by those who had been attracted to the movement by Houston's populist oratory and Prosser was assaulted by two members of Shoreditch branch.[55] With the rise of new men under

---

[53] PRO HO 144/20710/38–42.
[54] PRO HO 144/21062/282.
[55] PRO HO 144/20147/142–3.

Francis Hawkins, like Captain Donovan and U.A. Hick to control
the administration of the movement in London, so the emphasis
switched to the recruitment of anti-semitic elements and the
quality of the personnel deteriorated.[56]

Political anti-semitism in the East End of London had deep
social causes and utilized a historical tradition of anti-alien
hostility which had emphasized anti-semitism from the turn of the
century.[57] One-third of the Jewish population of Great Britain
lived there and the influx of refugees escaping from persecution in
eastern Europe between 1880 and the First World War had
exacerbated many of the social problems of this decaying inner
city area. Some Jews had been conspicuously successful in
adapting to British life and they undoubtedly brought a new
vitality to an economically declining region. They also came to be
blamed for the ills of the locality, including the use of sweated
labour by unscrupulous employers, rack-renting by slum land-
lords, and the increased crime rate. Both the Labour and Communist parties had already been highly critical of some Jewish
employers before the fascists arrived in the area. Both they and the
Jewish establishment argued that the best way to fight fascism was
to eliminate the festering sores allegedly caused by some Jewish
elements, by exhorting the whole community to adopt behaviour
patterns which would give no grounds for offence.[58] Some
nativist elements in the host community were critical of what they
saw as an assault on local culture by alien Jewish values and it was
this ethnocentric attitude to change, when allied to the existence of
genuine social grievances, which was to make some parts of the
East End a fertile reception area for racial populist and anti-
immigrant movements right through from the British Brothers
League in 1900, the BUF from 1936 to 1940, the League of
Ex-Servicemen and the Union Movement in the 1940s, to the
National Front in the 1970s.[59]

[56] PRO HO 144/21061/315.
[57] C. Holmes, 'Anti-semitism and the BUF', in *British Fascism*, ed. K. Lunn and R.
Thurlow, (London, 1980), pp. 114–34.
[58] Idem, 'East End anti-semitism 1936', *Bulletin of the Society for the Study of Labour
History*, 32 (Spring 1976), pp. 26–32; G.C. Lebzelter, *Political Anti-Semitism in England
1918–1939* (London, 1979), pp. 136–69.
[59] C. Husbands, *Racial Exclusionism and the City* (London, 1983), pp. 93–5; idem, 'East
End racism 1900–1980: geographical continuities in vigilantist and extreme right wing
political behaviour,' *The London Journal* 8, 1 (1983) pp. 3–26; N. Deakin, 'The vitality of
a tradition', in *Immigrants and Minorities in British Society*, ed. C. Holmes (London,
1978), pp. 158–85.

The increasing conflict in the East End in 1936 and the follow-up campaigns of the BUF developed as a result of the inter-action of fascist anti-semitism and Jewish counter-attack. It arose out of genuine social issues, not because there was a disproportionate number of prejudiced personalities living in the locality. The threat to the breakdown of law and order, which led to the passing of the Public Order Act in 1936, was more complex than the simplified picture of a battle between fascists and communists for control of the streets which both the BUF press and the Metropolitan Police records tend to convey. On both sides it was the rank and file members of the fascists, and the communists and the Jewish community, who demanded more vigorous action. Initially the fascists tried to present a respectable form of anti-semitism for the campaign in the East End. However, the success of Houston and the failure of Wegg Prosser, coupled with the emergence of East End populist orators like E.G. 'Mick' Clarke, combined with increased hostility by militant working-class and Jewish elements to bring about a rapid reversal of policy. Fascist resources became increasingly concentrated here and recruitment of anti-semitic elements and adolescents was actively encouraged.

The forces of government, the working-class organizations and the Jewish establishment wished initially to ignore Mosley and the fascists in the hope that this would deny him publicity and defuse a potentially explosive situation. However, some members of the Communist party and the Jewish community were increasingly concerned about fascist expansionism in Europe, Hitler's anti-semitic legislation in Germany, his destruction of the German Labour movement and Mosley's own move to anti-semitism. Since the Third International's change to a popular front policy in 1935, groups such as the Jewish People's Council against Fascism and Anti-Semitism, the International Labour Defence of Britain and the London Ex-Servicemen's Defence against Fascism were part-Communist party front organizations and part spontaneous working-class resentment against the incursion of the fascists into the East End of London. The Council for Civil Liberty, which later became the National Council for Civil Liberty, fulfilled much the same function for mainly middle-class people interested in this subject, and worried by the threat made by fascism to cherished freedoms.[60] Indeed, the leadership of the Communist party were

---

[60] J. Jacobs, *Out of the Ghetto* (London, 1978), p. 138.

more concerned with opposing fascism abroad, recruiting for the Spanish Civil War and developing trade union activity and housing associations than with fighting Mosley on the streets. However, their membership thought differently and Joe Jacobs and other militants backed up by massive popular support, forced the Communist party to organize the opposition to Mosley at the 'Battle of Cable Street' on 4 October 1936.[61]

What particularly enraged the East End labour movement and the Jewish community was the number of increased unprovoked attacks on Jews and communists by young hooligans in the Stepney, Bethnal Green and Shoreditch areas during 1936.[62] Together with these assaults, the breaking of shop windows, the desecration of Jewish cemeteries and synogogues and the massive spread of anti-semitic graffiti greatly heightened tension. While the IFL were responsible for some of the outrage, BUF members were behind much of the increased conflict. The growth of street corner meetings in 1936 where BUF speakers like 'Mick' Clarke and Raven Thomson made regular insulting remarks about the Jewish community inflamed passions still more. Fascists justified such behaviour as legitimate self-defence: it was they who had been first assaulted by razor gangs of alien Jews. The BUF argued that a West End bookmaker masquerading with a Scottish name had a fixed tariff of remuneration for the degree of severity of injuries his henchmen inflicted on Blackshirts.[63] Anti-fascists argued that whoever was to blame for the violence, the police and courts treated them more harshly, and the National Council for Civil Liberties certainly produced reliable testimony to back up those claims.[64]

It is against this background that the Battle of Cable Street must be viewed. Mosley wished to hold a march through areas in the East End of London where there was both a large Jewish community and elements who would be receptive to a fascist demonstration. The Labour movement and many in the Jewish

[61] Ibid., pp. 222–58; P. Piratin, *Our Flag Stays Red* (London, 1978); R. Skidelsky, 'Reflections on Mosley and British fascism', in Lunn and Thurlow, *British Fascism*, pp. 78–99; G.D. Anderson, *Fascists, Communists and the National Government* (London, 1983).
[62] PRO Mepo 2/3085, 2/3086, 2/3087.
[63] R.R. Bellamy, 'We marched with Mosley' (n.d.), p. 8.
[64] H. Peel to NCCL, 3 Oct. 1937, statement H. Ogrodovitch, 26 Oct. 1937, Box 40/5 NCCL archive.

community thought that the government, police and Jewish leaders were far too passive in their policy of ignoring Mosley. As a result a spontaneous movement whose leadership was seized by Jewish communist activists emerged. A petition organized by the Jewish People's Council against Fascism and Anti-Semitism collected 77,000 signatures in two days; it was felt that if there had been more time over a quarter of a million would have signed against Mosley's proposed demonstration.[65] When Mosley led his men towards the East End on 4 October he discovered that more than 100,000 opponents blocked his path. At Cable Street the counter-demonstrators broke into a builder's yard and a lorry loaded with bricks was overturned and used as a barricade. The police banned Mosley from proceeding with his march and 1,900 fascists marched westwards instead.

Consequently it was the huge anti-fascist demonstration that created the major problem of public order. The Bethnal Green police reported that truncheons were drawn and mounted police used against militant anti-fascists. The Hackney police stated that of the 85 arrests made by them, 79 were of anti-fascists. At least 73 police and 43 private individuals needed medical attention afterwards.[66]

Civil liberties and the Public Order Act of 1936

The Battle of Cable Street has entered left-wing mythology as a great triumph of militant anti-fascism. Certainly the fascists did not pass and the numbers involved showed the depth of popular hostility against fascism and anti-semitism. Yet the police reports suggest a different interpretation. It was the end of the first stage of a conflict which was to rumble on up to the Second World War. The first results of the demonstration and violence were much the same as after the Olympia meeting in 1934; there was an immediate stimulus to recruitment for both fascists and communists and Special Branch estimated the significant, if transient, boost to fascist membership in East London to be around 2,000.[67] The authorities became worried about the threat to public order

[65] PRO HO 144/21060/316.
[66] PRO HO 144/21061/92–101.
[67] PRO HO 144/21062/259.

and decided at last to act against both fascist paramilitary provocation and anti-fascist counter-violence, a decision influenced by deputations to the Home Secretary from the London Labour party and the Manchester watch committee. Whilst their more extreme suggestions were disregarded, the degree of concern was duly communicated to the government. Herbert Morrison was extremely unhappy about the degree of ethnic strife and fascist propaganda to be found even in the schools of the East End of London, and he suggested there should be non-partisan agreement between all other political parties in the area that fascist political activities should be banned.[68]

The Battle of Cable Street had led to further hostilities between fascists and militant communists, Jewish and working-class elements in the East End. A week afterwards fascist youths instigated the so-called 'Mile End Road Pogrom', when despite the presence of 2,000 special constables at a nearby communist victory rally, a gang of hooligans smashed windows of Jewish shops and houses and assaulted all those designated as Jews that they could lay their hands on.[69] As a result of the serious increase in the level of political violence the government rushed through the Public Order Act, which became law on 1 January 1937, in an attempt to contain the situation.

The Public Order Act represented the culmination of a long debate within the government about how increased civil disorder should be controlled. It was seen as necessary to increase police powers to ban and control demonstrations and marches and to remove ambiguities in the existing law. The Act was passed in response to the situation of conflict which had developed between fascists and anti-fascists in the East End, but had a wider purpose – to exert greater social control through increased police powers and the threat to public order posed by political extremism in general. In this sense it was aimed at the problems highlighted by the National Unemployed Workers Movement demonstration in 1932 as well as the fascist disturbances. Existing case law in *Beatty* v. *Gilbanks* (1882) and *Wise* v. *Dunning* (1901) left it unclear whether fascist demonstrations could be construed as a genuine attempt to convert people to a point of view or to provoke by

[68] PRO HO 144/21062/10–45.
[69] Cross, *The Fascists in Britain*, p. 161; PRO Mepo 2/3098.

insult.[70] The Public Order Act reflected the police concern about the use of uniformed paramilitary groups which might challenge their monopoly of law enforcement and maintenance of public order, together with more general worries about the necessity of maintaining social control and of preventing provocative behaviour against law-abiding citizens.[71]

Recently de-classified Home Office papers do, however, show that there was a fluid situation within the agencies of state on this question. In general the Home Office was more concerned with the issue of protecting civil liberty and public order, while the police wished to ban the fascist movement. In 1934 Lord Trenchard, the Metropolitan Police Commissioner, had written to the Home Secretary complaining that the BUF had passed false information with regard to a communist plot to attack the Holloway branch and an alleged IFL plan to attack the Chelsea headquarters, and suggested that this mischievous nonsense would best be dealt with by outlawing the fascist movement.[72]

The Home Office responded by stating that the same arguments which pertained ten years ago when General Horwood wished to ban the Communist party still stood today. While such movements should be closely watched, there was no argument for banning them. To do otherwise would be to break the long-established political tradition of allowing people to hold whatever views they liked, so long as they did not break the law or urge others to do so. Only if public order appeared to be on the verge of breaking down would the government contemplate restricting political liberty. Provided that people in this country believed they had an honest system of government which dispensed even-handed justice, then there was no need to tamper with the law unless public order was threatened. To do otherwise was to risk driving underground legitimate political expression, which would create worse problems in the long run.[73]

Nevertheless, despite this classic defence of the traditional liberal position of the Home Office, the Secretary of State was prepared to examine whether several aspects of the problem which

[70] Skidelsky, *Oswald Mosley*, pp. 418–21.
[71] R. Benewick, *Fascist Movement in Britain* (London, 1972), pp. 235–62; J. Stevenson, 'The BUF, the Metropolitan Police and public order', in Lunn and Thurlow, *British Fascism*, pp. 135–65.
[72] PRO HO 144/20158/107.
[73] PRO HO 144/20158/102–3.

worried the police could be dealt with piecemeal. Emphasis was given by the Home Office and Cabinet to the desirability of laws which banned the use of political uniforms and the establishment of paramilitary organizations, and research was concluded to see how other nations dealt with the problem.[74] In 1934 the Home Office twice re-drafted a bill banning political uniforms, but concluded that the difficulties involved in definition, and the need to protect the civil liberties of other groups who wore distinctive clothing, together with the expected nit-picking objections of MPs like A.P. Herbert who were concerned to protect civil liberties, outweighed any advantages to be gained from such legislation. The failure to gain the consent of opposition parties and the improvement in the situation led to the dropping of the second proposal in 1934 and the Cabinet then decided that the matter should be put on ice unless the position deteriorated and immediate legislation was thought necessary.

This situation occurred in 1936 after the Battle of Cable Street. However, the new Police Commissioner, Sir Philip Game, put forward fresh arguments when asked to comment. He still stressed the desirability of banning the fascists but he now stated that anti-semitism had added a new dimension to the problem since 1934. Sir Philip argued that anti-semitism appealed to a subconscious racial instinct which was almost universal, with the Colonel Blimps believing in the conspiracy theory, and that in East London it was envy of Jewish economic success which caused the problem; this development represented the only real danger of fascism. Although communists were a nuisance it was fascist anti-semitism which caused the real headache; if this were outlawed then the problem would be removed. Additions to the existing law which attacked the symptoms rather than the cause were useful: if the police were given the power to prohibit processions and meetings, to outlaw paramilitary defence corps and to ban political uniforms this would no doubt help, but suppression of fascist anti-semitism would be the best solution.[75]

Sir Philip Game's important contribution to the debate showed that police attitudes towards fascism altered considerably during the 1930s. Contrary to left-wing and anti-fascist claims, the police

[74] PRO HO 144/20158/310.
[75] PRO HO 144/20159/155–62.

at the highest levels were not biased in favour of fascism, even if there were problems of interpretation of the law in developing conflict situations at the street level amongst the junior ranks and local magistrates treated anti-fascists more harshly than fascists. Sir Philip argued forcefully that there were much stronger reasons for banning fascists than communists and that political anti-semitism should be outlawed. It was somewhat ironic that the Home Office moved from its traditional defence of political liberty into a law and order stance just as the main police spokesman was advocating more liberal and socially aware arguments. The Public Order Act was to reflect the traditional police palliatives, despite Game's lukewarm espousal of them, and was to ignore his more radical solution.

The terms of the Act forbade the wearing of political uniforms except on ceremonial occasions. The use of stewards was banned at open air meetings, and insulting words likely to cause a breach of the peace were declared unlawful in public speeches. The police were given the power to ban marches or alter their routes if in the opinion of the authorities they were likely to cause a breach of the peace. In addition this ban could be applied to all political parties in a locality for up to three months.

The Public Order Act was a necessary but highly controversial piece of legislation. It severely limited the right of free speech, a fact denounced both by fascists and communists. Yet it was not clear that the Act was successful in controlling the situation after 1937; in Germany the banning of political uniforms had little effect on the rise of the nazis. There was also the problem of defining the use of insulting words and behaviour. Although the police did successfully charge fascists for this crime after 1936 the punishment was often derisory, and police interpretation of the law was often inconsistent. Raven Thomson was deemed not to be insulting when he said at Bethnal Green in March 1937 that he had the utmost contempt for the Jews and that they were 'the most miserable type of humanity,'[76] but an Inspector Jones was overruled when he reported that Mick Clarke had used no inflammatory language at the same venue in June 1937, when other police shorthand notes stated that Clarke had called the Jews 'greasy Scum' and 'the lice of the earth'.[77] During the election

[76] PRO Mepo 2/3109.
[77] PRO Mepo 2/3115.

campaign of March 1937 there were numerous complaints that the police failed to take action against provocative statements and actions against Jews by the fascists. Numerous assaults, cases of window smashing and the dissemination of graffiti continued unabated.

The nature of the fascist impact in the East End of London was demonstrated in the first local elections of 1937. In the LCC elections of March 1937 the British Union, as it then called itself, attained 23 per cent of the vote in North East Bethnal Green, 19 per cent in Stepney (Limehouse) and 14 per cent in Shoreditch. Six months later in the municipal elections it fought eight seats in five London boroughs. In six seats it finished second, with a best performance of 22 per cent in Bethnal Green East. Outside London the British Union performed disastrously, with its candidates in Leeds, Manchester, Sheffield and Southampton all finishing bottom of the poll. Even in its stronghold of East London the BUF's impact was patchy. It never came close to winning an election anywhere and, despite the fears of Harry Pollitt, the Communist leader, it made little impact in London dockland around Wapping. Political anti-semitism attracted mass support for the BUF in a limited geographical area, but it engendered greater hostility within those same localities and had appalling consequences elsewhere. Mosley's dream of a fascist nation was reduced to the reality of a minority anti-semitic political sub-culture in some areas of the East End of London.

If the use of political anti-semitism can be seen as a crucial stage in the decline of the BUF from a national movement to a localized racial populist organization, then its attempt to resurrect its political pretensions in the Peace Campaign of 1938–40 merely hastened its inevitable total destruction. The campaign was at best only partially successful in recovering the fortunes of the BUF in 1938–9. As with earlier national campaigns against unemployment and the League of Nations policy of sanctions against Fascist Italy, the role of the BUF in the political history of the decision-making process was non-existent. However, in 1938 the 'Britons fight for Britain only' and 'Mosley and Peace' campaigns, although based on assumptions different from the government's appeasement policies and having no influence upon them, nevertheless harmonized quite well with the general drift of public opinion with regard to European intervention and the threat of war. From March 1939 the situation altered radically. With

Hitler's tearing up of the Munich agreement, with the invasion of the rest of Czechoslovakia and the threat to Poland, British public opinion began to distrust Hitler's word and the nature of nazism changed markedly. Mosley's opposition to this national change of mood meant that for the small minority who still wished to maintain the peace of Europe at any price, he was momentarily seen as an alternative leader who would keep Britain out of a war.

Such a policy led to a limited revival of the movement in 1939. According to Mosley, his great peace rally at Earls Court on 16 July attracted over 20,000 (the Special Branch claimed a figure of 11,000).[78] Most of the audience were respectable middle-class citizens who sported fascist badges. However, although new members flocked to the movement others resigned in protest against what was seen as the placing of fascist loyalties above patriotic considerations.[79] There had previously been problems in 1938 in Bethnal Green, Limehouse and East Ham when many members became anti-German.[80] Mosley now tried to collaborate with other anti-war forces, but to little avail although this activity was to prove disastrous for the BUF in 1940.

The impact of the BUF on British society in the 1930s was small; it was merely a minor irritant for the government. Although some success had been achieved through its radical economic, social and political programme in the early period, suspicions of the links with more sinister movements in Europe and the development of anti-semitism and political violence turned public opinion against the fascist movement. The BUF was contained by an unofficial publicity boycott in the media after 1934 and by the surveillance of the Security Service. When public order was threatened in 1936–7 the government hastily stepped in to implement palliative legislation limiting freedom of political expression, but this seemed to keep the problem within bounds. The pro-appeasement campaign of 1938–9 produced an accelerating recovery from a low base for the movement, but once war was declared this hastened its final destruction – although this is a complex story deserving separate consideration elsewhere. The important point, however, is that even in the dark days of May 1940 the Home Office was very reluctant to destroy the fascist movement, and the

[78] N. Mosley, *Beyond the Pale*, p. 153; PRO HO 144/21281/150.
[79] PRO HO 144/21429/18.
[80] PRO HO 144/21281/97.

Security Service joined the campaign to intern Mosley and the most important members of the movement only after information had been acquired which suggested secretive behaviour and links with potentially treasonable behaviour. The government in the 1930s saw the BUF as a nuisance which needed to be watched, but which was felt to have little impact on wider society and which suffered from grave internal weaknesses. It was seen more as a patriotic form of national self-expression than as a pro-nazi organization and hence was not closed down in September 1939 when war was declared.

6

The Boys in Black,
1932–1939

Source material for the BUF

The sources of information on the BUF are far from satisfactory.
Many of the important records were seized by the police in
1940 and have either been lost or not released. Those that were
returned by the authorities were later destroyed by bomb damage.
What reliable material we have can be divided into three
categories.

The first of these lies in the information recently released by the
PRO in the Mosley Papers. This Home Office material is mainly
concerned with issues relating to public order, the impact of the
BUF on British society, the attitude of the government and police to
the movement, and the internment of fascists in 1940. There are
some intelligence and chief constables' reports which tell us
something about the spatial distribution, membership, internal
politics, finance and structure of the BUF, but these tend to
supplement what we know from other sources rather than provide
much new information. In general the authorities' view of the BUF
was far more objective than the attitude it took towards left-wing
movements and the Communist party. The police sympathized
with the discipline and control of the Blackshirts at public
meetings unless provoked, although they disliked the threat posed
to themselves as a uniformed law-enforcement agency. However,
the quality of police intelligence varied considerably. Several
contradictory accounts of fascist meetings, an inability to perceive
where to draw the line between comment and abuse at such
events, and a tendency to be more concerned with anti-fascist
protest, leads one to doubt the complete reliability of the sources

of information on which chief constables based their reports. The
government never saw the BUF as a threat to Parliament and
thought it could best be handled by an unofficial boycott and
intelligence surveillance. However, the internment files have to be
viewed very carefully because charges against fascists were
hurriedly concocted in 1940 in an atmosphere of suspicion and
panic. They do, however, contain some useful personal information.

The second source of information comes from the personal
recollections of the fascists themselves, which vary from the
informative to the bland and unrevealing. Mosley's own memories
of the movement were nearer to the latter than the former
category. As one critic has alleged, Mosley was an 'expert
forgetter'[1] who systematically expunged much compromising and
dubious material from his own published views on the BUF.
Indeed, it appeared that Mosley adopted a rigorous counter-
subversion strategy from the outset, since he was fully aware that a
movement whose inspiration came from Italy and Germany would
be regarded as a potentially subversive organization and a security
risk. Mosley knew the identity of the main MI5 agent in the
organization, the ex-Ulster Unionist MP and managing director of
a large printing firm, W.E.D. (Bill) Allen,[2] who was heavily
involved with two of the more secretive aspects of BUF affairs, the
financing of the movement in the early years by Mussolini and the
Air-Time commercial radio project in 1938–9.

Mosley argued that Allen was a Walter Mitty figure with a vivid
imagination, whose use as an agent by the authorities would prove
to be unreliable. To a certain extent this was the case. Allen was
somewhat spasmodic in providing information, although there is
no evidence that it was of a fantastic or grossly inaccurate nature.
Although the gist of his most important intelligence, that Mosley
was being funded by Mussolini, was correct, the amounts he
suggested were involved probably understated the true total and
the authorities only became convinced of their reliability a year
after the payments became significant. This was so even though
Allen himself created the means by which Mussolini's money
could be channelled into BUF funds and his own secretary paid

[1] C. Welch, 'The white hope in the Black Shirt', *Daily Telegraph*, 3 Apr. 1975; R.
Thurlow, 'The Black Knight', *Patterns of Prejudice*, 9, 3 (May–June 1975), pp. 15–19.
[2] N. Mosley, *Beyond the Pale*, pp. 174–5.

most of this into the account. Although Allen was never a member of the BUF he did have sympathy with the reason for Mosley's revolt; his book, *BUF. Oswald Mosley, and British Fascism*, written under the pseudonym of James Drennan, was by far the best contemporary account of the movement. Whatever Allen's motives were, Mosley saw his use as a kind of double agent — somebody who would pass on sufficient material to convince the authorities that Mosley was not involved in any illegal or potentially treasonable activity.

There were other signs that Mosley was very conscious of the activities of the Security Service. In the late 1930s he kept the membership of Commandant Mary Allen in the BUF secret in the hope that her unofficial women's police force could provide advance intelligence if the authorities were about to move against the organization.[3] Many important areas of BUF finances and connections were hidden from the membership reflecting not only the style of fascist leadership but also an attempt to confuse the Security Service in their surveillance of the movement.

If Mosley deliberately obscured the nature and activities of the BUF, other ex-members have proved more informative, sometimes behind the cloak of anonymity. Studies using oral history interview techniques of ex-fascists in Lancashire, Yorkshire, Birmingham and elsewhere have provided useful material on the nature of fascism in the regions, although not all the material can be considered reliable. There is also an important gap in the lack of a fascist view of the anti-semitic campaign in the East End of London.[4] The material collected by Stuart Rawnsley is particularly revealing, as he is the first scholar to make use of the remarkable autobiography of Nellie Driver, the BUF women's section organizer at Nelson and Colne, and one of the driving forces behind fascism in Lancashire. Her unpublished work represented a detailed and sympathetic view of many aspects of the movement, being particularly informative about the membership and the bitter experience of internment.[5] The most successful and long-serving administrator in the north of England, R. Reynell

---

[3] PRO HO 144/21933/330.

[4] S. Rawnsley, 'Fascism and fascists in Britain in the 1930s', PhD thesis, University of Bradford, 1983; Trevelyan Scholarship Project, *The British Union of Fascists in Yorkshire 1934–40*; J. Brewer, *Mosley's Men* (London, 1984).

[5] N. Driver, *From the Shadows of Exile* (n.d.).

Bellamy, has also written an unpublished work which presents the
BUF view of the organization and the events of the 1930s, a small
section of which has been consulted for this work.[6] When used in
conjunction with the Mosley papers this material provides interesting source material which can be used to check and supplement
the accounts provided by secondary works on the movement.

The third source comprises the accounts provided by
contemporary opponents of the BUF. However, these were far
from objective and anti-fascist sources are more useful in
explaining the nature of conflict created by British fascism than
they are in producing an informed coherent view of the BUF,
although its bias in emphasizing the violent and unpleasant aspects
of the movement must not be ignored.

The membership of the BUF

Any account of the BUF must begin with an analysis of who the
fascists were and the size of the membership. Unfortunately these
have proved difficult to assess, owing to the dearth of a reliable
quantitative sample of social class profiles of membership and the
impressionistic nature of the evidence used to estimate numbers.
The Security Service calculated membership at periodic intervals
between 1934 and 1939, and some of these figures have been now
tabulated in a systematic manner.[7] Using this material and the
assumption that the ratio between active and passive numbers was
$1:1\frac{1}{2}$ for most of the 1930s, Gerry Webber has estimated that the
total rose from 17,000 in February 1934 to a peak of 50,000 at the
end of the Rothermere period (July 1934), and then collapsed to
5,000 in October 1935. After this date there was a slow recovery
to 10,000 in March 1936, to 15,500 in November 1936, to
16,500 in December 1938 and 22,500 in September 1939.[8] In
general, this supports Skidelsky's claim that the BUF was gaining

---

[6] R.R. Bellamy, *We marched with Mosley*, chap. 36.

[7] G. Webber, 'Patterns of membership and support for the British Union of Fascists',
Journal of Contemporary History, 19 (1984), pp. 575–606.

[8] *News Chronicle*, 6 Feb. 1934; PRO HO 144/20142/107–22; PRO HO
144/20145/14–17; PRO HO 144/20147/378–87; PRO HO 144/26062/403–7; PRO HO
144/21281/114; statement by Sir J. Anderson, HC Debs 25 July 1940, vol. 363, col. 966.

in strength prior to the Second World War and his revised estimate of 20–25,000 members in 1939.[9]

Undoubtedly these are by far the most reliable of the assessments we have of the size of membership. However, a slight revision of the size of the movement is in order. Webber's intelligent use of the Mosley Papers and sophisticated analysis of the intelligence reports need some qualification. Although his emphasis on the BUF's appeal to different groups in the population at separate times, on the fluctuating fortunes of the movement in various areas and on regional disparities, is most helpful, some of the assumptions may need to be modified. Local studies, for example, do not always support the argument of a steady recovery between 1936 and 1939. Brewer's work in Birmingham argues that apart from a few fascist tea parties and policy meetings the movement became moribund in the city after 1935.[10] Rawnsley's thesis suggests that the movement maintained its momentum in Manchester throughout 1934, and then declined steadily until the Munich crisis in 1938. Indeed, a Special Branch report of 17 June 1937 mentions that although Mosley was reasonably satisfied with the good progress the movement was making elsewhere, he was unhappy with the collapse of the movement in South Wales and Lancashire. In the whole of the north-west, including Manchester and Liverpool, there were no more than 100 active members in 1937.[11]

Similarly, the reliance on the Trevelyan Report for information on Yorkshire fascism probably overestimated the number of fascists in the late 1930s in that area. This study, although useful, accepts the estimated membership of the BUF in Leeds given by an ex-fascist and makes dubious assumptions that accurate totals can be calculated from the number of internees in 1940 in any given area. The main argument of the Report is that anti-semitism was the chief cause of the growth of fascism in Leeds, despite the fact that the period of its most spectacular development had ended before the BUF adopted anti-semitic policies, which leads one to doubt the total reliability of this source. Indirect evidence relating to the poor performance of fascist candidates in local elections in

---

[9] R. Skidelsky, 'Great Britain', in *European Fascism*, ed. S.J. Woolf (London, 1981), p. 275.

[10] Brewer, *Mosley's Men*, pp. 86–103.

[11] PRO HO 144/21063/4–7.

Leeds, Sheffield and Manchester in 1937 and 1938, to the North
East Leeds by-election in 1940, when the BUF candidate received
only about 2 per cent of the vote in a straight fight with the
Conservative, and the fact that the number of full-time
administrators for the whole of the north of England had been
reduced to one by 1938 and that little or no attempt was made to
advertise Mosley's Earl's Court meeting in 1939 throughout the
north, would suggest that Webber's estimate of 8,000–10,000
members in Yorkshire and Lancashire in 1939 was too high.[12]

In general a small downward revision of the total numbers may
be suggested and a slightly different spatial distribution.
Subjective impressions of ex-members that up to 100,000 people
joined for a time in the 1930s were probably on the optimistic side
despite the rapid turnover of membership. Indeed, the division
between active and passive supporters may have been misleading;
a better guide to the quality of membership is the length of time of
participation. On this we have only qualitative evidence. Most
observers agree that the movement built up steadily in 1933 to a
peak of 50,000 in the Rothermere period (January–June 1934).
The main areas of growth were in London and the north-west
around Manchester and Liverpool, although there were sizeable
local organizations in Birmingham, Leeds, South Wales, the
South Coast towns, Bristol, Reading, Edinburgh and Aberdeen.

The withdrawal of press publicity led to the rapid decline of the
movement in late 1934 and early 1935 in all areas outside the
north-west. In October 1935 MI5 estimated that there were no
more than 20,000 lukewarm or active supporters, although the
chief constables' reports indicated that there were probably less
than half this amount and many members existed only on paper.
In Cardiff only 7 of the 200 members were active and in Leeds 10
out of 66.[13] During late 1935 there was a large increase in
membership in the East End of London which more than
compensated for the decline in Lancashire. Indeed, between 1936
and 1938 it is likely that more than half the national membership
was concentrated in districts in the East End. Campaigns like the

[12] G. Webber, 'Patterns of membership', *Journal of Contemporary History*, 19 (1984),
p. 590.
[13] PRO HO 45/25385/38–49.

support for Edward VIII during the abdication crisis, anti-semitism and the peace campaign after 1937, maintained the momentum and the movement made slow progress in most areas of the country. From Munich onwards membership increase accelerated as Mosley's role in the peace campaign attracted more new converts to compensate for the loss of anti-German elements. The general impression was that the growth of support was much more pronounced in the south and east than in the north and west after 1937 and that total membership was probably approaching 20,000 again by the outbreak of war.

The spatial distribution of members suggested that apart from one or two isolated outposts of fascism in South Wales, Scotland and Ulster in 1934 the BUF was misnamed. The BUF was predominantly an English movement with its main area of strength in London and the south-east, although there was sizeable support in Manchester, Liverpool and Leeds in 1934. Unlike German nazism, it was mainly an urban movement which made little headway in rural areas despite the enthusiastic support of a few landowners. Throughout the 1930s problems of organization, administration and finance combined with the rapid turnover of personnel and the shifts of propaganda and programme to produce a constantly changing pattern of membership.

Although to a considerable degree the BUF became a catch-all organization appealing to a broad spectrum of political idealists, war socialists, authoritarian personalities, men of violence, anti-semites and cranks, there are certain generalizations about the nature of the membership which can be highlighted. In the period of rapid growth until June 1934 the movement appealed to a broad spectrum which cut across social class divisions. Mosley portrayed the BUF as a movement against the 'old gangs' of British politics and appealed to youth, the politically uncommitted and displaced idealists as well as those who were dissatisfied under the leadership of the political parties. Mosley appealed to maverick conservatives who were influenced by the style of *Daily Mail* patriotism. The BUF's uniform and discipline attracted many with war experience or military service as well as those who liked strutting about in neat apparel. In the Rothermere period fascism was politically fashionable, a temporary home for many who disliked either communism or the party system. According to the Security Service new members admired Mosley's stand for free speech;[14] a bizarre reason for joining, given that the BUF wished to close down all organizational forms of political opposition.

With the rapid decline after 1934 the focus of recruitment shifted to the north-west and for a time Mosley seriously contemplated moving his headquarters to Manchester. In Lancashire and to a certain extent Yorkshire considerable headway was made for a period in recruiting from the unemployed and working class, although they were only a small proportion of these groups in the population as a whole, and the anti-fascist numbers of these categories were always far more significant than those who were attracted to fascism even in these areas. The basis for this support was the positive economic programme of fascism which promised immediate action to cure unemployment; fascist propaganda was aimed directly at the industrial problems of localities with cotton and woollen textiles emphasized in Lancashire and Yorkshire and shipping in Liverpool. However, when northern fascism declined after 1935 attention was re-directed to London with the discovery that anti-semitism was a good recruiting tactic in the East End. From 1935 to 1938 marked gains were made here amongst some working-class elements, the self-employed, the lower middle classes, those below voting age and others prone to the anti-semitic appeals. There was a general movement towards street corner politics and those followers were attracted by activism and the appeal of political conflict and violence. However, although the BUF achieved its greatest political impact here with over 2,000 active members and much passive support, it probably never had a majority even in these groups and marked hostility was shown by organized labour, the Jewish community and by popular opinion in general.

In the later 1930s the gradual shift towards recruiting more middle-class, elderly and right-wing members was accentuated by the peace campaign. Disillusioned Conservatives and some pro-appeasement and anti-war protestors now joined the BUF. With a partial decline in the East End, Mosley's emphasis on 'Mind Britain's Business' and no entanglements in Europe led to renewed growth in the rest of London and the south and east of England generally. Intelligence reports in 1939 and 1940 suggest that Mosley's support was mainly from the middle and upper classes,

14 PRO HO 144/20142/115.

with up to 30 per cent of his audiences being women and only 5 per cent under the age of thirty at his meetings.[15]

In general, then, a pattern of rapid growth and a large turnover of membership in urban centres in 1933 and 1934 was replaced by an emphasis on regional movements in the north in 1934 and 1935 and the East End of London between 1935 and 1938. The peace campaign turned the BUF into more of a national movement again, although its greatest impact was to be in the south and east of England. In terms of its official ideology of war socialism, the commitment to this belief of its elite cadre of leaders (many of whom came either from the left of the political spectrum or from outside politics altogether) should be noted, even if the popular impact of such ideas was negligible in terms of its lasting impact on British society. After 1934 the BUF relied less on ideological appeal for recruitment and more on populist campaigns based on ethnic resentment and the peace movement. It degenerated from a political movement based on a serious, if eccentric, alternative view of the future of British society, to a series of single-issue pressure groups and propaganda campaigns, the most important of which were anti-semitism and opposition to the threat of war. Racial populism as the basis of recruitment for fascist and neo-fascist movements was to represent the main source of the revival of the tradition after 1945.

Home Office material and impressions of members themselves provide us with useful qualitative sources on the BUF. While it must be emphasized that police records tend to accentuate the dubious aspects of the movement, they nevertheless do suggest that the BUF did attract some individuals who exploited the lax administration and opportunities for criminal activity in the movement. The Brixton branch was organized as a brothel, the first leader of the women's section was dismissed for allegedly misappropriating funds, and the secretary of one of the Newcastle organizations was convicted of housebreaking.[16] Stuart Rawnsley has emphasized some of the more irresponsible proclivities of the northern membership at all levels of the movement. Blackshirts armed with coshes and razors attacked Jews and communists in Lancashire; the commanding officer of the BUF in Manchester in

---

[15] Report of British Union Luncheon at Criterion Restaurant, 26 Apr. 1940, C6/913/13 Board of Deputies Archive; PRO HO 144/21281/150.
[16] PRO HO 144/20140/251–2; PRO HO 144/20140/112; PRO HO 45/25385/38–49.

1934 was later charged in Westminster police court for stealing money from a restaurant; and another Manchester member absconded to Australia with all the proceeds of the National Fascist Fellowship Children's Charity.[17] Police records also comment on the fondness for the consumption of alcoholic beverages by many fascists. A.K. Chesterton was an 'inveterate drunkard' in the 1930s, although he underwent a successful cure for this affliction, and the leading officials in Cardiff were also heavy drinkers.[18]

The recollections of ex-members of the movement also mention the negative aspects of membership; Nellie Driver stated that for every normal member in Nelson and Colne there were several who were cranks or worse. One member spent five minutes selling *Blackshirt* and then ten minutes in the pub alternately and was as much concerned with shouting abuse at the Peace Pledge Union and Jehovah's Witnesses as he was in promoting fascism. Driver saw the membership as extremely varied and argumentative with Protestants clashing with Catholics, Methodists with members of the Church of England and anti-vivisectionists with Christadelphians.[19] Many members nationwide were literal social fascists who treated the local headquarters as convivial watering-holes and sporting clubs. Rawnsley, following Driver's and Reynell Bellamy's impressions, has argued that the high turnover of membership and lack of ideological commitment to fascism characterized the early period, but that those who joined in the later 1930s were more likely to be imbued with steadfast beliefs in nationalist economics, anti-semitism and Mosley's leadership.[20] He also argued that Mosley appealed to those who feared unemployment, to Irish immigrants who liked his opposition to the Black and Tans in the 1920s, and to Catholics.

Brewer has singled out for detailed analysis five ideal types from his small sample of fifteen. These purport to show that Mosley appealed to a cross-section of individuals from various social class backgrounds which included the working-class unemployed,

---

[17] Rawnsley, 'Fascism and fascists', pp. 105, 157.
[18] PRO HO 144/21063/5–6; PRO HO 144/21062/413.
[19] Driver, *Shadows of Exile*, pp. 21–2.
[20] S. Rawnsley, 'The membership of the British Union of Fascists', in *British Fascism*, ed. K. Lunn and R. Thurlow (London, 1980), p. 158.

wealthy landowners, the declining middle class, industrialists, and the young and politically inexperienced.[21]

However, although these qualitative examples provide graphic illustrations of some aspects of the profile of membership of the BUF, they have to be treated with caution. Rawnsley's use of the autobiographical recollections of Reynell Bellamy and Nellie Driver, with regard to Lancashire fascism, together with eleven interviews with ex-fascists, and Brewer's oral testimony from fifteen former members, can in no way be considered a representative sample. Even in impressionistic terms they are deficient in at least two highly significant areas if they are to be used to assess the national movement: there is no representative from the East End of London and little on the motivation of those who backed Mosley as the saviour of the peace of Europe. In regional terms the samples were mainly biased towards the north of England, the Midlands and other regions, all of which were relatively insignificant in the history of British fascism after 1935. There is also no way of knowing how typical the interviewees were nor, given the minute samples, whether they can be properly regarded as 'ideal types' of specific kinds of member.

Doubts must also be expressed about specific arguments drawn from impressionistic evidence. Although Mosley may have appealed to certain types of Irish immigrant or British Catholic it seems highly significant that he made little headway amongst Irish labourers in London dockland, an area of relative BUF strength.[22] Similarly, it seems doubtful whether many of those staid middle-class new members who backed Mosley to keep Britain out of war agreed with his radical economic and political policies, and could be considered as more ideological fascists than their predecessors.

Thus the general pattern of the nature of the membership shows a shift in emphasis from the recruitment of the politically alienated from all political classes, with propaganda aimed at youth, ex-military types and the unemployed in 1933 and 1934, to the use of anti-semitism in mobilizing discontented lower middle-class and youth elements in the East End of London, to the appeal to a mainly elderly middle-class audience in the peace campaign. There was a discernible shift away from a core ideology linking an

[21] Brewer, *Mosley's Men*, pp. 28–44.
[22] C. Husbands, *Racial Exclusionism and the City* (London, 1983), pp. 51–6.

authoritarian structure with ideas which had their root on the
political left, to an attempt to seize the leadership of a radical right
opposed to war. This transition was effected by the espousal of
anti-semitism which both provided an ideological affinity with the
nazis and hypothesized a Jewish conspiracy which supposedly
controlled the political left and allegedly usurped the traditional
right. Thus in terms of its membership and ideas the BUF moved
steadily to the right in the 1930s, even if the core beliefs of its
official ideology remained unaltered until 1945. The rapidly
changing nature of its appeal and sociological base reflected a
highly unstable mass movement in crisis.

The attraction of fascism

The basic appeal of the BUF was to those with initiative who had
for some reason experienced bottlenecks in mobility patterns in
society; this included cranks, criminals, alcoholics and worse. Rex
Tremlett resigned as editor of *Blackshirt* in 1936 and told friends
he no longer wanted to be associated with 'cads, thieves and
swine'.[23] However, to overemphasize this aspect of the movement,
acknowledged by ex-members themselves, would be misleading.
Amongst its committed membership at all levels was a large
majority of resourceful individuals whose spirit remained
undimmed by personal adversity and an inability to achieve their
full potential in a society where chances were blocked by the
effects of economic depression and the lingering after-effects of the
First World War. As in nazi Germany, members of the BUF saw
fascism as providing new opportunities for personal advancement
which would by-pass the closed avenues of traditional society.[24]
Although the BUF had a small appeal in all social classes, its
greatest impact was to be found amongst retired military gentlemen, some working-class elements, the lower middle classes and
'spirited' middle-class women.

This picture is as true for the leadership as for the membership
as a whole. Mosley has often stated that he attracted to the
movement some remarkable individuals of outstanding ability and

[23] PRO HO 144/20142/220.
[24] W.W. Jannen Jr., 'National Socialists and social mobility', *Journal of Social History*, 9
(Spring 1976), pp. 339–66.

that they compared favourably in intellectual ability and initiative with his colleagues in the Labour government of 1929–31.[25] There were indeed some interesting men in the BUF. Major-General J.F.C. Fuller was an original military strategist, A.K. Chesterton inherited more than his fair share of the family's considerable literary talent, William Joyce was a brilliant orator and Alexander Raven Thomson possessed a synthesizing mind of appreciable intellectual power.[26] And the main point of similarity between the diverse personalities and backgrounds of those in the leadership of the BUF was that most of them were outsiders; for reasons of personality or ideological opposition they were alienated from conventional establishment values. Mosley was later to see Colin Wilson's study of the alienated intellectual, *The Outsider*, of particular significance to the 1950s, although no doubt he also saw its relevance for the experience of the BUF in the 1930s.[27] What is of interest is that apart from the few Labour MPs, members of the ILP and the Ulster Unionist, W.E.D. Allen, Mosley failed to attract any significant support from establishment quarters once Rothermere had broken his connection. In spite of the BUF having its main roots on the political left, the Labour party was implacably hostile to Mosley. Anti-semitism mobilized significant support in one particular area, while his pro-appeasement and anti-communist policies appealed to a few right-wing Conservatives. However, Mosley's economic radicalism was viewed with suspicion by the right and his attitude to Mussolini and Hitler was viewed with hostility by the left. Aggressive anti-semitism and the political violence associated with the BUF was antithetical to the high politics tradition enshrined within the party system at Westminster. The constantly changing emphasis of Mosley's appeal merely added to the establishment view that he was unreliable, irresponsible and forever changing his loyalties; a man who was not to be trusted and beyond the pale.

A study of the parliamentary candidates chosen by the BUF after 1935 has emphasized the rootlessness of many of those attracted to the movement.[28] Their main characteristics were experience of

[25] O. Mosley, *My Life* (London, 1968), p. 318.

[26] A.J. Trythal, *Boney Fuller* (London, 1975); Baker, 'A.K. Chesterton. The Making of a British fascist', PhD thesis, University of Sheffield, 1982; W.A. Cole, *William Joyce* (London, 1964); A. Raven, *Civilisation or Divine Superman* (London, 1932).

[27] 'European' Colin Wilson's "The Outsider", *European*, 48 (1957), pp. 337–51.

[28] W.F. Mandle, 'The leadership of the British Union of Fascists', *Australian Journal of Politics and History*, Dec. 1966.

the armed forces, the high turnover of employment and the lack of previous political experience. Mosley appealed to those who could not settle down to the changed conditions of the post-1918 world. For some he was to be the embodiment of the creation of a new order based on new values, for others the reincarnation of an imaginary world which had never existed. Mosley's propaganda aimed at forming a new synthesis combining aspects of the political left and right – the creation of a third way in British politics. Unfortunately for him the methods by which he proposed to achieve this end proved unattractive in the political and economic condition of the 1930s. The National government contained the crisis more by luck than judgement; nevertheless even the small minority in the establishment who sympathized with the reasons behind Mosley's revolt saw no reason to foresake the party system to team up with a cavalier adventurer who was trying to turn a foreign tradition into a British political movement. Mosley was to appeal only to the politically inexperienced or the totally alienated. He was destined to become a marginal political figure linked by his creed to a lunatic fringe which he despised; his alliance with some of the ideological anti-semites in 1939 was to lead to his imprisonment and the destruction of British fascism.

The organization of the BUF

If the membership of the BUF exhibited a constantly changing profile, the same could be said of the organization of the movement. In 1936 British Intelligence discovered that a nazi agent called Colin Ross had reported to Hitler that the BUF was a fine movement and had a splendid leader but absolutely no organization.[29] Mosley claimed that he divorced himself completely from the organization and administration of the movement while he concentrated on meetings and the party programme. What is certain is that those responsible for organization lacked the competence to manage the growth of a political movement. This was partly due to Mosley's own faults. Whilst his political opponents criticized his lack of party loyalty those who were close to him saw that his major weakness was that

[29] PRO HO 144/21060/55.

he was too trusting and he had an inability to judge character.[30] Although Mosley did not suffer fools gladly he was taken in far too many times by political con men and he often failed to see through those with eccentric views until it was too late. In terms of the organization this flaw was disastrous. Those who had access to Mosley's ear realized that he was gullible in relation to propaganda about the growth of the movement and that the best way to advancement was to tell him what he wanted to hear, whether it was true or not. A.K. Chesterton later claimed that disastrous flops were always written up as great triumphs and that the toadying administrators of the movement had systematically prevented Mosley from hearing the truth.[31] The organizational flaws in the movement were to be found at all levels. Under the first deputy leader, Robert Forgan, financial control over the rapidly developing movement was to be non-existent with expenditure double the income and both petty corruption and fraud rife. It was Forgan's failure in this area as well as his disagreements with Mosley over anti-Semitism and political vio-lence which caused him to leave the movement.[32] F. M. Box, Forgan's replacement, told Mosley that the organization was in such a shambles that it would take at least ten years to build up a viable electoral machine.[33] Mosley was also badly advised about several crucial organizational matters. The decision to become a professional political organization from the outset meant a mas-sive financial outlay. The BUF paid top Fleet Street journalist rates and good comparative salaries throughout the organization. In 1936 the total wages bill exceeded £25,000 out of the total cost of £45,000.[34] Various estimates suggest that the BUF had spent between £60,000 and £80,000 in 1934. In a period after membership had rapidly declined, in late 1936, Special Branch reported that with 4,000 active and 6,000 non-active supporters, income from members (with employed workers paying one shil-ling a month and unemployed fourpence) was only £8–£10,000 per annum.[35] The obvious problems inherent in financing a

---

[30] Driver, *Shadows of Exile*, p. 31.

[31] A.K. Chesterton, *Why I Left Mosley* (London, 1938).

[32] C. Holmes and B. Hill, 'Robert Forgan', *Dictionary of Labour Biography* vol. VI (London, 1982), pp. 111–14; PRO HO 144/20145/222–5.

[33] PRO HO 144/20146/82–3.

[34] PRO HO 144/20147/378.

[35] PRO HO 144/21062/344.

political movement on such an insecure economic base, and the decline in external injections of capital in the later 1930s meant that the BUF was in a constant state of crisis. Severe cuts were made in 1935 when the Black House was dropped as a national headquarters, and in 1937 when half the major officials of the movement, all the paid speakers and most of the regional organizers were dismissed in a 70 per cent reduction of expenditure.[36] Further cuts in 1938 and 1939 reduced expenses to £13,000 per annum and marked a transition from a professional administration to a mainly voluntary organization.[37] The payroll was reduced from 350 to about 50 between 1936 and 1939.

While these severe reductions had important effects on the nature of the organisation, many of the fascist officials remained on a voluntary basis. However, constant reorganization and cuts in personnel meant that the highly imperfect administrative structure of the movement was in constant danger of collapse despite the valiant efforts of the few remaining administrators and the loyal volunteers in 1938 and 1939. Mosley's offhand attitude towards organization, and his belief that activism and commitment were the main criteria of advancement and promotion, failed to distinguish between creditable achievement and optimistic flattery. The highly bureaucratic administrative structure with its military overtones, organizational cliques, constant rationalization and re-deployment, merely institutionalized the problem.

The BUF was originally organized into areas, regions, branches, sub-branches and groups. At the local level they were further subdivided into companies, sections and units. If there were sufficient women members a separate female branch was founded and youth groups were also encouraged.[38] It prided itself on being a classless organization where merit and loyalty to the cause counted more than social privilege or the old boy network. In Lancashire an eighteen-year-old was a district leader and an unemployed ex-trooper had seniority over a mill-owner's daughter.[39] While this arrangement worked better in some areas than others, the real weakness in the system was that the

[36] PRO HO 144/21063/233.
[37] PRO HO 144/21281/121.
[38] PRO HO 144/20140/104–21.
[39] Driver, Shadows of Exile, p. 29; Bellamy, We marched with Mosley, chap. 6, p. 4.

administrative centre only exerted its influence in the provinces spasmodically and had little financial control. All branch associations and activities were supposedly self-financing and the movement's growth depended on the energy and activities of the local leadership. With the decline of the central administrative organization in the later 1930s local associations were left increasingly to their own devices, despite the valiant efforts of the remaining paid officials.

These financial and organizational problems were compounded by Mosley's basic misjudgements about the nature of the movement. The desire to create a classless organization based on merit, and the compulsory wearing of uniform to symbolize this fact and to instil discipline, were no doubt good ideas, but Mosley's choice of dress was less than inspired. The Blackshirt reminded the general public of Mussolini and the jackboots of Hitler, and was no severe loss when banned by the Public Order Act in 1936. Similarly, Mosley's attempt to palm off the use of the fasces and the flash in the circle as good old British traditions which had no connection with emulating continental examples, both in *The Greater Britain* and before the Advisory Committee on Internment in 1940, was amongst the least convincing of his arguments.[40] Mosley's dubious judgement of individuals and events, his impatience and uncertain temper, and his failure to see the limits of his power over language, along with the appalling lack of organization, proved his major weaknesses.

At first sight the abysmal picture of the finances of the BUF would lead automatically to the conclusion that Mosley had severe monetary weaknesses as well. This, however, is a misleading impression. Mosley's buccaneering spirit made him an ideal budding entrepreneur and he more than recovered the fortune he poured down the drain in the BUF in later life through his financial investments. The fact that Mosley supposedly divorced himself from all financial aspects of the movement from the outset[41] was undoubtedly a deliberate strategy. Not only did this free him to concentrate all his energies on speaking and policy, but enabled him to maintain the pretence that he was ignorant of the main sources of BUF finance. In particular it let him obscure the Italian connection and the fact that much of the cost of the dramatic

---

[40] O. Mosley, *The Greater Britain* (London, 1932), frontispiece; PRO HO 283/13/43–5.
[41] PRO HO 283/13/21.

period of growth until 1934 and the equally spectacular collapse in 1935 was underwritten by large financial subsidies from Mussolini, who provided the second largest source of income in overall terms during the 1930s, probably contributing over £60,000 between 1933 and 1936. Only Mosley, who spent £100,000 on the movement, subscribed more. Whilst there is some dispute over the amount Mussolini contributed, that it was substantial was beyond doubt. J. Chuter Ede's claim, as Home Secretary in 1946, that Mussolini had funded Mosley has been substantially proved by documents found in Italian archives.[42]

The obvious conclusion that can be drawn about Mosley's unconvincing and evasive answers before the Advisory Committee about the finances of the BUF were that his top priority was to obscure the sources of income for the movement from the outset, and the means by which this was achieved was a brilliant counter-intelligence operation. Mosley, despite the obvious suspicions that these obfuscating manoeuvres on finance aroused, nevertheless was able to maintain the fiction that he was unaware of the main source of funding in the early period until his death.

The fact that Mosley's top priority was to obscure the sources of his movement's income rather than exert tight financial control from the outset is detailed quite clearly in the movement's accounts. The Advisory Committee stated that they were in a most unsatisfactory state.[43] The Committee had the audited account of BUF Trust Ltd, the main financial company of the organization, for the years ending 28 February 1934, 28 February 1935 and 31 March 1936. These showed a small deficit in the first year and slightly larger surpluses in the two following years. However, the chartered accountants criticized all three accounts for not providing the means of verifying the amount of subscriptions and donations. The totals equalled £36,812 8s 2d, £75,606 12s 2d and £84,468 3s 9d respectively for the three years. The Committee also had access to the accounts from 1 September 1938 to 31 January 1940, which were properly prepared. These showed that in this period the BUF received over £34,000 of which £30,000 was from two people, £24,000 from Mosley himself. Presumably this was at least part of the accounts Mosley had before him when he wrote in

[42] David Irving, *Focal Point*, 30 Oct. 1981; N. Mosley, *Beyond the Pale*, (London, 1983), pp. 30–4.
[43] PRO HO 45/24891/40.

My Answer (1946), in response to Chuter Ede's accusation of Italian funding, that for a considerable period before the war they showed no evidence of this.[44]

However, the published accounts were not the only source of information about the BUF finances. W.E.D. Allen, who by 1940 was conveniently in Palestine, presumably tipped off MI5 that the main source of BUF funding in the first few years was via a secret account in the Charing Cross branch of the Westminster Bank. This acted as a conduit for foreign funds for the BUF and was operated in the names of Ian Hope Dundas, W.E.D. Allen and Major J. Tabor.[45] Special Branch obtained access to the records of the account in 1940 and discovered that in 1933 approximately £9,500 was paid in, in 1934 £77,800, 1935 £86,000, 1936 £43,320 and in 1937 £7,630, all in foreign currencies. At the Advisory Committee hearing it was pointed out to Mosley that most of the monthly deposits were fairly standard amounts, in 1935 between £4,000–£5,000 a month, the small differences seeming to reflect the currency fluctuation of lira and sterling.[46] MI5 interviewed Major Tabor in 1940. He was secretary to W.E.D. Allen between 1933 and 1937 and until 1936 a member of the BUF, where he had been in charge of providing food and supplies for headquarters. Although not very forthcoming, he told the authorities that he had frequently been given large packets of foreign notes for Allen to pay into the account. Robert Forgan told Colin Cross a similar story.[47] Tabor had once asked Mosley where the money came from but he had been very angry and refused to tell him.

Allen told MI5 that Mosley was receiving about £3,000 a month from Italian sources during 1935. However, the documents discovered by David Irving relating to the correspondence of Count Grandi, the Italian ambassador, suggest that in 1933 and 1934 Mussolini made four payments of about £5,000 as well as a special donation of £20,000. This would also fit in with the implications of the questioning concerning the regularity of similar monthly deposits in the banks in 1935. The fact that the total amounts deposited in the Charing Cross accounts were close to the

---

[44] O. Mosley, *My Answer* (London, 1946), p. 4.
[45] PRO HO 283/10/9.
[46] PRO HO 283/16/49.
[47] C. Cross, *The Fascists in Britain* (London, 1961), p. 91.

published income of the movement in 1934 and 1935 gave
credence to MI5's claim that in the middle 1930s the movement
was only kept going by Italian money.[48] The 'Mind Britain's
Business' campaign over the attempted League of Nations boycott
of Italy following the Abyssinian invasion of 1935 was a true *quid
pro quo*, the price of foreign funding. As F.M. Box pointed out,
'He who pays the piper calls the tune.'[49]

Irving's documents proved that Mosley received £40,000 in
1933 and 1934 from Italian sources. The likelihood is that he was
given substantial further support during 1935 from there. If Allen
is to be believed, this represented £3,000 a month which was
reduced to £1,000 a month in 1936. The fact that Mosley was
forced to abandon Black House and move to cheaper headquarters
in 1935, while not reducing significantly his professional staff until
1937, suggested a cut in funding rather than an absolute
withdrawal until its cessation in 1936 or 1937.

Mosley's counter-arguments to the Advisory Committee about
the funding of the BUF were that the means employed through the
secret bank account enabled British entrepreneurs and benefactors
to pay substantial contributions through foreign currency without
disclosing the source of such funds. Certainly Mosley did receive
substantial financial assistance from businessmen in his New Party
days and it is likely that some of this continued, at least for a time,
in the BUF. Mosley acknowledged that Lord Nuffield had paid
£50,000 to the New Party, Lord Portal £5,000, Cunliffe Owen
'the tobacco man' £5,000 and others various sums, to a total of
£80,000.[50] The Labour party argued in a research document
entitled 'Who Backs Mosley' that he had received financial
assistance from W.E.D. Allen, Lord Inchcape, Lord Nuffield, Sir
A.V. Roe, Lord Rothermere, Baron Tollemache, Air Commander
Chaumier, Vincent C. Vickers, Lord Lloyd, the Earl of Glasgow
and Sir Charles Petrie.[51] This list seems plausible, given Mosley's
known connections and interest in the aircraft industry. Other
sizeable contributions included A.C. Scrimgeour, a rich admirer of
William Joyce, who was alleged by Special Branch to have

[48] PRO HO 45/25385/38.49; letter from Count Grandi to Benito Mussolini, 30 Jan.
1934, photocopy in Nicholas Mosley's file on Mussolini's funding of the BUF.
[49] PRO HO 144/20145/12–13.
[50] PRO HO 283/14/8.
[51] PRO HO 144/20142/217.
[52] PRO HO 144/21062/282.

contributed at least £11,000 to party funds.[52] Dame Lucy Houston nearly gave Mosley £200,000 in 1934 as a result of his interest in Rothermere's National Air League, but decided against it after reading some unflattering comments about herself in *Blackshirt*. Some cotton manufacturers in Lancashire were also thought to have made some contribution to the movement.[53]

No doubt other contributions were made to BUF funds. Special Branch stated that one Conservative MP had given a donation of £500, for example.[54] Yet for the most part hard information about BUF finances is difficult to come by. Two facts, however, are fairly certain. First, that the gap between membership subscriptions and expenditure during the 1930s was not made up by British industrialists acting as political sugar daddies. In so far as this was achieved it was due mainly to Mussolini in the period before 1936 and to Mosley himself up until 1940. Second, Mosley made determined efforts both to hide the financial weakness of the BUF and to put its finances on a firmer footing.

The idea of using commercial capital to fund his political movement probably originated with Lord Rothermere. In 1934 Rothermere toyed with the idea of using the BUF as a distribution outlet for planned cigarette production.[55] To this end Mosley established New Epoch Products Limited and a factory was registered for production purposes. With an initial capital of £12,500, the articles of association included a Board of Directors which included two of Rothermere's journalistic associates, Sir Max Pemberton and G. Ward Price, as well as Sir Oswald Mosley and Ian Hope Dundas from the BUF. New Epoch Products was conceived on a grand scale. It was envisaged by Mosley as the basis of an industrial empire which would include manufacturing, banking, retailing and financial functions.[56] However, Rothermere changed his mind about the initial funding of £70,000 and the project proved still-born.

In the later 1930s Mosley tried to revive his political fortunes through planned commercial profit. From 1937 onwards much of his time not devoted to BUF affairs was concentrated on cornering

[53] Interview S. Rawnsley with G.P. Sutherst, 16 Feb. 1977.
[54] PRO HO 144/20140/117.
[55] P. Addison, 'Patriotism under pressure, Lord Rothermere and British foreign policy' in *The Politics of Reappraisal 1918–39*, ed. G. Peele and C. Cook (London, 1975), p. 269.
[56] PRO HO 144/20141/14–18.

the market in commercial radio franchises. Mosley told the Advisory Committee in 1940 that there were four new industries in the twentieth century which could generate great profits: newspapers, motoring, aeroplanes and radio advertising. From his standpoint the latter was most promising as it required less capital and offered more scope for quick returns. Mosley argued that at present less than £1 million was spent on radio advertising in this country compared with £20 million in the USA. In terms of relative population size there was a further £5 million worth of advertising to be won.[57] Following the establishment of Radio Normandie in France, in which he had no stake, Mosley systematically tried to establish a large interest in future commercial radio franchises. By the outbreak of the war Mosley had a 50 per cent interest in most advanced negotiations in Belgium, Ireland and Denmark and a 90 per cent interest in the concession from the Dame of Sark.[58] He had also persuaded Hitler to build him a radio transmitter in Germany. The aim was to syphon off the large potential profits from such operations for the funding of the BUF. These plans were so secret that few in the movement knew of them, since any disclosure would have created a political furore and wrecked Mosley's designs. The careful planning and single-minded dedication to putting such blueprints into practice showed that Mosley had imaginative plans for rescuing his financially ailing movement.[59] The commercial interest involved meant that Mosley also had less altruistic motives than matters of principle in his opposition to the war with Hitler in 1939.

The internal politics of the BUF mainly centred around the contentious issues of organization and finance and their links to ideological differences. The fundamental importance of the leadership principle, Mosley's own intellectual and moral stature within the movement and the lack of any credible alternative in the organization meant there was little coherent opposition in the period of growth. Such criticism as there was was dealt with in a military manner. Charles J. Bradford of the Industrial Propaganda Department, organizer of the Fascist Union of British Workers, was suspended for three months in 1934 for arranging a

[57] PRO HO 283/13/107.
[58] PRO HO 283/13/110.
[59] N. Mosley, *Beyond the Pale*, pp. 134–7.

conspiracy to split the organization and for attacking the deputy Chief of Staff, Archibald Findlay, while under the influence of drink.[60] Strict discipline was maintained in the organization and acts of spontaneous violence against opponents were discouraged unless there was any provocation for it.

However, with the twin problems of a collapse in membership and resultant financial difficulties, despite the benevolence of Mussolini, in the summer of 1934 a Court of Inquiry was established to stamp out increasing factional differences within the leadership. This tribunal had a strong military flavour, the Court of Inquiry comprising Captain Reavely, Major Lucas and Major Taylor. It centred on the linked problems of organization, finance and propaganda. It showed that there were two main factions within the leadership cadre who viewed the future of the BUF in different ways, although there were pronounced personal and ideological antagonisms on both sides of the argument. In general the dispute was between those who saw the BUF's future in terms of a military organization appealing to law and order, and emphasized a style of disciplined marches and demonstrations, and those who saw the need to expound propaganda and convert the masses to fascist ideology. The first faction was led originally by F.M. Box, his adjutant Neil Francis Hawkins and Ian Hope Dundas, the latter group by William Joyce, John Beckett and A.K. Chesterton.

Box, an ex-Conservative party agent, had been appointed by Mosley in 1934 as Forgan's replacement with the principle brief of reducing expenditure. His attempts to prune propaganda expenditure met the principled opposition of ideological fascists. Many of these wished to promote anti-semitism and to encourage physical force arguments in the organization, which was also anathema to Box. The outcome, although superficially a victory for Box, proved pyrrhic. Joyce was criticized for only holding 70 meetings instead of 300 planned and Mosley blamed this on him rather than on Box's expenditure cuts.[61] However, the open anti-semitism advanced after October 1934 and the move into the East End of London showed that the BUF was developing in the direction of Joyce and his associates. Box resigned, opposing both

[60] PRO HO 144/20142/314.
[61] PRO HO 144/20145/222–5.

the move to anti-semitism and increased physical force confrontation with opponents.[62]

This did not, however, end the argument. The case of the organizers against Joyce and his associates was taken up by a more redoubtable opponent, Neil Francis Hawkins. He became director-general of the BUF in 1936 and combined the characteristics of an inflexible personal loyalty to Mosley, an 100 per cent commitment to the cause and political skills at ingratiating his henchmen into key personnel positions. By such methods he was able to outflank Joyce and win the war for Mosley's ear. Francis Hawkins, a lineal descendant of the Elizabethan sailor, was an ex-opthalmic instrument maker who came into the movement from the British Fascists. A bachelor, he favoured promoting and working with unmarried men because they could commit more time to the cause. A workaholic himself, his attitude was one of the stated reasons why Mosley kept his marriage to Diana Guinness in 1936 a secret: Mosley told the Advisory Committee that there was a legend in the movement that married men did no work.[63] Francis Hawkins's opponents alleged that he was a homosexual, an occupational hazard for all bachelors in the movement and other fascist organizations since.

Francis Hawkins' chief opponent was William Joyce. He was a brilliant orator who rivalled Mosley in his eloquence and was a first-class teacher. Unfortunately he was both mentally unbalanced about the Jews, somewhat vain and a poor organizer. He had joined the BUF in 1933, and rapidly rose from being area administrative officer for the Home Counties to become Director of Propaganda in 1934, with responsibility for training and instruction of speakers, and for direction of the Research Department.[64] Whereas Francis Hawkins argued the importance of developing virile 'Blackshirts' and semi-military psychology, and contended that bands, uniforms, marches and general discipline were more effective than clearly defined political programmes, Joyce and his associates were for developing an electoral machine and securing adherents by propaganda in the factories and workshops. Joyce's abilities were initially appreciated by Mosley, who used them to good effect in the anti-semitic campaign in

[62] PRO HO 144/20146/82–3.
[63] PRO HO 283/13/116.
[64] PRO HO 144/21063/10–11.

1 Women Blackshirts listening closely to a speaker at a BUF meeting in Liverpool in June 1934. Women probably accounted for over 20 per cent of the membership of the BUF in the 1930s and for up to 33 per cent of those who passively supported Mosley, if inactive members are taken into account.

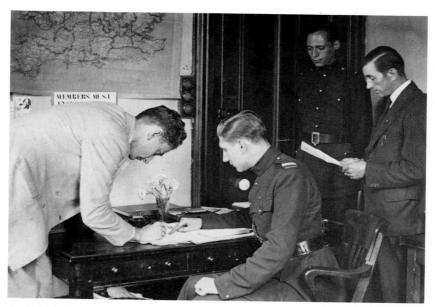

2 British fascists enrolling a recruit. There is some debate over how many members the BUF attained but if it is assumed that there were one and a half inactive supporters to every paid-up active member then the estimates that supporters in total amounted to between 40,000 and 50,000 in 1934, collapsed to about 5,000 in 1935 and gradually recovered to approach 20,000 by 1939, are probably accurate. If these assumptions are correct then MI5's claim that there were about 8,000 members between 1939 and 1940 would not necessarily contradict these figures.

3   The BUF 'Black House' recreation room. Some of the early funds of the BUF (partly supplied by Mussolini) were used to purchase the lease of Whitelands Teachers' Training College, Chelsea. This was the BUF's administrative headquarters between 1933 and 1935.

4   A fascist den at the Black House. Between 50 and 200 Blackshirts lived in Black House between 1933 and 1935 under military discipline. Black House was also used as the educational, social, operational and administrative headquarters of the BUF.

5   William 'Lord Haw Haw' Joyce was the most notorious British fascist. A member of the British fascists in the 1920s, he trained Mosley's speakers at Black House and was head of the political faction in the BUF leadership. Made redundant by Mosley in 1937, he formed the unsuccessful National Socialist League. In 1939 he went to Germany and became renowned for his broadcasts as 'Lord Haw Haw' during the war. He was hanged as a traitor on 3 January 1946.

6 'They shall not pass', Cable Street, Mark Lane, 5 October 1936. Residents repair the pavement after paving stones were ripped up and used as barricades to prevent Mosley's Blackshirts from marching through the East End the day before.

7 Barricades in Bermondsey 1937. Problems of law and order associated with fascist–communist confrontation did not end with Cable Street. In spite of the passing of the Public Order Act, the number of unprovoked assaults against Jews and communists and reprisals against fascists increased between 1937 and 1938.

8 Fascist march 1934. Paramilitary-style discipline and unarmed drill were the basis of fascist recruitment and campaigning. Mosley came to support the administrators' call for more marches and less political propaganda as the main recruiting tactics in the later 1930s.

9 'Marching with Mosley', Cable Street, 4 October 1936. Mosley, looking concerned, is flanked by Neil Francis Hawkins and A. K. Chesterton. About 1,900 BUF marchers were opposed by 100,000 anti-fascists in this demonstration.

10 (*above*) Blackshirts preventing an eviction 1934. Fascists involved themselves in issues of social justice both in individual cases, as here, and in organized propaganda campaigns, such as the tithe war in agricultural areas.

11 Fascist–communist violence in 1936. Attending to the injured following riots in Victoria Park. Although brutal assaults and attacks on Jewish property were commonplace in the East End between 1936 and 1939, it was remarkable that there were no deaths on either side as a result of the violence and guerrilla warfare. Unfortunately, such activity led to the emergence of an underground tradition which prompted similar violence among new ethnic minorities after 1945.

12 Internment 1940. A fascist arrested as a result of the Nazi invasion of Western Europe, the 'fifth column' scare and the aftermath of the Tyler Kent affair. Almost 800 members of the BUF and others on the fascist fringe of British politics were interned as security risks for varying lengths of time after May 1940. This action, together with the proscription of the BUF in July 1940, closed down British fascism.

13 (below) Fascism in Westminster 1932. Mosley unfolds the fascist flag. The axe and the bundle of sticks were a blatant imitation of the symbols and flag of Mussolini's Italian movement. Mosley's explanation that this was an old British symbol, in *The Greater Britain* and before the Advisory Committee on Internment in 1940, was one of the most unconvincing parts of his argument.

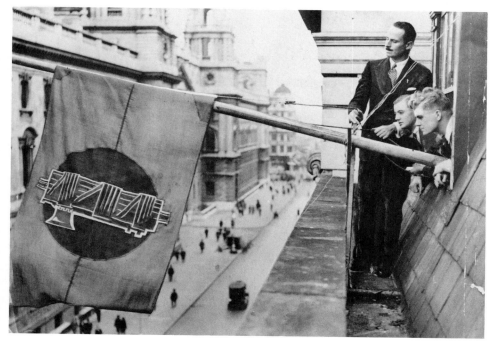

14 Oswald Mosley: 'Man of Destiny'. This horrific posed photograph exemplifies the cold penetrating arrogance of Mosley's revolt against the 'united muttons' of the 'old gangs' of British politics.

15 'Speaker' class, women's section, 1934. All fascist recruits including women were trained in the art of public speaking. Mary Richardson, the chief of the women's branch of the BUF, is standing in the background.

19 'The return of the demons'. Mosley speaking in 1948. Mosley returned to active politics as head of the Union Movement which saw a united Europe, rather than the BUF panacea of the British Empire, as the only hope for the future of Britain.

20 Mosley and friends 1948. The three on the left are Jeffrey Hamm, Commandant Mary
    Allen and Alexander Raven Thomson.

21 (*above*) 'Hail Mosley' 1953. The nature of Sir Oswald Mosley's East End support had changed little since the period from 1936 to 1939.

22 Sieg Heil! Colin Jordan and Françoise Dior in 1965. Jordan was the leader of the National Socialist Movement and the first world Führer of WUNS (World Union of National Socialists). He was later connected to the British Movement in its early years.

23 British fascism on the march. A member of the British Movement in full regalia.

24 Typical NF skinhead supporter. After the split with the Populists in 1975, Martin Webster led a successful recruiting campaign among the skinhead elements previously associated with the British Movement. This was a cause of the split with John Tyndall in 1979 and the violence increasingly associated with the NF.

25   John Tyndall and Martin Webster at an NF demonstration. Tyndall's imitation of Mosley's style with the use of flags, megaphone and inter-war economic and political programme is combined with a thinly disguised and cleaned-up version of Arnold Leese's obsession with *The Protocols of the Elders of Zion* and gutter racism. It is presented in the more acceptable language of the conservative fascist tradition with due homage to the influence of A. K. Chesterton.

London's East End. Gradually, however, Mosley came to support Francis Hawkins rather than Joyce for reasons of conviction and economy. Mosley increasingly began to see that the intellectual content of British fascism made few converts amongst the masses; populist campaigns based on activism and discipline attracted more support and the new recruits could then be converted to fascism. By 1937 Mosley had wholeheartedly adopted Francis Hawkins' strategy and it was the Joyce faction which felt the full weight of the economy axe. Joyce then resigned from the movement.

After leaving the BUF Joyce, in collaboration with the ex-labour MP John Beckett, formed the National Socialist League (NSL). This movement proved to be entirely inconsequential in itself, depending entirely on the donations of Joyce's benefactor Alexander Scrimgeour, and was never a serious rival of the BUF. Never having more than fifty members the NSL failed and soon Joyce's obsessional anti-semitism and Hitler worship led to a split with Beckett.[65] After Scrimgeour's death in August 1937 it rapidly became insolvent and disintegrated completely in 1938. However, Special Branch infiltrated its early London meetings and their verbatim reports shed more light on the factional splits in the BUF. At the first meeting in April 1937 Joyce argued that he had effectively been demoted in 1936 when Francis Hawkins had gained control of the training of the party speakers, leaving him as a glorified office boy. He then stated that the financial irregularities which had been charged against him were due to a forgery in order to blacken his reputation. Mosley's complete support for Francis Hawkins convinced Joyce that Mosley was in fact no longer the leader but merely a figurehead controlled by Hawkins.[66] A.K. Chesterton, the author of the BUF official biography of Mosley, later wrote a pamphlet published by the National Socialist League expressing much the same sentiments. Mosley's hagiographer here thought that the BUF was a parody of National Socialist thought and principles, and considered that Mosley had either been misled by Francis Hawkins or had deliberately used him to do his dirty work.[67]

The factional splits and acrimony of the latter stages of the BUF

---

[65] PRO HO 45/25690. Special Branch Report 2 April 1940.
[66] PRO HO 144/21247/4–11.
[67] A.K. Chesterton, *Why I Left Mosley*; PRO HO 144/21247/97–101.

represented the bitter backbiting of those who had committed their all to the fascist God that failed, and could not accept being discarded or the failure of Mosley. It should, however, be emphasized that many who lost their salary in 1937 remained as volunteers in the movement and followed Mosley to the end in 1940. Many fell by the wayside for various reasons but Mosley could always rely on a hard core of committed activists who unhesitatingly followed him even when the BUF became a scapegoat for the disaster of 1940 and most of the remaining leadership, both nationally and locally were interned, their 'crime' being that they were members of a now proscribed organization.

7

The Mutiny against Destiny

The BUF was almost unique among fascist movement in that its origin was marked by the publication of a coherent political programme and doctrine, in Oswald Mosley's *The Greater Britain* in October 1932. This outlined the rationale behind Mosley's revolt and the policies needed in his view to reverse Britain's decline. Although ideology came to play a less important role in the movement after 1935, Mosley nevertheless concentrated his energies in this sphere and in communicating his message to the British public, delegating administrative and financial organization to others.

The ideology and the movement

The importance for Mosley of rationally expressing an alternative political strategy to the party system and establishment values has been interpreted by commentators in various ways. Of those who have gone beyond a mere exposition of Mosley's and the BUF's basic ideas, Brewer has concentrated on his conception of crisis and explained it in sociological and psychological terms, rather than in terms of the economic and philosophical ideas from which it was derived.[1] Nugent has argued that a division should be made between the official ideas of the leadership and the less well

[1] J. Brewer, 'The British Union of Fascists, Sir Oswald Mosley and Birmingham: an analysis of the content and context of an ideology', M.Soc.Sci. thesis, University of Birmingham, 1975, pp. 1–171.

formulated motivating concepts of the rank and file.[2] Rawnsley, following Billig's distinction between an esoteric and exoteric ideology in the National Front, has suggested that members were recruited through various populist campaigns and then indoctrinated with a secret inner core ideology which emphasized the need for dictatorship, militarism, anti-semitism and the corporate state.[3] Farr has interpreted the emergence of the BUF as a watershed in the history of the British right: the development of a form of fascism with roots deep in a British national tradition which marked an integration of nationalist, socialist, imperialist and racist attitudes and had been formulated in the last stages of the New Party.[4] Skidelsky, in a brilliant and mainly convincing exposition, has analysed the development of Mosley's economic and philosophical ideas in a sympathetic manner, even if he attacked Mosley's establishment opponents in too cavalier a fashion and was not critical enough of his fascist ideas.[5]

All these interpretations have something to commend them, although Brewer's tautologies and arguments are difficult to follow at times, and he has not looked at the most interesting aspects of Mosley's conception of crisis. In this chapter I propose to examine Mosley's fascist ideas in terms of the historical development of his thought and relate this to the fortunes of the movement, and also to assess the practicality of such ideas and the role and function of the ideology to the movement, with some reference to the explanations already outlined.

Several facts need to be firmly emphasized before a detailed analysis of the ideas is undertaken. Firstly, Mosley's conviction that radical alternative economic and political policies were vital to halt what he saw as the inevitable decline and collapse of Britain was a constant and genuine belief which underlies all his actions. Having said that, however, the changing tactical and strategic shifts in policy necessitated by pragmatic political realities possessed one attribute in common. The turn from Conservative to Labour and the flirtations with the Liberals which made him so

---

[2] N. Nugent, 'The ideas of the British Union of Fascists', in *The British Right*, ed. N. Nugent and R. King (London, 1977), pp. 133–64.

[3] S. Rawnsley, 'Fascism and fascists in Britain in the 1930s', PhD thesis, University of Bradford, 1983, p. 48.

[4] B. Farr, 'The development and impact of right wing politics in Great Britain, 1903–32', PhD thesis, University of Illinois, 1976.

[5] R. Skidelsky, *Oswald Mosley* (London, 1975).

suspect to the establishment on the 1920s, and his switch to the leadership principle in 1931, all placed Mosley in the centre of events. Britain needed radical new policies which, if they could not be achieved through the democratic process by Mosley and his changing allies, would have to be solved by Mosley the dictator. His iconoclasm and egotism both pointed to Mosley as the big wheel around which all else revolved. In the 1930s he led the fascist revolution of youth against the 'united muttons' of the 'old gangs'.[6] In his old age he argued that there was no substitute for practical experience.[7] His whole political life was dedicated to two propositions: that the British Empire and/or Europe was in danger of collapse without drastic reorganization under firm leadership, and that he alone could provide the heroic flair and drive to restore the power that was being insidiously undermined by external and internal enemies.

Secondly, the distinction between official ideas of the leadership and unofficial fascist ideology of the rank and file was no different from the intellectual coherence of leaders and ideologists in most organizations with the reductionist transmission of such concepts. Fascism was a leadership movement, and although members influenced policy it was Mosley who brought the tablets down from the mountain to the membership. It was not true, for example, that the tactics of political anti-semitism and street violence were accepted by Mosley because of rank and file pressure. Mosley's own concept of personal honour and his rational analysis of the activities of some Jews against the BUF, and their role in British society, convinced him that assaults by enemies on the movement should be resisted by defensive force. Some members left because of the increase in violence and trend towards anti-semitism to which these tactics led; individuals were disciplined and expelled for unprovoked violence, or personally challenging the authority of the leader; but this did not constitute differences between official and unofficial ideology.

Thirdly, the core nature of fascist ideas remained remarkably consistent during the 1930s despite the various campaigns designed to appeal to popular sentiments and prejudices in order to draw people into the movement. Mosley's main statements of

---

[6] O. Mosley, *The Greater Britain* (London, 1934), pp. 149–50.
[7] Idem, *My Life* (London, 1968), pp. 128–36.

his beliefs in *The Greater Britain* (1932, revised 1934), *Fascism — One Hundred Questions Asked and Answered* (1936) and *Tomorrow we Live* (1938), all heavily accentuated the economic critique and political analysis of his alternative vision. Anti-semitism and foreign policy made no appearance in the first work and comprised only four and eight pages respectively out of seventy-two in *Tomorrow we Live*. The marked contrast with the space devoted to these themes in *Action* and *Blackshirt* after 1935, and the virulent political campaigns after 1936, inverted the emphasis between official ideology and populist rhetoric.

With the failure of official BUF ideology to provide a stimulus for recruitment after Rothermere's defection, populist campaigns appealing to local sentiment were the main weapons designed to restore the movement's collapsing fortunes. Racial populism and appeasement were used to recruit followers and those who became committed followers were converted to the basic beliefs of inner fascism. The vast majority of members in the 1930s were never wholehearted supporters of the full ideological package; only a small group of several thousand members were ever that. This gap between the true believers and the single-issue fascists helps to explain the widely differing estimates of numbers made by commentators on the movement in the 1930s.

To argue as Rawnsley does that there were different layers of ideology is correct, but unfortunately he does not take his analysis far enough. Whilst committed fascists believed in leadership, militarism, anti-semitism and corporatism, they did so in an entirely open and non-conspiratorial manner. These beliefs lay just below the surface of fascism and accounted for its notoriety and apparent addiction to physical violence, but the real inner core was something entirely different. This represented the concept of the new fascist man derived from heroic vitalist and creative evolutionist philosophies.[8] Man, through overcoming his own nature, would be able in a disciplined and socially responsible movement to transform himself and his society to create a new stage in the evolutionary development of mankind. This may have been utopian and the idea only fully rationalized by Mosley after 1945, yet sufficient contemporary evidence exists to suggest that

[8] E. Bentley, *The Cult of the Superman* (Gloucester, Mass., 1944); J. Drennan (W.E.D. Allen), BUF, *Oswald Mosley and British Fascism* (London, 1934), pp. 176–293.

these beliefs were at the root of Mosley's revolt in the 1930s. Both Robert Skidelsky and Nicholas Mosley have examined these ideas, the latter in a critical fashion, and have illuminated the beliefs behind British fascism in the most convincing fashion.[9]

Finally, the nature and content of Mosley's thought deserves special emphasis because its logical structure was far removed from British academic and intellectual traditions. Mosley's powerful mind produced stimulating ideas which were usually expressed in a coherent and rational manner. However, the development of his argument was dependent on continental methods of analysis rather than on British traditions. Although not an original thinker, he was a strong believer in synthesizing ideas, no matter how disparate, to produce new thought at a higher level.[10] While the intellectual justification for this was not developed by Mosley until after 1945, it was characteristic of the way his mind worked in the inter-war period. Thus although British fascism was strongly rooted in relatively weak national traditions, its political expression and intellectual justification were much more strongly influenced by European examples.[11] If Marx's ideas represented a fusion of English economics, French politics and German philosophy, Mosley's system, at a lower level of analysis, represented a fusion of English radical economics, fascist politics and German idealist philosophy. The links were to be in philosophical method, as Mosley's insistence on idealism and psychological roots of behaviour were to contrast with Marx's materialism. For Mosley, Marx's materialism denied man's spiritual and evolutionary potential.

Mosley and other BUF theorists presented their case both in terms of sweeping away the old parliamentary system of government and of the need to replace it with a new fascist conception based on leadership and personal responsibilities. Mosley was perfectly serious when he talked of the need for a revolution.[12] Britain was facing a crisis and was in a steady decline which could only be checked by the forming of an instrument of steel.[13] The

[9] Skidelsky, *Oswald Mosley*, pp. 299–316, 465–80; N. Mosley, *Beyond the Pale* (London, 1983), pp. 35–42.

[10] O. Mosley, *My Life*, p. 91.

[11] R. Thurlow, 'The Return of Jeremiah', in *British Fascism*, ed. K. Lunn and R. Thurlow (London, 1980), pp. 100–13.

[12] *Blackshirt*, Feb. 1933.

[13] O. Mosley, *Tomorrow We Live* (London, 1938), p. 10.

immediate problem was to solve growing unemployment, which reached 3,000,000 in the last months of 1932. However, this was only a symptom of the more insidious collapse of British power in the twentieth century which had been accelerated by the First World War. These twin problems demanded radical new economic policies and a new political system of government if Britain were not to decline to the level of Spain.[14] To reverse the situation required a different type of leader and the development of a community imbued with cohesive and coherent national values. Thus for Mosley and the BUF new political, economic and philosophical ideas were necessary to prevent long-term trends turning into terminal decline. The BUF was at base an attempt to defy the trend of history, a 'mutiny against destiny' as James Drennan (W.E.D. Allen) called it.[15] Blackshirts in the Black House in the Rothermere period had an almost chiliastic belief in the BUF attaining power within a few months.

Mosley did not produce a systematic theory of why Britain had declined from her peak as an imperial and industrial power in the eighteenth and nineteenth century until after 1945.[16] He then developed an interesting historical and psychological critique of the British ruling class. In the 1930s the demands of British fascism left him little time for new constructive thought and the intellectual content of his argument against the British ruling class at this time often degenerated to the level of crude propaganda and virulent political abuse. He had lost patience with the British establishment and became totally alienated from the methods of parliamentary government and its apparent inability to solve the fundamental problem of political decline. His failure, outside a small and diminishing coterie of convinced followers, to persuade any political party or government until 1931 to commit themselves to radical policies to fight a war in peacetime against unemployment, convinced him that parliamentary democracy could not solve Britain's fundamental problems. Although some radicals sympathized with this analysis, few of any consequence were prepared to follow Mosley and work outside the system. Mosley therefore concentrated on the economic analysis of the reasons for Britain's decline and the philosophical justification for,

---

[14] *Parliamentary Debates*, vol. 239, 28 May 1930.
[15] Drennan, BUF, *Mosley and British Fascism*, p. 200.
[16] O. Mosley, *The Alternative* (London, 1947).

and political blueprint of, the proposed fascist utopia. During the 1930s, apart from some interesting comments on Spengler, Mosley left the historical justification for British fascism to others.

The BUF argued that the principles of British fascism were embedded deep in British history, and that it was the dominant Whig interpretation that had distorted the historical textbooks.[17] Taking their arguments from a recently published modern history of England, they argued that the founding of the history schools at Oxford and Cambridge had been a propaganda stunt to justify the Hanoverian dynasty and were endowed in order to write Whig history.[18] To Bill Allen, for instance, the National government of 1931 was another long Walpolean lassitude, a revived Whigdom. Modern conservatism, despite its turn to Protectionism, had failed to develop national planning to make the policy effective. The BUF by contrast saw itself as a continuation of a tradition which linked feudalism, the guild system, Tudor centralized authority and the spirit behind the achievement of Empire to their own conception of the corporate state.[19]

In particular, it was the vital spirit of endeavour that so characterized the Elizabethan age which the BUF tried to emulate. They believed that the Tudor nation-state concept which had produced the basis of British world supremacy had been undermined during the seventeenth century by the victory of parliament over the centralized authority of monarchy.[20] As a result liberal capitalism and the dominance of powerful vested interests had replaced the needs of the state as the paramount influence on government. As David Baker has shown, other fascists, like A.K. Chesterton, also saw in the Elizabethan age the model for fascist revolt. For Chesterton, it was not the lessons of history but the aesthetic appreciation of the plays of Shakespeare which provided a guide to political action.[21]

This dubious attempt to place the BUF within the mainstream of British history was seen by Mosley as the explanation of why the

[17] A.L. Glasfurd, 'Fascism and the English tradition', *Fascist Quarterly*, 1, 3 (July 1935), p. 360.

[18] G.R. Stirling Taylor, *A Modern History of England 1485–1932* (London, 1932), p. 28.

[19] Drennan, BUF, *Mosley and British Fascism*, p. 16.

[20] Ibid., p. 30.

[21] D. Baker, 'A.K. Chesterton. The making of a British fascist', PhD thesis, University of Sheffield, 1982, pp. 146–217.

political establishment had failed to adopt his, or anybody else's, radical policies to solve the immediate problems: the British ruling class had become ossified and was unable to meet the rapidly changing circumstances of the post-war world. His near apocalyptic gloom and doom foreboding was partly based on a rational economic critique, but was also partly a critical reaction to Oswald Spengler's *Decline of the West*.

BUF *ideas and society*

Mosley's economic ideas in the late 1920s had gradually moved from a mildly socialist and strongly Keynesian criticism of orthodox finance and Treasury policy to a belief in conservative planning within a protected national framework.[22] The failures of the Mosley Memorandum and Mosley Manifesto had led him to turn his back on party politics and with the defeat of the New Party to move outside parliamentary politics altogether. By 1931, Mosley's economic analysis was no longer tempered by the constraint of the pragmatic realities of parliamentary politics and the narrow limits within which governments could operate in economic policy before that time. His increasingly utopian prognosis was no longer subject to the critical gaze of Cabinet committees and government colleagues and nobody of influence now took any notice of his ideas. Skidelsky has pointed out the seminal influence of Keynes and the arguments of his *Treatise on Monetary Reform* on Mosley in the 1920s; with Mosley's fascist economic ideas came a reversion to some of the themes of J.A. Hobson as well as the economic nationalism common to all fascists.

Mosley's fascist economic programme derived from the main ideas of his socialist and radical synthesis of the 1920s transposed into an ultra-national context. For Mosley, the basic problem was that the ability of the industrial system to expand production far exceeded its propensity to consume the excess output. Unemployment was caused by a failure of demand to meet the productive potential of industry, and there was therefore an

---

[22] A. Oldfield, 'The growth of the concept of economic planning in the doctrine of the British Labour Party 1914–25', PhD thesis, University of Sheffield, 1973, pp. 225–47.

immediate need to institute consumer credits amongst the low-paid in order to raise purchasing power. Britain's liberal economic system's only response to this problem was to export excess goods. As industrializing nations increasingly put up protectionist barriers so the British economy became dependent on third world markets, on the need to 'find enough Negroes to sell bicycles to'. Worse still, Britain had exported her own capital to ensure that the overseas markets upon which Britain was dependent could now industrialize themselves. Britain, which more than any other country was dependent on overseas trade, had pursued policies leading to a continuous decline in its export potential.

To Mosley the situation was so serious that palliatives like the Conservative protection policy were totally inadequate.[23] What was needed was a planned economy under firm governmental direction which could utilize the resources of the British Empire in an efficient manner. While the capitalists ensured the necessary incentives for rewarding personal initiative, an increased role for the state was necessary to ensure that production and consumption were brought into proper balance and that a scientific mechanism for ensuring permanent economic growth could be developed. The liberal economics of successive British governments had meant that the economy had become dependent on world markets. These in turn had become controlled by finance rather than productive enterprise, particularly since the First World War when Wall Street had replaced London as the world's leading financial centre. Scientific protection and firm leadership were now needed to insulate the British Empire from both world conditions and the power of finance over industry. In Mosley's view, fascism was needed because only a 'modern movement' could revolutionize the British economy; the short-term palliatives like his own and Lloyd George's public works projects of 1929 and the tentative moves towards protection and reflation of the National government were now totally inadequate to meet the growing seriousness of the problem.[24]

Mosley believed that the breakdown of the liberal economic order heralded the doom of parliamentary government and political democracy. What was needed to restore Britain's power

---

[23] O. Mosley, *The Greater Britain*, p. 89.
[24] Ibid., pp. 98–147; idem, *Tomorrow We Live*, pp. 23–52.

was a rationalization of government as well as industry. To create national investment boards and planning mechanisms to equate production with consumption would be inadequate unless government were given the authority to act to solve the pressing economic problems. Although fascism would come to power by entirely constitutional means, the first action of the elected fascist government would be to pass a General Powers Bill which would enable the prime minister and a small inner cabinet of five to initiate legislation without recourse to Parliament. MPs were to have the constitutional check of being able to pass no-confidence motions when it was deemed necessary to call Parliament, but the talking shop and blocking powers of the party system were to be abolished. If a no-confidence motion was passed the king would create a new prime minister who would ask for the support of parliament. Political parties would be abolished and the second parliament of the fascist utopia would have MPs elected on a corporate basis.

Mosley's view of the function of MPs was that they would assume the leadership of local government. In the same manner as the prime minister would be responsible for the national government, so the MPs would control local politics. The constitutional mechanism would significantly alter under fascism. MPs would no longer be elected on a geographical franchise; in the new corporate state each industry and profession would elect its own representatives to a National Chamber of Corporations. A corporation would also be established for each industry, comprising a third representation for labour and capital, with the consumer interest and government holding the balance of power.[25] Mosley argued that the average voter did not understand the complexities of national politics and the current bartering for votes by the national parties was a farce. The electorate was only concerned with and interested in the issues which immediately confronted them at work. National politics would best be understood by the technical experts who would gravitate towards the highest echelons of the corporate state, and whose importance would be institutionalized further by representation in the Assembly of Notables which would replace the House of Lords. Mosley saw British fascism as part of a managerial revolution.[26]

---

[25] A.R. Thomson, *The Coming Corporate State* (London, n.d.).
[26] O. Mosley, *The Greater Britain*, pp. 17–35; idem, *Tomorrow We Live*, pp. 9–22; L.P.

If fascism meant a revolution in the British state, then its future depended on the full utilization of the resources of the Empire. Mosley viewed the fascist Empire as a mercantile super-state where the dominions and colonies would happily supply primary products and raw materials in return for British manufactured goods. A Council of Empire would formulate policy for British imperial interests as a whole. What the political relationship should be between fascist Britain and the dominions was not spelt out as Mosley assumed that it was inconceivable that they could refuse the offer of preferential access to the British market. Mosley argued also that the 'backward and illiterate populations' of the colonies were totally unsuited for self-government and that both India and British African territories should remain under the tight political control of our imperial interest.[27] The other fascist empires of Germany, Italy and Japan were considered to be Britain's 'natural' allies in the world-wide spread of fascism. These countries should be encouraged to develop their own closed economic systems with adequate access to raw materials and it was argued their geographical expansion would not compete with British imperial interests.[28]

This ideological core of fascism was philosophically rationalized from the outset. Raven Thomson, Bill Allen and Mosley all argued that the heroic vitalist tradition behind Oswald Spengler's grand panoramic vision of the rise and fall of civilizations and the imminent prophecy of the doom of the 'Faustian culture' of Europe was of vital importance to the understanding of contemporary history. Raven Thomson, who was much influenced by Spengler's organic method, argued that the processes of nature were a series of biological integrations, and that with each new synthesis old natural laws ceased to have their applications and new forms emerged; the highest form was civilization, which was a super-biological force directing the actions of men to its higher aims, the very realization of the Superman.[29] Soon after writing this Thomson came to see fascism as the twentieth-century

Carpenter, 'Corporatism in Britain 1930–45', *Journal of Contemporary History*, 11 (1976), p. 4; A. Booth and M. Pack, *Employment, Capital and Economic Policy* (Oxford, 1985), pp. 29–34.

[27] O. Mosley, *Tomorrow We Live*, pp. 42–3.
[28] O. Mosley, 'The world alternative', *Fascist Quarterly*, 2, 3 (1936).
[29] 'A. Raven', (Thomson) *Civilisation as Divine Superman* (London, 1932), p. 33.

expression of the will to infinitude and Mosley as the leader who would transform the world.

Mosley and Bill Allen both argued in typical fascist fashion that Spengler's prognosis was far too pessimistic. Although he had correctly analysed the cyclical pattern of history and the forces which led to the rise and fall of civilizations, his prognosis of the fate of the Faustian culture was wrong. Whereas Spengler had argued that the emergence of new caesar figures could only delay the decline of the west, Mosley argued that his misunderstanding of the potentialities of modern science has led him to mistaken conclusions. For Mosley, caesarism and science could renew the youth of western culture and fascism was the only political system which could create a new civilization.[30] Without fascism Spengler was right and Europe was doomed, a prey to the money power, its instrument democracy, and the predations of outer barbarians, particularly Russia. Mosley saw himself as one of the great 'fact men' of history leading us on to a higher destiny.[31]

If Mosley rationalized his historical vision with reference to a critical reaction to the writings of Oswald Spengler, then his philosophical justification was based on his interpretation of the writings of Nietzsche and George Bernard Shaw. In Mosley's view fascism represented a synthesis of Nietzschean and Christian values, of the will to power exemplified by the athleticism and discipline of the individual striving to become Superman, being harnessed into service for the community. The fascist movement was to represent the heroic elite who would guide and educate the rest of a society to a higher stage of evolution, where national planning and co-operation could lead to material and spiritual progress. For Mosley, each Blackshirt was to become the individual cell of a collective caesarism.[32] Nicholas Mosley has argued that his father's interpretation of Nietzsche sometimes failed to recognize the ironic attitude of the Superman concept. He often confused the need for self-control with power over others and he failed ultimately to resolve the problem of the function of evil.[33] Whether or not this interpretation of Oswald Mosley's view

---

[30] Drennan, BUF, *Mosley and British Fascism*, pp. 176–202; O. Mosley, *Tomorrow We Live*, pp. 69–72.

[31] R. Thurlow, 'Destiny and doom, Spengler, Hitler and "British" fascism', *Patterns of Prejudice*, 14, 5 (Oct. 1981), pp. 17–33.

[32] O. Mosley, 'The philosophy of fascism', *Fascist Quarterly*, 1, 1 (Jan. 1935), p. 43.

[33] N. Mosley, *Beyond the Pale*, pp. 38–9.

of Nietzsche is correct is beside the point. The fact is that Oswald Mosley took very seriously indeed the philosophical justification for his political career. At root the BUF was envisaged as the prototype of a new kind of humanity, and Mosley was a neo-Lamarckian who believed that through action and conscious striving man could create a better society. That the BUF failed to live up to these standards was clear enough, however the political idealism and belief in creative evolution which lay behind it was fundamental to Mosley's revolt against the political establishment.

The most notorious aspect of BUF ideology was the development of anti-semitism. This was not part of the initial programme of the BUF and only became pronounced after Mosley's speech at the Albert Hall on 28 October 1934. Even then it took over a year for it to become a central part of a political campaign. Anti-semitism had been a potent force beneath the surface of BUF ideology since its inception and fascist journalists had often commented on the 'alien' menace in *Blackshirt* and *Fascist Week*, despite frequent pronouncements that Jew-baiting was forbidden 'by order'.[34]

Contrary to the claims of several authorities, the use of political anti-semitism by the BUF has to be seen as a genuine belief rather than a cynical device to prop up an ailing movement. Mosley was not an ideological anti-semite but he became convinced that some Jews were acting against the British national interest through their role in international finance, and that others were trying to destroy the BUF through physical violence. Mosley presented his case against the Jews in terms of these 'well-earned reputation' arguments.[35] The anti-semitic campaign of the BUF can best be understood as a result of the interaction of bitterly opposed fascist and anti-fascist elements, rather than simply a reaction to fascist scapegoating of Jews.[36]

Unlike the other major ingredients of fascist theorizing, Mosley's attacks on the Jews were not highly conceptualized nor did anti-semitism ever represent a total ideological explanation. The criticisms of 'big Jews' and 'little Jews', of the alleged Jewish control of international finance and the British media, and the

---

[34] 'Britain for the British. The alien menace', *Blackshirt*, 30 Sept.–6 Oct. 1933; 'Fascism and the Jews', *Blackshirt*, 1 Apr. 1933.

[35] 'Blackshirts take up the challenge thrown down by Jewry', *Blackshirt*, 2 Nov. 1934.

[36] C. Holmes, 'Anti-semitism and the BUF', in Lunn and Thurlow, *British Fascism*, pp. 114–34.

supposed Jewish dominance of the Communist and Labour party opposition to the fascists was never developed beyond the loosest of conspiracy theories in Mosley's populist rhetoric. Mosley thought the *Protocols of the Elders of Zion* was a silly forgery and that the existence of a world-wide secret conspiracy throughout the ages was a ludicrous fantasy.[37] However, despite a toning down of social and economic arguments against Jewish immigrants after 1937, he still declared the Jews to be largely responsible for the deterioration in Anglo-German relations in 1938–9.[38]

In so far as Mosley possessed a perspective on the Jews it probably derived from Spengler's influence. Mosley, like Spengler, believed that culture rather than race determined behaviour and that the 'Oriental' Jew was more alien to the British than any European nation.[39] Spengler's belief that different cultures could not be transposed on or influence each other was at the heart of the traditional hatred between Jews and Christians in European society. From such beliefs Mosley was to develop an apartheid perspective both with regard to Jews in the inter-war period and Africans after 1945. That he developed into an anti-semite in the 1930s was admitted before the Advisory Committee in 1940: In the fascist state, Special Commissions were to be set up to decide whether individual Jews were more Jewish or British in their attitude, and those who failed to pass the test would be expelled.[40]

If Mosley's anti-semitism was less well conceptualized than most of his beliefs, this did not apply to some of his followers. True believers in anti-semitism, both as an ideology and political weapon, were to be found at all levels of the BUF. In terms of ideology, special mention must be made of William Joyce's 'Letters from Lucifer' in *Blackshirt* and two of the most virulent of all anti-semitic diatribes in the inter-war period. Major-General Fuller's 'The Cancer of Europe' and A.K. Chesterton's 'The Apotheosis of the Jew'.[41] As an hierarchical leadership movement

[37] O. Mosley, *My Life*, p. 342.
[38] O. Mosley, 'For Britain peace and people – no war for Jewish finance', *Action*, 2 Sept. 1939.
[39] O. Mosley, *Tomorrow We Live*, p. 59.
[40] PRO HO 283/13/38–42.
[41] Major-General J.F.C. Fuller, 'The cancer of Europe', *Fascist Quarterly*, 2, 1 (1935), pp. 65–81; A.K. Chesterton, 'The apotheosis of the Jew', *British Union Quarterly*, 1, 2 (1937), pp. 45–54.

Mosley's views set the tone for the BUF, but discipline often broke down under confrontation situations and unofficial violence and co-operation with more extreme groups often resulted, particularly in the East End campaign.

The reactions to Mosley's ideas in British society were mainly of a moral and ethical nature. Few, if any, were prepared to discuss the practicalities or necessity of Mosley's vision outside the fascist movement. The reaction from the British establishment was almost entirely negative. Stanley Baldwin's view that Mosley was a cad and did not play the game was symptomatic of Conservative attitudes; from the left Beatrice Webb argued that Mosley's paternalistic approach to the working class ran counter to trade union and co-operative traditions, and that he was 'loose with women', which offended both her and presumably the working class's puritan sensibilities.[42] Organizations like the January Club may have afforded some links to the establishment but had little lasting impact, given the negative view of British fascism taken by respectable opinion after the Olympia fiasco. Ideas such as the need for fascist man with new values cut no ice with traditional party politics and parliamentary government.

In so far as the establishment found it necessary to respond to the positive content of Mosley's ideas, the view taken was represented by the Cabinet Committee's rejection of the Mosley Memorandum in 1930 (see pp. 40–2). Neither local government, nor landowners, nor planning authorities would have the necessary time for consultation in terms of immediate action on necessary public work projects. Improvements to transport infrastructure would have to take place in terms of a co-ordinated integrated national policy. There was also no guarantee that unemployed workers wanted public works projects which would involve uprooting men and their families from their homes or of the necessary trade union co-operation in terms of the dilution of national agreements that would presumably result from such activity. Overlapping jurisdiction between the Inner Cabinet and its technical experts with the traditional machinery of government would also cause friction.[43]

The establishment viewed Mosley's ideas for economic nation-

[42] Passfield Papers; B. Webb, unpublished diaries, vol. 44, p. 60, entry 29 May 1930, quoted in Oldfield, 'Economic planning', p. 247.
[43] PRO Cab. 24/203/104 (29).

alism as a non-starter for two reasons. First, Mosley's memorandum represented a direct challenge to the Treasury view of economic policy in the 1930s and to the Labour government's financial policy. Mosley argued that a sound domestic economy was a pre-requisite for our other problems to be solved. The Treasury and the Labour government took the view that, given that one-third industrial production was dependent on international trade and that we were not self-sufficient in the production of raw materials for our industry, our international commitments should be given the first priority. Hence the much maligned (by Mosley) Lord Privy Seal, J.H. Thomas, circulated a memorandum arguing that the real objection to financing public works through large public loans was that it hindered the chances of conversion of part of the War Loan debt to a less oppressive level, and that large public expenditures were the policy of those who wished to reduce real wages by inflation.[44] While these arguments were not so important after the collapse of the Gold Standard in 1931, Mosley had exaggerated when he argued that underconsumption was a root cause of unemployment. Real wages had remained constant in the 1920s whilst retail prices fell from 110.8 to 105.1 (1930=100).[45]

Second, the establishment would have viewed Mosley's plan for economic nationalism as entirely impracticable. As early as 1902 Joseph Chamberlain had proposed to the Colonial Conference that the Empire should be an economically insulated unit similar to the German Zollverein and had been rebuffed by the Canadian prime minister. When Milner had proposed a Council of Empire to co-ordinate policies of foreign policy and defence in 1907 the idea was met with hostility by both Canada and South Africa.[46]

In the 1930s Mosley's autarkic solution was even more of a pipedream. It went totally against the Empire's economic interests. Dominions since the 1850s had been given the right to impose customs duties and had used this freedom to discriminate against the import of manufactured articles in order to protect their own nascent industrialization. At Ottawa in 1932, the dominions wished to continue to discriminate against British goods, which

[44] PRO Cab. 24/211/120.
[45] D.H. Aldcroft, *The Inter-war Economy* (London, 1970), p. 352.
[46] Farr, 'Right wing politics', p. 12; A.M. Gollin, *Proconsul in Politics. A Study of Lord Milner in Opposition and in Power* (London, 1964), p. 139.

would have been anathema to Mosley. Similarly the economies of the national states of the Empire were by no means complementary, particularly given the steep turn in the terms of trade against primary producers in the inter-war period and Mosley's insistence that the needs of British farmers should come before those of the Empire. How Australia was to diversify out of wool, which represented nearly half her exports, without industrialization and at the same time run a full-employment high-consumption economy was not explained by Mosley.[47] Canada was supposed to exchange wheat for British coal in Mosley's model, but how this was to rebound to Canada's advantage was obscure, given the obvious geographical and economic advantages which coal from the USA would give Canada.

The National government in fact did take some tentative steps in the direction advocated by Mosley, but these were achieved within the democratic framework and the pragmatic constraints of the economic system. Mild reflation after 1932 led to economic recovery with growth rates once more reverting to mid-Victorian norms. Protection was introduced for most imports in 1932 and the system of Empire Preference was evolved. Trade did switch from other markets to the Empire. The proportion of British exports sent to the Empire rose from 22 per cent to 47 per cent[48] while the percentage of imports from non-Empire sources fell from 80 to 61 per cent.[49] Almost one-quarter of the new capital raised in London was sent to the Empire.[50] Mosley's assumption that most of the British capital exported overseas had been sent to finance sweated labour in third world countries was misleading, as was his total misrepresentation of the function of overseas investment.[51] The British Cabinet spent more time discussing matters of economic policy than any other aspect of imperial affairs.[52]

Thus the British government did in fact prove to be highly flexible within the limits of practical politics and did co-operate

---

[47] W.K. Hancock, *Survey of British Commonwealth Affairs II, Problems of Economic Policy Vol. 2 Pt. 1*, (London, 1940), p. 251.
[48] I.M. Drummond, *British Economic Policy and the Empire 1919–39* (London, 1972), p. 18.
[49] Ibid., pp. 20–1.
[50] Ibid., p. 29.
[51] O. Mosley, *Tomorrow We Live*, pp. 23–36.
[52] I.M. Drummond, *Imperial Economic Policy 1917–39* (London, 1974), p. 426.

with the dominions in trying to restructure the collapsing international economy. Mosley's draconian solution of establishing an authoritarian state with drastically reduced individual liberties, expelling minorities, anti-semitism and the abolition of political opposition, was of little appeal to the bulk of the British people. The implied tightening of control over the dominions and colonies on which the system was based was totally unrealistic and would have been violently resisted by the rest of the Empire. Above all, Mosley's prognosis of the imminent collapse of the economy and democracy proved to be unfounded. Mosley was perhaps unfortunate in that he founded his movements at the depth of the Depression. His mistaken economic analysis failed to account for rising real wages for those in work, as income fell less than the price level, the emergence of new industries which led to a sustained economic recovery in the 1930s and falling unemployment apart from the worst regional blackspots. The National government proved to be acceptable to most of the population and the Labour party recovered from the débâcle of 1931. Even if Britain's relative decline was only checked in the 1930s, the British people preferred democracy and political liberty to the fantasies of Mosley's Spenglerian dreams.

8

The Hitler Fan Club

Among the most controversial areas of the study of British fascism has been the relationship, if any, between the various anti-semitic and fascist movements and German nazism and Italian fascism, and the reasons for the internment without trial of over 750 individuals connected with these organizations for varying lengths of time after 1940. In particular the shadow of Sir Oswald Mosley's lawyer has loomed large in previous discussions of these subjects. But while Mosley can be criticized for the secretive nature of his dealings with the fascist powers, and the fact that he was evasive and ambiguous about both the financing of the BUF and his relationship with other fascists, anti-semites, or peace movements in 1939–40 before the Advisory Committee, there is little evidence that fascists in Britain were directly implicated in potentially treasonable behaviour before they were interned.

Fascists or traitors?

Previous literature has dealt very delicately and with varying degrees of illumination about these sensitive subjects. The most important work on the first of these themes, Richard Griffiths's *Fellow Travellers of the Right*, has shown that for much of the 1930s there was a widespread mood in sections of British public opinion that was not only strongly in favour of appeasement, but saw some positive virtue in the fascist regimes. Only with the collapse of the post-Munich euphoria did the extremists, who included the fascists, become isolated from the dramatic change of opinion about Hitler in influential circles.[1] Praise of this admirable work nevertheless requires qualification with regard to its description of the fascist fringe, partly as a result of the release of new material. For instance, Griffiths's assumption that individuals like Mosley and Sir Barry Domvile were nazi enthusiasts, primarily because of ideological sympathy, is questionable; both in fact saw friendship with Germany as a necessity if their primary consideration, the security of the British Empire, was to be maintained. Griffiths also fails to discuss adequately the crucial events of the phoney war period, particularly the secret meetings between representatives of most of the extremist organizations mentioned in his text, and how they were interpreted by the authorities.

Equally, Mosley's version of these matters can be criticized. His exceptional reticence about many aspects of British fascism was shown in his autobiography where he merely justified his public attitude towards Hitler and British isolationism.[2] He provided little new material for Skidelsky's stimulating analysis of BUF views on foreign policy in the 1930s.[3] Nicholas Mosley stressed his father's patriotism and, despite emphasizing his secretive behaviour, his partial covering up of the sources of funding of the BUF, and his ambiguous use of language, implied that although Sir Oswald may have been misguided in some of his actions, he was certainly no traitor.[4]

Recent releases of Home Office material on British fascism, the discovery of an important diary of an internee, Sir Barry Domvile, which was successfully hidden to avoid being taken by the Security Service in 1940, and work on the history of MI5 and its agents, have provided sufficient new information for a reassessment of these questions. Although much of this material must be viewed critically, particularly with regard to events in May 1940, it nevertheless provides a fascinating insight into the death throes of inter-war British fascism.

At the outset two general points need emphasizing. First, for many British fascists there was a conflict of interest between their

[1] R. Griffiths, *Fellow Travellers of the Right* (London, 1983), pp. 334–67.
[2] O. Mosley, *My Life* (London, 1968), pp. 377–97.
[3] R. Skidelsky, *Oswald Mosley* (London, 1975), pp. 423–46.
[4] N. Mosley, *Beyond the Pale* (London, 1983), pp. 168–78.

ideological sympathy with Italian fascism and German nazism and their deep sense of patriotism and British nationalism. Although Mosley assumed no conflict between Britain's world-wide commitments and the continental imperialism of other fascist powers, Arnold Leese became critical not only of Mosley's views but of Hitler's actions in the Second World War. Many who desired peace at any cost joined the BUF in 1939, while others left because they could not equate their primary commitment to British patriotism with either Mosley's position or their ideological sympathy for fascism.

Second, there was little relationship between the strength of commitment to anti-semitism or racial nationalism and support for Hitler. William Joyce and A.K. Chesterton were two of the most virulent anti-semites in the BUF in the 1930s, yet while the former was found guilty of treasonable behaviour in working for the nazis in the war as the infamous Lord Haw Haw, Chesterton fought against Hitler in the British army in East Africa.[5] Other anti-semites such as Douglas Reed were also vehemently anti-nazi.[6] Indeed both the Social Credit movement and Reed during the war came to see Hitler as a Jewish agent whose function was to destroy Europe by placing it under the hegemony of the 'golden international' – Wall Street finance, the alleged power behind American imperialism, and Russian communism.

If fascists and anti-semites were not necessarily Hitler's friends, then both the policies of the nazis and the attention of the Security Service allowed little scope for the emergence of a fascist-inspired fifth column in England. It is now clear that Hitler saw Britain as a potential ally until 1937 and forbade the Abwehr to develop an intelligence network there. After that date the efficiency of F2 branch, which was responsible for the surveillance of nazi intelligence operations, and the relative success of Maxwell Knight's B5b section of MI5 in infiltrating suspect organizations like the Link and the Right Club, and with partial effect the BUF, meant that the Security Service was always in control in monitoring both suspect 'aliens' and native fascists.[7] The mass internment of both

[5] D. Baker, 'A.K. Chesterton. The making of a British fascist', PhD thesis, University of Sheffield, 1982, pp. 351–8.

[6] R. Thurlow, 'Anti-Nazi anti-semite', Douglas Reed file, Times Archive.

[7] N. West, *MI5 British Security Service Operations 1909–1945* (London, 1983), pp. 96–136; A. Masters, *The Man who was M* (Oxford, 1984), pp. 55–75.

groups in 1940 was unnecessary; they were made scapegoats by the new Churchill government which was determined to maintain collapsing morale by a show of action in the face of the nazi onslaught in western Europe in April and May 1940. This represented an *ad hoc* response to crisis, not a conscious conspiracy orchestrated by the Security Service and the War Office.[8]

Similarly, it is not at all clear that the implications of BUF policy, if not its assumptions, with regard to nazi Germany were radically different from that of the British government until March 1939. Griffiths has shown that there were a large number of fellow-travellers who held favourable views of the dictators. Indeed, it was also true that Mosley's continuing demand for appeasement still had considerable support even during the phoney war period. Revisionist accounts of British foreign policy in the 1930s suggest both that appeasement of the dictators was a popular policy and that public opinion fully supported the government position, at least until the dismemberment of Czechoslovakia in March 1939. Even then, when the active appeasement policies which culminated in the Munich Settlement were shown to be a disastrous mistake, at least in terms of accepting the reliability and good faith of the dictators, Chamberlain was still able to keep control of the government and the support of his followers until the collapse of Norway in April 1940.

Appeasement had been based on economic, political and strategic motives, stemming from the need to limit the costs of rearmament and the impact this would have on domestic welfare expenditure. The policy accepted the justice of German demands for a revision of the Versailles treaty, and the need for a settlement to ensure the peace of Europe and encourage the opening up of German markets for British exports. Appeasement reflected too the growing independence of the British dominions and their fear after the Chanak Crisis of being embroiled in further European conflict, and growing suspicion of French attempts to create a network of alliances in eastern Europe which had little relevance for Britain's essential strategic interests. These factors were probably uppermost in Chamberlain's mind when deciding to move

[8] P. and L. Gillman, *Collar the Lot* (London, 1980), pp. 115–30; R. Stent, *A Bespattered Page* (London, 1980), p. 253; PRO FO 371/25253/138–40.

from Baldwin's passive appeasement policy to more active attempts to produce a European settlement in 1937.[9]

The complete reversal of this policy followed, with the guarantee to Poland and other eastern European countries in 1939 after the collapse of Czechoslovakia. This was brought about both by the growing belief that Hitler had to be stopped, justified in terms of the traditional balance of power within Europe, and the government's fear that the Labour party would seize the popular initiative in advocating a collective security policy in order to attempt to block the dictators.[10] What is particularly interesting for our theme is that British fascists only began to diverge from the implications of government policy after March 1939. Although appeasement had been rooted in the moral and ideological dogma of liberalism[11] while BUF ideas were based on the nationalist and neo-mercantilist beliefs in state power which had been resurrected in Die-hard and national efficiency ideas of the Edwardian era, the implications for foreign policy were similar up until 1939 with regard to the need for an understanding with the European dictators.

Even after March 1939 it was not at all clear to what extent popular opinion followed the government's lead. Although fascists were as divided as other sections of the community in response to the growing crisis in 1939, Mosley's claim that his peace campaign produced a large increase in membership appeared to be accurate, although it also provoked significant defections as well. Those early attempts at gauging public opinion, the Mass Observation surveys and Home Office intelligence reports on civilian morale, suggested that there was considerable support for a negotiated peace with Hitler during the phoney war period.[12] Only with the German invasion of Norway and the attack on western Europe did public opinion harden, and Mosley was physically assaulted at the

---

[9] W.R. Rock, *British Appeasement in the 1930s* (London, 1977), pp. 41–53; Royal Institution of International Affairs, *Political and Strategic Interests of the United Kingdom* (London, 1939), pp. 3–99; M. Cowling, *The Impact of Hitler* (Cambridge, 1975), pp. 97–208; W. Mommsen and L. Kettenacker (eds), *The Fascist Challenge and the Policy of Appeasement* (London, 1983), pp. 79–206 and 223–251.

[10] M. Cowling, *The Impact of Hitler*, pp. 257–92; W.R. Rock, *Appeasement on Trial* (Hamden, Conn., 1966), pp. 31–45.

[11] M. Gilbert, *The Roots of Appeasement* (London, 1966), pp. 4–5; C. Barnett,

[12] File 39, Silvertown by-election, Feb. 1940, p. 12; File 59, North East Leeds by-election, Mar. 1940, p. 1, *Mass Observation File Reports*; I. McClaine, *Ministry of Morale* (London, 1979), pp. 34–61.

Middleton and Prestwich by-election the week before he was interned in May 1940.[13] Poor organization and the failure to get his message across to the electorate accounted for the dismal performance of the BUF in the first two by-elections they fought in 1940, not popular opposition to his call for a negotiated settlement. It was the fifth-column scare after the rapid collapse of western Europe and the fact that public opinion, quite wrongly, perceived Mosley as a potential Quisling, which accounted for the drastic change in public perception of the BUF in May of that year.

Of the groups operating on the fascist political fringe it was the 'reactionary right' who changed their admiration for Hitler into outright hostility at the onset of war. It was *The Patriot*, the journal started by the Duke of Northumberland in 1922, and the Militant Christian Patriots who seized on the Nazi-Soviet Pact of August 1939 as the sign that Hitler could not be trusted.[14] Nesta Webster, who since 1933 had been praising Hitler because his anti-semitism showed that he was undermining the power behind Prussian militarism, and because he had cleared out all the pornographic literature from Germany,[15] now changed her mind. In her view the position of *The Patriot* had always been the correct one. Hitler had been wonderful for Germany but he had now sold his soul to the devil; evil influences around him, notably Goebbels, Streicher and Rosenberg, had gained the upper hand as the old Prussian vices reasserted themselves. Germany could no longer be trusted and Mr Chamberlain was forced to declare war against German aggression.[16] What this signified was that the reactionary right's approval of Hitler's attack on alleged Jewish power was withdrawn because of the pact with Bolshevism, and the old Die-hard fear of Germany re-asserted itself.

If the conservative fascist tradition was able to show that its basic patriotism outweighed its admiration for nazi anti-semitism, the problem was much more difficult for racial nationalists and extreme anti-semites. There was a thin dividing line between patriotism and treason, as the case of William Joyce was to testify. Yet the main organizations – the IFL, NL, RC and NSL – were all to

[13] File 154, Middleton and Prestwich by-election, 30 May 1940, pp. 10–12, *Mass Observation File Reports*.
[14] PRO HO 144/21382/297.
[15] N. Webster, *Germany and England* (London, 1938), pp. 3, 18.
[16] Idem, 'Germany and England', Series II, *The Patriot*, Nov. and Dec. 1939.

resolve the problem in different ways despite some derisory and bitter division. It was to be the activities of one of these groups, the Right Club, trying to resolve this dilemma under the alert gaze of MI5, which finally led the government to put up the shutters on British fascism.

The IFL provided an interesting example of the predicament of racial nationalists. For a man reputed to be the most rabid anti-semite in Britain, Arnold Leese adopted an increasingly critical view of Hitler's actions in 1939–40 and of the 'more German than the Germans' faction in the IFL.[17] Before the beginning of the war attitudes to Hitler had not caused any problem within the organization. Delegates from the IFL had attended Nuremberg rallies at the invitation of Streicher in 1935 and 1936. The IFL had close relations with nazi organizations and agents in Britain, and the Brown House in Munich had arranged for IFL literature to be translated into various languages. However, although MI5 used almost the full range of their techniques to observe the IFL, including the use of agents and postal intercepts, F3 branch found little of significance. The nazis provided no funds, nor did they use the organization to infiltrate agents into Great Britain. The close interest of the Security Service did lead to the production of a fascinating report, however, on the nature of the organization in 1942, from which much of our knowledge of this subject is derived.[18]

Leese stated at the outset of the war that his primary loyalty was to king and country. It was indeed the supposed insult to his patriotic instincts which led to his violent reaction to the order for his internment in June 1940. He avoided detention for over four months and was only arrested after a violent struggle. He then proceeded to smash up his police cell in protest at the loss of his liberty without due process of law. He wrote later to one of his followers that he was amazed that patriots like Ramsay and Domvile had co-operated with the Security Service and appealed to the Advisory Committee, although this action was only to be expected from Mosley and Raven Thomson.[19] For Leese, Mosley was an ideal candidate for an English Quisling, and he meant this as a term of abuse. He also thought no man of honour would have

---

[17] *Weekly Angles*, 9 Sept. 1939.
[18] PRO HO 45/24967/105.
[19] Letter, A.S. Leese to A. Gittens, '30 Oct.', n.d., File 3574, Britons Library.

done what Joyce had done.[20] Leese was proud to have taken the same attitude to the Security Service as Rudolf Hess and one or two minor fascists like Knott.

For Leese the Second World War was quite simply a 'Jew's War'. It had been caused by the internationalism of the Jewish money power and its object was to destroy the one oppositional force to its world hegemony. However, this did not mean that Hitler should be supported unreservedly. Leese was against giving back the mandated territories and he criticised 'big money' (Mosley) fascism for suggesting it.[21] He was also against the Nazi-Soviet Pact and thought Hitler had taken leave of his senses by allying with Jewish Bolshevism. This mistake was compounded by the nazi invasion of the 'holy ground' of Finland and Norway in 1939–40. As he stated to Beamish, Hitler had been a marvel but was no longer one.[22] Leese's attitude to Hitler and Joyce was to alter significantly by 1945, but in 1940 he was highly critical of both.

Leese's attitude to Hitler in 1940 was not shared by all his followers. Many in the IFL (or the 'Angles Circle' as it called itself after September 1939) placed hatred of the Jews and admiration for Hitler above patriotism in their response to the war. Individuals like Harold Lockwood, Elizabeth Berger, Tony Gittens and Bertie Mills were openly critical of Leese at IFL meetings. All these were later interned. The most significant of these in relation to the events of 1939–40 was Mills. He was to be one of the most active in the attempt to form a united alliance of the fascists, anti-semites and some of the peace movements in this period. The position of many in the IFL was summed up by a correspondent of Leese in 1940, who argued that he did not want to be ruled by Germans or other foreigners but that was nevertheless preferable to being ground under the heel of the Jewish financier and his pimps and proselytes.[23]

For the NL the war quickly led to a cessation of activities. Like most of the other fascist, anti-semite and pro-German organizations, apart from the BUF, the NL officially disbanded soon after the outbreak of war but its leading members continued to

---

[20] *Weekly Angles*, 24 Feb. 1940.
[21] *Weekly Angles*, 2 Mar. 1940.
[22] PRO HO 45/24967/105.
[23] Ibid.

meet in the house of Oliver Gilbert until his internment on 22 September. Two members of this extremist organization, William Joyce and Margaret Bothamley, had already gone to Germany and many of the other members had difficulty reconciling their extreme anti-semitism with their basic patriotism. There was a wide range of views amongst them on how they were to react now their country was at war. Few were willing to bear arms against Germany but the majority felt that nothing should be done which would prejudice Britain's interest. They should play their part in civilian defence and humanitarian work but should try to convince those with whom they worked of the 'real nature' of the causes of the war. Some, such as J.C. Vaneck, Oliver Gilbert and Aubrey Lees, were prepared to go further and Captain Archibald Maule Ramsay MP enlisted their support in the continuing dissemination of anti-semitic propaganda. This was to be distributed among MPs, clubs and the Services and leaflets and adhesive labels were to be distributed secretly during the night.[24] At a meeting on 11 September it was agreed to disband the NL and to encourage all members to sink their former differences with Mosley and join the BUF.[25]

Ramsay's other secret society, the Right Club (RC) continued in a clandestine form. Its original aim of purging the Conservative party of all Jewish influence and of infiltrating the establishment had been reduced to a secret operation of disseminating Ramsay's anti-semitic and pro-nazi propaganda.[26] Ramsay's concern was that the Jews as a result of a world-wide conspiracy were forcing on Europe a war in which millions of gentiles would be slaughtered. For him it was a patriotic crusade 'to save this country from the strangling tentacles of the Jewish octopus'.[27]

The other small racial nationalist and extreme anti-semitic organization of some relevance for this theme was the National Socialist League (NSL). This was the main vehicle for William Joyce's politics in 1937–8 after his split with Mosley, and was led jointly by John Beckett and himself. Joyce argued in *National Socialism Now* that Hitler was a great German patriot but that an English national socialism was needed for this country.[28] After he

[24] PRO HO 144/21382/298.
[25] PRO HO 144/22454/85–6.
[26] PRO HO 144/22454/87.
[27] PRO HO 144/22454/109.
[28] W. Joyce, *National Socialism Now* (London, 1937), p. 15.

fled to Germany in July 1939 he wrote that England was now
morally decaying and in terminal political decline and that only
Hitler's Germany could provide the leadership and drive for the
reconstruction of Europe.[29] His defeatist propaganda as Lord
Haw Haw on Radio Hamburg was to provide entertainment and
an alternative source of information for many during the phoney
war period, but once the war started in earnest he was to be
perceived as more sinister than amusing.[30]

Yet before his decision to replace Mosley with Hitler, Joyce had
been involved with Beckett in an attempt to broaden the influence
of national socialism through an alliance with Lord Lymington's
pseudo-left-wing peace organizations. The formation of the British
Council against European Commitments at the height of the
Czechoslovakia crisis directly linked the NSL with Lymington's
English Array. Although Joyce soon left, Beckett became deeply
involved with Lymington and his *New Pioneer* magazine in 1939.
Together with A.K. Chesterton, H.T. Mills, Lymington and
George Lane-Fox Pitt Rivers, this group published a mixture of
pro-German, anti-semitic and economic reform articles.
Lymington followed the romantic occultist and back-to-the-land
beliefs of Rolf Gardiner's native volkish movement, English
Mistery, and Pitt Rivers was a colonial administrator and
anthropologist who was strongly influenced by eugenics and a
belief in the conspiracy theory of history.[31]

In the summer of 1939 Beckett left to form a new political
movement, the British People's Party (BPP) with Lord Tavistock
(later the Duke of Bedford), Ben Greene and John Scanlon.
Greene, Beckett and Scanlon were all ex-members of the ILP, and
the latter two were ex-followers of Mosley. Together with
Tavistock's commitment to Social Credit, the new party was
dedicated to the cause of social reform at home and peace
abroad.[32] Its ideas were similar to those of the *New Pioneer* group
but had a more radical tinge. Its significance was that it provided
an alternative focus for the peace movement to that given by
Mosley. Even though some left-wing opponents could tar it with

[29] Idem, *Twilight over England* (Metairie, n.d.), pp. 129–42.
[30] 'Survey of broadcasts from Hamburg, December 1939 BBC', J.W. Hall (ed.), *Trial of William Joyce* (London, 1946), pp. 302–7; File 65, p. 2; 'Public and private opinion on Haw Haw' Mar. 1940, 29, *Mass Observation File Reports*.
[31] R. Griffiths, *Fellow Travellers*, pp. 319–29.
[32] Ibid., pp. 351–3.

the same fascist brush, the presence of Beckett as Tavistock's right-hand man meant that potential collaboration between the two movements would always be difficult, for Beckett still felt bitter hostility for Mosley since being made redundant from the BUF in 1937.

Of all the groups on the fascist fringe of British politics it was only Mosley's BUF that developed the coherent and systematic views on foreign policy which Skidelsky has seen as providing a genuinely credible alternative to government attitudes towards the dictators in the 1930s. Mosley argued that national socialism and fascism were essentially nationalist doctrines whose substance differed more widely between nations than international creeds in the past.[33] The BUF's policy was born of British inspiration and reflected her commitments alone, and was governed by the necessity of protecting Britain's vital interests in her Empire. Because Britain had world-wide imperial duties her power depended on protecting her geographically diffuse territories so it was vital for Britain to be on friendly terms with other potential rivals. She should no longer interfere in quarrels which did not clash with her vital interests, namely the development of the Empire. Mosley was particularly critical of the moral and international approach to foreign affairs of the dominant liberal ethos, and the British obsession with the balance of power in Europe, which he saw as irrelevant to her strategic requirements. He told the Advisory Committee in 1940 that he did not actively oppose the fact that Germany occupied Czechoslovakia, Poland, Austria, Belgium, Holland and France,[34] because European politics were not Britain's vital interest.

According to Mosley the fascist powers, namely Germany, Italy and Japan, should be encouraged to expand. German and Italian expansion, particularly in eastern Europe, were of no interest to Britain and their growing power would lead eventually to the collapse of the USSR, particularly if it was encircled through an alliance with Japan.[35] Japan should be encouraged to expand in northern China, thus avoiding a conflict with Britain's Far Eastern interests.

Mosley argued that these nations with their disparate interests

---

[33] O. Mosley, *Tomorrow We Live* (London, 1938), p. 2.
[34] PRO HO 283/14/83–4.
[35] O. Mosley, 'The world alternative', *Fascist Quarterly*, 2, 3 (July 1936), pp. 377–95.

had no incompatible problems which would lead to conflict between them. Hitler viewed Britain as a potential ally and we should encourage good relations by offering to return to Germany the mandated territories given to us at Versailles.

Even if his assessment of relations between fascist powers should prove optimistic, Mosley declared, the insurance policy of a thoroughgoing rearmament would deter any potential aggressor from attacking the British Empire. Since 1933 he had called repeatedly for a rapid expansion of all the Armed Services so that the resources of the Empire could be adequately protected.[36] Mosley contrasted this 'appeasement from strength' policy with the flaccid weakness of the National government's position in the 1930s, whose failure to start a rearmament policy early enough meant that by 1940 England was in danger of being reduced to a 'dungheap'.[37]

Mosley's views represented an alternative foreign policy which was totally ignored by the political establishment. This no doubt derived from the unofficial boycott in the media of his ideas after the 1934 Olympia meeting and from the natural suspicion that Mosley was a tool of Italian fascist and German nazi propaganda. It was also a reflection of the fact that Mosley had broken the rules of the political game and now operated outside the parameters of conventional discourse. The content of Mosley's views was based on very different assumptions to those of the political and diplomatic world. Not only was he opposed to the strategic basis on which British foreign policy since the eighteenth century had been formed, and the dominant ethos of liberal moralism and internationalism with which it had been conducted, but he presented his arguments in terms of an economic explanation of political decision-making which often degenerated into crude anti-semitism, particularly at movements of crisis. Thus an interpretation of the National government's foreign policy in terms of the Hobsonian theory of imperialism, which itself had no explanatory value in terms of what was really happening in the international economy in the 1930s, degenerated into the argument that Britain had been forced into war by a quarrel of Jewish finance against Germany because the nation was controlled

---

[36] *Blackshirt*, 24 June–1 July 1933; *Fascist Week*, 26 Jan.–1 Feb. 1934; *Blackshirt*, 5 July 1935.
[37] PRO HO 45/24895/10.

by Jews. Poland was supposedly a Jewish-controlled state under which millions were oppressed and the Nazi-Soviet Pact represented a Jewish communist plot to create war between Britain and Germany.[38]

Mosley was later to justify his foreign policy stand in the 1930s by arguing that it was the only credible alternative which would avoid the mass slaughter of European population and would save the continent from American imperialism and Russian communism. He argued that this was a patriotic policy designed to preserve the integrity of the British Empire. Mosley's arguments were close to the case put forward by Admiral Sir Barry Domvile, whose pro-German Link organization and connection with the Anglo-German Fellowship was based on the assumption that Britain needed to be friendly with the expansionary fascist powers if she was to preserve her Empire.[39] Domvile was to write for *Action* in 1939–40 and to co-operate closely both with Mosley and with other elements of the patriotic neo-fascist fringe in the British Council for Christian Settlement in Europe. The major difference between Domvile and Mosley was purely technical; the former emphasized the importance of the navy whilst the latter stressed air power as the most important part of Britain's defences.

There can be little doubt that the views of Mosley and Domvile on foreign policy and defence were sincere and persuasively argued. The Advisory Committee itself acknowledged this and said that Mosley's views and actions were not illegal. However, apart from the increasing moral revulsion with which politicians and significant public opinion came to view the dictators' actions after Munich showed their word could not be trusted, there were a number of factors which meant that Mosley's outlook could not be seen as a credible alternative. Most important was the fact that the constant British attempts to unify dominion attitudes had met with increasing rebuffs in the inter-war period. Not only were Canada and South Africa showing marked differences to British interests in political policy, but Australia and New Zealand were very concerned about Japanese intentions in the Pacific since the lapse of the Anglo-Japanese treaty.[40] The Empire, hardly a figment

---

[38] PRO HO 144/21429/6; HO 45/24895/22.
[39] Admiral Sir B. Domvile, *Stand by your Moat* (London, 1937).
[40] R. Thurlow, 'The Return of Jeremiah', in *British Fascism*, ed. K. Lunn and R. Thurlow (London, 1980), p. 107; Barnett, pp. 121–234.

of the imagination in terms of power politics, was nevertheless a disunited force containing disparate beliefs. Mosley's view of the Empire was to impose British interests and the fascist system of government on the dominions, the colonies and India, but the reality of growing independence within and between various elements meant that only a very loose confederation based on consent not force was a tangible option. Mosley's view of leadership was alien not only to the British political tradition but to the development of the dominions as well.

If Mosley's assumptions could be criticized as unrealistic in the political world of the 1930s, they could also be attacked from the nationalist perspective. Mosley seemed unaware that the leading British geopolitical theorist, Halford Mackinder, who based his analysis on similar neo-mercantile assumptions as the fascists in relating economic resources to strategic interests, had come to diametrically opposed conclusions. For Mackinder the control of the heartland of Eurasia, a combined German–Russian empire, would directly threaten Britain's interests and because of the geographical concentration of resources such a combination would be a more powerful force than the scattered units of the British Empire.[41] It was Hitler and not Mosley who was influenced by this view.

It is now clear that although there were lingering suspicions, the Government and the Security Service accepted much of Mosley's explanation that his actions derived from genuine patriotic motives. His appeal before the Advisory Committee on Internment in 1940 developed mainly into an examination of the charge of foreign influence on the BUF. Mosley valiantly defended himself, arguing that even the most obvious similarities between BUF style, uniform and policy and their foreign counterparts in fact derived solely from British roots. The Committee was not convinced by such explanation,[42] and was very suspicious of the arrangements the BUF made to pay foreign currencies into a secret account and the supposed lack of knowledge Mosley professed about the sources of the movement's finances. They viewed rather more

---

[41] P. Hayes, 'The contribution of British intellectuals to fascism', in Lunn and Thurlow, *British Fascism*, pp. 183–4; H. Mackinder, 'The geographical pivot of history', *Geographical Journal*, 23, 4 (Apr. 1904), pp. 421–44; idem, *Democratic Ideals and Reality* (London, 1919), pp. 191–235.
[42] PRO HO 45/24891/40–5.

charitably Mosley's explanations of his negotiations, via his second wife the former Diana Mitford, with the nazis to set up a commercial radio station to beam programmes to Britain from Germany. The commercial profits from this were to be used to fund the BUF. They also concluded that Mosley's policy of opposing the war while asking his followers not to take any action which would hinder its prosecution was the product of a very clever mind determined to keep the BUF within the law.[43]

The general conclusion of the Advisory Commission was that Mosley had been frank with them when it suited his purpose and evasive when he wished to hide or cover up his actions. We now know that Mosley was indeed funded by Mussolini in the early years of the movement and that the BUF's 'Mind Britain's Business' campaign in support of the Italian invasion of Abyssinia was more than an altruistic display of sympathy. Similarly, Mosley's sincere opposition to the Second World War nevertheless had a material side, since war meant the loss of his investment and ingenious plans to corner the market in commercial radio advertising. Mosley's secrecy and the covering-up activity showed his obsession with minimizing the damage the Security Service could inflict. As well as hiding the laundering of Mussolini's lira, the secret negotiations over the wireless franchise and his wedding in Berlin in 1936, Mosley went out of his way to confuse the Security Service. When he discovered a nazi agent in the organization in 1936 he immediately sacked him and he ostentatiously avoided the German embassy and known nazi agents in England. Presumably he was unaware that Joyce was sending highly unreliable intelligence about the BUF to Berlin in 1936.

It appeared that the BUF had no links with the nazis and they certainly received no financial assistance from them. Diana Mosley was a personal friend of Hitler and she was instrumental in gaining the wireless franchise but there is no evidence of other links to them. Mosley's later comment that he would rather die fighting for his country against invaders than be a Quisling is understandable, as was his belief that long before that situation would have arisen after an invasion he would have been killed by the Security Service.[44] Mosley was only interested in power after

[43] PRO HO 45/24891/63.
[44] N. Longmate, *If Britain had Fallen* (London, 1975), p. 116.

a negotiated peace which left the integrity of the British Empire intact. Hitler's attitude to defeated nations and most other fascist movements in western Europe made that eventuality unlikely.[45]

The Patriots International, 1939–1940

If German influence and connection proved to be problematic, the committal of illegal behaviour by fascist groups in the war was even more negligible. Only a handful of minor cases of BUF personnel trying to help the Germans were discovered by the Security Service.[46] Mosley told the Advisory Committee that he thought only 5 per cent of the membership of his organization were suspect. MI5 officers told the Home Secretary that between one-quarter and one-third of members were security risks.[47]

Even with the imminent danger of a German invasion and the fifth column scare this vague accusation seemed insufficient evidence for making members of the BUF the main victims of the Tyler Kent affair, an event with which they had no connection whatsoever and which will be fully discussed in the next chapter. This fact makes the enigmatic secret annexe to the Cabinet minutes of 22 May 1940 more mysterious. This argued that Ramsay had been involved in 'treasonable practices' and was 'in relations with' Sir Oswald Mosley although on another matter. Whether Tyler Kent is viewed as an American patriot, an isolationist or a Soviet agent, he was obviously a serious security risk. Ramsay too was in a position to inflict great damage if he made public Tyler Kent's documents. Yet Mosley had been assessed by MI5 as at worst a clever but misguided patriot and the Home Secretary had only recently emphasized in the Cabinet that he was very clear in his instructions to members not to impede the war effort.

Anthony Masters has argued that the linking of Ramsay with Mosley represented an attempt by Maxwell Knight and MI5 to convince the War Cabinet that a major right-wing coup was being planned, and that there was no concrete evidence for this accu-

---

[45] D. Littlejohn, *The Patriotic Traitors* (London, 1972), pp. 335–8.
[46] West, *MI5 Operations*, pp. 161–3.
[47] PRO HO 283/16/88.

sation.[48] A close survey of the first three releases of Home Office papers on British fascism does produce one document which throws some light on this matter. This is a Special Branch report of 25 June 1940, in the Commandant Mary Allen file. It states that when Aubrey Lees was detained on 20 June 1940 under DR 18b he was found to be in possession of two typewritten letters, unheaded and unsigned, concerning meetings at 48 Ladbroke Grove, W11, in March, April and May 1940. Lees refused to discuss the object of these meetings but said they were secret affairs and stated that amongst the people attending were Sir Oswald Mosley and Commandant Mary Allen. What was described as 'a very reliable informant' reported that these meetings were convened by Mosley and Ramsay and attended by leading members of the various pro-nazi and anti-semitic organizations in Britain. The object was to secure the greatest possible collaboration between them and make preparations for a *coup d'état*.[49] On her Advisory Committee appeal Commandant Allen denied having attended such meetings but thought the address was the home of Mrs Dacre-Fox who ran an anti-vivisection society.[50] This was a known fascist front organization and Professor Dacre-Fox was later interned.

One other released Special Branch report refers to a secret meeting between prominent fascists and anti-semites on 7 February 1940. This was convened by Mosley and amongst those who attended were Francis Hawkins, Domvile, Lane Fox Pitt-Rivers, Aubrey Lees, the Earl of Mar and Norman Hay. This was similar to a previous meeting held on 9 November 1939. The chief decision taken at the 7 February meeting was to fight Silvertown and Leeds North East by-elections.[51] The important point about this report is that its reliability with regard to who attended the 7 February meeting can be confirmed from an independent source, the diary of Admiral Sir Barry Domvile. The entry for 7 February 1940 states that Domvile attended a Mosley meeting and that amongst others attending were Lane Fox Pitt-Rivers, Francis Hawkins and Aubrey Lees.[52] Domvile also attended another

[48] Masters, *The Man who was M*, p. 90.
[49] PRO HO 144/21933/330.
[50] PRO HO 144/21933/418.
[51] PRO HO 45/24895/16.
[52] Dom. 56, 7 Feb. 1940.

Mosley meeting on 8 November (the discrepancy of one day was probably accounted for by the fact that Special Branch reports were sometimes written the day after events took place). The most interesting fact about this meeting was that Mosley and Ramsay were the main speakers.

The evidence in Domvile's diary suggests that he was one of the motivating forces behind the initiative to gain a greater degree of unity amongst the fascist and anti-semitic movements. Indeed, his organization the Link was aptly named. Not only did it provide a channel for Ribbentrop and Goebbels to influence British public opinion,[53] but Domvile saw his role as the key link man between the various groups. He wrote for the BUF newspaper under the pseudonym 'Canute' or 'Naval Expert', he spoke for the BPP candidate in the Hythe by-election, he was on friendly terms with Ramsay, Norman Hay, Lane Fox Pitt-Rivers and Tavistock, as well as founding the Link. As a retired admiral, an ex-assistant secretary to the Committee of Imperial Defence 1912–14, Director of Naval Intelligence 1927–30, and president of the Royal Naval College at Greenwich 1932–4, his patriotism and the accuracy of his diary seem beyond reproach. His daily addiction to the writing of his diary spanned his long active life from the 1890s to the early 1970s; it can now be consulted at the National Maritime Museum at Greenwich. What information can be gleaned from the Home Office Papers confirms much of the detail of Domvile's account, as do the internment files on Aubrey Lees and Neil Francis Hawkins.

Domvile's diary for the phoney war period is a significant document because it lists many of the people who attended the meetings he was at, as well as some cryptic references to the discussion. The general picture which emerges from the diary is that there were loose connections between fascists, anti-semites and peace movements from before the war. Many BUF members helped H. St John Philby, the diplomat and noted Arabian explorer, when he obtained 578 votes for the BPP at the Hythe by-election in July 1939.[54] Domvile attended a dinner with Mosley when Ramsay was also present on the 26 July 1939.[55] In the early phoney war period the diary lists the meetings of the British Council for Christian Settlement in Europe with ex-

[53] S. Wiggins, 'The Link', MA diss., University of St Andrews, 1985, p. 6.
[54] Dom. 56, 14 and 21 July 1939.
[55] Ibid., 26 July 1939.

Mosleyites like Gordon Canning, ex-members of the closed Link and NL, and members of the BPP.[56] After this attempt to rally public support for a peace campaign had been exposed as being dominated by well-known fascists and anti-semites, Domvile took the initiative in persuading Mosley to organize meetings of the pro-nazi and anti-semitic organizations and other fellow-travellers of the right who desired an end to the war.[57]

These meetings took place at fortnightly intervals between October and December 1939.[58] The first on 26 October, when it was decided to hold regular meetings of the group, was attended by the leading members of the BUF, the Link, the BPP, the *New Pioneer* group, Information and Policy, the RC and the NL. Those who attended some of these meetings represented many of those categorized as extremists in Griffiths's *Fellow Travellers of the Right*. They included Ramsay, Domvile, Lymington, Lane Fox Pitt-Rivers, Mills, Lees, C.G. Grey of the *Aeroplane*, Commandant Mary Allen, Major-General Fuller, Francis Yeats Brown, A.P. Laurie, Norman Hay, Lady Pearson, Lady Dunn and Francis Hawkins. The meetings were deliberately kept secret as all present were very worried by the threat of internment should their activities be made public. From Domvile's list it is possible to deduce that the BUF, the Link and the NL appeared to be more enthusiastic participants than the Tavistock and Lymington groups.

After Christmas 1939 Domvile's diary is less suggestive. He attended fewer meetings, which may not be that significant as the handwriting deteriorates and he appears to have been ill for part of the winter. What is significant is that Ramsay was not mentioned as attending the two meetings of 17 January and 7 February although other ex-members of the Link and the NL were.[59] A fresh impetus to the flagging peace hopes of the extremists was provided by Lord Tavistock as a result of his obtaining Hitler's draft peace proposals from the German legation in Dublin and the published correspondence resulting with the Home Secretary.[60] This set off a flurry of activity and Domvile

---

[56] Ibid., 19 Sept. and 18 Oct. 1939; PRO HO 144/22454/87–8.
[57] Dom. 56, 26 Oct. 1939.
[58] Ibid., 26 Oct. 1939, 8 Nov. 1939, 22 Nov. 1939, 6 Dec. 1939.
[59] Ibid., 17 Jan. 1940, 7 Feb. 1940.
[60] Tavistock, *The Fate of a Peace Effort* (High Wycombe, 1940).

arranged a meeting between Mosley, Tavistock, Mills and himself on 13 March. At this meeting Mosley was reported as saying that Lloyd George would have to come back and lead a 'Peace Government'.[61] However, apart from attending a few Information and Policy meetings and reports of tea with Mrs Ramsay there are no significant reports of meetings before his internment.

It is also apparent from 'Dom 56' that Domvile was well aware of the significance of this volume of his diary. Although he held eccentric views on Hitler and the Jews, which were transformed into a peculiar personal conspiracy theory by the experience of internment, Domvile was certainly no fool with regard to intelligence matters. He was highly critical of British Intelligence when Director of Naval Intelligence and he blamed falling out with Vernon Kell, the Head of MI5, between the wars as one of the causes of his early retirement. The reason why volume 56 of the diary can now be consulted is because, as he explained inside the original cover of the book before it was rebound, it was hidden under the henhouse just before Special Branch arrested him, and although gnawed by rats, it was then taken indoors by the 'faithful household'.[62]

Domvile was fully aware of the significance of the list of names and meetings he produced in his diary. Yet the very fact that he felt able to write about them at the time, given his previous intimate experience of the Security Service, strongly suggests that nothing of an illegal nature could have been discussed at these meetings. The fact that he was the instigator of these secret meetings and that he mentioned in his diary some relevant details of the first of them (where MI5 alleged treasonable activities were discussed on 15 March), would support this interpretation. Domvile knew that fascists and fellow travellers were prime candidates to be made scapegoats to public opinion for the fifth column scare, and the immediate crisis which faced the British government in April and May 1940.

Ramsay too was well aware of the risks he was taking with his continued anti-semitic campaign, and indeed he gave Tyler Kent the membership list of the RC because he thought he would have diplomatic immunity. This, however, did not prove to be the case.

[61] Dom. 56, 13 March 1940.
[62] Dom. 56, original cover.

There is evidence that Ramsay co-operated closely with Mosley during the last half of 1939. Not only does the Domvile diary suggest that Ramsay played a leading role in the peace campaign, but Special Branch reported that the NL side of Ramsay's operations closed down and several ex-members joined the BUF, most notably at the Maida Vale branch.[63] Much the same appears to have occurred to the anti-semites and fascists who were in the Link. Special Branch reported that Mosley and Ramsay had reached agreement on 16 September on a common policy towards the war. They agreed on a continued peace campaign whilst avoiding engaging in activity which could be construed as treasonable. The RC were, however, apparently more suspicious of Mosley and unlike the NL were unprepared to sink former differences and regard him as their new leader.

The split response to Mosley as a unifying leader of the anti-semitic and fascist groups campaigning for a negotiated peace with Hitler was typical of Ramsay's judgement. As the intelligence reports of NL meetings signified, he oscillated between a wild extremism which appeared to sanction the use of force against the Jews, the need to purify the Conservative party by whatever means came to hand, and a rigid constitutionalism which warned his followers not to use illegal methods. His failure to use the Tyler Kent documents showed similar indecision. There appeared to be an unresolved tension between his fanatical hatred of the Jews, which developed in 1938, and his undoubted patriotism. The Security Service argued that he wished to co-operate with the Germans in the conquest and government of Great Britain,[64] but his contact with Germany appeared to be limited to one dinner at the German embassy and such sentiments were against his deepest instincts. Ramsay was an eccentric patriot, a brave soldier who had been injured in the First World War, and for whom the concept of treason was anathema. Yet virulent hatred of the Jews led him to sympathize with the rationale behind nazi anti-semitism. He wished to cleanse Britain of Jews without the help of the nazis.

The apparent decline in the contact between Mosley and Ramsay after Christmas 1939 may have represented a cooling in

[63] PRO HO 144/22454/86.
[64] A.H.M. Ramsay, *The Nameless War* (London, 1952), p. 102.

relationships. At no stage was Mosley impressed by the crude anti-semitism of Ramsay, and the latter or his supporters may have been resentful of the intellectual and political leadership of the BUF. Alternatively they may have reached a conscious decision to try to confuse the Security Service, with Mosley and Ramsay deciding not to meet together but with the latter's interests being looked after by Aubrey Lees or other ex-NL members. Whatever occurred, there are signs that Mosley and the BUF began to see the NL as an infernal nuisance and as a potential lightning conductor for increased public hostility to the BUF after April 1940. Raven Thomson suggested at a BUF meeting that a propaganda attack should be made on the NL people, accusing them of being nazi traitors while emphasizing the BUF's absolute loyalty to Britain and the Empire.[65]

Mosley's own explanation before the Advisory Committee of his political behaviour in the 1939–40 period represented another area where he was evasive and told less than the whole truth. There were elements of ambiguity in the explanation he offered. On relations with Ramsay he said quite truthfully that he knew nothing of the 'American business', as he called the Tyler Kent affair, until he was told Ramsay's version of it in Brixton. He claimed that he did not get to know Ramsay until they were interned, as he ran his own show, although he had been to see him to ask questions in the House of Commons. On another occasion he said that Ramsay had been to see him four or five times in the office to discuss questions of mutual concern such as anti-semitism. He now liked Ramsay personally but implied that he had very violent views about Jews and freemasons.[66] He admitted to working with Domvile, who would often visit him in his office and published articles by him in *Action*.[67] Mosley's views of the NL were more vitriolic. He thought they were a parasitic organization who took to extremes the views of the BUF, and that they made the whole principled stand of the peace campaign look foolish.[68]

What was clearly evasive in Mosley's answers was that he never at any stage admitted holding meetings with other organizations,

[65] PRO HO 45/24895/34.
[66] PRO HO 283/14/85–6.
[67] PRO HO 283/14/91.
[68] PRO HO 283/16/72.

THE HITLER FAN CLUB

despite the long list of such events chronicled in Domvile's diary. Occasionally some intimations of these occasions emerged in his answers. Thus his various attacks on the NL and other small societies, whom he portrayed mainly as those who had been thrown out of the BUF, included a very interesting comment on one who had attended NL and BUF meetings. This was Aubrey Lees, in whose possession Special Branch found the invitations to secret meetings. For Mosley, Lees was 'absolutely certifiable', although whether this was a result of his extremist views or of the fact that he opposed Mosley's line on every occasion is not clear from the context in which he made the remark.[69] It is clear, however, that although Mosley painted others as extremists and himself as thoroughly patriotic, Ramsay told the Committee of some of the details of the conversation he had with him, one of which related to Mosley inviting Ramsay to take over Scotland 'in certain circumstances'.[70] The Advisory Committee used this example as an indication of their belief that Mosley had been far from frank with them.

If Mosley was somewhat reticent about his relations with other fascist groups and fellow travellers before the Advisory Committee, others were more forthcoming. Neil Francis Hawkins said that he had met Lord Tavistock about co-ordinating the activities of those groups who had views about the war similar to the BUF. Various meetings were held in the early part of the war to concentrate the efforts of those who believed in the movement for negotiating peace. Francis Hawkins who had represented the British Fascists in the merger talks with the New Party in 1932 and had experience of such activities was a natural choice for Mosley to make as the BUF's chief negotiator. Hawkins also told the committee that at one of these meetings Lord Lymington, Sir Barry Domvile, Lord Tavistock and Bertie Mills were present.[71]

Aubrey Lees also convinced the Committee that there was nothing untoward in the three meetings he attended. According to Domvile's diary these were on the 8 November, 6 December 1939 and 7 February 1940, and indeed Lees categorically stated to the Advisory Committee that he attended no more meetings after the

[69] PRO HO 283/13/73.
[70] PRO HO 45/24891/49.
[71] PRO HO 45/25700. Advisory Commission Report on Neil Francis Hawkins 29 July 1940.

latter date. Lees said that at the first meeting, to which he had been invited by Ramsay, Mosley read out a long statement relating to a BUF internee named Thomas and that the meeting was about the preservation of civil liberties. He attended the second for personal reasons in order to see Domvile who through his naval and military connections might be able to get him an army post to release him from his new appointment as a colonial civil servant on the Gold Coast. A Special Branch report suggested the third meeting was about supporting BUF candidates in by-elections. Lees persuaded the Committee that there was nothing wrong or unusual about any of these three meetings, and it was this fact and because he had been wrongly accused of being a member of the BUF which led to the Home Secretary agreeing with the Advisory Committee that he should be released from internment in October 1940.[72]

Lees' files also contain further information on the three meetings in March, April and May 1940 which Special Branch were so concerned about. These relate to meetings on 13 March, 17 April and 29 May 1940.[73] Domvile's diary shows that there was a meeting on 13 March attended by Mosley, Domvile, Mills and Tavistock about the desirability of a negotiated peace. There is no mention of Lees being present and the evidence in Domvile's diary appears to confirm that he was honest to the Committee about attendance at such meetings. There is no mention in Domvile's diary of the alleged meetings of 17 April and 29 May 1940. Indeed, given that many of those who would have been invited to 29 May meeting were already interned by that date and others would have been concerned about their own immediate future, it is extremely unlikely that the last meeting ever took place. In general, then, the evidence in Domvile's diary and the released internment files strongly suggests that the so-called secretive behaviour of fascist groups decreased rather than increased between the autumn of 1939 and the spring of 1940, and that collaboration between the groups, which was never very great, proved to be of no significance during the crisis of spring 1940.

Whatever the complex truth about the nature of the Patriots International in 1939–40 it is quite clear that the relationships

[72] PRO HO 283/45. Advisory Commission Report on Aubrey Lees 5 Sept. 1940.
[73] PRO HO 45/25728. Special Branch Report 22 June 1940.

between the individuals and organizations concerned were far from harmonious. The mixed collection of fascists, anti-semites, pacifists, Social Credit enthusiasts and neo-nazi extremists had little in common except a burning desire to bring the war to a negotiated peace as quickly as possible and to maintain the integrity of the British Empire. A very reliable informant told the authorities that some collaboration resulted from these meetings but those present could not agree who should be leader.[74] Hardly surprising, such meetings failed dismally to produce a coherent united front or influence the public. Although all the organizations concerned adopted a common programme of opposing the war while doing nothing to upset Britain's vital interests, the public, in so far as they were aware of the fascist political fringe, viewed them at best with suspicion. Even though there was considerable evidence that public opinion was not wholeheartedly behind the war effort in the phoney war period, the fascists were unable to capitalize on this fact at that time.

[74] Ibid. Special Branch Report 8 June 1940.

9

Internment, 1939–1945

> Within those walls confined at night
> I often heard them cry
> Although my woes were far more light
> My own eyes were not dry,
> It seemed that justice came that way
> And haughtily passed by.
>
> Nellie Driver, 'The Ballad of Holloway Gaol'

The story of the internment of British fascists has been conveniently swept under the carpet with the tacit agreement of most of the parties involved. An obsession with secrecy has characterized all British governments in the twentieth century with reference to national security considerations, even with regard to British fascism which has no relation to current problems in that area. Such reticence is justified also by the need to protect sources of information in intelligence-gathering activities and to cover up the sometimes dubious methods employed in security and espionage operations. Whatever the merits of such a policy in security terms, they are a nuisance to historians of British fascism. Of the surviving Defence Regulation 18b internment files, 18 out of 54 have not been released in the HO45 series and 19 out of 49 in the HO283 series. In addition to this many subfiles and some transcripts of Advisory Committee hearings within the released material have been kept by the Home Office. Practically the whole of this material is retained under Section 3(4) of the Public Records Act, which means there is no present intention of

releasing it in the foreseeable future. About 15 individuals who
were associated with fascist groups have had their files released.

The information given by fascists on internment also has
notable gaps. It is informative on prison conditions and aspects of
physical deprivation but less than helpful on the reasons why the
government felt it necessary to lock up fascists and fellow travellers in the first place. While there is no doubt that the vast
majority of internees imprisoned under DR 18b (1a) were unjustly
incarcerated, the deafening silence about the stupidity of Maule
Ramsay and the secretive behaviour of Mosley and others on the
fascist and anti-semitic fringe in the phoney war period is
suspicious to say the least. In particular the fact that there is not
one word on the Tyler Kent affair (see p. 194) in either Sir Oswald
or Lady Mosley's autobiographies, or in Skidelsky's or Nicholas
Mosley's biographies, is highly significant. In one sense it is
understandable, of course. The Mosleys had no connection
whatsoever with Tyler Kent and only learned about his activities
in prison. However, the significance of this event and its rami-
fications most certainly would have been immediately recognized
by Sir Oswald Mosley. There appears to have been a sophisticated
cover-up operation ever since to deny the secret meetings across
the fascist political fringe in 1939–40 and the links between
Mosley, Maule Ramsay and others, which has continued to the
present day, even though Maule Ramsay died in 1955 and Lady
Mosley has recently discussed some aspects of the Tyler Kent
affair with Anthony Masters. Given that the balance of the
evidence suggests that Mosley and most of the fascist fringe were
not indulging in illegal behaviour in 1939–40, the fact that so
much has been deliberately obfuscated for so long increases rather
than decreases whatever suspicions remain.

Yet the internment of British fascists is obviously an important
episode: fascists and fellow travellers were the main native victims
of internment during the Second World War, along with a few IRA
members and pacifists. Not only that, internment destroyed British
fascism, and its later resurrection in various revisionist or
derivative forms was compromised from the outset by the smear of
the necessity for preventive detention for fascists in the Second
World War and the fear of infiltration by MI5 agents. The *de facto*
suspension of habeas corpus with regard to interned fascists also
represented one of the darkest pages in Britain's liberal tradition;
unlike the IRA in the 1940s and 1970s the vast majority of interned

fascists were British patriots not engaged in subversive or terrorist activities. The fact that the government felt that such a draconian change of policy towards the fascists was necessary demands fuller explanation than it has so far received.

The background to internment

The Second World War, with Britain at conflict with the two major fascist powers by 1940, placed native fascists in an invidious position. Most of the fascist and pro-nazi organizations apart from the BUF immediately closed down in September 1939 to avoid possible official retribution. The government had already rushed through Parliament on 24 August 1939 an Emergency Powers Act which empowered it to make regulations by Orders in Council for the Defence of the Realm. These sweeping powers enabled the government to promulgate Defence Regulation 18b on 1 September 1939; this allowed the authorities to detain those whom they had cause to believe were capable of prejudicial acts against the state. Its effect was to remove the main defence to civil liberties provided by the Habeas Corpus Acts. This legislation represented an instinctive response by government to the threat of war. In fact the authorities had no plans to intern large numbers of aliens or native fascists; the Home Office under Sir John Anderson wished to maintain as great a degree of civil liberty as the necessary emphasis on national security would permit. His primary objective was not to repeat the mistakes of the First World War when public pressure had led to the internment of 32,000 aliens and the repatriation of 20,000 others.[1]

Apart from the wish not to follow the same path in internment matters as in the First World War, there was one essential difference between the security situation in 1939 and that in 1914. This was the fact that there had been no important native pro-German organization in 1914, whereas in 1939 British fascists could be assumed by the uninformed to have close ideological affinities with the German nazis which would compromise their patriotism. In fact this problem did not arise until May 1940. During the phoney war the BUF failed to capitalize on the less than

[1] C. Andrew, *Secret Service*, pp. 181–2.

wholehearted public support for hostilities. Mosley's highly successful rallies at Ridley Road, Dalston, Kingsway, Bethnal Green and Manchester's Free Trade Hall during the autumn and winter of 1939–40,[2] and the British Union Luncheon at the Criterion Restaurant as late as 26 April 1940 with over 400 in attendance,[3] did not reflect significant public opinion. The poor performances of the British Union candidates in the three by-elections fought at Silvertown, North-East Leeds and Middleton and Prestwich in 1940 was rather more typical. They all received miniscule votes representing less than 3 per cent of those who voted either in straight fights with the 'old gang' party whose seat it was, or in a three-cornered contest with the communists as the other participants. Indeed in Silvertown, in an area adjacent to its area of greatest strength in the East End of London in the late 1930s, the BUF received only one-sixth of the communist vote.

The fact that the DR 18b powers were seen more as a weapon of last resort than as immediately applicable was seen in the early history of the legislation. In the first months of the war only 12 were arrested under its sweeping powers, including four with British fascist connections. All detainees were given the right to appeal to an Advisory Committee whose function was to advise the Home Secretary regarding the internment of DR 18b prisoners, and the internment and repatriation of enemy aliens detained under the Royal Prerogative (until 7 June 1940).

This Advisory Committee was hurriedly set up under the chairmanship of Sir Walter Monckton. However, he was soon transferred to the Ministry of Information and was replaced by Norman Birkett KC. Under Birkett the Committee was to conduct its most important hearings in 1940. The Advisory Committee was a strange legal hybrid set up to provide a safety net for those who could prove that the authorities had earlier made a mistake in interning them or who could show they were no longer a threat to national security. As there was little in the way of precedent for such an institution it made its own rules up as its work expanded. Its first meeting on 21 Septeember 1939 decided that appellants should present their appeals in person and not be assisted by counsel or solicitors.[4] After the Committee heard a case it passed

---

[2] *Action*, 12 Oct. 1939, 19 Oct. 1939, 23 Nov. 1939, 8 Feb. 1940.

[3] C 6/9/3/13, Board of Deputies Archive.

[4] PRO HO 283/22, memorandum on work of Advisory Committee by Norman Birkett, 5 Mar. 1941.

its recommendation regarding the detainee to MI5, who then either agreed to or rejected its findings before sending them on to the Home Secretary who made the final decision on whether the detention order should be extended.

The release of two personal files relating to fascists who were detained and the review of all the Orders made before the revision of DR 18b on 23 November 1939 give some insight into the security situation regarding the supposed threat posed by British fascists at this time. Only one of the fascist detainees, E. J. Thomas, was a member of the BUF in 1939 and the Advisory Committee recommended his release after the hearing, a decision upheld by the Home Secretary. It was the Thomas case, and the threat posed by DR 18b, which led Mosley to attempt co-operation with other fascist groups in the phoney war period. Oliver C. Gilbert, an ex-member of the BUF and member of the NL who had visited Germany with Thomas in May 1939, was detained for 4½ years for having 'hostile associations' with German and Japanese agents in London, for preventing Thomas making anti-nazi sentiments on his return to London for fear of damaging the BUF, and for knowing that Hoffman of Munich provided nazi propaganda for distribution at NL meetings.[5] In its review of the case the Committee admitted there was no convincing proof that Gilbert had ever committed an illegal act.[6]

The other two cases involving fascists also raised serious questions about the infringement of civil liberties. Quintin Joyce was interned for nearly four years on the grounds that he was a friend of a known nazi agent called Christian Baur who lived in England between 1934 and 1937, that he was a member of the NSL and brother of William Joyce and might try to communicate with him in Germany, and because of his admiration for Hitler.[7] The Committee were highly suspicious of Joyce's correspondence with Baur in June 1939 when the latter asked for British African stamps of Somaliland, South and East Africa for a friend. The Committee suggested that in certain circles stamps were a euphemism for maps.[8] Victor Rowe, a strongly pro-nazi member

---

[5] PRO HO 45/25692, report of Advisory Committee on O. C. Gilbert, 23 Oct. 1939.
[6] PRO HO 45/25758, review of Orders made before the revision of 18b.
[7] PRO HO 45/25690, petition from Edwin Quintin Joyce.
[8] PRO HO 45/25690, report of Advisory Committee on E. Q. Joyce, 25 Oct. 1939; PRO HO 283/43, transcript of Advisory Committee hearing E. Q. Joyce, 16 Oct. 1939, pp. 17–19.

of the NL, was interned for over four years for boasting that he could or did travel by air from Croydon to Germany without passing through airport control and further that he was an import agent of German goods and well supplied with finance which did not originate in his own business. Rowe argued that although he festooned his flat with nazi regalia his claims were made out of bravado and he had never been to Germany, and the Committee concluded that he was generally unreliable and mentally unstable.[9]

If these cases represented the most blatant examples of British fascist connections with the enemy then it is clear that the Security Service had the home front well under control and that growing dissatisfaction with the infringement of civil liberties during the phoney war period was justified. In fact in all four cases the authorities could not prove any illegal activity whatsoever. As a result of back bench pressure the government was forced to amend DR 18b on 23 November 1939 to the effect that the authorities must have reasonable cause to believe the hostile origins or association of individuals or that internees must have been recently concerned in actions which had compromised national security. This change was to cause problems when the grave military situation in May 1940 led the new government to a drastic alteration in security policy and the decision to intern not only most aliens but British fascists as well.

The decision to intern

The decision to terminate the activities of British fascism and to intern the leading members of the various organizations represented the conjunction of several influences. The collapse of the dominoes in western Europe before the nazi blitzkrieg in April and May 1940, with the fall of Norway, Denmark, Holland and Belgium and the failure to stop the attack on France, brought to an end the complacency of the phoney war period. This was succeeded by a 'fifth column' scare, manufactured by credulous diplomats in Holland and reinforced by a hysterical Rothermere press, which threw suspicion on all aliens, fascists and fellow

[9] PRO HO 45/25758, review of Orders made before the revision of 18b.

travellers as potential traitors. The same spy fantasies which had been projected by popular novelists like William Le Queux and E. Phillips Oppenheim before 1914 suddenly seemed much more plausible in 1940.[10] Fascism was now seen as a potential nazi Trojan horse within Britain. Given what had happened in Norway, the public leaped to the conclusion that Mosley was a prime candidate for a potential British quisling, and overnight indifference to his person turned into outright hostility as signified by the physical assault on him at the Middleton and Prestwich by-election in May 1940.

This was the background as to why the new prime minister, Winston Churchill, who had succeeded Chamberlain after the Norway fiasco on 10 May, thought there should be a very large round-up of enemy aliens and suspect persons in Britain.[11] However, the Home Office resisted the extension of internment to mass detention of a group of British citizens. While ostensibly seeing the wisdom of such a move, Sir John Anderson pointed out to the Cabinet that the police would be overtaxed just processing the aliens, and as there had been no evidence of fifth column activities by either fascists or communists he would not proceed to move against either of these groups at present. This was a view he maintained at both the Cabinet meetings of 15 and 18 May when the issue was discussed.[12]

This resistance was overridden by the implications of the Tyler Kent affair, which proved to be the trigger mechanism for the immediate internment of British fascists. The Tyler Kent affair arose when MI5 agents in the Right Club uncovered a real breach of national security. They discovered a link via a member of the RC, Anna Wolkoff, between a cipher clerk at the American Embassy, Tyler Kent, and the Italian Embassy. They also discovered that Wolkoff and Kent had shown crucial intercepted documents between 'Naval Person' (Churchill) and President Roosevelt to Maule Ramsay. Maxwell Knight, the head of B5b in MI5 and in charge of placing agents in fascist and communist groups in Britain, linked such information to the belief of the Government's Code and Cipher School's intercept system that the German ambassador in Rome, Hans Mackenson, had been look-

[10] Andrew, *Secret Service*, pp. 34–5.
[11] PRO Cab. 65/7 WM 123 (40), p. 139.
[12] PRO Cab. 65/7 WM 128 (40), p. 177.

ing at Churchill's correspondence with Roosevelt.[13] As Churchill's correspondence was carried on without the knowledge of the Cabinet, if Kent published his material in a pro-isolationist publication in the United States, or Maule Ramsay asked a question about it in the British Parliament, there was a real possibility that the secretly pro-interventionist Roosevelt would not be re-elected and that Churchill's government would fall. Roosevelt although supporting American isolationism in public was working behind the scenes to increase aid to the beleagured British.

The Security Service decided to act and Tyler Kent was caught red-handed on 20 May 1940, not only with a girl friend in bed but also with copies of 1,500 secret documents, including the Roosevelt-Churchill correspondence, and the 'red book', the list of members of the RC. It was these discoveries coupled with supposedly reliable information that Maule Ramsay and Mosley were 'in relations',[14] and that attempts were being made to unify fascist, anti-semitic and peace groups, which led the Cabinet and the Security Service to strike at the entire anti-war neo-fascist fringe and not just the RC.

The Security Service had claimed that Maule Ramsay was organizing meetings of the pro-nazi and anti-semitic groups with Mosley, and Anderson later confirmed that one of the main reasons why the fascists had been interned and the communists left free was because of the secrecy surrounding the former's activities and the open manner of the latter. During the phoney war the BUF and the communist party both opposed the war. The authorities, not noted for their belief before June 1941 that communists were fine upstanding patriotic gentlemen who eschewed secretive subversive activity, undoubtedly had other motives. The decision to intern fascists and to leave communists free reflected the rise of the Labour party to share power in a coalition government. Whereas Labour was militantly anti-fascist, the left wing of the party had been co-operating with communist popular front policies since 1935. Although there is no evidence to suggest that interning the fascists was one of the conditions of coalition – indeed it was Churchill and Chamberlain who were the main

[13] A. Masters, *The Man who was M* (Oxford, 1984), pp. 86–7.
[14] PRO Cab. 65/13 WM 133 (40), 22 May 1940.

supporters of such a move according to Cabinet minutes – the decision to keep a substantial number of key fascist personnel interned after the crisis was past in the autumn of 1940 did reflect Labour pressure. The influence of communists in the labour force in key strategic industries and the role they played in the forefront of the demand for social reform also made the government think twice about banning the party.

The authorities had a more relaxed attitude to the communists than to Mosley after 1939 because MI5 had successfully infiltrated communist headquarters in King Street and knew far more about their activities than about the BUF. Since late 1938 when W. E. D. Allen had quarrelled with Mosley over the Air Time project, MI5 had had no effective agent near the centre of the BUF. The fact that Mosley had covered his tracks so successfully meant that internment became more likely as suspicions increased. Given Mosley's formidable record in the Law Courts, where he had never lost a case, the fact – as Anderson continuously emphasized to the War Cabinet – that the evidence against him was so flimsy meant he could only be kept under lock and key if the emergency powers were invoked. Thus although the authorities had unfounded worries about either a joint anti-war or anti-semitic campaign by communists and fascists, it was decided to differentiate between the two groups in the action taken against them.

In the end a half-way house of stopping communist propaganda by banning the *Daily Worker* and *The Week* was decided upon. This was used as a warning to the communists not to disrupt war production. With the nazi invasion of Russia in the summer of 1941 this became academic, since overnight the communists became virulent anti-nazis once more. They also resumed the leadership of a vitriolic anti-Mosley campaign; their opposition had been muted since the Nazi-Soviet pact in August 1939 and the lack of militant opposition partly explained the success of Mosley's anti-war rallies during the phoney war period. Only during the Silvertown election was there much evidence of fascist-communist hostility at this time.

In his comments to the Cabinet Committee on Communist Activities on 20 January 1941 on the different treatment of the two major anti-war groups, Sir John Anderson argued that although there was no evidence which could justify the prosecution of fascists there had been reason to believe that they were preparing secret plans which would enable them, in the event of an invasion of this country, either to range themselves on the side of the enemy, or by a *coup d'état* to seize power and make terms with them.[15] The Home Office now viewed the BUF as a highly organized conspiracy whose object was to overthrow the government and make peace with Germany. Both Mosley and Maule Ramsay were supposedly obsessed with a 'march to power'. Mosley had predicted at the outset of hostilities that a revolutionary situation would develop against the 'Jewish War'.[16] However, there was no definite proof of subversive activity. Indeed the Home Secretary and the law officers decided after the 22 May meeting when the War Cabinet were told of the Tyler Kent affair that it would be unwise to prosecute Maule Ramsay under Section 1 of the Official Secrets Act of 1911 as it was unclear whether an offence had been committed. This was undoubtedly the correct decision, for when Mrs Christobel Nicholson of the RC, wife of Admiral Nicholson, was charged for photocopying the classified documents which Ramsay had handled she was found not guilty of the charge under the Official Secrets Act. Maule Ramsay said he only read the documents and had taken no copies because he did not find in them the evidence for which he had been looking of sinister Jewish activities.[17]

Interning rather than charging Maule Ramsay also meant that the authorities could freely interrogate him about his links with nazi Germany and Mosley,[18] and avoided his claims that as an MP he could only be tried by his peers. As the evidence against fascists was even more flimsy than with Maule Ramsay the use of DR 18b against them was seen as the best way of allowing MI5 the free opportunity to discover through interrogation the nature of the fascist threat to national security. Although Anderson still argued, even at the 22 May Cabinet, that there was little evidence to substantiate the claims of subversive fascist activity and that there was nothing illegal in the pronouncements of Sir Oswald Mosley, which although anti-war were couched in patriotic language, it was nevertheless decided that 25–30 leading members of the BUF should be interned. New laws were immediately promulgated to

[15] PRO Cab. 98/18, Committee on Communist Activities, 1st meeting 20 Jan. 1941; p. 3; N. Branson, *History of the Communist Party of Great Britain* (London, 1985), p. 318.

[16] PRO HO 45/25754, minute of Home Office meeting, 18 Sept. 1940; PRO Cab. 66/35 WM 148 (43), p. 5.

[17] PRO HO 45/25748, undated Home Office minute on Ramsay.

[18] PRO Cab. 65/7 WM 133 (40), p. 219.

allow for internment of fascists on 22 May. The use of DR 18b, brought in as much as a counter measure to the threat of sabotage and terrorism in a renewed IRA campaign as to potential nazi-inspired activity, was amended in DR 18b (1a) which allowed for internment without trial of members of organizations which were subject to foreign influence or control, or whose leaders had or had had associations with leaders of enemy governments, or who sympathized with the system of government of enemy powers. No longer did the government have to prove that subversive activity was being contemplated or had been committed before fascists could be interned. On 10 July 1940 under DR 18b (AA), the British Union was declared a proscribed organization.

The closing down of British fascism by the authorities in the spring of 1940 reflected the deteriorating war situation. The government were determined to leave nothing to chance and for reasons of security and to allay public fears all suspect groups with the exception of the communists were put under lock and key. The total lack of influence of fascists in society or the armed services should have convinced the government that the whole idea of a fascist fifth column was a figment of the imagination – a ludicrous fantasy. As it was, many innocent aliens and fascists were unjustly interned as a result of the government's loss of a sense of proportion, and became the scapegoats for the desperate situation in which the new government found itself. No evidence at any stage was ever produced to show that the BUF, or any other fascist group, had ever sanctioned illegal behaviour, despite the devious tricks and intimidation later applied by the Security Service during the interrogation process. During the Second World War a few individual fascists were sentenced to terms of imprisonment for trying to help the enemy,[19] and several others became conscientious objectors after telling the Advisory Committee that they wished to be released from internment in order to fight for Britain. Many members of the BUF performed valiant service for Britain's armed forces during the war. The evidence produced by the government of actual unpatriotic behaviour in England before 1945 by members of the BUF was scanty.

However, despite the undoubted patriotism of many associated

---

[19] N. West, *MI5. British Security Service Operations 1909–45* (London, 1983), pp. 161–3.

with the BUF, several ex-members were convicted of serious offences at the end of the war. Punishment included four death sentences, two of which were commuted to life imprisonment. These related to individuals who were either prisoners of war who had gone over to the enemy, or who were in Germany at the outbreak of hostilities. Some of the more serious offences involved ex-members of the BUF who had broadcast on German radio, such as William 'Lord Haw Haw' Joyce, had joined the Waffen SS, who had assisted German intelligence or who had been responsible for helping to recruit prisoners of war for the Legion of St George or the British Free Corps units in the German army to fight the Soviets on the eastern front.[20] No current member of the BUF in 1939 was thought to be involved in such treasonable behaviour.

Although 24 of the 66 MI5 renegade files sent to the Director of Public Prosecutions have been retained by the Home Office under Section 3 (4) of the Public Records Act, the released files show little active involvement by such individuals in fascist organizations. The files relating to those who were members of the British Free Corps confirm Rebecca West's impressions at the treason trials; that weak-willed individuals, those who had chips on their shoulders and disreputable characters were as likely to commit treason as those with ideological affinities with the nazis.[21] A fascist traitor was, however, uncovered by the Special Operations Executive in France. The agent 'Bla' claimed to have infiltrated SOE on behalf of Mosley's fascists and was executed by the French resistance on the orders of British Intelligence after admitting betraying a cell in Paris and operating a 'Double Cross' radio source for the Abwehr in 1942.[22] The actual evidence of treasonable behaviour by the fascists tends to suggest that Mosley's estimate that 5 per cent of his membership were potential security risks was more accurate than the estimate of 25–30 per cent by MI5 to the Home Secretary on 22 May.[23]

[20] R. West, *The Meaning of Treason* (London, 1952); R. Seth, *Jackals of the Reich* (London, 1973); M. de Slade, *Yeoman of Valhalla* (Mannheim, 1970); 'Roll of Honour, British Union of Fascists', NCCL 1946, Lazar Zaidmann Papers, PRO HO 45/25798, PRO HO 45/25805.

[21] PRO HO 45/25834–25836, PRO HO 45/25817/25819/25820.

[22] M. M. Fourcade, *Noah's Ark* (London, 1973), pp. 146–53.

[23] PRO Cab. 65/13 WM 133 (40), 22 May 1940; PRO HO 283/14/88.

case and the statement of Mary Stanford, in the Norah Briscoe case was known in the RC as 'Miss Marjorie Amor'.[25] The role ascribed to Joan Miller in *The Man who was M* was taken by another agent at the trial, a Belgian girl called Helene who testified that she took a letter, from Anna Wolkoff to William Joyce, to Maxwell Knight. This presentation of the evidence may have represented deliberate policy on the part of MI5 in an attempt to shield Joan Miller. However, the case was held in camera and Helene too was later apparently used again by the Security Service. Joan Miller did not give evidence at the trial although her activities were mentioned. The Joan Miller version sounds plausible, but there is no independent source which would verify her account. It would be better to interpret her revelations not as the product of her own role but as the combined operations of all three agents. Joan Miller had a chip on her shoulder concerning her treatment by Maxwell Knight and the Security Service and her story probably over-dramatizes the contribution she made, particularly as Marjorie Amor was involved with the RC for a longer period of time than herself.

The revelations of Joan Miller have also overstated the significance of the RC. Agents are not trained to assess the significance of their work. Although the Tyler Kent affair represented a breach of national security there is no hard evidence that either Kent or Maule Ramsay contemplated breaking the law by publishing their information. In fact as a secret society the RC exhibited farcical rather than sinister aspects. Kent told the court of a meeting with a man introduced to him as 'Mr Macaroni' from the Italian Embassy. Marjorie Amor said the group around Maule Ramsay represented the inner circle of the RC and Kent that Helene had given him the secret symbolic badge of an eagle and snake to mark this fact. Indeed, the part of the RC still operating in May 1940 that was implicated in the Tyler Kent affair appears to have consisted of Maule Ramsay, Kent, five women with eccentric views and three MI5 agents. Anna Wolkoff was convicted only as a result of one of the informers acting as an *agent provocateur* by supplying her with the means to communicate with William Joyce in Germany. Wolkoff, who appears to have been the source in the RC of the information about secret meetings between Mosley and

[25] Transcript of the Tyler Kent Case, 23–8 Oct. 1940, PRO HO 45/25741; statement of Mary Stanford to Special Branch, 21 March 1941.

Maule Ramsay, would only have known about such events at second hand. Like the rest of the RC apart from Maule Ramsay, they viewed Mosley with suspicion and the Domvile diary does not mention Wolkoff or her female cronies like Enid Riddell, Mrs Nicholson or Mary Stanford. Her lunatic fringe views on Jews and nazis also fails to inspire confidence in her credibility. As against that, however, the information gathered from her by the MI5 agents on Tyler Kent was highly reliable, at least to the extent that he proved to be a serious security risk.

Joan Miller's account is misleading too in its implication that the RC agents were the chief source of information on secret meetings between fascists and fellow travellers. Joan Miller's main work in the RC was between March and May 1940 at a time when co-operation between most of the fascist fringe was becoming less significant and Maule Ramsay and his secret societies appeared to have lost interest in combined activities. Although it is not possible to say with certainty what MI5 agents in the RC found out on this matter, a new source of information can be pinpointed through analysis of declassified Home Office files, the Domvile diaries and the research of Anthony Masters. This suggests that several agents operated on the fringes of the BUF, the Nordic League, the Link and the British Council for Christian Settlement in the autumn and winter of 1939–40. An important source of information on these organizations and assessment of its quality can be deduced from information in the released personal files of Aubrey Lees and John Beckett, and agents' reports in the Norah Briscoe case.

Aubrey Lees was a colonial civil servant who was deputy governor of the Jaffa district in Palestine. While home on leave in 1939 he had contacted anti-semitic groups like the NL, IFL and BPP and passed on details of alleged Jewish atrocities in Palestine. He also lived with a woman member of the BUF which probably accounted for the crucial mistake MI5 made in the stated reasons for his internment. The evidence he gave about secret meetings to the Advisory Committee has already been mentioned (see p.186). A letter to the Advisory Committee Chairman in his file names the intelligence agent who gave information against Lees. This letter was in response to information given to Lees by Birkett who told him that 'Mr. James Hughes (P. G. Taylor of the B.U.) is an intellegence agent.'[26] Lees claimed he met him regularly, and the

---

[26] PRO HO 283/45, Aubrey Lees to Norman Birkett, 26 Aug. 1940.

implication is that he was a source of the information on the NL decision to close down and Maule Ramsay's decision to collaborate with Mosley, as Lees's attitude is mentioned in the report. Special Branch knowledge of the secret meetings in the phoney war is confined to the three meetings Lees attended and not the others listed in Domvile's diary and the three meetings Lees was invited to but did not attend between March and May 1940. The fact that Lees was wrongly accused of being a member of the BUF in the reasons for his internment suggested that the 'very reliable source' in this case passed on inaccurate information.

What appears to be the same man is also mentioned in the John Beckett file. Beckett, whose collaboration with William Joyce in the NSL in 1937–8 meant he was regarded with deep suspicion by both MI5 and the general public, and whose quarrel with Mosley in 1937 led him to be viewed with equal hostility by the BUF, singled out an 'agent provocateur' called P. C. Taylor (sic) whom he regarded as responsible for many of the allegations in his case.[27] Anne Beckett, his wife, wrote to Birkett claiming that at a meeting in their flat early in 1940 between Mr Taylor, Beckett and herself propaganda alleged to have been made by her husband was in fact made by Taylor in an apparent attempt to elicit information.[28] The Committee decided that they were unable to deny or confirm MI5 allegations but in general were impressed with Beckett's case.[29]

However, Taylor was not the only source of such allegations. Ben Greene, who was also involved in the British Council for Christian Settlement, had introduced Beckett to a 'Mr. Court', a young German, who later confessed that he had given untruthful evidence in the Ben Greene case; Beckett now demanded in January 1942 that 'Court's' evidence should not be held against him.[30] The government had been forced to release Ben Greene when Oswald Hickson, his solicitor, proved that Harald Kurtz, one of MI5s agents, had indeed passed on false information and the case was to undermine Maxwell Knight's credibility.[31] Herbert Morrison, the Home Secretary, admitted the justice in Beckett's claims. Evidence

[27] PRO HO 45/25698, MI5 report on John Beckett.
[28] PRO HO 283/26, Anne Beckett to Norman Birkett, 14 July 1940.
[29] PRO HO 45/25698, Advisory Committee Report on John Beckett, 10 July 1940.
[30] PRO HO 45/25698, John Beckett to Norman Birkett, 19 Jan. 1942.
[31] Masters, The Man who was M, pp. 141–67.

which suggested that Beckett would join the anti-parachute corps, would harbour escaping pro-nazi Germans, had contacted the armed services and had been in communication with the German government would have to be disregarded for much of it was supplied by Kurtz. Morrison, who thought that Beckett was a 'proletarian gone wrong', still thought in 1942 that he should remain interned, however, because it was likely that if released he would form an organization of the various malcontents.[32]

Further evidence on agents' operations and the methods employed is provided in the Norah Briscoe case. Here the court allowed two MI5 agents to use code names as Agent Q and Agent X when giving evidence, because the wife of one had a mother living in Germany and the other was a German national. Q described himself as a British subject who had been employed under Major Maxwell Knight since 1936. Under his direction he was associating with persons belonging to various fascist or pro-nazi organizations including the BUF, the IFL, the RC and the Link.[33] X said he was 27 years old and was born in Germany although his mother was half English. He had lived in England since January 1937 and had worked under the direction of Major Knight since May 1938.[34] X can be positively identified as Harald Kurtz from the description of him in *The Man who was M*.[35] Q may have been 'Taylor' or an unknown third agent.

The Norah Briscoe case in 1941 represented MI5 tying up the loose ends of the RC. After the Tyler Kent affair most of the active members of the RC were interned. However, Mary Stanford's appeal to the Advisory Committee was successful and she was released in September 1940. An informant reported that 'Molly' (*sic*) Stanford, who had just been released, and Aubrey Lees were soon active in proposing various schemes to aid internees and the proposed dissemination of peace propaganda.[36] Q, who had attended a meeting of the RC at Marjorie Amor's flat in April 1940 at which Maule Ramsay, Anna Wolkoff, Mary Stanford and Jock Houston amongst others were present, was now directed back into the RC. His purpose was to monitor the activities of Stanford.

[32] PRO HO 45/25698, minute from Herbert Morrison, 6 Jan. 1942.
[33] PRO HO 45/25741, statement of Witness Q to Special Branch, 21 Mar. 1940.
[34] PRO HO 45/25741, statement of Witness X to Special Branch, 21 Mar. 1940.
[35] Masters, *The Man who was M*, p. 141–2.
[36] PRO HO 45/25728, informant's report on Aubrey Lees, 20 Nov. 1940.

According to Q's testimony, Stanford introduced him to Mrs Briscoe, a typist in the Ministry of Supply. She lived with Gertrude Blount Hiscox, Jock Houston's girlfriend. According to Q, Stanford knew that Briscoe had photocopies of classified documents which she wished to pass to the Germans. Q introduced Briscoe and Hiscox to X, a supposed nazi spy.

The denouement of the episode followed when X met Briscoe and Hiscox in his flat and received the classified documents which dealt with relatively trivial matters like the transfer of equipment to Northern Ireland and details of goods from Australia lost at sea. Meanwhile Special Branch Officers took shorthand notes of the conversation between Hiscox, Briscoe and X and attempts were made to record the proceedings with primitive equipment. Maxwell Knight and a Special Branch officer then appeared and arrested Hiscox and Briscoe. Although they had no evidence against her, apart from the claims of Agent Q, Mary Stanford was re-interned. With Briscoe and Hiscox receiving 5-year sentences at their trial, MI5 finally succeeded in closing down the RC. Although Briscoe and Hiscox were obviously culpable in wanting to impart information to the nazis, Q and X had acted as agent provocateurs in the operation. Such activity was reminiscent of the techniques of Oliver the Spy, who set up and helped close down the Pentridge rising (1817) and Cato St Conspiracy (1820).

The other major case where an agent played a key role in the internment decision was with Admiral Sir Barry Domvile. In his account of the episode Domvile argued that the proceedings of the Advisory Committee were amongst the most unsavoury episodes in English history. His initial hearing on 22 October 1940 he reported passed off very pleasantly. However, he was recalled on 5 November and the barometer was no longer 'set fair' but was 'stormy'.[37] The minutes of the Home Defence (Security Executive) on 6 November sheds some light on this. Birkett had decided that the Advisory Committee need not see agents but would accept the word of intelligence officers as they wished to do nothing which would compromise the sources of information available to the Security Service.[38] They would therefore not wish to see the agent who had provided the evidence against Domvile. The implication

[37] Sir B. Domvile, 'From Admiral to Cabin Boy', p. 108, Dom. 84, Sir Barry Domvile Papers.
[38] PRO HO 45/25754, minutes of Home Defence (Security Executive), 6 Nov. 1940.

was that Domvile was interned mainly as a result of the allegations of an unknown agent whom MI5 had produced after the first hearing and whose credibility and veracity were never tested.

Other sources and the survival of documents from the weeding process in released files provides us with the minimum of information from which assessment can be made of why this material is so sensitive. At the outset it must be stated that much of the material that has been released is embarrassing for the authorities. The assessment of the RC material too, suggests that the response of the government to the Tyler Kent affair was that of taking a sledge-hammer to crack a nut. The activities of MI5 agents and the willingness of the Advisory Committee to accept uncorroborated evidence from unknown agents without giving the defendant the chance to cross-examine or allow him legal support at his hearing was a black episode in English legal history. So too were the House of Lords judgements in the test cases brought before it in relation to the operation of DR 18b. In effect these meant that even where it could be shown that the grounds for detention were false it had to be demonstrated that the arrest represented bad faith by the Home Secretary, before the courts were prepared to challenge DR 18b.[39]

This undermining of individual civil liberties could only be justified by the war emergency and the invasion scare. Bearing this in mind, the performance of the Advisory Committee in exceptionally difficult circumstances perhaps deserves more praise than blame and a case can be made that it successfully stood up to the Security Service and kept the erosion of civil liberties to a necessary minimum. The position of the Security Service needs to be seen in perspective too. The propaganda whipped up by the Rothermere press over the fifth-column issue meant pressure on the Security Service to block off all potential allies for the nazis in the event of an invasion. Although the home front was well under control, MI5 and its agents had to cut corners and find imaginary fifth columnists in some numbers to maintain morale and provide scapegoats to explain the nazi threat. Aliens and native fascists became the victims of such pressures; many of the aliens were anti-nazi and only a small minority of fascists could be seen as

---

[39] Times Law Report, 14 Nov. 1941, *Liversedge* v. *Anderson*, *Greene* v. *Secretary of State*; C. K. Allen, 'Regulation 18b and reasonable cause', *Law Quarterly Review*, 58 (1942), pp. 232–42.

pro-German. Major General Liardet in charge of defensive preparations in Kent even went so far as to suggest there were large numbers of disloyal British subjects in his area who should be moved out of the county and the aliens restriction zone.[40]

The pressures on MI5 to obtain results and its obsession with secrecy to protect sources mainly accounts for the sensitivity of the fascist internment files. The fact that Mosley had always adopted an anti-subversion strategy within the BUF and that even when W.E.D. Allen had been in place as an MI5 agent his reports may not have been reliable become significant factors when knowledge of fascist activities become more important during 1939. Several of the closed files on the BUF probably relate to unorthodox and possibly illegal methods used by MI5 in obtaining information about Mosley and the organization. It is also true that relatively few personal files on BUF members have been released, about a dozen out of the 750 or so who were interned. Mainly this is because the large majority of them have been lost – but the fact that within the released material there are a significant number of subfiles which have been retained suggests that sources are being protected on a large scale and that certain MI5 operations are being covered up. As next to nothing has been released on the RC and the Link the same conclusions apply even more strongly.

Other sources and stray comments within released material enable more to be said on this issue. MI5 operations for example involved both the bugging of Mosley's cell in Brixton prison in 1940 and the use of postal intercepts on some fascists. All correspondence of internees was censored but prior to internment the mail of Arnold Leese and Richard Findlay was intercepted, as was Cola Carroll's on his release in 1943.[41] Findlay was a member of the Council of the NL, and the RC, the vice-chairman of the Central London branch of the Link, who corresponded with Mosley, and he had resigned his commission in the RAF in 1936 in protest against the abdication of Edward VIII. He was not released from internment until 1945. Carroll, the editor of the *Anglo-German Review*, was closely associated with Domvile and the Link. Although it is not known whether Carroll's and Findlay's files are amongst those not released, Arnold Leese's file has been retained.

---

[40] PRO HO 45/25758, Major-Gen. Liardet to Chief Constable of Kent, 2 June 1940.
[41] PRO HO 45/24967, MI5 report on IFL 1942; PRO HO 283/26, MI5 to Home Secretary, 4 May 1944.

Similarly the files of Alexander Raven Thomson, one of the leaders of the BUF, have not been opened by the Home Office. Whatever the reasons for this it is certain that part of the explanation can be accounted for from an article he wrote in *Union*, one of Mosley's post-war publications, in 1948. As another member of the BUF, J. L. Battersby, refers to the same matter in a published account, the events described, if not their interpretation, can be verified. This relates to the interrogations of fascists by military intellegence at Latchmere House, Ham Common, during August and September 1940.

According to Raven Thomson a group of BUF leaders, including himself, were taken to Ham Common in an attempt to obtain information about the organization. To begin with fascists were placed in solitary confinement and when let out for exercise were not allowed to communicate with each other. Food rations were minimal and only just enough to survive on. After this softening-up exercise groups of fascists were allowed to congregate in a room and allowed to talk for a quarter of an hour. The fascists, suspecting there were hidden microphones, spent most of their time denouncing their captors. Sometimes fascists were awoken late at night and subjected to interrogation by a military tribunal under fierce arc lighting. One fascist burst into uncontrolled laughter when he saw the set-up and denounced the tribunal for its ludicrous Gestapo tactics. The whole range of techniques of psychological warfare was allegedly used in an attempt to break down the fascists. Men were threatened with being shot one moment and the next offered immediate release and financial recompense if they would give information against the leaders of the movement. At other times the alleged confessions of other fascists were used in an attempt to elicit information. At the end of a gruelling five-week ordeal Raven Thomson had lost two stones in weight. Mosley, when he heard of what was happening, immediately instituted legal proceedings and the whole grisly charade quickly came to an end. Fascists claim that military intelligence learned nothing from the experience because there was nothing to tell.[42]

If MI5 interrogation techniques have been wholly covered up then some material has filtered through about how information concerning interned fascists was gained in prisons and the camps

---

[42] A. Raven Thomson, 'Ham Common', *Union*, 19 June 1948; J. L. Battersby, *The Bishop said Amen* (Poynton, 1947), p. 29.

although the significance of this still remains a secret. The use of a 'very secret and delicate source'[43] to obtain in advance details of Mosley's defence before the Advisory Committee suggests that his cell in Brixton was bugged. Prison warders were present at all visits to internees and reported on conversations. The presence of R. List, described as a 'camp informer', amongst the permanent residents of Brixton gaol in April 1942 suggests either that he was transferred from the Isle of Man to elicit information,[44] or that his cover had been blown at Peveril. Just prior to this his activities in the camp were referred to in a report from the Senior Intelligence Officer where List provided the information about the nature of internee St Barbe Baker's religious meetings.[45]

No doubt there are many more reasons why the internment files on British fascists have proved to be so sensitive. What is clear is that the cover-up relates to traditional security considerations and not to a desire to hide any potentially embarrassing connections between the mainstream of British politics and fascist activity. Apart from a few minor figures in the Conservative party who were interested in Mosley for a time, there is no evidence, apart from the disastrous Maule Ramsay connection, that British fascism had any significant links to the establishment after 1934.

DR 18b (1a)

The story of the internment of British fascists has also to be seen in the perspective of the parallel internment of aliens. While the fascists after 22 May 1940 were interned under DR 18b (1a), most aliens of enemy origin were interned under the Royal Prerogative and neutrals under Article 12 (5A) of the Aliens Order 1920 (as amended in 1940). There were 1,300 interned under DR 18b of whom about 750 were associated with the BUF, and 22,000 German and Austrian aliens and about 4,000 Italians.[46] The vast majority of these were interned between May and July of 1940. As

---

[43] PRO HO 283/6/7.
[44] PRO HO 45/25752, 18b (1a) detainees in Brixton and Holloway gaols, April 1942.
[45] PRO HO 214/45, religious meetings in Camp, 2 Apr. 1942.
[46] M. Kochin, *Britain's Internees during the Second World War* (London, 1983), pp. 22–7; R. Stent, *A Bespattered Page* (London, 1981), pp. 83–94; Andrew, *Secret Service*, pp. 478–80.

some of the aliens were refugees who had come to Britain to escape nazi persecution the treatment they received has to be regarded as more scandalous than that meted out to British fascists. Indeed, if some dubious behaviour can be pointed to amongst a small minority of British fascists and suspicious activities of its leaders in the eyes of the authorities, then the evidence of pro-nazi operations by aliens is negligible. The fact that such large numbers were suddenly interned created grave administrative problems for the authorities which led to overcrowding and poor facilities in the prisons and internment camps, at least in the short term.

For the Advisory Committee which had been set up to deal with the problem of aliens and DR 18b internees the new situation was a nightmare and after the beginning of June 1940 it narrowed down its field of operations to deal only with DR 18b cases. Even this created a difficult situation and eventually four separate committees under different chairmen had to be employed to hear all the cases. The decision to intern 25–30 leading members of the BUF on 22 May had been extended to include 350 local officials on 4 June.[47] This probably represented one of the first decisions of the security revolution with the sacking of Kell and the establishment of the Home Defence (Security Executive) to co-ordinate counter-subversion activities. However, the security authorities were over-zealous in their work and 750 persons were detained because of association with the BUF in the summer of 1940.[48] Of these detentions 216 were originated by the Security Service, between 20 and 30 by Special Branch after consultation with MI5, and the rest by Chief Constables.[49] However, the information available to F Division's nominal index in the central card file of MI5's registry was supplemented by information passed to it by the Board of Deputies of British Jews at the outbreak of war. This material was supplied by an informant within the BUF who provided every week a complete file of fascist activities and their programmes. By such means the Board of Deputies claimed they not only knew the venue of all fascist meetings indoors and outdoors in advance, so that counter-measures could be devised, but they also obtained a full list of members of the party. Many of these names were quite

[47] PRO Cab. 65/7 WM 130 (40), p. 188.
[48] PRO Cab. 66/35 WP 148 (43), p. 6.
[49] PRO HO 45/25754, minutes of the Home Defence (Security Executive), 6 Nov. 1940.

unknown to the authorities. The Board of Deputies mole was code-named 'Captain X' and was an Irish ex-officer and supporter of Sinn Fein who had joined the BUF because of Mosley's support for Irish Independence.[50]

Fascists claim that arrests were carried out indiscriminately and that in so far as there were suspect persons in the organization the wrong people were arrested. A police source who attended MI5 conferences in London claimed that the basis for arrest was uniform.[51] The truth probably lies between the two. The authorities certainly went over the top in manufacturing evidence for detainment and in arresting double the number of fascists they were instructed to. Members were even arrested in the armed forces and interned after fighting the Germans or returning from bombing raids. The aim was to destroy the organization both nationally and locally and in this they were certainly successful.

Mosley had made contingency plans to protect the administration of the organization if he was interned. The authorities discovered in the papers of Mrs Elam, who ran the London and provincial anti-Vivisection society as a Mosleyite cover organization, and Hector McKechnie, a leading administrator of the BUF, a list of eight individuals whom Mosley trusted to do as they thought fit if he was arrested. The others mentioned were R. Temple Cotton, Commander C. E. Hudson, K. E. Marsden, J. H. Hone, E. Dudley Elam, N. Francis Hawkins and B. D. E. Donovan.[52] Most of these were interned for varying periods of time. The list of prominent persons interned[53] included most of the leading Mosleyites and several of those like Domvile, Ramsay, Hay, Lees, Gordon Canning, Greene and Beckett who had been involved in the various secret meetings or peace organizations to which the authorities attached such significance. The list did not include Lord Tavistock or any prominent individuals rumoured to be connected to the RC. Several of the interned fascists were to complain that socially influential supporters of Mosley were not interned while ordinary members were.

[50] Information from Nigel West; S. Saloman, 'Now it can be told', C 6/9/2/1, Board of Deputies of British Jews.
[51] Trevelyan Scholarship Project, 'The British Union of Fascists in Yorkshire', p. 19.
[52] PRO HO 283/48. Note in Hector McKechnie file.
[53] PRO HO 45/25747. Prominent persons arrested.

With such vast numbers of aliens and native fascists to process the authorities had to draw a fine line between administrative convenience and national security considerations. They rapidly had a change of heart over aliens and once the invasion scare receded after September 1940 the majority of them were gradually released. The DR 18b Advisory Committee recommended release for over 60 per cent of the internees it processed in the autumn of 1940. Most of the DR 18b prisoners were first interned in Brixton and Liverpool gaols. However, it was found necessary to open two camps to deal with the overflow and with aliens. In July 1940 a camp at Ascot racecourse was brought into use for the accomodation of internees and a second camp was opened at York in October. Many were then moved to a council estate in Huyton, Lancashire. In May 1941 the bulk of the prisoners were transferred to the Isle of Man and settled in two separate camps, one for men and one for women. The overcrowding problem was so serious that in July 1940 the Cabinet discussed whether interned fascists should be sent to overseas camps in the Dominions or Colonies. It was decided that this was not practical when the Law Officers informed the Cabinet that the government had no power to ship British subjects overseas against their will and without trial, nor did it have the power of jurisdiction once an internee had landed on the shore of a self-governing Dominion. The Cabinet then dropped the suggestion that internees be sent to Australia, New Zealand or St Helena.[54] There is no evidence that the recent sinking of the *Arandora Star*, which led to the deaths of many innocent interned aliens being sent to Canada, played any part in the decision.[55]

In the summer of 1941, of the 671 DR 18b internees still in custodial detention over 500 were in the Isle of Man camps. Of the remainder 44, including Sir Oswald Mosley and nine other leaders of the BUF, were in Brixton prison and 24 women were detained in Holloway. Some 18 had been removed to Walton gaol, Liverpool, for disciplinary reasons from the Isle of Man. Mosley and his leading lieutenants were not sent to the Isle of Man because the authorities thought he would have an undesirable influence on other detainees by hardening their fascist attitudes.[56] However, it

---

[54] PRO HO 45/25767. Proposal to send BUF internees overseas.
[55] PRO HO 215/205. Arandora Star.
[56] PRO Cab. 66/20 WP 279 (41), p. 3.

was decided to allow both the Mosleys and Domviles to visit each
other in Holloway gaol in 1941. Lady Domvile was soon released
and the authorities then moved Mosley to live with his wife in
Holloway, rather than the Isle of Man. During 1943 and 1944 the
authorities released many of the more serious cases, as they termed
them, including Mosley, Sir Barry Domvile, John Beckett, Archibald Maule Ramsay and Mrs Nicholson.[57] Only 45 British
subjects were interned on the Isle of Man until the end of the
war.[58]

The task of the Advisory Committee was to assess who should
remain interned. It had to balance the administrative problems
involved in keeping such a large number of individuals interned
without trial with the national security arguments. Although the
final decision rested with the Home Secretary who took into
account wider political and security factors, in practice the
Advisory Committee was the most important source for decisions
on continued internment. The Home Secretary had the powers
under DR 18b (1) and DR 18b (1a) to make a detention order.
Under DR 18b (2) he could suspend the order subject to specified
conditions. He also had the power to revoke the suspension order
if either the conditions of suspension were flouted or the safety of
the realm was at issue.[59] As the law officers considered that
provided the request was not frivolous an individual could appeal
as many times as he liked about his internment or the conditions
relating to the suspension of the order,[60] in practice the work of
the Committee was concerned almost wholly with internment
orders until 1943 but increasingly after that date became
concerned with the conditions of suspension.[61] Although it used
its powers sparingly certain suspension orders were revoked and
individuals re-interned. The case of Mary Stanford (see p. 205)
and Arthur Marson fell into this category. Marson was re-interned
after becoming a conscientious objector when conditionally
released, and failing to notify the authorities of a change of
address.[62]

[57] PRO Cab. 65/40. 156th Conclusion, Minute 4 (Confidential Annexe 14 Nov. 1943).
[58] PRO HO 215/495, Herbert Morrison to Edward Harvey MP, March 1945.
[59] PRO HO 45/25754, memorandum by chairman of Advisory Committee on the
Administration of DR 18b, 1941.
[60] PRO HO 45/25754, law officers' opinion on DR 18b, 21 May 1941.
[61] Ibid.
[62] PRO HO 45/25736, Arthur Marson.

The Advisory Committee's guidelines for recommending release of internees was dependent on four variables. They recommended release when the order had been made as a result of incorrect information as in the case of Aubrey Lees (released 1940). Similarly if further information had come to light or the Home Secretary had acted on information which was not quite up to date; the case of J. Smeaton Stuart (released 1940), who left the BUF in 1937 and joined the local Conservative Association, falls into this category.[63] Again, the committee recommended that if a man could be shown to have changed his views since the invasion of the low countries he should be released. This was a very difficult area as the committee were aware that some fascists might tell untruths in order to obtain release. The case of Captain Dudley Evans (released 1941) fell between the last two categories. He held the view that the BUF ought to have discontinued its activities when war began and that when the country was at war national unity was essential.[64] Conversely, those who appeared unrepentant in their pro-nazi sympathies were punished with continued detention. Harold Lockwood and Thomas Guillaume St Barbe Baker were treated in this manner, the latter's case being compounded by his organizational abilities which made him potentially dangerous in the eyes of the committee.[65] Both were to be interned until 1945. Finally, comparatively unimportant members of fascist organizations who would probably have been frightened by internment could be released.[66] In practice this last point explained the release of the vast majority of internees in 1940.

In practice too, wider political considerations were also important in the decision to continue detention or to release the most important internees after 1940. This however did not affect the decisions of the Advisory Committee. Fascists complained that the Advisory Committee was little more than a public relations exercise whose legal basis was extremely dubious. It accepted evidence from the Security Service without evaluating the reliability of its sources, it failed to allow for legal representation

[63] PRO HO 283/64, J. Smeaton Stuart.
[64] PRO HO 45/25727, Dudley Evans.
[65] PRO HO 283/46, Harold Lockwood; HO 283/28 Thomas Guillaume St Barbe Baker.
[66] PRO HO 45/25754, Home Office Minute, 31 Oct. 1940.

of the accused and it recommended continued internment for individuals even though no evidence had been produced that any crime had ever been committed. Its Jekyll and Hyde façade, with its peculiar improvised procedure which seemed to combine elements of a court martial and a vicarage tea-party, was certainly hostile to the internee. Certain hearings were more ritualistic than judicial; it went through the motions of a scrupulously fair hearing, with Mosley, for example, before reaching its pre-ordained conclusion that he should not be released. As Robert Skidelsky has pointed out, the government never had any intention of letting Mosley go free.[67]

The fact that the authorities' suspicions about Mosley's secretive behaviour were only obliquely referred to in the lengthy hearings and that his replies on such matters were not subject to a rigorous cross-examination raises immediate doubts about the Advisory Committee's function, as does the failure to question the political judgement of Mosley and his wife in negotiating with Hitler to build a wireless transmitter when diplomatic relations between Britain and Germany were deteriorating rapidly after March 1939. Similarly the fact that MI5 allowed the Advisory Committee access to its files on Mosley and supplied it with advance information on the nature of his defence pointed to closer links than was usual between the prosecution and judicial process in the English legal system.

All this suggests that the released PRO material on internment and the Advisory Committee needs to be handled with a great deal of care. The stated reasons for internment in the personal files, for example, should not be taken too seriously. These were hurriedly concocted after the individuals had been arrested, and were for the most part dependent on unsubstantiated allegations, local gossip, and the use of *agents provocateurs* and whatever dubious insinuations could be hastily cobbled together. Nellie Driver patiently explained to her Advisory Committee hearing that the people accused of visiting her at night for secret meetings were respectively the insurance agent, the landlord, the trade union collector and an uncle. One of her friends was closely questioned about a book of maps she had drawn as a child 50 years ago. Another woman was asked about the significance of the words

---

[67] R. Skidelsky, *Oswald Mosley* (London, 1975), p. 449.

'Bob's your uncle' in a letter to her brother.[68] John Ellis, managing director of a firm of motor distributors in Yorkshire, was questioned about why bays, harbours, golf links and ferries were marked in ink on his maps; he explained that these showed places with quiet beaches where he could take the children for a holiday.[69] Another BUF member allegedly wrote in his diary, 'the Queen must be replaced.' He explained to the Committee he was a bee-keeper.[70] Diana Mosley stated in her autobiography that she did not take the Advisory Committee seriously and from an examination of her internment hearing one can see what she meant. Her bland and not very revealing answers on her relationship with Hitler and other nazi leaders appeared to have much the same significance for the Committee as the rather more fatuous probing into her behaviour at a 'Boycott German goods' rally in 1934 in Hyde Park.[71] The most plausible explanation of this is that W. E. D. Allen had convinced the authorities that the Mosley's connection with Hitler was purely a commercial one.

Although the anger and frustration of the fascists was fully justified an examination of the released Home Defence (Security Executive) minutes gives a different perspective on the performance of the Advisory Committee. The Home Defence (Security Executive) had been set up on 28 May 1940 to co-ordinate all aspects of national security under the chairmanship of Lord Swinton (until 1942). It comprised three independent members, and representatives from the armed services, the Home Office, War Office, MI5, MI6, the Advisory Committee and other security organizations. It established the framework of policy within which the Advisory Committee functioned. The minutes of the meetings of 15 October, 31 October and 6 November 1940 make it quite clear there was a significant battle for the control of internment policy between the Advisory Committee and MI5 with regard to DR 18b detainees which the former won. Of the first 317 cases heard the Committee had recommended continued detention in 118 cases and release in 199. Of the latter the Security Service had agreed in 88 cases and disagreed in 111. As a result of a

[68] Nellie Driver, 'From the Shadows of Exile' (n.d.), p. 57.
[69] PRO HO 45/25726, John Ellis.
[70] Sunday Telegraph, 16 Feb. 1986.
[71] D. Mosley, Life of Contrasts (London, 1977), p. 177; PRO HO 144/21995/17; Driver, 'Shadows of Exile', pp. 51–2.

conference MI5 had agreed not to make further representations in 96 of these cases and only to press the other 15.[72] A Home Office minute signed by one of their representatives on the Executive stated that it had been agreed, with MI5 dissenting, that subject to special circumstances in individual cases the Home Secretary should be advised to accept the recommendations of the Advisory Committee, that the armed services would have the right to refuse employment to ex-internees, that all those released should give an understanding not to engage in political activities for the duration of the war and that in special cases orders imposing restrictions on the movement of individuals would be invoked.[73] It was also agreed that the Advisory Committee would send a copy of their recommendation to the Home Secretary and MI5 at the same time, thus cutting down on administrative delays in the resolution of cases.

What this signified was a decisive victory for the Home Office over MI5 for the political control of national security. With the defeat in Cabinet of Sir John Anderson's reluctance to impose blanket internment measures on aliens and fascists, the insistence by Birkett and the Advisory Committee that as many internees should be released as soon as possible contingent on national security considerations and that MI5 should not have an effective veto on who was released enabled the Home Office, with its liberal tradition in civil liberty issues, to minimize the repercussions of the fifth column scare and the backwash of the Tyler Kent affair. Although fascists would with justification continue to feel aggrieved with their treatment, the situation would have been much worse for them if the Advisory Committee had lost this political battle. Sir John Anderson and Herbert Morrison, the two Home Secretaries involved, accepted 400 of the 455 recommendations for release by the Advisory Committee, 86.6 per cent of the total by 6 February 1941.[74]

Yet if the Advisory Committee can be stoutly defended in its role and for the large number of cases it conscientiously processed, it could perhaps be criticized for not making greater use of its powers to recommend the release of internees under conditional

---

[72] PRO HO 45/25754; minutes of the Home Defence (Security Executive), 15 Oct., 31 Oct. and 6 Nov. 1940.
[73] PRO HO 45/25754, minute from A. S. Hutchinson, Home Office (n.d.).
[74] PRO HO 282/22, memorandum by Norman Birkett, 5 Mar. 1941.

terms which would keep them out of alien restriction zones and their home areas, and limited their movements to within five or ten miles of their residence. Oswald Hickson, the solicitor of a group of DR 18b internees, suggested to the Home Office in August 1940 that they should be released conditional on them accepting restrictions on their movements and reporting to the local police. In one case it was seriously suggested that an internee would volunteer to assist at communist meetings and sell copies of the *Jewish Chronicle* as a punishment.[75] This request was turned down on the grounds that the police had too many duties in the national emergency situation to worry about the whereabouts of fascists, and that internment represented the most efficient use of resources in the total security context. As the fortunes of war changed, such conditional release of supposedly serious cases was, however, to become the main solution to the authorities' security dilemma.

The Advisory Committee in retrospect was a fig leaf which tried to provide a respectable judicial gloss for an aberration in the tradition of the English legal system. Although the fascists regarded its deliberations with hostility and contempt they should perhaps be thankful that its recommendations stood between them and the much harsher response proposed by MI5. Fascists saw the Advisory Committee as a dark episode in English legal history in which they were the main victims; others could point to its valiant battle to minimize the damage inflicted to civil liberties and the rule of law in the grave national emergency of 1940 by successfully standing up to MI5 pressures. Whatever view is the more relevant in the perspective of hindsight, proscription and internment represented an ironic fate for members of a political party which had announced that it would silence all opposition to itself if it ever gained power, and that it would have used similar commissions to the Advisory Committee to decide whether Jews were patriotic Englishmen or not.[76] Those who failed that test would not have been interned but expelled from the country. Perhaps not too many crocodile tears should be shed for the wartime fate of British fascists.

---

[75] PRO HO 45/25758, Oswald Hickson to Sir Alexander Maxwell, Home Office, 21 Aug. 1940.
[76] PRO HO 283/16/28.

The internees

The effects of detention on the internees and the security clamp-down produced a variety of responses ranging from a loss of belief in fascist activity, to sullen acceptance or militant hostility. Although conditions were initially worse in some of the internment camps used exclusively for aliens, owing to their greater numbers, nevertheless fascists experienced severe overcrowding and deteriorating conditions in the prisons and internment camps, and the role of the Advisory Committee became one of thinning out the number of internees so that acceptable conditions would prevail for those who remained.

The Home Office always maintained that DR 18b was preventive and custodial in character and not punitive. It issued instructions in 1940 which attempted to make the conditions of confinement seem less oppressive. Internees were allowed to associate with one another at meals, labour and recreation, visitors were permitted at least one visit a week and, subject to censorship, internees could write two letters per week. They could receive as many letters as were written to them. Regular outdoor exercise, games and recreation were encouraged. Smoking was allowed at exercise and recreation except during the hours of associated labour.[77] The logistics of overcrowding and the exigencies of the war situation were to make the conditions of confinement more oppressive than intended and for those incarcerated for long periods of time was to lead in many cases to a deterioration in health.

The living conditions at the initial detention centres at Brixton, Liverpool and Holloway gaols were deplorable. The mass influx of internees led to the opening up of little-used wings in Brixton and Holloway, and to the reopening of the old female prison at Liverpool. Many of the male internees at Brixton went into C Wing which was lice-infested. Only after interrogation and appearance before the Advisory Committee did they graduate to the more tolerable conditions of E Wing. No doubt this repre-sented a peculiar mixture of administrative difficulties and psychological warfare.[78] Holloway was extremely dirty, with

[77] PRO Cab. 66/20 WP 279 (41), p. 1.
[78] Sir B. Domvile, 'From Admiral to Cabin Boy', p. 107.

walls running with damp, filthy mattresses and disgusting lava-
tories.[79] At Liverpool the authorities admitted that the general
conditions of detention for internees were initially much less
comfortable than those which would normally be enjoyed by
ordinary prisoners. However, they saw most fascist internees as
'lazy and shiftless' persons, who failed to keep their rooms
properly cleaned, expected to be waited on by the prison staff and
deliberately put material down the drains in order to block
them.[80] Food was unappetizing in all institutions and had a low
nutriment value. Vegetables were unwashed and unprepared, the
meat tasted like horse and even the cats refused to eat the fish
pie.[81] Nightly air raids meant blackouts and prisoners locked up
often for 23 hours a day in 1940.[82] At Liverpool five ordinary
prisoners were killed by a bomb when some of the internees were
in residence.[83] A prison wardress's report at Holloway stated that
Diana Mosley felt that she and her class were tortured by living in
such close confinement and that it was very different for the
working classes who were used to living in the dirt and noise.[84]

Conditions in the internment camps in the Isle of Man were
generally less onerous but the monotonous routine, futility and
poor rations sapped morale. From the accounts which survive it is
possible to deduce that internment was less harsh for fascists than
for the alien refugees who were first sent there, that the facilities
were better and terms of confinement less oppressive for the
women than the men. The men were in the Peveril Camp, in a
section of the promenade at Peel which was cut off from the sea
and town by barbed wire 15 ft high and 6 ft deep. Food rations
were rudimentary and were based on porridge, bread and salt fish,
with two small meat rations per week. Basic educational facilities
were provided in the mornings.[85] The women were interned at the
Rushen Camp at Port Erin. Here there was no barbed wire and
there were kindly landladies. The British fascist women comprised

[79] D. Mosley, *Life of Contrasts*, p. 177; Driver, 'Shadows of Exile', pp. 51–2.
[80] PRO HO 45/25753. Note on conditions of detention of 18b detainees at Liverpool, summer 1940.
[81] Driver, 'Shadows of Exile', p. 58.
[82] Sir B. Domvile, 'From Admiral to Cabin Boy', p. 96.
[83] PRO HO 45/25753, Liverpool prison governor's annual report, 1940.
[84] PRO HO 144/21995/108.
[85] Battersby, *The Bishop said Amen*, pp. 37–40. C. Chappell, *Island of Barbed Wire* (London, 1986).

only a small proportion of the total inmates and there was a camp restaurant for all internees, both fascist and alien, which was subsidized by the German government through the Red Cross.[86]

The most severe effects of such conditions on the health of internees was the combination of inadequate heating facilities in winter with poor diet. Sir Oswald Mosley blamed the flaring up of his phlebitis on the failure to heat the annexe at Holloway during the coldest part of the winter in 1942 and 1943, the general long-run effects of two years' imprisonment and worry about his wife's health.[87] Richard Findlay, the camp leader at the Peveril (M) Camp, complained in 1943 that accommodation in the lower group of houses which were cold and damp was to be kept open, whilst those higher up which had fewer problems were to be closed for economy reasons. This he claimed would worsen the health of many of the elderly internees.[88] Some of the long-term internees were moved to better accommodation in 1944.

The resistance to internment by fascists was of both an active and passive nature. Fascists were at a disadvantage because the authorities merely extended the detention orders for those they considered dangerous or who refused to co-operate. Given this, the range of response was quite extensive although some alien internees gave the authorities more problems than the fascists. Of the general files on internment released by the Home Office only three relate to DR 18b fascist internees, and they appear to be very rarely mentioned in the 500 other files in the HO.215 series. The first reaction by DR 18b detainees was to use the legal system to argue that their detention broke the law of the land. However, the judgements in *Re Aubrey Lees* (1940), *Liversedge* v. *Anderson, Greene* v. *Secretary of State for Home Affairs* and *Smeaton-Stuart* v. *Anderson*[89] (all 1941) all went against the plaintiff and established the precedent under the Emergency Powers that provided the Home Secretary thought there was subjective cause as a result of information accepted in good faith the government could intern whom it deemed necessary.

Mosley and Maule Ramsay both used the legal system in an attempt to protect their reputations, with varying degrees of

[86] Driver, 'Shadows of Exile', pp. 85–101.
[87] PRO HO 45/25753, O. Mosley to prison governor, Holloway, 17 Oct. 1943.
[88] PRO HO 214/67, Richard Findlay to Home Secretary, 30 Nov. 1943.
[89] PRO HO 45/25714, John Roland Smeaton-Stuart.

success. Mosley sued or threatened to sue all those who impugned his patriotism, including on one occasion Beverley Nichols who had written a sympathetic article in the *Daily Express* which contained one ambiguous phrase. Maule Ramsay sued the *New York Times* in July 1941 for implying he was a traitor; the judge awarded token damages to him and said that although he did not understand what fifth column meant he thought that Maule Ramsay had been disloyal to the Crown.[90]

Others took more direct action against the threat of internment. Arnold Leese and Jock Houston both went underground to avoid capture. Leese avoided capture for four months and Houston for over six months.[91] Others like E. G. 'Mick' Clarke, Arnold Leese and John Beckett tried to ignore the conditional terms relating to their release.[92] Others broke prison or camp discipline and appealed at every available opportunity to the Advisory Committee. John Beckett was punished for three minor offences when held at Stafford prison, and removed from the Isle of Man back to Brixton gaol after conflicting with BUF detainees. He petitioned for release on the grounds that he had been framed by *agents provocateurs* and wanted to know why the Duke of Bedford had remained free whilst he was interned. He even complained about the nature of his conditional release: he thought it unfair that he should be restricted to a five-mile radius from his home whilst Mosley and others were allowed ten miles.[93]

More direct resistance was rare. Probably the most daring exploit was the escape from the Peveril Camp of three DR 18b prisoners with fascist and IRA connections in 1941. They managed to tunnel under the fence and escaped in a motor boat from which the sparking plugs had been removed. Even so they managed to get within a few miles of the Irish coast before being recaptured. According to the authorities they were given food on the boat on the return to camp and then interrogated. The camp inmates thought the escapees had not eaten for three days and when they were brought back to Peveril the refusal of the camp authorities to give them immediate rations provoked a riot. Shots were fired in

[90] 'Lest We Forget', Captain A. H. M. Ramsay, Rogues Gallery, C 6/9/3/2, Board of Deputies of British Jews.
[91] PRO HO 283/41, Richard Alastair (Jock) Houston.
[92] PRO HO 45/25713, BU members released under a suspending direction; PRO HO 283/26; MI5 to Advisory Committee, 4 May 1944.
[93] PRO HO 45/25698, John Beckett.

the air and after this disturbance was brought under control, and on the following day when Osbert Peake, a parliamentary under-secretary, was jostled, about 20 alleged ringleaders were sent to Walton gaol.[94] This incident was to lead to the replacement of the military authorities by the Metropolitan Police as the main upholders of security at the camps.[95] Mock fancy dress balls, which were introduced as a diversion for fascists and other inmates at Holloway at Christmas 1940, were hastily terminated after an internee who had successfully imitated Hitler and Sir Anthony Eden on such occasions dressed up as a nun and tried to escape.[96] Jeffrey Hamm, who had been interned on very dubious grounds in the hulk of a ship in Port Stanley harbour on the Falkland Islands in 1940, was also involved in an ironic variant of the attempted escape British prisoner of war drama; he was active in tunnelling at Leuwkop internment camp in South Africa just prior to his release.[97]

The other major episode of active resistance to internment involved Frederick Bowman, a member of the BPP. He was force fed in Brixton gaol in 1942 as a response to a hunger strike following punishment after trying to pass uncensored mail out of the prison. His case was taken up by Ramsay who led a deputation to the Governor and asked the Home Secretary a parliamentary question on the matter. Ramsay wanted to know whether forcible feeding should be used as a punishment in cases where a prisoner has expressed his willingness to take the nourishment in question. After a verbal protest Bowman submitted quietly. Another detainee then tried the same procedure as Bowman but when told he would be fed artificially unless he took the diet ordered he changed his mind and took his punishment.[98] Bowman however exacted his revenge by refusing to accept conditional terms for his release in 1942 and the authorities decided to release him uncon-

---

[94] Battersby, *The Bishop said Amen*, pp. 44–5; S. Rawnsley, 'Fascism and fascists in Britain in the 1930s', PhD thesis, University of Bradford, 1981, p. 216; PRO HO 215/492, *Mona's Herald*, 23 Sept. 1941.

[95] PRO HO 215/493, Home Secretary's Report on Incident at Peveril Camp, 2 Oct. 1941.

[96] Driver, 'Shadows of Exile', p. 51.

[97] J. Hamm, 'Other concentration camps', *The European*, 8, 5 (Jan. 1957), pp. 313–19; idem, *Action Replay* (London, 1983); PRO HO 45/25740, Jeffrey Hamm.

[98] PRO HO 45/25729, Frederick H. U. Bowman; PRO HO 45/25700, note by W. H. Lines (governor) of meeting with Maule Ramsay, Domvile et al., 4 Nov. 1942.; PRO HO 45/25753, note on the forced feeding of H. U. Bowman.

ditionally in 1943 as they regarded him as an unimportant detainee whose stroppy behaviour made him an undesirable influence in prison.[99] Arnold Leese claimed too that he went on a hunger strike where he was forcibly fed in protest at not being told the reasons for his detention.[100] There is no confirming evidence of this but given Leese's general attitude it is certain he resisted the authorities as far as he could.

A more dignified expression of protest was displayed by the released internee, Charles Watts. He was district leader of the Westminster branch of the BUF and organized the cab drivers group of members which allegedly contained 1,000 members. He had been released in 1941 with restrictions applied to his freedom of movement. On 16 November 1942 he helped organize a party to celebrate Sir Oswald Mosley's birthday. At this function, at which he appeared in the illegal Blackshirt uniform, Watts made an impassioned speech saying there was far too much suspicion and distrust amongst the members of British Union, who instead of uniting in one party were now forming numerous small groups which were wary of each other. He then stressed the point that British Union must be regarded as a British organization, and any adherent harbouring pro-German thoughts was a menace and thoroughly deserved detention under DR 18b.[101]

A minor sign of resistance from some internees was shown by the adherents of St Barbe Baker's new religion. St Barbe Baker was a victim of the First World War, where he had obtained an MC as well as the after-effects of shell shock and gas poisoning. He was an able man who was responsible for the advertising for the British Empire exhibition in 1923. His poor health, alcoholism and variable mental state meant he only found irregular employment in the inter-war years. His behaviour at the outbreak of war, when he joined the BUF as 'Colonel' Moore-Hope – he was in fact a captain – and his propaganda at the meetings of Maida Vale BUF and NL members that the *Royal Oak* had been sunk by enemy bombing and not a submarine and that Hitler was about to unleash his secret weapon against France by unlocking the flood-

[99] PRO HO 45/25729, unconditional revoking of detention order, 7 Apr. 1943.
[100] A. S. Leese to Earl Winterton MP (n.d.), note on my internment file 3573, Britons Library.
[101] PRO HO 45/25702, Special Branch report on Charles Watts at Mosley birthday party, 20 Nov. 1942.

gates of the Rhine, brought him to the attention of the authorities.[102] He was interned and the Committee, although recognizing his eccentricity, formed the opinion that his pro-Hitler beliefs and organizing abilities and his evasive behaviour made him a potentially dangerous man if released. He was to be interned until the end of the war.

At Peveril Baker began preaching a new religion which glorified Hitler as Christ returned to earth. He emphasized that the Jews should be pitied and well treated and he was distrusted by some anti-semites. However, he had a certain amount of success in converting other detainees to his peculiar views. On one occasion, Baker and one of his converts, J. L. Battersby of the BUF, told the camp commandant after reading him a passage from the Acts of the Apostles that if he followed the wisdom of St Paul's gaoler and let them go free, he and his family would be saved from eternal damnation.[103] St Barbe Baker in 1942 held religious meetings in camp where the diehard nazis, according to the camp informant, interpreted Baker's quotations from Isaiah, which said that rulers and kings would pay tribute to a man who lived on the mountain and that when he came 'Joybells would be rung', as Hitler living at Berchtesgaden and the ringing of church bells in the event of an invasion.[104] Needless to say St Barbe Baker's religious meetings seem to have been rapidly closed down by the authorities after two meetings.

If active resistance was minimal, the most sustained response was a passive resistance to the boredom, physical deprivation and increasing mental strains of internment brought about by the seemingly never-ending ordeal for those who failed to gain immediate release from the Advisory Committee. In spite of using prison and camp warders as informants and the bugging of Mosley's cell, little of consequence was learned by the prison and internment authorities about supposed fascist treason. Indeed, the prison governor at Brixton later commended BUF internees on their patriotism and their support for the RAF against the Luftwaffe in the nightly air raids.[105]

Although it is dangerous to draw too many conclusions from

[102] PRO HO 283/28, MI5 report on Thomas Guillaume St Barbe Baker, 1940.
[103] PRO HO 45/25732, report on St Barbe Baker, 1945.
[104] PRO HO 214/45, Religious Meetings in Camp, 2 Apr. 1942.
[105] Skidelsky, Oswald Mosley, pp. 455–6.

anecdotal evidence a few tentative points can be made about the effects of internment of DR 18b detainees. Lengthy internment undermined the constitutions of even the fittest and healthiest, but it should be remembered that many recovered physically from the ordeal. For example, Mosley lived to be 84 and Domvile survived into his 90s. However, the long list of internees who were released mainly on health grounds included Mosley, Leese, Domvile and Beckett amongst others. All internees lost weight and were physically debilitated by the experience, but most survived without permanent undermining of their health. The mental scars, however, produced more long-term effects in some cases. Sociological and psychological literature on the institutionalization of individuals, and the growing use by historians of such material, has suggested that reductionist models of behaviour patterns have to be treated with a great deal of scepticism.[106] This is certainly the case too with internment and it could of course be argued that such personality change as was noticed could have had other causes.

Of those who survived the experience, some of Mosley's closest followers adjusted well to the post-internment world. Although Francis Hawkins never re-entered active politics, a coterie of prominent and junior members of the BUF whose commitment to Mosley and his ideas had been strengthened by internment persuaded him back into politics in 1948 against his better judgement. Mosley and his wife also endured the experience without noticeable psychological scars. Mosley used his enforced rest in prison to read widely; he learned German and his main interest became ancient Greece. Through a correspondence with his eldest son, Nicholas, his pronounced classicism gradually shaped out the forms of his radical new post-1945 ideas. This correspondence was to develop the intellectual basis of the non-materialist evolutionism whose roots were in Jungian psychology and the new physics of Jeans and Eddington,[107] views which were later to be developed in *The Alternative*, where the evolution of the 'Thought-Deed' man was to be contrasted with the 'will to comfort' type prevalent in the puritanical ethos of British capi-

[106] S. Elkins, *Slavery* (Chicago, 1976); A. J. Lane (ed.), *The Debate over Slavery* (London, 1971); R. Fogel and S. Engerman, *Time on the Cross* (Boston, 1976); P. David and P. Temin, *Reckoning with Slavery* (New York, 1976).
[107] N. Mosley, *Beyond the Pale* (London, 1983), pp. 216–27.

talism and its ruling class.[108] These ideas were to be much better thought out than the activism behind fascist ideology.

Ironically, these new ideas were to be closer to European revisionist fascist ideology, mainly deriving from Waffen SS propaganda, the nazi colonial bureau and the ex-South African Minister of Defence, Oswald Pirow, whose Europe-Africa colonial ideas were to influence the survival of European neo-fascist views after 1945, than BUF ideology had been to either German nazism or Italian fascism in the 1930s. Internment helped turn Mosley into a European. This derived from the experience of internment tempered by the realization that his movement had been too totalitarian and nationalistic in the 1930s.

The majority of internees, however, retired from active political life after the war. Nellie Driver argued that most fascists drifted off after the war because some had suffered too much for the cause; others like herself found new enthusiasms, in her case Roman Catholicism. She herself found it impossible to get a job for three years after she was released, and practically all the internment files comment on the difficulty fascists had obtaining employment when they were released. Francis Hawkins's appointment at the Medical Supply Association in 1945 led to a threatened strike by the staff and his dismissal.[109]

For some the scars of internment were to be more pronounced. Certain of the 'Jew wise', for example, became hardened in their eccentricity. Maule Ramsay, who had congratulated the Advisory Committee on having no Jewish members,[110] immediately on his release tried to reactivate in Parliament an ancient thirteenth-century statute which would have introduced Nuremberg-type laws for the Jews in Britain. Leese appeared to revel in being persecuted for his adherence to fanatical anti-semitism and his one-man crusade was intensified. Admiral Sir Barry Domvile now became a much more committed adherent to the conspiracy theory of history; for him Judmas (a combined Judaeo-Masonic plot) was responsible for the calamities of the modern world. His objections to the way the Intelligence Community functioned and his peculiar attacks on specialists in the Royal Navy which he thought had

---

[108] O. Mosley, *The Alternative* (London, 1947), pp. 25, 289.
[109] PRO HO 45/25700, *Jewish Chronicle*, 4 May 1945.
[110] PRO HO 283/45, Advisory Committee hearing with Aubrey Lees, 29 July 1940, p. 17.

eventually led him to be pensioned off in 1934, were now rationalized in terms of his refusal to be recruited by a Jewish freemason while he was Director of Naval Intelligence.[111]

Some of the less exalted internees also suffered from long-term mental aberrations. Harold Lockwood, the second man of the IFL, commented on the essential truth behind the DR 18b detainees propaganda pamphlet, *It might have happened to you* (Glasgow 1943). He said he had seen men slowly losing their grip and sanity, becoming physical wrecks as a result of internment.[112] Although Lockwood was an extreme anti-semite whose judgement can be questioned he was not entirely wrong in his assessment. One of St Barbe Baker's converts, J. L. Battersby, published privately after the war a pamphlet describing Hitler as the champion, redeemer and saviour of the Aryan people in their relentless struggle with the Jews. The Germans were the God-appointed lords of the earth and 'The God has indeed come down from heaven and his name is Adolf Hitler.'[113]

The release of Mosley

If the effect of internment on the fascists was varied, for the communists the release of Mosley in November 1943 produced an outbreak of emotion which momentarily threatened to disrupt war production. The whole sorry saga of internment produced a peculiar inversion of the normal political responses to the vexed question of civil liberties. Whereas usually it was the political left who criticized the government for infringement of fundamental liberties, now it was the Communist party and the Council for Civil Liberties (the precursor of the NCCL), which they partly controlled, who were at the forefront of the demands to keep Mosley interned. Harold Nicolson resigned from the Council over its general reaction to Mosley's release, on the grounds that he thought it illogical that such a body could support a belief that a citizen could be kept in prison without trial.[114] There were 38

---

[111] Domvile, 'From Admiral to Cabin Boy', p. 73; idem, *By and Large* (London, 1936), pp. 175–80; Domvile to A. K. Chesterton, 15 Aug. 1965.
[112] H. H. Lockwood, 'Not finished yet', *People's Post*, Dec. 1945.
[113] J. L. Battersby, *The Holy Book of Adolf Hitler* (Southport, n.d.).
[114] Harold Nicolson to CCL, 23 Dec. 1943, Box 41/4 NCCL Archive.

other resignations over the same issue. While there was an understandable case for locking up fascists in 1940, the logic of the argument became progressively weaker as the fortunes of war changed and the threat of invasion receded; and given the fact that the Communist party had played a less than glorious role in the phoney war period when they too advocated an anti-war policy, it was not surprising that the authorities viewed these protests in a somewhat cynical manner.

Although the communists provided the froth of the anti-Mosley campaign, it was the attitude of the Labour party and Trades Union Congress which accounted for the longevity of internment. Since 1940 Richard Stokes, the Labour MP for Ipswich, and a few other members had persistently demanded the release of Mosley and the fascists on the grounds of the continuing infringement of his civil liberties. In the eyes of such critics Mosley should either be tried as a traitor or set free. The objections of the left were summed up in two letters to Herbert Morrison from the Transport and General Workers Union and the TUC in the furore following Mosley's release in November 1943,[115] which argued that to release Mosley then would reduce civilian morale as Mosley had come to symbolize fascism and nazism for most of the British people.

Although the British government was very sensitive to issues of civilian morale, Churchill and the Conservatives were equally concerned about foreign, particularly American, opinion. It was thought to be somewhat incongruous to be fighting a war against an allegedly unspeakable tyranny when the government were imprisoning British citizens without trial. From the autumn of 1940 onwards the Advisory Committee was consciously used as a device for reducing as quickly as possible the numbers interned. The government was particularly concerned that DR 18b prisoners should not have their health undermined and where this appeared to be occurring internees were released. General debility or threat to life were the reasons why 'serious' cases were released, and when Mosley's phlebitis started to spread in 1943 the medical authorities informed the Home Office there was a threat to Mosley's life, particularly given the fact that the conditions of

[115] PRO HO 45/28492/252 and 257.

internment had already reduced his weight from 14 stone 7 lbs to 11 stone 4 lbs.[116]

It was in the light of these facts that the Cabinet decided to release Mosley in November 1943. The Left organized a series of demonstrations in November and December 1943, although Special Branch argued that these were mainly planned by the Communist party or front organizations.[117] At least 21 anti-Mosley meetings in London were reported to the authorities in the month following his release, with attendances rising to 1,300 and several over 1,000.[118] Following one demonstration an empty quart beer bottle was delivered to the Home Secretary labelled 'Rat Poison' and 'Cure for Phlebitus' (sic).[119] On 23 November over 1,000 demonstrators yelled outside the Palace of Westminster: 'We've got to ged rid of the rat M-O-S-L-E-Y.'[120] The government was more worried by the 14 days' notice of strike action at nine Glamorgan collieries over the issue, although it appears these did not take place.[121]

The virulence of the opposition, with London as its epicentre, reflected both the degree of popular hostility felt in the capital to Mosley following the blitz, and the fact that the Communist party had organized tenant associations and front organizations in local communities, particularly in the East End. The government were particularly concerned about the growth of anti-semitism during the Second World War and the possible role fascists might have in fanning its embers.[122] This arose partly as a result of criticism of alleged involvement by some Jews in black market activities. This was one of the reasons why the conditional release of many fascists did not allow them access to the Metropolitan Police District. However, even before the end of the war there was conflict between communists and ex-fascists and the meetings of Jeffrey Hamm's League of ex-Servicemen were to bring alive once more the tensions of the 1930s in parts of the East End for a short period after 1945.

---

[116] PRO HO 45/24892/129.
[117] PRO HO 45/24893/3–4.
[118] PRO HO 45/24893/11.
[119] PRO HO 45/24893/6.
[120] PRO HO 45/24893/110.
[121] PRO HO 45/24893/114.
[122] Aaron Goldman, 'The resurgence of anti-semitism in Britain during World War II', *Jewish Social Studies*, 40, 1 (1984), pp. 37–50.

Thus internment brought the official history of British fascism to an abrupt conclusion. The BUF and IFL were never to be reformed. Yet fascism did not die; like the leopard, it changed its spots. Its resurrection in a greatly altered post-war world was to be achieved in revisionist forms.

Few were to emerge from the sorry saga of internment with any credit and the continuing obsession with secrecy by both the authorities and those who suffered make a final assessment of it difficult. What can be said, however, is that internment, which began as a response to a political and military crisis in 1940 and was introduced on the grounds of national security, after 1941 was maintained as a political act; the purpose of internment subtly changed from preventive detention of an arguably potential fifth column to the maintenance of public morale through the punishment as scapegoats of those in British society who appeared to resemble most, at least superficially, the nazis and what they stood for. It was ironic that the Communist party, who turned from an anti-war party to super-patriots overnight in June 1941, exhibited far more signs of foreign control than the fascists ever did; although Mosley had received significant finance from Mussolini for a few years in the 1930s, this was no more reprehensible than the financial support and rigid direction that Moscow had always provided for the communists. If the Zinoviev letter, whether forged or not,[123] and the funds provided for the *Daily Herald* suggested attempted Moscow influence behind the British Labour movement, the Security Service completely failed to produce clear evidence of any close control of British fascism by the more successful European movements, at least insofar as their activities in 1939–40 were concerned.

[123] Andrew, *Secret Service*, pp. 298–338.

10

New Wine for Old Bottles, 1945–1960

Inevitably the end of the Second World War marked a watershed in the history of British fascism. Although fascism had not been banned, the use of DR 18b (1A) and DR 18AA against the BUF, and the wholesale internment of many of the leading members of the BUF, IFL, NL, BPP and the Link, meant that the state had squashed flat the political activities of these organizations. After the war only the BPP was to survive under the aristocratic patronage of the Duke of Bedford.

Post-war revisionist fascism

For those whose faith in British fascism remained undimmed the realities of the post-war world had to be taken into account. A new consensus had formed. State and society were hostile to all forms of political activity which could be seen as friendly to or influenced by nazism. Prior to the Second World War, apart from organized labour and militant Jewish movements, there had been widespread indifference to fascism provided that public order was not threatened. The experience of 1940 and the war to the finish against Hitler had radically altered that perspective.

This was shown in the assessment of public opinion in the Mass Observation files, where the two main surveys of anti-semitism in 1938 and 1943 showed a marked difference in attitude on the part of the researchers, from an anthropological oddity to a serious social problem.[1] Reactions to Mosley changed from indifference in the first two by-elections fought by the fascists in 1940 through the physical assault of Mosley in May 1940 and popular support for the mass internment of fascists to the marked hostility to Mosley's release in late 1943.[2] Indeed, although Tom Harrison probably under-estimated the extent to which the Communist party orchestrated this event, his comment that his researchers found stronger feelings on this last subject than on any other that they had examined since 1937 did reflect a change in public sentiment.

After 1940 British fascism faced the domestic equivalent of the mood which wanted to hang the Kaiser and squeeze Germany until the 'pips squeaked' after the First World War. It was in this light that the new Labour government in 1945 set up a committee on fascism. This was in response to Mosley addressing a meeting of about 600 DR 18b internees on the 15 December 1945. However, although the first meeting of the committee assumed it would be a good thing to ban fascism, the Home Secretary, J. Chuter Ede, soon changed his mind.[3] It was thought too difficult to define the concept and, if it were outlawed, either far too wide a range of opinion would be suppressed or such movements would marginally alter their beliefs to move outside the range of definition. The new committee also found it very difficult to obtain material to support charges of seditious conspiracy against Leese, Ratcliffe and others who were still actively propagating anti-semitic doctrines, in the wake of the repeal of the Defence Regulations.[4] Chuter Ede considered that vigilance and informed discussion of democratic principles was all that was needed to defeat fascism. Thus the Labour government, although taking note of such groups as the London Trades Council, who wished to ban all fascist activity and put Mosley back in gaol in 1947, reverted to the classic liberal line of the Home Office in the 1930s to maintain

[1] File 12, Anti Semitism Survey 1938, File 1669, 'On overcoming Anti-Semitism 1943', *Mass Observation File Reports.*

[2] File 39, Silvertown By-election, Feb. 1940; File 59, Leeds NE By-election, March 1940; File 154, Middletown and Prestwich By-election, 1940; File 135, Reactions to Internment of Mosley; File 2011, Mosley and After, *Mass Observation File Reports.*

[3] PRO HO 45/25399/89. PRO Cab 128/2 Cab 63 (45) Minute 3, PRO Cab 128/5 Cab 31 (46), Cab 129 CP (46) 137.

[4] PRO HO 45/25399/123.

freedom of speech while closely watching the suspect organizations who were creating public disquiet.[5]

Thus fascism had caused an ironic reversal of attitudes in British society. While the Labour movement and the NCCL were calling for a reduction in the freedom of speech, the government was valiantly defending the right of all groups in society to liberty of expression provided that public order was not threatened.

Thus if the government was reluctant to suppress fascism, the fascists were aware that they would have to move very carefully to avoid reprisals. The hanging of William Joyce provided further bad publicity. Although Mosley called him an 'offensive little beast' and Chesterton thought he deserved to be hung as a traitor,[6] the public linked by association the smear of Joyce's treachery with British fascism. Whatever the doubts about Joyce's British citizenship and whether it was legally valid to hang him,[7] amongst the leading proponents of the tradition only Arnold Leese, in a reversal of his position in 1940, was prepared to defend him. Leese wrote to the Home Secretary saying that Joyce had no treachery in his heart and his only motive was to bring Britain and Germany closer together in a great European civilization.[8] Later, Chesterton was to write six articles on Joyce's treachery when he was employed by Beaverbrook in 1953, but at the last moment it was decided to reduce the story to one article which was subedited down to a bowdlerized version which did little justice to Chesterton's meticulous use of the material given him by Margaret Joyce, John Macnab and Aubrey Lees. Even so, the article in the *Sunday Express* created a furore, with accusations that Chesterton was trying to whitewash Joyce. Chesterton, with the judgement of hindsight and researched knowledge, now considered that Joyce's defence on legal technicalities was a strong one but that nevertheless he was still morally guilty of treachery.[9] Even though Mosley and Chesterton were both horrified by Joyce's action during the war, the fact that they had both been closely connected with him in the 1930s was to compromise their reputations as judges of

[5] PRO HO 45/25399/320–2.

[6] PRO HO 283/13/63. 'The National Front. Its formation and progress', p. 7, 6 July 1945, Ivan Greenberg papers, 170/5, Mocatta Library.

[7] J.W. Hall (ed.) *The Trial of William Joyce* (London, 1946).

[8] Letter, Leese to Chuter Ede, n.d., File 3574, Britons Library.

[9] A. K. Chesterton, 'The strange case of William Joyce', Article 6, p. 11, in A. K. Chesterton papers.

men; guilt by past association was to cloud, however unfairly, their future activities.

This extremely negative perception of all kinds of fascist activity after 1945 meant that all those who took a less fundamentalist line than Arnold Leese were very wary and security-conscious. Mosley, ever mindful of the case of William Joyce, was exceptionally careful not to become associated with extremist lunatics who advocated sabotage and armed insurrection. Although he kept rigidly to a legal and constitutional line and expelled from the Union Movement (UM) (see pp. 244–5) those who advocated illegality, the very fact that it took him so long to see through many dangerous extremists in the first place was disquieting, as the case of Francis Parker Yockey and his associates was to prove. Chesterton told the National Front after Victory group (NF after V) in 1945 that he had received a letter from the IFL proposing the formation of an underground movement which possessed arms and ammunition dumps, with a strict discipline enforceable by death. Chesterton's line, which he held consistently throughout his career, was to arm privately if in defence of the king but not otherwise.[10] Leese and some of his followers were gaoled in 1947 for being involved in a conspiracy to help escaped Dutch Waffen SS prisoners of war.

The other major factor which led public opinion to detest all movements which appeared to have any connection with the nazi regime was the grim revelations of the survivors of Belsen and the death camps in Poland. From 1945 onwards the chief accusation to be hurled at all varieties of fascists by opponents was their supposed commitment to the physical extermination of Jewry. In terms of two of the major political survivors of British fascism this accusation was untrue. Mosley had never advocated anything beyond the physical separation of Jews and Englishmen and the forced expulsion of Jews from England. Chesterton's position was equally clear; his opposition to nazism after March 1939 and friendship with individual Jews like Joseph Leftwich led him to a partial realization that his rabid anti-semitism before 1939 could be construed as genocidal. Indeed, in his confused state in 1939 he more than once ended his arguments at meetings with statements which implied exactly that. Yet although his anti-semitism was to

[10] 'The National Front. Its formation and progress', p. 11.

remain a lifelong obsession, he was to recoil from the implications
of his extremism before 1939 and to argue that those responsible
for the gas chambers and the horror of the concentration camps
should go to the gallows.[11] His own conspiratorial anti-semitism
was seen as part of an Anglo-American tradition which
presumably was supposed to have milder consequences than the
nazi version. What these were was never spelt out and he failed to
understand the contradiction between the logic of his arguments
and the moral revulsion he felt about the excesses of nazism.

Arnold Leese's bias, in contrast, hardened significantly. For him
the nazi defeat, despite his earlier misgivings about Hitler, was
now seen as an unmitigated disaster and represented the triumph
of the forces of international Jewry and Zionism. His genocidal
beliefs were strengthened by the war and he was to advocate these
arguments again after 1945.[12] Cranky views like those of Leese
were to have no impact on society after the war. Leese had become
a one-man band whose main impact was through the Britons
Society. Post-war fascism was to see an oscillation of fortunes
between purveyors of revisionist forms of fascism and the classic
nazi mantle assumed by Leese after 1945.

Both Mosley and Chesterton vehemently denied that they were
fascists after 1945. Mosley argued that the narrow nationalism of
fascism was no longer appropriate to the need to create an
integrated European state whose government supposedly would
be more amenable to democratic controls than the pre-war fascist
conception. Chesterton, presumably regretting his pre-war hero-
worship of Mosley and the embarrassing attempts to transfer this
mantle to Lord Lymington or Maule Ramsay in 1939, was no
longer filled with the need to worship at a leader's feet. Yet their
politics, although they developed in radically different directions,
were both rooted in separate aspects of the inter-war tradition,
and both reflected developments in the attempt to revive the
phenomenon on the continent after the war. In short, both can be
viewed as separate revisionist forms of fascism even if their

---

[11] A. K. Chesterton and J. Leftwich, *The Tragedy of Anti-Semitism* (London, 1948), pp.
150, 212–13; *London Tidings*, Nov. 1947; D. Baker, 'A. K. Chesterton. The making of a
British fascist', PhD thesis, University of Sheffield, 1982, pp. 392–93.
[12] C. Holmes, 'Historical revisionism in Britain; The politics of history', Trends in
Historical Revisionism, Centre for Contemporary Studies Seminar, May 1985, p. 4–8.

experiences had led them to emphasize the need for legality and democratic forms.

Revisionism in this sense has been seen almost entirely in terms of those who have argued that the Holocaust never happened.[13] This view has been put by non-fascists but it has assumed a central role in the case of certain contemporary self-proclaimed nationalist or neo-nazi organizations. Its origins date from the war and some of its earliest proponents were anti-nazi anti-semites.[14] Yet the chief survivors of the British fascist generation believed that Hitler had committed foul crimes against European Jewry, even if Leese argued that the Holocaust was a Jewish myth. For Mosley and Chesterton new responses of the fascist generation were needed after 1945 to meet the changed political conditions of the post-war world, and it was their very different ideas which represented the revisionist link between two generations of fascists. It was only through the smokescreen of hindsight that later apologists for Hitler in the NF and BM felt bold enough to promote a cover-up of nazi atrocities and attempted Jewish genocide through so-called 'revisionist' works – a euphemistic label for a historical fairy tale.

The fascist revisionism of Mosley and Chesterton arose partly from continental and American influences and partly from the logic of the situation in Britain. Mosley had spent some of his enforced rest during the war in learning German and catching up on his reading. The similarity between many of the ideas outlined in *The Alternative* (1947) and the emergence of proposals for a Nation Europa and Eurafrika in the underground and semi-legal nationalist movements in post-war Germany appeared to be related to these facts.[15] *The Alternative* was translated into German and was more widely read in that country than in Britain. The FBI noted that the UM in 1948 had a European Contact Section and a German adviser called Alfred Francke Kriesche who had links with the Bruderschaft, an elitist underground society of ex-SS officers.[16] Such contacts, no doubt, were the reason why

[13] Ibid.

[14] D. Reed, *A Prophet at Home* (London, 1941), p. 94; idem, *The Controversy of Zion* (Durban, 1978), p. 400.

[15] K. P. Tauber, *Beyond Eagle and Swastika* (Middletown, Conn. 1967), pp. 208–38.

[16] CG100–25647, FBI files, K. Coogan, 'Francis Parker Yockey and the Nazi International. A preliminary report' (1982), Appendix.

the British government refused to give Mosley back his passport until 1949.

Similarly there was a parallel between Mosley's later new ideas on 'European socialism', advocating syndicalist forms of organization in industry, and Mussolini's attempt to return to his roots in the Republic di Salo in Italy in 1944.[17] This may have represented a similarity of response by men who came to fascism from the political left, or the influence of Italian contacts with the UM. It was indeed ironic that a man who spent most of his time arguing before the Advisory Committee how British his movement was, should now turn intellectual somersaults in a so-called extension of patriotism to merge some of his pre-war beliefs into a European superstate concept.

Chesterton's revisionism was at first sight less dramatic in its new orientation. He did not lose his basic patriotism as the cornerstone of his beliefs. Yet his anti-semitism showed important changes. No longer did he indulge in violent anti-semitic abuse, and he inveighed against the nazi influences of Houston Stewart Chamberlain's 'clotted nonsense' and Rosenberg's 'racial rubbish'.[18] However, this attack on nazi nordicism did not also apply to anti-semitic conspiracy theories. Although Chesterton's views were rationalized in terms of Anglo-American influences they were also very similar to Rosenberg's. Rosenberg's 'golden international' alliance of Jewish capitalists and Soviet communists became an obsessional bogey-man in his revisionist ideas, and even the *Protocols*, forgery or not, were to be used as evidence of what really happened in the world. In the 1950s racial abuse was transferred from the Jews to coloured immigrants and Africans, where an odd mixture of colonial paternalism and virulent racialism symbolized his attitude to the new scapegoat which was seen as a threat to the remnants of the British Empire and way of life.[19]

Chesterton's new ideas like Mosley's were a reflection of the changed geopolitical realities in Europe and the British Empire after 1945. Europe and Britain were exhausted and it was the two

[17] A. J. Gregor, *The Ideology of Fascism* (New York, 1969), pp. 283–303.
[18] A. K. Chesterton, 'Why Patriotism', *Candour*, Apr. 1971; idem, 'The myth of race', *Truth*, 4 Aug. 1950.
[19] R. C. Thurlow, 'Ideology of obsession', *Patterns of Prejudice*. 8, 6 (Nov.–Dec. 1974), pp. 23–9.

new superpowers, the USA and USSR, who were the main factors in international politics. Fascists whose anti-Bolshevism had always been a motivating force now, like Mussolini in the 1920s, saw the USA as an equally dangerous enemy. Chesterton's conspiracy theory was to highlight the supposed role of Jewish financiers in US policy and how it was designed to destroy the British Empire. However, although he was to be as virulently anti-American as his German friend, Otto Strasser, Chesterton was never influenced by Strasser's ideas for European confederation, Eurafrika or pro-Soviet sympathies.[20]

The survival of political forms derived from inter-war fascism after 1945 in a hostile Britain was to depend not only on the tenacity of those involved but on financial resources as well. The most influential groups were those who possessed sufficient capital to publicize their views. In this sense Mosley, with his own financial resources and personal magnetism, was in a position to survive once he decided to re-enter active politics in 1948. Arnold Leese, too, who had carefully husbanded his own resources in the inter-war period, inherited part of the estate of H. H. Beamish after the war. After paying succession duty he received £3,350 from this source,[21] which was used to help finance *Gothic Ripples* and the Britons Society.

Chesterton, a professional journalist who was deputy editor of *Truth* from 1944 to 1953, and literary adviser to Beaverbrook in the latter year, was able to form his own newspaper *Candour* in late 1953 thanks to receiving a cheque for £1,000 from an eccentric ex-patriate millionaire from Chile called R. K. Jeffery. During the next few years until Jeffery's death in 1961, Chesterton was reputed to have obtained £70,000 from this source and these bequests were used to fund *Candour* and the antics of its political offshoot, the League of Empire Loyalists.[22] Jeffery had read Chesterton's pamphlet, 'Truth has been murdered', an account of how that journal was turned into an orthodox Tory publication when bought by a Conservative MP. The dispute over Jeffery's will, which was mysteriously altered at the last minute to deprive

---

[20] D. L. Baker, 'A. K. Chesterton, the Strasser brothers, and the politics of the National Front', *Patterns of Prejudice*, 19, 3 (1985), pp. 23–33; O. Strasser, *Germany in a Disunited World* (Eastbourne, 1947), pp. 26–31.

[21] Estate of H. H. Beamish, H. H. Beamish Correspondence etc., File 3571, Britons Library.

[22] Baker, 'A. K. Chesterton' (thesis), p. 370.

Chesterton of the estate, stopped the National Front from receiving a massive injection of funds, reputed to be over a million pounds, in its early years.[23]

Many of the problems emphasized here were to be experienced in one of the early attempts to revive the tradition in 1945. The NF after V group was a still-born operation which formed a patriotic, anti-semitic nationalist movement in revisionist clothing. The ever-alert Board of Deputies of British Jews reactivated their mole who had successfully burrowed into the innermost recesses of the NL in 1939 in order to infiltrate the organization. In a classic whistle-blowing operation, the Board of Deputies arranged for Lord Vansittart to make a speech in the House of Lords to condemn the revival of fascism so as to prevent a merger between this group and the BPP, the effect of which was to destroy the organization.[24]

The agent's reports of the meetings of this group, in which he was part of the small team who negotiated the merger with the BPP, provided much valuable information on the psychology and mood of such organizations. The driving force behind the NF after V group was A. K. Chesterton. He was not one of those who, in the euphemistic words of John Beckett at the merger talks, had been 'held together' during the war. Although he was suspect in some quarters because he was not interned it is thought that this was because MI5 had intercepted Chesterton's indignant refusal to be recruited by the nazis to broadcast propaganda to Britain in 1939.[25]

The group, which was formed in 1944, spent much of its time watering down Chesterton's original proposals, which were to represent his basic political position for the rest of his life. Talk of impeachment of political leaders who did not put the best interests of Britain first and guarding against the further extension of Jewish power and influence were replaced by more euphemistic expressions. Many of the original members, like Major-General J. F. C. Fuller, dropped out of the organization, not because they were against its principles but, as Chesterton pointed out, because they wished to hide behind a barricade of mumbo jumbo. The

[23] *Sunday Times*, 30 Mar. 1969.
[24] S. Saloman, 'Now it can be told', p. 7, C6/9/2/1, Board of Deputies of British Jews Archive.
[25] Baker, 'A. K. Chesterton (thesis), p. 364.

group contained several internees, including H. T. Mills and Ben Greene, the latter merged his English Nationalist Association with the group. The BPP negotiating team also numbered several internees including John Beckett, ex-BUF and NSL, Aubrey Lees, ex-NL, and Harold Lockwood, ex-IFL. The NF for V, which was always short of cash, approached such well-known far right benefactors as Gordon Canning and Lane Fox Pitt-Rivers for support. The significance of the group lay in its name; Chesterton was to suggest it, plus much of its original programme, as the basis of the National Front when it was formed in 1967.[26]

The new groups and immigration

There can be little doubt that fascism would not have survived as a political irritant in Britain after 1945 if those who adopted revisionist forms of the pre-war doctrine, or who still saw Hitler as the saviour of European civilization, had not latched on to the problems created by the influx of new commonwealth immigrants in the 1950s and 1960s. The actual fascist, nazi or revisionist doctrines at the core of the various movements since 1945 were like a political dodo, dead from the outset. Neither Mosley's Europe-a-Nation campaign, the japes and stunts of the League of Empire Loyalists (LEL), or Leese's vitriolic anti-semitic venom, had any political influence whatsoever. In so far as they had any minimal significance at all it was the role played in the nativist response to what was to be called coloured immigration. In the 1960s racial populism was to fulfil the same function as the BUF's anti-semitic campaign in the East End of London from 1935–8. It was to be the UM, the LEL and the political legacy of Arnold Leese which were to act as the prototypes of the full range of negative political responses to the issues posed by coloured immigration.

Since the Second World War western Europe had attracted a migratory flow of labour to fuel the boom years from 1945–73 and to prevent a labour shortage. Britain's experience, with its imperial past, citizenship rights of Commonwealth immigrants, lower rates of economic growth and nativist resentment over fears of economic competition, housing shortages and cultural clashes,

---

[26] 'The National Front. Its formation and progress', pp. 1–11.

produced earlier conflict than elsewhere. In particular, the lack of controls on the flow of new commonwealth immigrants created hostile feelings. If the net migration to the UK was only 12,000 between 1951 and 1961 and negative thereafter, the steady build-up of immigrants, mainly from the West Indies, after the arrival of the first shipload in the *Empire Windrush* in 1948, led to many social problems in areas where they settled. Numbers had risen from 2,000 a year in 1953 to 136,000 in 1961.[27] Significant racial violence had occurred in the Nottingham and Notting Hill riots of 1958 and in attacks in Birmingham, Liverpool, Deptford and Camden Town.[28] Cyril Osborne, Conservative MP for Louth, was to galvanise a campaign in Parliament, the Conservative party and amongst public opinion to end immigration. In this latter area he was to be aided both by the rapid growth of nativist organizations and by the racial populism of UM and the heirs of Arnold Leese.

The return to active politics of Sir Oswald Mosley after the war had an air of theatricality about it which suggested a degree of stage management behind the spontaneity. Three separate movements, the 18b detainees' aid fund, the League of ex-Servicemen and the Mosley Book Clubs, coalesced in the UM in February 1948 when Mosley finally, politically, came out in the revivalist atmosphere of one of his old East End haunts. The 18b detainees' aid fund had been founded with the laudable purpose of helping the families of those who had been unfairly imprisoned without trial during the Second World War under DR 18b. The League of ex-Servicemen had been developed in the immediate post-war years by Jeffrey Hamm, a minor BUF figure in 1939 whose internment hardened his commitment to the Mosleyite cause; the experience was to turn him into a follower who eventually rose to the position of Mosley's political secretary after the death of Raven Thomson in 1955. Hamm's vigorous defence of Mosley and his criticism of his Jewish opponents led to outbreaks of violence at his meetings in London between 1948 and 1951 when the 43 group and the Association of Jewish ex-Servicemen (AJEX) interrupted his oratory with organized heckling and physical violence. The Mosley Book Clubs were

---

[27] Z. Layton Henry, *The Politics of Race in Britain* (London, 1984), pp. 16–29.
[28] Ibid., p. 35.

designed to introduce his followers to his new thought – the result of his reading and cross-fertilization of ideas with new German contacts.

The German contacts of Mosley are mentioned in FBI files on Francis Parker Yockey. Yockey was a nazi agent who, incredibly, was employed in the US legal team at the Nuremburg War Crimes Tribunal. After his dismissal from this position he came to London and made contact with Mosley in 1947. According to the FBI he became one of Mosley's paid officials and was employed in the European Contact Section of what was later to become the UM. Mosley, who was unaware of Yockey's nazi past, was impressed with his intelligence. Within UM Yockey quickly became a disruptive influence. He gathered around him a group of extremists who were influenced by his plans to create anti-American hostility in Europe and to establish links with the Soviet Union for funding propaganda and sabotage. After reading Yockey's *Imperium*, a geopolitical epic which synthesized nazi and Spenglerian themes, Mosley refused the offer that it should be published in his name. Realising now that Yockey was a dangerous contact Mosley dropped him. Mosley suffered neither fools nor madmen gladly and being accused by Yockey of being an American agent and tool of Churchill placed him in that category. Yockey's breakaway group, the European Liberation Front, was to include some whose aims were to infiltrate other nationalist groups and foster extremism and sabotage. Such individuals were later to be associated with the LEL and the Northern League.[29]

Given the fact that Mosley would inevitably initially attract such extremists as Yockey, UM emphasized that the leopard had indeed changed his spots. Mosley jettisoned much of the nationalist baggage and style of the BUF and started political life anew with a pronounced commitment to more democratic European ideals. It was the force of his personality which attracted some of the survivors of internment back to the cause. Others whose belief in the Empire or extremism were stronger than their personal loyalty to Mosley were to drift off to join the LEL or the more radical forms of 'nationalism' favoured by a new generation of militants. However, few significant new faces were to be found in Mosley's entourage and UM was to exhibit an increasingly elderly

[29] CG100–25647, FBI files.

profile of aging revolutionaries amongst its functionaries. The new generation were to find their inspiration and sustenance elsewhere.

The history of UM was to represent a low-key variant of that of the BUF after 1934. Whilst media attention gave it bad publicity for its racial populist campaigns, its serious political programme was totally ignored. Since 1935 the BBC had responded to government pressure to allow neither fascists nor communists access to wireless or television, and this was to continue until Mosley published his autobiography in 1968;[30] the press continued its unofficial boycott of Mosley's meetings, and reported only the conflict and violence.

The UM cut no populist ice with its 'Europe a Nation' and 'Europe-Africa' campaigns, though its attacks on immigration gave it some impetus in parts of east and north London. In the 1940s this was aimed at immigration from eastern Europe. Headlines in *Union* to the effect that 'Life blood flows out, sewage flows in'[31] were used to argue that every spiv and shark in eastern Europe was determined to get into Britain. Occasionally reminders of the past surfaced and more blatant anti-semitism obtruded following the findings of the Lynskey tribunals and the murder of British servicemen in Palestine.[32] Mosley later told the Anti Defamation League that UM could get by without name-calling. Whereas previously he had attacked international Jewish bankers, his followers knew exactly whom he was talking about when he now criticized American capitalists,[33] and this front of respectability enabled UM to permeate the other political parties. Although anti-semitic sentiment surfaced during the Suez crisis of 1956, memories of 1940 meant that UM was amongst the first to volunteer to fight for Britain.

If anti-semitism was toned down in comparison to pre-war attitudes, more strident racial views were noticeable. Mosley told the UM conference in 1949 that European investments in Africa should never be threatened by African governments of witch doctors and ju-ju men.[34] It was amongst the first to take up the issues posed by coloured immigration and after his partial

[30] R. Skidelsky, *Oswald Mosley* (London, 1975), p. 517.
[31] *Union*, 11 Sept. 1948.
[32] *Union*, 5 Feb. 1949.
[33] *The ADL Bulletin*, Mar. 1954.
[34] *Union*, 12 Feb. 1949.

retirement, after moving to Ireland in 1951 and later to Paris, this was the issue which was to bring Mosley back to political campaigning in the later 1950s. The UM first attacked the 'coloured invasion' in 1951 and *Union* regaled its readership with tales of the coloured work-shy, dope peddlars, molestation of white women and black crime.[35] As early as 1952 UM was fighting local elections primarily on an anti-immigrant platform, demanding a 'white Brixton'.[36]

The UM directed its main organization into the new reception areas and moved out from its old stamping ground of the East End into parts of south and west London like Brixton and Notting Hill. Antipathy and prejudice against the new immigrants and social disorders in 1958 led Mosley to attempt a political comeback in the 1959 general election in North Kensington. In fact UM had not been responsible for the encouragement of antipathy. The main area where UM was active was Notting Hill and even here, as *The Times* pointed out, the methods employed were strictly legal and constitutional and did not involve the advocacy of violence against coloured immigrants.[37] However, as in pre-war days, racial populist politics appealed to youthful activism and teddy boys were defended by UM speakers.

Mosley's campaign in 1959 was an odd mixture of economic radicalism and racial prejudice; the high road of 'Europe a Nation' and the low road of 'Kit-E-Kat' politics which criticized immigrants for their supposed love of catfood.[38] The voters of North Kensington were supposedly strange hybrids: willing to accept the most drastic economic and political changes including the merging of British sovereignty into a European State, the 'wage price' mechanism (an early form of prices and incomes policy), and 'European Socialism' (a syndical form of organization for industry); yet on the other hand so socially conservative that cultural pluralism was projected as a dire threat to the British way of life. UM propaganda was relatively restrained and did not overtly incite racial harassment although demands for forced repatriation of coloured immigrants, even if this was coupled with vague references to forms of compensation and building up the

[35] *Union*, 7 July 1951, 5 Apr. 1952, 19 June 1954.
[36] *Union*, 15 March 1952.
[37] *The Times*, 8 Sept. 1959.
[38] Skidelsky, *Oswald Mosley*, p. 513.

Caribbean economy, did nothing to calm the fears of the emerging black community. However, while Mosley thrived at synthesizing the contradictions in his political programme at a higher level of thought, the voters of North Kensington not surprisingly found it all rather confusing. After his canvassers had promised him a narrow victory Mosley lost his deposit with 8 per cent of the poll. Attempts to prove electoral malpractice foundered for lack of evidence.

After the air of unreality surrounding the North Kensington fiasco Mosley turned his attention back to his European dreams. With the help of contacts abroad Mosley tried to form a unified National Party of Europe at a conference in Venice in 1962, where he addressed a motley assortment of ex-SS officers and representatives of Europe's neo-fascist movements. In his autobiography this is presented as a resounding triumph.[39] The reality was rather more mundane. All that the representatives of the Italian and German groups agreed to do was to set up a permanent liaison office. They were not prepared to merge themselves into a National Party of Europe and many of the most significant neo-fascist European organizations were not represented at the conference.[40]

The re-emergence of Mosley and the rise of a more virulent new generation of racial nationalists led to more conflict between the survivors of the changed fascist tradition, a new generation of racial populists and neo-nazis, and the Labour movement and Jewish community. Groups such as the 62 group and Yellow Star movement created disturbances at UM meetings and public disorder resulted, including at least one physical assault on Mosley. Such confrontation led to the growth of UM with a maximum membership of about 1,500 and inactive support of about 15,000 in the early 1960s. It was this violence, plus a reduction of his vote to 4 per cent in the 1966 election and the less than brilliant performance of his candidates elsewhere, which led to Mosley retiring from active politics in that year.

The mainly favourable reception given to his autobiography ushered in the last semi-respectable phase of his career.[41] Given some access to the media once more, he crossed swords with some

[39] O. Mosley, *My Life* (London, 1968), pp. 434–40.
[40] Tauber, *Beyond Eagle and Swastika*, p. 221.
[41] Skidelsky, *Oswald Mosley*.

redoubtable past and present opponents and provided evidence that old age was no handicap for one of Britain's most formidable political debaters of the century. His reviews for *Books and Bookmen* and occasional articles in the *Daily Telegraph* colour magazine meant that he ended his days in 1981 with a small improvement in political status – from beyond the pale to the margin of respectable society.

When fascism eventually re-emerged after 1945 it did so slowly and furtively. Various extensions of pre-war fascism and anti-semitism during the 1940s organized themselves politically. Amongst the most significant of the non-Mosley groups were the so-called North West Task Force, an anti-semitic group active in Hendon and Edgware in 1946–7, the Britons, and the National Party. All these had links with the political activities of Arnold Leese and in 1948 the IFL tradition was reactivated when the new management at the Britons, now partially funded by Maule Ramsay and Arnold Leese, formed the National Workers Movement, with a journal called *Free Britain*. At its inaugural meeting Leese sent a message to his old followers urging them to eschew quarrels amongst themselves, forget old feuds and to recollect that a 'Jew wise' man or woman was a rare and precious phenomenon.[42] However, Tony Gittens and Anthony Baron later fell out with each other at the Britons, Leese's plea was disregarded and the movement collapsed in the early 1950s.[43]

The significance of the National Workers Movement was that it enabled the Leese tradition of racial nationalism to survive into the 1950s in political form. In itself it had no importance, being a vehicle for about thirty ex-IFL members to vent their spleen against the Jews in private and to give the nazi salute at the end of their meetings.[44] It was decided at one of these events that any Briton who willingly associated with a Jew was guilty of treason and a suitable punishment was being devised for any member of the group who ever gave sanctuary to one. The main difficulty was to find suitable venues for such meetings as local vicars were none too keen to rent church halls for gatherings which disseminated nazi propaganda. The other problem was that the retirement of Leese meant a leadership void for Britain's racial nationalists.

---

[42] PRO HO 45/24968/116.
[43] Note from A. S. Leese, 31 Jan. 1951, File 3571, Britons Library.
[44] PRO HO 45/24968/116.

Although hardly potential Führer material himself, Leese had been able to achieve some semblance of discipline amongst the highly argumentative racial nationalists before the war. The search for a new leader in the racial nationalist tradition was to lead to developments in the 1950s which strengthened these extremist sentiments. Organizations like the National Workers Movement and the Britons provided a cultural transmission of ideas from an increasingly elderly and embittered pre-war generation to an emerging dynamic new leadership of young 'nationalists' who were to make racial nationalism, in its revisionist conservative fascist clothing, the most important strand in the post-1945 revival.

The spirit of inter-war conservative fascism, that of the British Fascists and the ideas of Nesta Webster, was reasserted by the LEL. Although the fascist tradition was explicitly disowned as being outmoded, discredited, and associated with political violence and genocidal policies, its real pedigree was in little doubt. Autocratically led by the ex-BUF propagandist A. K. Chesterton, who controlled the purse strings of the Jeffery largesse and the LEL's weekly newspaper *Candour*, it represented a forlorn rear-guard action against the demise and changing nature of the British Empire. It regarded the Conservative government of the 1950s, particularly the Macmillan administration, as a collection of traitors who deserved to be hung like William Joyce.[45] The LEL believed in publicity-seeking stunts and demonstrated at public events although it disowned political violence and terrorism.

Chesterton's old argument with the dominant martinet clique in the BUF after 1935 also explained his tactics; the LEL was organized as a League, not a party, and believed in disrupting opponents' meetings through publicity stunts rather than by holding demonstrations and marches itself. The LEL was a halfway house between an open reactionary right political movement and an underground clandestine operation fomenting civil disobedience, although not open terrorism. Its significance lay partly in its ability to attract figureheads – retired military gentlemen, ex-colonial administrators, anti-communist and anti-semitic Roman Catholics, alienated scions of the Conservative establishment and energetic upper-middle-class ladies – to be a

---

[45] *Candour*, 14 Feb. 1958.

respectable front for rather dubious activity behind the scenes. Indeed, one chairman of the organization resigned when he considered the LEL's operation had gone beyond the bounds of legality in 1959.[46] It was to be the ideas of A. K. Chesterton, and the growing realization by some of this group that extremist and nazi ideas could be given a veneer of respectability through being expressed in more moderate language, which was to be the central importance of the LEL.

Without the financial backing from Jeffery, whom Chesterton never met, it is certain he would never have been able to start either *Candour* or the LEL. Indeed, once funds from this source had dried up after Jeffery's death in 1961, the LEL and *Candour* had difficulty continuing their operations and political activities were on a much reduced scale. However, between 1955 and 1961 the LEL had often been drawn to public attention in the media as a result of its antics. Members blew bugle horns at Conservative party conferences, interrupted state occasions by shouting that Anthony Eden had just shaken hands with a murderer when Kruschev and Bulganin arrived at Victoria Station in 1956, gate-crashed the Lambeth Conference in 1958 by dressing up as Greek Orthodox bishops, and interrupted meetings of the Movement for Colonial Freedom and Anti-Slavery Society amongst many others.[47] Renegade ex-members denounced the movement and its schoolboy pranks with its amateurish counter-subversion strategy against the Security Service.[48] Although it possessed up to 3,000 members at its peak in 1958, by the early 1960s this had fallen to a few hundred; the LEL was to gain support from both the remnants of the Die-hard tradition, who were dismayed by the collapse of the British Empire, and ex-fascists who resented Mosley's new European idea. In spite of its old-fashioned political tactics its role was to be seminal in the founding of the National Front in 1967.

As well as disruption and more clandestine activity, the LEL presented more conventional challenges to the establishment in a series of by-elections. It stood as the conscience of a form of

[46] Letter from Chairman of LEL to A. K. Chesterton, 20 May 1959, A. K. Chesterton papers.
[47] *The Times*, 13 Oct. 1958; *Candour*, 27 Apr. 1956; *Guardian*, 5 July 1958; *The Times*, 28 June 1956; *The Times*, 24 June 1960.
[48] *The People*, 29 Jan. 1961.

traditional Conservatism, as the Die-hard remnant of the Tories. It attacked as treason the withdrawal from Empire, the scuttle at Suez and Macmillan's 'wind of change' policy towards Africa. With a peculiar mixture of anti-Americanism, anti-communism, crude racialism and colonial paternalism, all woven together by a conspiracy theory of how politicians were merely pawns of the American Jewish financial establishment, the LEL had little impact on the electorate. Only at the North Lewisham by-election in 1957 did they have the moral triumph of having the best candidate, according to several observers.[49] Politically, however, they sank without trace; their candidates all lost their deposits.

Mosley, Chesterton, Leese and the 'new' fascism

In terms of the relevance of their respective ideas to new forms of British fascism for Mosley, Chesterton and Leese, there was to be an inverse correlation between the quality of such thought and its impact on 'nationalist' movements and society. Mosley during both his enforced rest from active politics in the Second World War and much of his semi-retirement read and reflected widely. Both the nature and content of his writing after the war was much more interesting than anything he had achieved as a fascist in the inter-war years. But apart from a small coterie of devoted followers nobody took any notice of what Mosley was saying. Although several elements within his ideas were to remain pernicious in terms of assessment by liberal humane values, and others hopelessly utopian and unrealistic, the synthesizing power of Mosley's mind has to be respected and the nature of his arguments have some intellectual interest. The same cannot be said of the work of Chesterton and Leese; both became increasingly obsessed by supposed Jewish plots, and although there was a certain elegance in Chesterton's journalism, the all-pervading conspiracy fantasies and different kinds of virulent racism meant they had no significance except to fascists, where their post-1945 impact was much more important than that of Mosley.

At the root of the differences between Mosley, Chesterton and

[49] *Evening Standard*, 12 Feb. 1957.

Leese were their varying assessments of the nature and function of evil in society. Although, as Nicholas Mosley argues, Sir Oswald's view, based on an interpretation of Goethe's *Faust*, a critical appreciation of Shaw's view of Wagner's Ring Cycle, and Nietzsche's philosophy, can ultimately be rejected because a person cannot manipulate ends and means as if they were words,[50] it was nevertheless a sophisticated attempt to explain and rationalize his own ideas and actions, and of a totally different order to the simplistic and reductionist views of Chesterton and Leese, neither of whom could see human activity except in stark black and white terms. Mosley argued that Faust's quest for beauty and achievement could only be realized by ceaseless striving and that once contentment was reached so man's evolutionary urge was extinguished and death ensued. Man's restlessness could be harnessed for positive achievement, like the draining of the marshes, even if this led to the death of innocent victims. For Mosley 'evil' could be harnessed for 'good' in both art and life.[51] This interpretation of *Faust* meant that for Mosley Wagner in his Ring Cycle saw further than either Nietzsche or George Bernard Shaw. *The Twilight of the Gods* was not mere grand opera, as Shaw claimed, but the inevitable destruction of the hero once mere adventure replaced the evolutionary urge to higher forms.[52] Perhaps here there is an ironic unconscious commentary on the history of the BUF. Mosley inevitably failed once he had allowed his revolutionary programme to be sidetracked into a pointless quarrel with the Jews.

Chesterton, however, could not handle the complexity of evil except in crude terms. Although he was not interned, the trauma of the abject failure of the British fascist political revolution turned Chesterton into a conspiracy theorist. Searching for reasons to account for the collapse of his fascist faith, Chesterton found an explanation in the writings of the political underground. Studying both the occult explanations of Father Denis Fahey and Nesta Webster and the materialist interpretations of A. N. Field, Douglas Reed and C. H. Douglas, Chesterton came to explain

---

[50] N. Mosley, *Beyond the Pale* (London, 1983), pp. 39–41.

[51] O. Mosley, 'Which inheritance? Goethe or "The Vicar of the Minster of Basle"', *European*, 2 (Apr. 1953), pp. 37–49.

[52] O. Mosley, 'Wagner and Shaw: a synthesis', *The European*, 37 (Mar. 1956), pp. 51–61.

complex political events in terms of the occult powers of Jewish conspirators behind the scenes to manipulate government and society mainly through their control of the money power.[53]

With a prodigious journalistic output, Chesterton outlined in *Truth* and *Candour* and in several pamphlets and books the details of this conspiracy. In essence, American Jewish financiers under Bernard Baruch and his henchmen Paul and Max Warburg were not only responsible for financing all social unrest since the Russian Revolution, but were behind the dastardly plot to destroy the British Empire and set up a one-world Jewish superstate based on the Bretton Woods and Dumbarton Oaks agreements and its derivative agencies like the World Bank and United Nations. All American-inspired international organizations like the Council of Foreign Relations, the Trilateral Commission or the Bilderberg Conferences were seen as front organizations for the conspirators. Unlike Mosley's complex philosophical and psychological ideas, Chesterton's simplistic conspiracy theory saw good and evil in Manichean terms, with traitors and agents of the devil in control of events.

Leese's perception of the complexity of the modern world was even less sophisticated than Chesterton's. For him it was axiomatic that the *Protocols of the Elders of Zion* explained the evil forces at work in society, and everything he disliked was ascribed to the machinations of Jews. After his dramatic fight against internment his views became more rigid and extreme. Great Britain was infested with Jews and rotten with freemasonry.[54] The Second World War was a Jewish war of survival and the end result was the death of Europe. Leese's Manichean views and his total intransigence suggested not only a prejudiced personality but his increased willingness to suffer persecution for his strange beliefs hinted at a progressive form of abnormality.[55]

If there were marked differences in the style and sophistication of Mosley, Chesterton and Leese with regard to their views of the role of evil and the nature of the political process there were also fundamental differences with their attitudess on the nature of man. This was particularly marked in relation to their views on

---

[53] A. K. Chesterton, *Menace of the Money Power* (London, 1946), frontispiece; idem, *The New Unhappy Lords* (Liss Forest, 1965), pp. 247–8.

[54] *Gothic Ripples*, 11 Apr. 1946.

[55] C. Holmes, *Anti-Semitism in British Society 1876–1939* (London, 1979), p. 231.

race, culture and evolution. Sociological theories of race relations have suggested that two types of determinist belief system are symptomatic of those who believe in racial ideologies; racism, which is the belief in different biological, physical and genetic factor endowments between races, and ethnocentrism, which is the variation in cultural development between groups as defined by the subjective observer.[56] This can be expressed in terms of theoretical conceptualism or common-sense.[57] There is some dispute over whether ethnocentrism is merely a functional equivalence of racism in an intellectual environment where racism has become discredited. More recently it has been suggested that where both racist and ethnocentric attitudes are seen as outmoded what is misleadingly called the 'new racism' is developed as a functional equivalent.[58] This argues merely that cultures are different, and not superior or inferior to each other, but the fact that such variations exist creates conflict and hostility between groups in society. Mosley, Chesterton and Leese were to develop varying aspects of these types of racial ideologies to justify discriminatory policies towards Africans and coloured immigrants.

Mosley's view of race developed significantly from his view in the inter-war period that racial hatred was not a desirable policy for the British Empire. In essence they were close to the racial views of Italian fascism, and the concept of the nation as a race cradle which developed from the English anthropologist Sir Arthur Keith.[59] Its main assumptions were that race formation was a dynamic historical and political process within the confines of the nation state and that the derived characteristics of the nation-race could be acquired by the interaction of heredity, environment, culture and education over historical time. This was essentially Mosley's position.[60]

As a Lamarckian Mosley believed that culture rather than race was the major factor behind evolution. However he derived from Spengler a belief that different cultures should be separated from each other because contact brought decay and not growth. These

---

[56] M. Banton, 'Racism', New Society, 10 Apr. 1969, pp. 551–4.
[57] J. Rex, Race Relations in Sociological Theory (London, 1970), p. 138.
[58] M. Barker, The New Racism (London, 1981), pp. 12–29.
[59] Gregor, Ideology of Fascism, pp. 258–9.
[60] Mosley Right or Wrong? (London, 1961), pp. 115–31.

ideas were developed with the help of Oswald Pirow, the ex-South African Minister of Defence, into an apartheid perspective which in 1948 envisioned European control over African development and in 1953 rigid separation of White and Black Africa;[61] it was cultural difference and not a notion of superiority which made this inevitable.[62] With such a view he argued that coloured immigrants could never be harmoniously integrated into Britain and should be involuntarily repatriated with some compensation. The obvious contradiction that a belief in evolution implied an encouragement of wide outcrossing from the original stock and contact with a wide variety of cultural forms showed the basic incompatibility between his Lamarckian and Spenglerian beliefs.

To a certain degree this contradiction can be explained in Mosley's linking of the Faustian culture of Europe and its potential for evolutionary development towards the Superman concept, the 'Thought-Deed' man.[63] This brought Mosley per-ilously close to some nazi ideas and during the early post-war years he justified his views in terms of the underlying reality of race as representing the base of European unity and the close similarity between the peoples of Britain, northern France, Germany and Scandinavia.[64] Mosley also used crude arguments; in the same way that you only produced disaster if you attempted to cross horses with cattle or cabbages with roses, so you would get the same result if the races and cultures of mankind were mixed.[65]

If Mosley's was essentially a mixture of an intellectualized ethnocentrism and new racism attitude towards racial questions, both Chesterton and Leese developed views at a much lower level of conceptualization. Chesterton eschewed all theory and relied on instinct to tell him that so-called race mixing was an abomination.[66] He exhibited a strange mixture of racial pater-nalism and race prejudice in his attitudes towards Africans and coloured immigrants. To Chesterton, the African had no culture and was little more than a savage.[67] Similar animal imagery to

[61] O. Mosley, *The Alternative* (London, 1948), pp. 143–70; 'European' (Mosley), 'The African problem', *The European*, Apr. 1954.
[62] Idem, 'Underlying realities', *Union*, 10 Apr. 1948.
[63] O. Mosley, *The Alternative*, p. 289.
[64] Idem, 'Races. The first reality of European unity', *Union*, 15 May 1948.
[65] *Union*, 10 Apr. 1948.
[66] Chesterton and Leftwich, *The Tragedy of Anti-Semitism*, p. 72.
[67] *Candour*, 15 June 1956.

Mosley's was also used on occasion comparing race-mixing with attempts to cross mastiffs and Yorkshire terriers or Siamese cats and African elephants.[68]

Leese was even cruder than before the war. His views on Negroes were shown in his 'Nigger notes' in *Gothic Ripples* and his references to all educated men of colour as 'babus'. Jews were encouraging coloured immigration to dilute Britain's racial stock so that Aryan civilization could be destroyed.[69] In Leese's view, there was no difference between the face of Jomo Kenyatta and that of a gorilla.[70] Leese's racial hierarchy saw Aryans as the superior race responsible for creating all culture and civilization and the Negro was the most inferior type of mankind. Jews were not human at all and like Hitler he viewed them as a racial mishmash, an anti-race. The war had represented the triumph of Jewry and the last remaining strongholds of Aryan ascendancy were in danger of dying out as the Nordic elements merged with the 'scrub population'.[71]

In terms of the political programmes of these three men there were two main kinds of contrast; first, that of the European emphasis of both Mosley and Leese in their very different ways, and the continued belief of Chesterton in the British Empire, and secondly, while Mosley concentrated on outlining his positive political programme both Chesterton and Leese spent most of their time writing about their negative obsessions, and in particular the alleged Jewish conspiracy.

Mosley's political object in the UM was to campaign for a union of European peoples, to resist communism and finance, to fight for a new civilization and way of life, to attain power by vote of the people, to develop Africa for the benefit of Europeans and not Africans, to abolish class, privilege and hereditary wealth and to encourage hereditary service in creative enterprise.[72] The war had destroyed the political power of Europe which could only be restored through the voluntary co-operation of European peoples. The urgent need was to remove the outside power of the USA and USSR from Europe and for the new European superpower to

---

[68] A. K. Chesterton, 'The myth of race', *Truth*, 5 Aug. 1950.
[69] *Gothic Ripples*, Dec. 1952.
[70] *Gothic Ripples*, May 1953.
[71] *Gothic Ripples*, 11 Apr. 1946.
[72] *Mosley News Letter*, 13 Dec. 1947.

develop Africa for her own benefit. These arguments outlined in *The Alternative*, together with his creative evolutionist ideas about the Thought-Deed man, were very similar to the revisionist ideas emerging in the nationalist groups in the Western Allies' occupied zones of Germany. In essence Mosley's European idea had certain similarities with nazi New Order European propaganda during the Second World War and some elements of its racial philosophy after the Nordic school had been discredited.[73] Given the contacts Mosley had at this time, it should be viewed more in this light than as a precursor of the democratic idea of the EEC. It probably had some influence in turning some German nationalists away from co-operation with the Soviet Union.[74]

During the 1950s Mosley was less concerned with the geo-political grand design and he returned to his original preoccupation with economics which had led to his fascist revolt in the first place. Now the new ideas were 'European socialism' and the wage-price mechanism, which were interesting attempts to redistribute wealth through syndical forms of organization and ownership and a highly complex and somewhat bureaucratic prices and income policy.[75] However, like Mussolini, who also became an economic radical once his fascist utopia was blown away, and Jose Antonio Primo de Rivera in Spain, Mosley became the hero in the empty room; the grand theorist to whom nobody of importance listened. The British fascist tradition was to pay more attention to Leese's post-1945 'ideas' than to Mosley's interesting new synthesis, though indeed Leese had nothing positive to contribute to new post-fascist views except his monomaniacal conspiracy beliefs and vicious racism.

Chesterton, however, became the key originator of what was to become the main surface tradition in post-1945 British fascism. At the end of the war he had been mainly responsible for the programme of the NF for V and was also involved in writing the policy of the BPP. It was these ideas which were to represent the core of his positive beliefs as expanded in the programme of the LEL and National Front in 1967. For Chesterton the NF after V movement in 1945 was a revolutionary organization in that the

---

[73] R. Herzstein, *When Nazi Dreams Come True* (London, 1982); A. J. Gregor, 'National Socialism and race', *The European*, 1958, pp. 273–91.
[74] J. Guinness with C. Guinness, *The House of Mitford* (London, 1985), p. 546.
[75] O. Mosley, *Europe Faith and Plan* (London, 1958); idem, *My Life*, pp. 432–46.

solution of the problems facing the British people was outside the range of existing politics. Chesterton believed that Britain's problems would be solved by contracting out of the international financial system and by building up a strong national and Empire economy. Purchasing power would be related to productive capacity within the nation and private enterprise preserved. Agitation against the national sovereignty would be an act of high treason and every political leader who did not put the best interests of Britain first would be impeached. Lastly there was the need to guard against the further extension of Jewish power and influence in Britain.[76]

This programme represented in essence Mosley's inter-war BUF programme superimposed on Chesterton's re-vamped and more rationally expressed conspiracy theory anti-semitism. Chesterton himself was to become obsessed with his conspiracy theory and neglected to develop his positive programme, and indeed most of his contemporaries in the LEL and National Front were to do the same. Younger elements were to find Chesterton's programme and rationally expressed conspiracy ideas an ideal camouflage for more extreme sentiment; they became a kind of code to hide nazi ideas.

Similarly the clandestine activities of the LEL, although originally designed for juvenile pranks and stunts, were adapted to more sinister purposes in the NF once Chesterton left. The old Leese underground tradition of the 'Tough Squad', premeditated racial violence, and paramilitary groups, became a reality for the NF as well as the British Movement. Indeed, this development was beginning to alarm Chesterton before he died. In one of his last letters he wrote to John Tyndall, who had proposed making him President of the NF, saying he was concerned about the participation of some NF members in an operation called 88.[77] In terms of the British fascist political tradition, Chesterton's ideology and clandestine operations were used as a smokescreen by others to promote the Leese/nazi mode of expression and operation which differed in degree and not kind. Had Chesterton lived and realized what was happening in the NF he would have been horrified. In the 1970s the Leese tradition dressed in

---

[76] A. K. Chesterton, 'Proposed policy of the National Front for Victory', *The National Front: Its Formation and Progress*, Ivan Greenberg papers 110/5.

[77] Letter from A. K. Chesterton to John Tyndall, 17 May 1973, A. K. Chesterton papers.

Chesterton's clothing was to be the dominant historical tradition operating in the NF. Mosley, who was incomparably the most interesting British fascist, and from whom John Tyndall learned his oratorical style and his inter-war economics, was a long-forgotten failed fascist to be remembered only in a gushing obituary in *Spearhead*.

11

National Socialists and Racial
Populists, 1960–1967

The 1960s saw both the decline of revisionist neo-fascist
movements with their leadership rooted in inter-war groups
or personalities, and the rise of a new generation of young racial
nationalists and nazis who revived the tradition in militant form.
Although never able to escape the negative perception of fascism
by state and society, many of the young 'nationalists' were to
emphasize Hitler worship, anti-semitism, a virulent anti-
immigrant racial populism, political activism, mass politics, anti-
Americanism, anti-communism, militant nationalism and covert
and conspiratorial behaviour which sanctioned offensive violence
and illegal methods against opponents where legal and political
means were considered ineffective. The 1960s saw the emergence
of the main outlines of such small but militant neo-fascist groups
in blatant form.

The new nationalists of the 1960s and 1970s

In essence the new generation were to be united in their opposition
to the political system, their anti-semitism and their virulent
hatred of coloured immigrants, but bitterly divided on most other
aspects. The most important contrast with the inter-war period
was that there was nobody who possessed the moral authority, the
intellectual power or political experience of Sir Oswald Mosley to
pose as a credible leader of a new fascist tradition. As a result the
new movements were riven by personality conflicts, ideological
disputes and leadership struggles which were to be repeated on a

broader canvas in the National Front in the 1970s. The new groups were to represent an alliance of racial populism, a vicious *ad hoc* response to coloured immigration, with the political legacy of Arnold Leese.

The political extremism and the nazi influence on several of the new organizations meant that they were regarded as little more than a nasty lunatic political fringe in British society.[1] Certainly in terms of numbers none of these groups were of any consequence; the British National Party (BNP), which was ambivalent about nazi connections, was probably the largest group with about 1,000 members in 1967.[2] Yet size was to be relatively unimportant, for it was one of the smallest groups, the Greater Britain Movement (GBM), with a distinct nazi heritage and just 138 members, which was to play the most important role in the National Front (NF) during the 1970s. The most blatantly nazi of these groups, the National Socialist Movement (NSM), and its successor the British Movement, were to remain outside the umbrella of the NF and to remain relatively small; but it was to have close links with an emerging political underground which fomented racial violence and had connections with European fascist political terrorists.

In general terms the new generation thought that the political methods and ideas of Mosley and Chesterton were outmoded. They were failed politicians from whose experience much could be learned but who were definitely yesterday's men. Mosley's attempt to build up a mass party, and Chesterton's tactics of a genteel form of political disruption, could be developed. It was the political intransigence of Arnold Leese, his refusal to compromise with political reality and his willingness to martyr himself for his beliefs which provided the main spur from the fascist political tradition for extremists like Colin Jordan, John Tyndall and Martin Webster. In particular, Leese's identification in his last years with the nazi heritage and the policies of Hitler was to be of seminal significance.

Other new recruits were critical of the nazi appreciation society from the outset. The racial populists of the BNP were to dispute the wisdom or desirability of linking British nationalism so directly to the swastika; Tyndall and Webster were later to justify their split

---

[1] G. P. Thayer, *The British Political Fringe* (London, 1968).
[2] M. Walker, *The National Front* (London, 1977), p. 67.

from Jordan in 1964 by stressing that English rather than German traditions needed to be emphasized. This division was to be accentuated by the relative emphasis placed on anti-semitism or opposition to coloured immigration by the various groups.

The revival of racial nationalism after 1945 derived from Arnold Leese's one-man band, the publishing activities of the Britons Society and its political offshoot the National Workers Party, and some of the disaffected Mosleyites. An organization called Natinform, with links to the covert nazi underground and the Socialist Reich Party in West Germany, was developed which opposed Mosley's Europe a Nation and the Catholic anti-semitism of the Britons, now under the management of Tony Gittens. Natinform believed that only the re-establishment of the German Reich to the primary power position in Europe would lead to success in the battle against Bolshevism. Its geopolitical dreams supported the Pirow plan for Europe Africa in which South and East Africa were to be the preserve of the white man.[3] This Anglo-German movement, which had marginal impact even in nazi German circles, disintegrated in 1953, but one of its main organizers was later to become an associate editor of the *Northlander*, the journal of the Northern League, an extremist group based in Holland, dedicated to the nazi nordic ideal and with links to both German and American nazis. This played an important role in promoting international nazism.

Of the various nazi enthusiast soap-box orators noticed by Special Branch after 1945 the only significant one was to be Colin Jordan.[4] After wartime service in the Army Education Corps, Jordan read a history degree at Cambridge and later formed a nationalist club in Birmingham. He made contact with Arnold Leese and became an avid disciple. The Britons published several of his anti-semitic pamphlets and his book *Fraudulent Conversion* in 1954, but relations with Gittens were less than harmonious. When Leese died in 1956 his widow was to make Jordan his political heir, to allow him to use Leese's property at 74 Princedale Road in London for political activity, and eventually to make him the sole selling agent when it was sold in 1968, much to the annoyance of the Britons.[5] As well as the tangible assets from the

[3] K. P. Tauber, *Beyond Eagle and Swastika* (Middletown, Conn., 1967), pp. 246–7.
[4] PRO HO 45/24968/120.
[5] Undated letter from solicitor to Gittens, File 3570, Britons Library.

Leese inheritance, Jordan's political education was to be furthered in the LEL, for which he was Midlands Organizer in 1955–6.

Most of the leaders of the second-generation racial nationalists received their political baptism in the LEL. Jordan, John Bean, John Tyndall and Martin Webster, all later prominent in the tradition, joined Chesterton's movement in the 1950s. Bean was an industrial chemist and editor of a trade journal and Tyndall and Webster salesmen whose variable hours of employment enabled them to develop their political interests. Tyndall was born in 1934, the same year as Mosley's Olympia meeting as he later noted; his obsession with military disciplines probably originated in his days of national service. All became highly critical of Chesterton's style of leadership, his old-fashioned political methods, his obsession with the British Empire and the cranky stunts with which the movement was associated.

Jordan was the first to go in 1956 when he formed the White Defence League (WDL). In 1957 Bean and Tyndall left to form the National Labour Party (NLP). Jordan wished to promote a nazi movement and to forge links with continental groups and Bean and Tyndall to emphasize an English national socialism rather than the Die-hard conservatism of the LEL. All were accused of disloyalty by Chesterton, and Bean's behaviour in trying to steal a copy of the membership list of the LEL was seen as particularly reprehensible, a factor which was to impede the negotiations on the formation of the NF in 1966.

The WDL and the NLP rapidly became much more extremist in their orientation than the LEL. The major difference was they were both more pronounced in their explicit racialism, in attacking coloured immigration rather than bemoaning the collapse of the British Empire. Jordan's *Black and White News* was amongst the most scurrilous publications promoting race hatred, and John Tyndall in the earliest editions of *Combat* demanded the 'elimination' of the Jewish 'cankerous microbe' in our midst.[6] Both movements too became associated with particular localities; Jordan's base in Notting Hill enabled more racial provocation by the WDL than could be achieved by the better-organized and disciplined UM. John Bean was later to develop his connections in Southall in the BNP.

---

[6] *Combat*, Apr./June 1959.

In 1960 the WDL and the NLP merged to form the BNP. Both movements had tangible assets. Jordan and his mentor, Mrs Leese, had premises in Notting Hill and the NLP had *Combat*. In the new movement Jordan was to be national organizer and John Bean was to edit *Combat*. Andrew Fountaine, a Norfolk landowner, was to be president and Mrs Leese vice-president. Fountaine had fought for Franco in the 1930s, had risen to the rank of Lt-Commander in the navy in the Second World War and had been adopted as a Conservative parliamentary candidate for Chorley in 1949. However, after an embarrassing speech at the Conservative Conference in which he criticized the party for allowing Jews to achieve positions of public importance, he was disowned and lost the candidacy. He stood instead as an Independent Conservative, split the Tory vote and only lost the 1950 election by 341 votes.[7] In 1958 he had formed his own shortlived National Front.

The immigration issue

The philosophy of the BNP was based on racial nationalism, on the need to preserve the northern European folk, predominantly nordic in race, and to free Britain from Jewish domination. All non-northern European immigration was to be terminated and racial aliens repatriated.[8] However, tension soon developed between Bean and Fountaine on the one hand and Colin Jordan on the other. Jordan's increasing nazi stance led to a split in the movement in 1962 when he and Tyndall left to form the National Socialist Movement (NSM). Henceforth the BNP was to concentrate on local political activity and building up a strong political base in constituencies like Southall and Deptford which saw growing coloured communities. In 1964 John Bean was to attain over 9 per cent of the poll in the general election, the highest until then by a radical right candidate in Britain since 1945. Its increasingly racial populist tone and the strident racialism of *Combat* were to make the BNP emphasis on opposing coloured

---

[7] Walker, *The National Front*, p. 28.
[8] *Combat*, May/June 1960.

immigration the main propaganda weapon for both them and the NF.

Indeed, it was to be the issue of coloured immigration which was to make the emergence of racial populist, neo-fascist and nazi movements in the 1960s more significant than a mere lunatic political fringe. The Commonwealth Immigrants Bill of 1962 had failed to check nativist resentment and anxieties, and maverick Conservatives as well as the radical right accentuated the issue. The general election of 1964 was notable not only for Bean's performance, but for the election of the 'parliamentary leper', Peter Griffiths, at Smethwick, where against the national swing Patrick Gordon Walker was unseated, and for the defeat of Fenner Brockway, the noted campaigner against colonialism and racial discrimination, at Eton and Slough. The failure to elect Gordon Walker in a safe Labour seat at Leyton and the highly illiberal 1965 White Paper, *Immigration from the Commonwealth*, showed how sensitive the government was to the issue. The latter severely cut back on New Commonwealth immigration and reduced it to only 8,500 in a period of labour shortage. The narrow Labour parliamentary majority of four was thought to be due to the failure of the party in the west Midlands, where its more liberal ethnic policies than those of the Conservatives had a negative effect. Only by neutralizing the issue by highly illiberal policies could the Labour party defuse the issue in time for the 1966 election.[9]

The fact that public opinion was so sensitive to the matter was not to go unnoticed amongst the racial populist and neo-fascist organizations. Although the rapid growth of such groups was not to occur until 1968, the political issue of race relations in the early 1960s alerted the radical right to its political significance. Both Mosleyites and the BNP saw not only a revival of racialist sentiment but also of militant hostility by the left against the resurgence of fascism. Anti-fascist movements such as the '62 group and Yellow Star attacked Mosley rallies for the first time since the 1948–51 campaign, and increased hostility against the BNP and in particular the NSM. As in the 1930s, political violence was to be a catalyst for recruitment and with a much greater

[9] Z. Layton-Henry, *The Politics of Race in Britain* (London, 1984), pp. 59–64; P. Foot, *Immigration and Race in British Politics* (London, 1965), pp. 124–94.

public antipathy towards immigration in the 1960s than in the 1930s even the more eccentric nature of the new form of fascism was given greater credibility. The new radical right were also to learn from the growth of mass politics on the political left. Although completely opposed to the cause of nuclear disarmament, fascists and racial populists saw that the Campaign for Nuclear Disarmament had shown that mass political activism could be organized around single issues. 'Stop immigration now' was to become the fascist and racial populist slogan equivalent of 'ban the bomb' on the left.

However, before the new breed of fascists were to use racial populism as the great recruiting sergeant of the radical right, Colin Jordan was to attempt to organize an open nazi organization, whose blatant anti-semitism alerted both the Jewish community and the Home Office to renewed concern about public order and race relations in British society. In 1961 Special Branch was already interested in John Tyndall's Spearhead group in the BNP, which engaged in paramilitary training. When the NSM held its first rally in Trafalgar Square in 1962 the anti-fascists disrupted the meeting and the police arrested Tyndall and Jordan for insulting words likely to cause a breach of the peace. Jordan argued at this meeting that Hitler was right and that we should have been fighting world Jewry and its associates in the Second World War and not Germany. Tyndall was even more blunt. He said that the Jew was the 'assassin of Europe' and like a 'poisonous maggot' in society.[10] For these offences Jordan received two months in jail and Tyndall six weeks. Tyndall's sentence was later reduced to a fine after he argued on appeal that what he said about Jews was no worse than Aneurin Bevan's charge that the Tories were vermin.

Prior to his first trial Jordan had created more publicity by announcing that the NSM was to organize a summer camp where an international nazi conference was to be held. As a result of pressure from Labour, the trade unions and the Jewish community, international delegates to the conference were banned from entering the British Isles; but Jordan and Tyndall were able to smuggle the American nazi leader, Lincoln Rockwell, into the country although he was deported before the camp.

[10] Transcript of speeches of Colin Jordan and John Tyndall, NSM rally, 1 July 1962, File 144.8, NCCL archive.

The object of the conference was to set up a World Union of National Socialists. Those who eventually attended elected Colin Jordan as world Führer and Rockwell was named his heir. In the 'Cotswold Agreement' the object of WUNS was stated to be to form an international 'combat efficient' organization to oppose international Jewish communism and Zionism and to promote the Aryan race. There was a long-term objective of the unity of white people in a world order with complete racial apartheid. What differentiated WUNS and the NSM from other organizations on the extreme right was that it acknowledged the spiritual leadership of Adolf Hitler and demanded a 'final settlement' on a world-wide basis of the Jewish problem.[11]

Such blatant extremism led the authorities to move against the NSM by charging four of its leading members with offences committed under Section 2 of the Public Order Act. This related to the paramilitary antics of NSM recruits in the Spearhead group organized by Jordan and Tyndall. They were found guilty of causing reasonable apprehension that they were training for the use or display of force in promoting political objectives. Jordan was sentenced to nine months, Tyndall six months and Roland Kerr Ritchie and Denis Pirie for three months each. Prosecution evidence at the trial included allegations that Tyndall had purchased sodium chlorate weedkiller, suitable for making exposives. One of these tins had 'weedkiller' crossed out and replaced by 'Jew-Killer'.[12]

After this conviction the unofficial self-protection units of the neo-fascist and racial populist political fringe were forced to conform, at least outwardly, to the law. Uniforms and paramilitary training were now outlawed, but the later Leader-guard of British Movement, and the Instant Response Unit and Colour Party of the National Front, were allowed to function. However, the extremists who believed in both offensive and defensive use of physical force went underground into more conspiratorial organizations like Column 88, named after the Austrian nazi group that had gone underground when national socialism was banned in that country in 1934.

The preparations for the trials, the prison sentences and the publicity associated with the antics of the NSM, led to the revival

---

[11] Walker, *The National Front*, p. 41.
[12] Transcript of Spearhead Trial, File 172.2, NCCL archive.

of militant anti-fascist activity in the early 1960s. As the NSM lost its leadership as a result of the jail sentences it was the Mosleyites who bore the brunt of new anti-fascist anger. Mosley had already made tentative suggestions that Bean and Jordan should become the national organizers of UM in 1962, but this was ignored.[13] Neither Bean's racial nationalism nor Jordan's 'racialist twaddle', as Mosley was later to call it, represented the mainstream of UM beliefs. However, the hostility of anti-fascist groups and the attempt by the state to crush the NSM led to a reassessment of tactics once the jail sentences were served.

Personal factors also became involved in an increasingly bitter feud between Jordan and Tyndall for the leadership of the NSM. The cause of this was the French heiress Françoise Dior, who had joined the NSM in 1962. Courted by Jordan, she became engaged to Tyndall while the former was still in prison. On Jordan's release there was a competition for her affection which Jordan won. Jordan and Dior were married in a strange ceremony complete with nazi regalia, but separated after a few months. Briefly reconciled, they were finally divorced in 1967. Tyndall never forgave Jordan for stealing Dior's affections. Jordan was equally incensed. He accused Tyndall and Webster of making disgusting telephone calls to his wife whilst she was in Paris to try and terrorize her.[14]

These increasingly bitter personal feuds and growing ideological disagreements as to how far open support for nazi policies was detrimental to the growth of the NSM in British society led to a split between Jordan and Tyndall in 1964. Tyndall, together with Webster and most of the headquarters staff, departed to form the GBM, leaving Jordan with the NSM name and the premises at Princedale Road. Tyndall began a new magazine, *Spearhead*, which was to be his main base in the future history of the radical right.

The split led to a battle over which of the two organizations, the NSM or GBM, would be recognized by WUNS. Jordan had been forced to hand over his position of world Führer to Lincoln Rockwell during his jail sentence and both Tyndall and Jordan did their best to smear each other in their attempt to woo Rockwell.

[13] Walker, *The National Front*, p. 44.
[14] NSM, 'Internal Bulletin', May 1964.

The world Führer, now called the Commander, who was already under great pressure from so-called mutineers within the American Nazi Party, instinctively sided with Jordan. For him, internal dissidents were greater enemies to national socialism than even the Jews.[15] He was also suspicious of Tyndall's plan to drop the swastika as a nazi symbol, believing that true nazi vanguard organizations did not disguise or camouflage their intentions.[16] Tyndall, disappointed with his failure to convince Rockwell, then established contact with 'White Power' and the National States Rights Party, both highly critical of the supposed growing moral depravity and political tactics of the American Nazi Party. They alleged that Rockwell surrounded himself with homosexuals and kept a mistress in nazi headquarters.[17]

Between 1964 and the formation of the NF in 1967 the open stance of Jordan and Tyndall was to show a marked contrast. Prior to the GBM split, it had been Tyndall and not Jordan who had made the most vituperative and obscene anti-semitic outbursts in public, although both had been equally crude in the pages of *National Socialist*. After 1965 Tyndall's language became more measured and reasonable in tone and he presented his argument in more rational terms. As he explained in letters to American nazis, one could adhere to the principles of fascism and nazism whilst presenting them in a manner in which Britons could identify with the cause of their own country. In any merger with any other group Tyndall was not worried about losing overall control of the movement, provided he had control over premises and publication.[18] Both for tactical reasons, and because of the need to avoid prosecution under the new Race Relations Act of 1965, it was expedient to use coded language when expressing ideological opinions.

Jordan was becoming more outrageous as Tyndall camouflaged his extremism. He stood against Gordon Walker at the Leyton by-election in 1965 and engaged in flamboyant political stunts to embarrass the government. A follower dressed up as a black and white minstrel and tried to register as Mr Walker Gordon the 'race mixing' candidate who would 'make Britain black'.[19] A member

[15] Lincoln Rockwell to John Tyndall, 6 July 1964, *Searchlight* Files.
[16] Matt Koehl to John Tyndall, 14 Sept. 1964, *Searchlight* Files.
[17] Open letter to George Lincoln Rockwell, 15 Sept. 1964, *Searchlight* Files.
[18] John Tyndall to William Pierce (23 March 1967), quoted in *Searchlight*, Aug. 1978.
[19] *Leytonstone Express*, 15 Jan. 1965.

of the NSM dressed up as a monkey while another held a placard stating that the immigrants were going to vote for Gordon Walker.[20] Colin Jordan interrupted a House of Commons debate from the gallery by shouting that Harold Wilson was betraying Britain's interests by allowing coloured immigration.[21]

More worrying than the open propaganda was the conspiratorial secretive aspects of the NSM and GBM, whose members were implicated in racial attacks, arson and sabotage. This again appeared to derive from the Leese tradition. Both organizations were implicated in such behaviour. NSM members were jailed for attacks on synagogues in Clapton, Ilford, Kilburn and Bayswater;[22] from evidence given at one of these trials Françoise Dior was given an eighteen-month sentence in 1968 for conspiring to burn a synagogue. Martin Webster was jailed for assaulting Jomo Kenyatta when he came to London in 1964, an act which was Webster's idea although Tyndall authorized its implementation.[23] Beneath the vitriolic personal hostility, the differing tactics and style of the two movements was a frightening militancy which often spilled over into violence and conspiratorial and subversive behaviour.

There is no evidence that either movement was ever significant in numerical terms. A police search of Jordan's card index in 1966 discovered that there were only 187 full members in the movement's history, of whom 35 were still paid-up and active in 1966. There were also 271 active supporters and 114 subscribers to the *National Socialist* magazine.[24] *Searchlight*, however, has reliable information that up to 1,200 were associated with the movement in the course of its history, with 680 at its peak in late 1962. There were never more than 138 members of the GBM, many of whom would also have been in the NSM at an earlier date.[25] It would be ridiculous to argue that they were chiefly responsible for Britain's deteriorating race relations in this period, but they nevertheless raised the political temperature considerably. The leadership struggles between Bean and Jordan in the BNP and Jordan and Tyndall in the NSM, the discovery by Bean that racial

---

20 Ibid., 5 Feb. 1965.
21 *Sun*, 16 Feb. 1965.
22 *Jewish Chronicle*, 11 Feb. 1966; *Guardian*, 9 Nov. 1966.
23 Letter from J. Tyndall to M. Koehl, 25 Sept. 1964, *Searchlight* Files.
24 Walker, *The National Front*, p. 41.
25 Ibid., p. 47.

populism and the issue of coloured immigration could turn an obscure fanatical sect into a potential mass movement, and the tactics of Tyndall which showed that nazi ideology could be presented in more acceptable form which might appeal to a much wider audience than the blatant Hitler worship of Jordan, provided important lessons for the young generation who were preparing to usurp the leadership of the tradition.

Apart from the open nazi organizations and the racialist BNP, racial populist groups were sprouting in areas where strong local cultural traditions acted against the growth of new immigrant communities. The various immigration control organizations in the Midlands and south were loosely linked in the Racial Preservation Society (RPS). This combined elements which had links to extremist groups like the BNP and Northern League and, at the other end of the spectrum, the Conservative party. It also had several wealthy private backers who helped fund a range of publications including the *Sussex News*, the *Midland News*, the *British Independent, New Nation* and *RPS News*. It has been estimated that this group was responsible for publishing over two million copies of various types of literature between 1965 and 1969.[26] The RPS was significant because of its financial backers and its links with orthodox politics; it was not a fascist organization but a confederation of racial populist associations who militantly opposed immigration.

While the level of much of the propaganda output of the new generation of nazis and racial populists made Arnold Leese by comparison seem an intellectual giant it was of some significance in forcing the government to tighten up the loopholes in the law which made it so difficult for the authorities to act against group libel or even racial incitement. Although it was far from the only factor involved, both Conservatives and Labour being mainly concerned about increased anti-immigrant feelings within their own parties, the passing of race relations legislation in 1965 and 1968 was directed partly against the scurrilous abuse and group libel with which such extremist groups fomented racial hatred. A bi-partisan consensus developed which became highly illiberal in terms of New Commonwealth immigration into Britain, but which tried to improve race relations by attempting to outlaw the

[26] Ibid., p. 60.

worst forms of published material which promoted race hatred. The loophole in the law which Leese and others had highlighted was now to be closed. Not all Conservatives agreed to such an approach, however, and mavericks such as Enoch Powell were to oppose such legislation.[27]

The difficulty of enforcing and interpreting such laws was to be demonstrated in a test case at Lewes in 1968, when the NF and the Britons Society were to organize a successful defence of individuals charged under the new legislation.[28] Although successful prosecutions were to be brought against explicit racist material disseminated by neo-fascist organizations in the 1970s and 1980s, much blatant propaganda from such groups was still published. Such use of the law has led to the closing down of *Bulldog*, the NF journal aimed directly at recruiting youth to the party through virulent racialist propaganda. Such legislation was a factor in John Tyndall's newfound caution, but others such as Chesterton claimed not to have altered their style or arguments in any way as a response to the new legislation.

Jordan and Tyndall

The open nazi ideology of Colin Jordan was explicitly based on racial nationalism. In his NSM days it was directly modelled on the crudest form of nazi nordicism and anti-semitism.[29] It was through the 'malignant' and 'satanic' ambition of world Jewry to achieve world domination that the Jews had manipulated democracy to cause national decline, and the whole structure of white civilization was to be replaced by a 'mongrelised world system'. The British state should protect and improve the 'Aryan, predominantly Nordic blood' of the British and all non-Aryans, including all Jews, would be expelled and would not be permitted to have sexual relations with Britons. All marriages between Aryans and Jews would be dissolved and measures taken to prevent the reproduction of defective 'stock'.[30]

As well as equally scurrilous sentiments, John Tyndall's early

---

[27] P. Foot, *The Rise of Enoch Powell* (London, 1969), pp. 66–128.
[28] A. K. Chesterton, *Not Guilty* (London, 1969).
[29] G. C. Field, 'Nordic racism'.
[30] Colin Jordan, *Britain Reborn* (London, n.d.).

contributions to the ideology of racial nationalism included a pamphlet on the nature of the new Aryan utopia. This was published both by the BNP and NSM and was called 'The Authoritarian State'. In contrast to the virulent public outbursts which led to his prosecution, Tyndall here used relatively measured and seemingly rational arguments to attack the Jewish money power behind both democracy and communism. In his view this had caused the decline of Britain, whose resurgence could only be accomplished by the creation of an authoritarian state under the command of a leader. For Tyndall no other principle could meet the challenge of the modern age; for him only 'The best will rule' – presumably John Tyndall.[31]

What was significant about this expression of extremist ideas was its use of fairly primitive coded language to present obvious nazi sentiments in a seemingly more rational form. After his break with Jordan in 1964 Tyndall was to develop this euphemistic use of language. He announced his intention in the first issue of his new journal *Spearhead*, which became the mouthpiece of the GBM, arguing that it would not differ in sentiment from *The National Socialist* except that it would relate to the supposed needs of the British people rather than nazi antecedents.[32]

Whilst Tyndall wrote portentous articles which combined the arguments and style of *The Protocols of the Elders of Zion* with those of Mosley's *Tomorrow We Live*, 'Julius' (Martin Webster) specialized in gutter anti-semitism which attacked the 'unheroic, greasy, shifty-eyed, sickly moneylenders, rent racketeers, pornographers and big business wide boys'[33] in language which was at least as bad as that published by the NSM. This division of labour, with Tyndall writing seemingly respectable, rationally expressed articles using euphemisms and coded language to hide extremist and nazi sentiments while Webster graduated from gutter anti-semitism to virulent racialist abuse of New Commonwealth immigrants, was to be continued in the NF.

The presentation of Tyndall's ideas was to become more sophisticated in the progression of his thought in the 1960s and 1970s. From open Hitler worship and barely disguised expression of such ideas in the NSM, through the 'English' form of national

---

[31] J. Tyndall, *The Authoritarian State* (London, 1982), p. 20.
[32] *Spearhead*, Sept. 1964.
[33] *Spearhead*, Dec. 1964.

socialism in the GBM, to the expression of such sentiments clothed in apparently respectable form in the NF, Tyndall was to retain the basic extremist views which had always characterized his thought. Webster meanwhile acted as the drummer boy, the disseminator of crude propaganda which would appeal to the alienated.[34] Both learned from the mistakes of the 1960s; Tyndall discovered that open nazism was counter-productive; Webster that the potential for racial populism in British society was in directing racist propaganda against coloured immigrants rather than Jews. Neither was to lose their basic anti-semitic obsessions; they merely learned to project them in a seemingly less counter-productive manner. The growth of anti-fascism, which paralleled the growth of the NF, was to ensure that nobody forgot their disreputable political past; and in the end it was to catch up with both of them.

---

[34] M. Billig, *Fascists* (London, 1978), pp. 344–50; N. Fielding, *The National Front* (London, 1981), pp. 86–104.

12

The Grand Synthesis,
1967–1985

The formation of the National Front in 1967 was the most significant event on the radical right and fascist fringe of British politics since internment. It represented the culmination of a process whereby the various strands of revisionist neo-fascist and racial populist politics came together in an attempt to form a national mass party which, although anti-Mosley, had distinct roots in the BUF of the later 1930s. The NF was never an explicit fascist party; indeed it had spent most of its history vehemently denying the significance of the blatant past fascist associations of some of its leading members. Much of the internal feuding of the movement and the bitter struggles for power have centred around this theme. Its dramatic growth, which led some observers to see it, quite improbably, as Britain's fourth political party and a serious challenger to break the mould of British politics, testified to the significance of the issue of immigration in British politics in the 1970s. This was so despite the complete shambles of the political structure of the NF; the forces making for disintegration, and personal and ideological differences within the leadership, lost the movement the great opportunity presented for the emergence of a racial populist movement in the 1970s.

The rise and fall of the National Front

Although some credit for the growth of the NF has to be shared between the unholy alliance of John Tyndall and Martin Webster and their rivals in the mid-1970s, the 'populist' ex-Conservatives,[1] the major reason for its expansion was due to the failure of the Conservative party to make much political capital of the immigration issue. Although they were responsible for the restrictive Immigration Act of 1971 which made right of entry for New Commonwealth citizens much more difficult, Edward Heath's government was more liberal in some ways than the Labour administrations which preceded and succeeded it. For example, it allowed if somewhat reluctantly, the inflow of Ugandan Asians in 1972 fleeing from Idi Amin's atrocities; the Labour government had proved less accommodating over Kenyan Asians in 1968.[2] The right wing of the party, the Monday Club, and many traditional party supporters felt intensely alienated by the attitude of the Heath administration and made their opposition felt through their support of Enoch Powell.

Powell had been unceremoniously dismissed from the Shadow Cabinet in 1968 as a result of breaking the bi-partisan consensus in his notorious 'River of Blood' speech at Birmingham, where he said we must be literally mad to allow 50,000 dependants of immigrants into the country each year. His successful campaign to block the inflow of Kenyan Asians and the enormous popular support for his restrictive position on this matter, which totally contradicted his liberal views on other economic and social issues, made him deeply suspect in the eyes of the Conservative establishment. The tone of his speech, with its apocalyptic scenario, the apocryphal tale of little old ladies having excreta pushed through their letterboxes, and its reference to 'wide-eyed, grinning piccaninnies',[3] brought the language and arguments of the neo-fascist political fringe into the heart of the establishment. Although spurned by the authorities, the enormous popular impact of Powell's outburst forced the government to be highly restrictive in its attitude to immigration from then onwards. Isolated by the Conservative leadership, Powell ignored the racialist political fringe. However, they, and particularly the NF, made political capital of Powell's impact and racial populism moved from the gutter to the centre of politics in inner city areas.

The other important issue which affected the growth of racial

---

[1] M. Walker, *The National Front* (London, 1977), pp. 133–202.
[2] Z. Layton-Henry, *The Politics of Race in Britain* (London, 1984), pp. 75–86.
[3] P. Foot, *The Rise of Enoch Powell* (London, 1969), p. 115.

populism was the Race Relations Act of 1965. Although the authorities were spasmodic in their use of the law, the fact that racialist propaganda could now be seen as incitement to racial hatred made some, although not all, radical right and neo-fascist organizations more careful in their use of language; it was certainly a factor in John Tyndall's move from extremism to a more rationally presented expression of similar sentiments. Through a legal loophole, publishers of racist material like the Britons Society kept in business by making their customers members of book clubs and societies (they kept links with the NF through publishing *Candour* for A. K. Chesterton).

However, it was to be amongst those who either spurned the NF or who were not permitted to join that the impact of the Race Relations Act was most pronounced. Colin Jordan's position as the British Führer was undermined by his refusal to martyr himself to the new law; some of his ex-followers now went underground to set up Column 88, which was faithful to the nazi inheritance. This subversive paramilitary group infiltrated many far-right organizations including the NF and was to be implicated in illegal activity and the encouragement of racial violence. The NF was to represent the revisionist political expression of the British fascist tradition, with nazi elements barely camouflaged behind racial populist policies and struggling for power with renegade ex-Conservatives. The more sinister clandestine operation, also with its inspiration in the Leese tradition, was to have important financial links with international nazi groups and political terrorism abroad.[4]

In terms of the British fascist tradition, its part in the NF may be seen as an attempt to synthesize the mass politics and economic and political programme of the BUF with the ferocious anti-semitism and racial populism of Arnold Leese which, however, was presented in the more respectable and seemingly rational guise of the conservative fascism of the survivors of the Die-hard inheritance. This in essence is what the NF became, although its early years and much of its development were spent in trying to distance itself from its obvious associations, since the NF aimed at recruiting both discontented Conservatives and the alienated white inhabitants of inner city areas, both of which would have

---

[4] *Searchlight*, May 1975; P. Wilkinson, *The New Fascists* (London, 1981).

failed to have been attracted by open fascist propaganda. This was well understood by the practitioners of the new political game. When members of the GBM were allowed into the NF in 1968 as individuals, they were quite happy to serve a probationary period. Tyndall was prepared to eschew thoughts of immediate leadership and to invest in the future with secure premises and *Spearhead* as his main base in the party. Through their hard work and dedication ex-members of the GBM were to become the most significant faction in the NF despite their lack of discipline; their camouflaged extremism and rapid rise to positions of influence in the movement meant that they saw themselves as controlling events from behind the scenes, a mirror image of their conspiracy theory mentality. This appeared to be Tyndall's grand design; but unfortunately the pawns failed to make their allotted moves.

The origins of the NF have to be seen as a compromise between mutually suspicious parties. In essence the NF represented a merger between the LEL and BNP, to which were added individual members of the RPS. Tyndall, who had urged a reunification of the non-Mosleyite groups since 1964, was kept waiting in the wings, partly because he was in jail for illegal possession of a firearm and, with his notorious immediate past, he was neither forgiven nor forgotten by his ex-colleagues in both the LEL and BNP. His enthusiasm for a more moderate presentation of extremism had been increased when Lincoln Rockwell refused to reconsider his allegiance to Jordan in WUNS in 1965.

For Chesterton merger with the BNP was desirable because it had more relatively successful political experience and appealed more to the working class than the LEL.[5] The LEL was also concerned about the emergence of the Monday Club on the right of the Conservative party, which was siphoning off their dwindling support. Although he still disliked populist methods and preferred an elitist group to a political party, Chesterton was forced to compromise to stop the threatened collapse of one of the last outposts of the British Empire.

For the BNP the attraction of a merger with the LEL related to the premises operated by Chesterton in central London and the lure of the Chilean gold which would benefit the NF if the Jeffery inheritance was finally procured. Although the president of the

---

[5] A. K. Chesterton to John Bean, 1 Nov. 1966.

BNP, Andrew Fountaine, was a rich man his wealth was tied up in land and was not available to the movement. For Bean and other militants the LEL was a piece of Victoriana, an outmoded relic of a bygone age which had no political relevance for the contemporary world. His own acrimonious departure from the LEL in 1957 meant that he was suspicious of Chesterton, whose coterie of devoted followers he instinctively distrusted. He accused them of being sycophants and Chesterton of authoritarian behaviour.[6] Bean would have like to have welcomed Tyndall back to the fold in 1967 but Fountaine would not countenance such a suggestion. Chesterton, who had been impressed by the suitably patriotic and rationalist tone of Tyndall's *Six Principles of British Nationalism*, was also coming round to the idea of allowing him to join the party for a probationary period. The fact that the RPS had several wealthy backers and connections to the Conservative Party made their members a more desirable immediate addition to the coalition.

There can be little doubt that the NF would not have survived if Enoch Powell had not unwittingly given it such a helping hand in its infancy. The early history of the NF from when Chesterton became the first chairman of the Directorate in 1967 until his resignation in 1970 was a period of mutual backbiting, suspicion and paranoia by practically all the participants of the merger. Almost the only person who did not get involved in the accusations and intrigue was John Tyndall, who after being admitted to the movement in 1968 was a model of diligence and correct behaviour.

In this period there was a power struggle between Chesterton and Fountaine. This involved Chesterton in legal battles with both Robin Beauclair of the RPS and Fountaine. The issues were personal incompatability, mutual recriminations about inefficient administration and authoritarian behaviour, disputes about jurisdiction on disciplinary powers within the movement, and ideological differences. Behind this were BNP suspicions of Chesterton's lack of commitment to mass politics, criticism of his winter visits to South Africa for his health, his refusal to merge *Candour* and his LEL office into the movement and allegations about improper use of funds. For his part Chesterton criticized

---

[6] Internal memo to council members, BNP, 9 Oct. 1966.

Fountaine's call to help the police if there was an insurrection in 1968 as alarmist and found him totally impossible to work with, as he kept up a barrage of criticism in which nobody was spared. After this power struggle, which Chesterton eventually won, a second battle was fought with a so-called Action Committee of new young members of the Directorate who blamed Chesterton for the poor election results of 1970 and the lack of direction of the movement. This blew up immediately after Chesterton had left for his winter visit to South Africa and he resigned in high dudgeon, with the rest of the LEL remnant soon following him into the political wilderness. What was interesting about these early disputes, which effectively removed the main protagonists involved in the original merger, was the fact that there was so much factional strife at a time when the movement was expanding rapidly. The degree of mutual hostility and suspicion in what was a relative success story for a young political movement was a congenital weakness of the non-Mosley fascist fringe and helps to explain its lack of political credibility. Indeed, the fact that Chesterton was prepared to use bugged conversations of members of the movement, that he employed not only his own cronies but also Tony Gittens to act as an intelligence agent for him within the NF while he was in South Africa, and that like several others he saw potential MI5 agents everywhere, illustrated the degree of insecurity and the awareness of the methods of infiltration by the authorities which had always characterized the fascist tradition.[7]

There has been a tendency in some accounts of the NF to see a deep-seated machiavellian plot organized by John Tyndall and Martin Webster to gain control of the party through infiltrating their personnel into key administrative positions and by monopolizing the movement's propaganda, which could then be used to indoctrinate members and the public by clothing nazi sentiments in more euphemistic language which over a period of time would anaesthetize critical faculties and make more extremist solutions acceptable – the technique pioneered by Goebbels to develop the logic of the genocidal model of anti-semitism in nazi Germany. This thesis has been most notably argued by Michael Billig,[8]

---

[7] A. K. Chesterton to Andrew Fountaine, 27 May 1968, Report 1, Conspiracy against A. K. Chesterton, A. K. Chesterton to A. Gittens, 11 Dec. 1970.

[8] R.C. Thurlow, 'Racism in British society', *Patterns of Prejudice*, 13, 4 (July–Aug. 1979), pp. 1–8.

whose impressive value analysis of NF publications and use of sophisticated psychological models of personality development gives credence to such a thesis as far as the original intentions of Tyndall and Webster were concerned. However, it may be doubted that ex-Conservatives, members of the Monday Club, and the working-class voters attracted by racial populism who flocked to the NF in the early 1970s in such numbers, were secret or even potential nazis. Certainly the persistence of anti-nazi arguments in the criticisms of Tyndall and Webster throughout the 1970s appeared to derive from more than tactical cynicism.

The other main problem with such a case is that when it is viewed in terms of the actual historical development of the NF then the model fails to fit. Although the ex-GBM members did play a key role in the NF, the evidence suggests that they were more of a group of mutually hostile individuals whose actions lacked discipline and owed more to the principle of anarchy than conspiracy. Even the obsessively conspiratorial Tony Gittens, no friend of either Tyndall or Webster, failed to find evidence to connect them with the plot to oust Chesterton, even though the organizer of the *coup*, Gordon Brown (*né* Marshall) was ostensibly Tyndall's right-hand man and the landlord of GBM's headquarters. In the great power struggle with the 'Populists', Gordon Brown was later to give his casting vote to ex-Conservative John Kingsley Read rather than Tyndall. In the showdown in 1980, after the 1979 election *débâcle*, Tyndall and Webster were to split, the former going off to form the New National Front and later the BNP. Three years later Webster was booted out after another ex-GBM member, Andrew Brons, sided with the third generation 'Strasserites' against him.

There is also considerable evidence that Tyndall and Webster, as chairman of the Directorate and activities organizer of the NF for much of the 1970s, spent as much time squabbling with each other as in organizing a unified movement. Thus for example when Tyndall proposed that Chesterton should be made president of the NF in 1973 Webster, according to the former, was opposed because of almost pathological hatred for the old LEL founder.[9] In 1976 a memorandum from the Policy Committee of the NF noted that Webster supported the maintenance of parliamentary democ-

---

[9] J. Tyndall to A.K. Chesterton, 6 June 1973.

racy while Tyndall was opposed to it.[10] After the split in 1980 Tyndall attacked Webster for incompetence, sloth and mal-administration as well as his responsibility for the indiscipline of what he now called the 'gay National Front'.[11]

The performance of the hard-line ex-nazis in the NF suggested that personal animosities, jealousy and ideological and tactical disagreements were as rife amongst second-generation racial nationalists as they had been in Arnold Leese's day. Far too many had dreams of the Führer's mantle to give more than grudging support to either Tyndall or Webster, although Tyndall with his obsession about leadership could lay some claim to the succession, particularly as he had isolated Colin Jordan outside the NF. Jordan, forsaken now both by the newly respectable GBM within the NF and despised by the hardliners after what they regarded as his failure to confront the Race Relations legislation and his imprisonment for stealing ladies' underwear from a high street store, made a partial comeback through his British Movement, which was later taken over by younger enthusiasts. Compared to the NF, the British Movement was not impressive. Its major significance was in mobilizing groups of young toughs and skinheads in inner city areas in direct action against the left and coloured immigrants in the 1970s. In this it was to be copied by the NF. Martin Webster saw skinheads and football hooligans as suitable material to engage in both defensive and offensive vio-lence against anti-fascists and the British black community, but Tyndall's elitism and attempts to give a veneer of respectability to the NF thoroughly disapproved of such a move; this was another cause of the friction between himself and Webster in the NF.

If the history of the NF was to be riven by conflict between the ex-fascists, it was also to be characterized by the instinctive closing of ranks against greater democracy in the movement. During the early 1970s the Ugandan Asian influx, growing inflation and the oil crisis of 1973 had all undermined the credibility of the Heath administration in the eyes of some right-wing Conservatives and members of the Monday Club. Some of these joined racial populist groups which had links to the NF while others entered the movement openly or had friendly contacts with it through some local branches of the Monday Club. There can be little doubt that

---

[10] Memorandum from Policy Department to National Directorate National Front, *Searchlight* 38 (1978).

[11] *Spearhead*, July 1983.

this development was a two-way process. The NF developed its own counter-subversion strategy which saw infiltration of the political establishment as a mirror image of the activities of the Security Service. The Conservative Central Office in particular became especially keen in blocking off contacts between the party, its affiliates and racial populist and extremist movements like the NF. Groups such as WISE (Welsh, Irish, Scots, English) and local immigration control associations, many affiliated to the RPS, still maintained contacts with both groups, however.

There were certainly links between such groups and some right-wing Tory MPs in the 1970s and 1980s which can be compared to the interest of a few Conservatives in Mosley in the 1930s. Some older supporters such as Oliver Gilbert used the old Mosleyite technique of infiltrating fascist arguments into local round table debating societies and mock parliaments. Gilbert was one of the first fascists interned under DR 18b. He was also a member of his local Conservative association after the war, as well as being connected to the NF. Other individuals like Chesterton, Frank Clifford, Ted Budden and Alan Hancock linked the old Mosleyite tradition to the contemporary far right.

The main effect of the sudden influx of ex-Tories into the party was to inject some much-needed electoral experience of mainstream politics into the movement. In inner city areas and in neighbourhoods where strong local cultural traditions were potentially threatened by an influx of immigrants the ex-Tories used racial populism to attract support, but they became highly critical of the past nazi associations of the leadership of the NF after Tyndall had taken over from John O'Brien, who had a caretaker role after Chesterton's resignation. They were also suspicious of the centralization of power in the movement by Tyndall and his activities organizer Martin Webster. Thus began the battle for power between the so-called 'populists' and John Tyndall. Ex-Tories like John Kingsley Read and Roy Painter managed to out-vote Tyndall at Directorate meetings when some ex-GBM members and their associates began to side with them. The expanded membership also strongly supported the Populists and John Kingsley Read replaced Tyndall as chairman in 1975. Control of the movement was shifted away from the ex-nazis by non-fascist and ostensibly more democratic elements.[12]

[12] Walker, *The National Front.*

However, Tyndall had learned from previous leadership skirmishes. From his own experience with Jordan and having observed Chesterton's tactics in the NF, he realized that the key to success in intra-party feuding lay in control of propaganda, in having a secure organizational base within the movement and using the legal system to one's own advantage. For a revolutionary party which wished to overthrow the state, the NF has frequently used the state's detested legal system to settle the increasingly bitter disputes which have affected the movement; despite the NF's grand talk of attaining state power, most of these disputes have seemingly been petty squabbles or arcane disputes about control of property and legal costs. They can be explained by the fact that Tyndall had correctly perceived that fanaticism, hard work and control of administration and propaganda were the key to power in the NF.

With his own relatively secure organizational base, Tyndall attacked and tried to discredit the main propaganda weapon of the Populists, *Britain First*. In this he was aided by a new ally, Richard Verrall. Verrall was the Front's intellectual, who possessed a first class honours degree in History. From 1976 until 1980 he became editor of Tyndall's journal *Spearhead* and was a member of the Directorate. In an important article in *Spearhead*, Verrall portrayed the Populists' demands for greater democracy in the NF as leftist propaganda,[13] which sparked off an internal row leading eventually to the mutual expulsion of Read and Tyndall, with the latter retaining his journal and the name National Front and maintaining the allegiance of the majority of constituency organizations. Read and the Populists split away and formed the National Party which gradually sank into oblivion in the late 1970s.

In retrospect it is more accurate to see the Populists as pseudo-Conservative racial populists rather than as syndicalists or left fascists as portrayed by Verrall. The real leftist heresy was to raise its head two major splits later: Tyndall was forced to take the blame for the poor general election performance in 1979 and was ousted when Webster sided with a new populist faction demanding more street politics and confrontation tactics. NF infiltration of football hooligans and skinhead 'bovver boys' was

---

[13] R. Verrall, 'Left wing shift in the National Front', *Spearhead*, Dec. 1975/Jan. 1976.

now the new political tactic, with Webster determined that the NF should kick its way into the headlines. However, the bad publicity which these tactics had brought, and the continued personal attacks on Webster by Tyndall in *Spearhead*, undermined his position and he was ousted when Andrew Brons, the ex-GBM chairman of the Directorate, sided with the 'Strasserites', the young third-generation British fascists who derived their ideas from the opposition within the nazi party to Hitler.[14] Webster was finally expelled from the NF in February 1984.

Meanwhile Tyndall had established the New National Front, which he portrayed as the authentic voice of British nationalism; it became the British National Party in 1982 after an alliance with a breakaway faction of the British Movement, ex-members of the NF and the British Democratic Party. The grand design to produce a unified radical right grouping under fascist control had irredeemably fractured into two warring factions more concerned with fighting each other than any common enemy.

In retrospect, three important factors can be singled out to explain the decline and fall of the NF in the 1970s and 1980s, which to a certain extent paralleled the experience of the BUF in the 1930s. First, as in the 1930s, the rise of what was perceived as at least in part a neo-fascist mass political party was met by marked hostility by the left, immigrant organizations, the Indian Workers Association, the Board of Deputies of British Jews and the Association of Jewish Ex-Servicemen. An umbrella protest organization, the Anti-Nazi League continued the tradition of mass opposition to incipient fascism in Britain whenever it had posed a threat since the 1930s. As then, the political violence associated with confrontation led to the growth of both right and left extremism in the short term, much to the concern of the authorities; the climax of this street conflict occurred with the deaths of Kevin Gately and Blair Peach. The NF too were to have a martyr: Albert Marriner became the British Horst Wessl. Street politics between the militant left and right was to be as bitter in the 1970s as in the 1930s.

The decline of the NF after 1974 was partially due to the successful undermining of it by the Anti-Nazi League. When the

---

[14] D. Baker, 'A. K. Chesterton, the Strasser brothers and the politics of the National Front', *Patterns of Prejudice*, 19, 3 (July 1985), pp. 23–33.

latter itself was blatantly taken over by the Socialist Workers' Party the organization folded as the bulk of the membership refused to tolerate being controlled by a notorious factional hard-line Trotskyist group. The left, however, was still able to keep abreast of developments on the fascist political fringe, thanks to *Searchlight* magazine and Gerry Gable's intelligence activities, which appeared to find out more about the extreme right than the fascists knew themselves. *Searchlight* has more recently helped to organize the Campaign against Racism and Fascism and Anti-Fascist Action.

The second factor was the emergence of Margaret Thatcher as the new leader of the Conservative party in 1975, which marked the end of what later became known as the dominance of 'wet' Toryism. Her forceful aggressive leadership, her uncompromising stance on law and order, the stand against the unions and the illiberal attitude towards immigration meant that many on the right of the party could now identify with what they saw as traditional Conservatism, despite her liberal economic policies.[15] The Falklands War showed that patriotism was still a powerful underlying force in British politics and that Mrs Thatcher's Conservatism could fully tap that source. Since 1975 the NF experienced a steady decline as a result. Attacked by the left, undermined by the state and having its appeal to patriotism made unnecessary by the actions of Mrs Thatcher, the racial populist neo-fascist right had nowhere to go. The highly fragile stability of the NF and other groups disintegrated as a result and the deep fissures which appeared led to the collapse of a coherent fascist tradition. The sight of ex-nazis in party political broadcasts at general elections draping themselves in Union Jacks did little to restore their credibility.

Third, the activities of the state and private intelligence agencies severely damaged the far right. While the authorities faced severe criticism from the left and immigrant communities for not doing more to act against the increase in racial violence which was partly inspired by neo-fascist propaganda,[16] the Public Order Act (1936) and Race Relations Act (1965) had been used against some of the more blatant acts of incitement to racial hatred. However, more

[15] A. Gamble, *Britain in Decline* (London, 1981), pp. 207–26.
[16] Z. Layton Henry, 'Racial attacks in Britain', *Patterns of Prejudice*, 16, 2 (1982), pp. 3–12.

worrying was that the failure of the more open political campaigns of the neo-fascist revival had driven the real hardliners underground; and that a covert and violent secret tradition, which involved illegal paramilitary training and links with wanted European neo-fascists suspected of terrorist activity, secret nazi funds, and connections with the Ulster Defence Force in Northern Ireland, was much more difficult to deal with.

Fascists underground: British fascism today

The growth of the underground tradition was characterized by a large increase in racial attacks by hooligans against New Commonwealth immigrants during the late 1970s and 1980s. Although it was not the only source of such violence, nevertheless both the NF and British Movement were implicated in such assaults and the authorities found the guerilla warfare against Asians and West Indians difficult to contain. Indeed, one of the root causes of the breakdown of police-community relations in inner city areas in the 1980s has been the failure by the authorities to perceive racial motives in the increased violence against New Commonwealth immigrants. Obviously black unemployment, social and economic deprivation, drug-related offences and hooliganism provided the immediate background to the race riots of 1981 and 1985, as the Scarman Report emphasized in the former case. Yet at least some of the reason for the lack of confidence in the police shown by the black community has been due to their failure to even perceive that racist motives, some deliberately fomented by extremist organizations, have been behind at least a proportion of the large increase in crime in such areas.

The traditional Home Office policy of surveillance and legal action against the most blatant offences proved insufficient with the neo-fascist revival. Although the fascist groups were nowhere near as skilled as Mosley in adapting security measures to minimize the impact of MI5 surveillance, or in disseminating propaganda and the use of infiltration tactics in the way that Domvile had with the Link, sporadic terrorism was far more difficult to handle.[17]

---

[17] P. Wilkinson, *Terrorism and the Liberal State* (London, 1977); 'The murderers are amongst us', *Searchlight*, Special Issue, Nov. 1985.

Whilst the Security Service had been responsible for the termination of the activities of inter-war fascists, the most significant damage to the post-war revival was caused by the intelligence activities associated with *Searchlight*. This occurred when the journal managed to 'turn' Ray Hill, an ex-member of the NSM in the 1960s, when he returned from South Africa in the late 1970s. He was run as a mole inside the British Movement, and when he had led much of its most active membership out of the organization, he joined the BNP in the 1980s. When he finally came out the exposure of his activities, which had already led to the break up of British Movement, severely weakened the new BNP. Hill was also able to penetrate the underground secret tradition and make contact with the European fascist underground and its sources of finance.

The activities of Ray Hill led to the exposure of a gunrunning operation to Northern Ireland involving members of the National Democratic Party, the thwarting of a plot to explode a terrorist bomb at the 1981 Notting Hill carnival, and the passing of information to the authorities of the provision of 'safe houses' for wanted German and Italian terrorists, who in return (it was alleged) were providing paramilitary training and proceeds from previous bank robberies on the continent. Hill provided evidence that practically all of Britain's nazis were implicated in some of these activities, including the British Movement, the League of St George and Column 88. More recently the Strasserite ruling group in the NF has been connected to the community of Italian fascist terrorists in London.[18]

What has differentiated the membership and electoral support of the NF from inter-war fascism has been both the key issue of immigration in NF propaganda and politics and the much greater willingness to take part in the electoral process. Indeed, this latter fact has led some observers to see the NF as a much more significant fascist threat than the BUF ever was. This, however, is a misleading analysis. At its peak the NF had an active membership of less than half that of the BUF in 1934 – about 17,500 to 50,000. Even at the outbreak of war BUF members, on the most reliable estimates, were higher than at the peak of NF activity. The fact that the NF were able to mount much more significant electoral

---

[18] *Searchlight*, 106, 107, 108 (Apr., May, June 1984).

campaigns than the BUF is mainly accounted for by a quirk in the electoral process – that the NF were identified with a social issue, that of immigration, which touched a raw nerve in the electorate in the way that no campaign, except locally, of the BUF ever did. It was also far easier to find the electoral deposit of £150 in the 1970s than it was in the 1930s, after the ravages of inflation. Where the NF undoubtedly scored over the BUF was in its electoral organization; Tyndall and Webster appeared to have had more success in this area than Mosley's administration.

The best analysis of NF membership and the electoral process casts further doubt on whether it can be seen as simply a fascist party in sheep's clothing. Christopher Husbands' impressive book *Racial Exclusionism and the City* showed that NF growth came about as a response to several issues of urban politics. There was no high correlation of areas of high immigrant settlement to strong NF presence. However, the spatial distribution of NF support represented a reaction by the resident host community to a perceived threat to strong local cultural traditions by immigrants rather than a reflex response to economic issues like housing, class or employment competition. Areas like the East End of London which have maintained an almost unbroken cultural tradition of racial populist politics from the early 1900s to the present day have been the most significant localities for such policies. The NF has also helped spread such resentment into other areas threatened by so-called cultural 'swamping', most notably in the west and east Midlands, Lancashire, west Yorkshire and in areas of south and north London.

In terms of its membership and support the NF was similar to the middle period of the BUF; an urban working-class racial populist party which had a much wider impact in geographical terms than Mosley's movement, because the influx of immigrants was more visible and geographically widespread. For an alleged nazi party, the support of the NF had a peculiar sociological profile; the nazis' greatest strength was amongst the rural agricultural areas and Protestant small towns in Germany;[19] in the cities its greatest support came from the upper middle classes.[20] The NF also differed from neo-fascist revivals on the continent since 1945: in

[19] C. Husbands, *Racial Exclusionism and the City* (London, 1983), pp. 140–1.
[20] R. Hamilton, *Who Voted for Hitler* (Princeton, 1982).

Germany, Italy, Switzerland, and France until recently, there has been no correlation between radical right and racial exclusionist politics and urban working-class support.[21]

While the membership figures of the NF have not been released, *Searchlight* has produced the most reliable estimates. This suggests a period of growth from about 4,000 in 1968 to a peak of 17,500 during the Ugandan Asians crisis in 1972 and a gradual falling away to 15,000 by the time of the Populist split which lost the NF several thousand members to the National Party so that at the time of the 1979 general election membership was around 10,000. With the poor performance in 1979 and the split between Tyndall and Webster, the numbers collapsed and were only partly checked by the recruitment of ex-British Movement activists. After the removal of Webster, membership slumped to reach 3,148 on 1 October 1984,[22] and fell precipitously to just under 1,000 in January 1985, but has since made some recovery to about 2,000 by the autumn of 1985. The British Movement, given the volatile nature of its membership, is more difficult to estimate, but probably had several thousand members at its peak. However, this collapsed after an internal struggle for power.

The financing of the NF is an even more closely guarded secret. Paid-up membership in recent years has probably accounted for one-half of its total income from normal subscriptions and donations. About one-third of local branches are thought to have a 'good fairy' who give sums of up to £100 a month and will pay for candidates' deposits at elections. There is also a profit from publications and other NF sales. Individual donations of up to £20,000 have also been provided and there is some overseas funding; the NF's old headquarters building in East London was more than half purchased by a £16,000 donation from friends in France. Arab funding for revisionist and anti-semitic literature has also been provided for the Historical Review Press, as have funds from German revisionist historians to print material.

Although no adequate sample of membership has been constructed, the impressionistic interviews of Taylor, Fielding and Billig have indicated a mixed impact of the attempt to influence the

---

[21] C. Husbands, 'Contemporary right wing extremism in western European democracies: a review article', *European Journal of Political Research*, 9, 1 (1981), pp. 75–99.
[22] 'The financial structure of the National Front', *Searchlight* files.

NF with nazi propaganda.[23] The most that can be said about this complex topic is that some members have been converted to the conspiracy theory mentality and others have shown an increased tolerance to its implications, while others either do not understand it or regard its simplistic logic as a personal idiosyncracy of some of the more dedicated and hard-line members of the movement.

Electoral support for the NF has been more marked in local than general elections. Most of the evidence suggests that in both cases the NF vote was a protest vote against immigration and the assumed links to cultural decline and urban renewal, and had little or nothing to do with any perceived or hidden fascist political programme. Even allowing for this, the performance of the NF should not be exaggerated. Only two local councillors in Blackburn were ever elected as candidates of the racialist right and only in one parliamentary by-election, in West Bromwich in 1973, did any NF candidate ever retain his deposit.

In local elections the NF peak came in 1977 when the average NF vote was a high as 17.8 per cent in Tower Hamlets, 13.9 per cent in Hackney and 12.5 per cent in Newham. They also received 12.6 per cent at Leicester, 11.3 per cent in Oadby and Wigston and 10.6 per cent in Wolverhampton in the seats contested in that year. In general elections the performance of the NF declined throughout the 1970s. In February 1974 NF candidates received an average of 3.17 per cent of the vote in the seats which were fought and 3.12 per cent was the mean for the ninety candidates in October 1974.[24] In 1979 the average for the 303 seats fought was 1.5 per cent and in 1983, of the 58 seats 1.1 per cent. The rival Tyndall BNP was well under 1 per cent in 1983.[25] The perceived poor performances by the NF at all general elections since 1970 have led to power struggles and the removal of Chesterton (1970), Tyndall (1975 and 1980) and Webster (1983) from the movement as a result. On the other hand, Tyndall used the local election campaigns of 1973 and 1976 successfully to heal developing rifts in the party.

[23] S. Taylor, *The National Front in English Politics* (London, 1982), pp. 96–107; N. Fielding, *The National Front* (London, 1981), pp. 137–56.
[24] AJEX Defence Bulletin No. 4, Oct. 1974, p. 3.
[25] *Spearhead*, June 1983.

The ideology of the National Front

If the title of this chapter appears to exhibit more than a little of the conscious irony inherent in several others, then its essential purpose can be more readily comprehended by an examination of the ideology of the movement. As has already been intimated, it is dangerous and somewhat misleading to write the history of the NF from the perspective of the inversion of the conspiracy mentality of *Spearhead*. Nevertheless, it remained true that the ideology and propaganda of the NF was dominated by the ex-GBM faction until the split between Tyndall and Webster in 1980, and the intellectual support it received from Richard Verrall. However, this reflected an attempt to portray the essentials of nazi ideology in more rational language and seemingly reasonable arguments, representing Tyndall's intellectual debt to A. K. Chesterton from the discussions which preceded the formation of the NF, which left him a semi-respectable if controversial figure within the coalition while Jordan was left in the political wilderness.

Essentially the presentation of NF ideology was on three levels. In *Spearhead*, Richard Verrall (its editor from 1976 to 1980), provided the intellectual core of a seemingly academic presentation of NF racism and conspiracy theory. At the intermediate level Tyndall argued in forceful but rational language the conspiracy, leadership and racial themes which barely disguised more extremist sentiments. Martin Webster in *National Front News* concentrated on racialist abuse of coloured immigrants interspersed with a few conspiracy themes designed to appeal to the racial populist beliefs of the rank and file.[26]

The political programme of the NF has represented the synthesis of Mosley's inter-war economic ideas, Chesterton's conspiracy theory and Leese's racial nationalism,[27] being anti-immigrant, anti-semitic, anti-American, anti-European Economic Community, anti-liberal, and anti-communist;[28] its most notorious policy was the compulsory repatriation of New Commonwealth immigrants. It tried to blend Mosley's positive utopia with the dreary negative obsessions of those who fell under the spell of *The*

---

[26] M. Billig, *Fascists* (London, 1978), pp. 124–90.

[27] R. Thurlow, 'The witches' brew', *Patterns of Prejudice*, 12, 3 (May–June 1978), pp. 1–8.

[28] 'For a new Britain', The Manifesto of the National Front, 1974 election.

Protocols of the Elders of Zion. The programme and ideology of the NF was essentially designed to broaden the outlook of the vast majority of members who had been attracted to the movement by its anti-immigrant policies. Indisputably its function was to convert racial populists into fascists. Given the very high turnover of members and the evidence of only partial success amongst those who remained, it did not achieve these aims. Neither did the near monopoly of propaganda output of the Tyndall-Webster clique after the expulsion of the Populists silence opposition within the NF. Factional opposition to Tyndall and Webster began to crystallize around Andrew Fountaine in 1978, as he once more became openly critical of the barely concealed nazism of the leadership, the growing involvement with skinheads and football hooligans, and the emergence of quite a high level of homosexual proclivities amongst members. He too was to split after the débâcle of the 1979 election to form the NF Constitutional Movement.

Bearing in mind the less than monolithic unity achieved by the ideology and propaganda, it nevertheless remained true that its purpose was to instil fascist and nazi beliefs into the NF in disguised form, as was most blatantly shown in Tyndall's version of Aryanism. Tyndall had cultivated connections not only with the Northern League and European nazism but through them with the racist States Rights party in the United States as well. The link between such geographically diverse groups was 'Anglo Saxonism', the British race.[29] For Tyndall it was the Anglo-Saxons who were solely responsible for all culture and civilization; without them, we should all still be living in mud huts, art would consist of primitive scrawlings and literature would speak to us 'in grunts'.[30]

A similar masking of basically nazi ideals was evident in Tyndall's critique of liberalism. For this Tyndall adapted the ideas of Oswald Spengler and applied them in what was a basically nazi critique of liberal society. The contradictions in such a synthesis of ideas were ignored since Spengler's emphasis on culture was incompatible with nazi racial determinism.[31] Tyndall adapted the

---

[29] J. Tyndall, 'In the cause of Anglo-Saxonism', *Spearhead*, Oct. 1979.
[30] Idem, 'Tyndall speaks, on Anglo-Saxon heritage' (tape NNF, 1981).
[31] R. Thurlow, 'Destiny and doom, Spengler, Hitler and "British" Fascism', *Patterns of Prejudice*, 15, 4 (Oct. 1981), pp. 17–33.

interpretation of Spengler, and his American interpreters Francis Parker Yockey and Revilo Oliver, to conclude that liberalism had sapped British national pride, willpower, the sense of destiny and awareness of race.[32] Verrall, like Arnold Leese before him, was to point out the incompatibility of Spengler's ideas with racial nationalist thought. For him there was a contradiction between the quest for infinitude by Faustian man and Spengler's pessimistic conclusion of the inevitable death of the culture; for racial nationalists race created culture, not the other way around.[33]

Tyndall also tried to make his anti-semitism more respectable. He tried to distance himself from what he termed gutter forms of anti-Jewish behaviour, while believing that there was a Jewish Question which should be openly and candidly discussed.[34] This did not relate to the problem of the State of Israel but to alleged Jewish power within the nation states of the world. The updating of the conspiracy mentality and the attempted removal of its *Protocols of the Elders of Zion* and nazi connotations was to be further developed by Verrall, who was to write several articles on a conspiracy theme suggesting the role of Jewish money behind the Bilderberg meetings of influential people, the Jewish and communist influences behind the 'race equality charlatans', and the importance of Lamarckianism in social thought.[35]

Verrall's most notorious contribution to NF propaganda was as the author 'Richard Harwood', whose 'Did Six Million really Die' was the most important of all the falsifications of history perpetrated by so-called revisionist historians with regard to Jewish genocide. For the NF it was important to deny the Holocaust because it was the attempted genocide of the Jews which had made racism such a disreputable subject since 1945. It was also more difficult to project the Jews as a threat if it was admitted that up to 6,000,000 of them had been slaughtered in the war. 'Harwood' was also the editor of 'Holocaust News', which quickly folded after he left the Directorate of the NF. His identity,

---

[32] J. Tyndall, 'Spengler updated', *Spearhead*, Aug. 1982; J. Tyndall, 'Spengler revisited', *Spearhead*, Mar. 1985; F. P. Yockey and R. Oliver, *The Enemy of Europe and The Enemy of our Enemies* (Reedy, W. Virginia, 1981).

[33] R. Verrall, 'What does Spengler have to say to us', *New Nation*, 2 (Autumn 1980).

[34] J. Tyndall, 'The Jewish Question; out in the open or under the carpet', *Spearhead*, Mar. 1976.

[35] R. Verrall, 'Technique of the "race equality" charlatans', *Spearhead*, Jan. 1978; idem, 'Karl Marx's Piltdown men', *Spearhead*, Feb. 1978.

long suspected by observers of the far right, was definitively proved when he sued the publishers, Historical Review Press, for royalties. This organization has now replaced the Britons Society as the chief publisher and distributor of neo-fascist, conspiracy and racialist literature; it has links to both the Northern League and the NF. Verrall's views on race and their relatively sophisticated presentation appear to be influenced by the interconnected American and European academic network which embraces the *Northlander* (Northern League journal), *Mankind Quarterly, Neue Anthropologie* and *Nouvelle École*.[36]

If the negative anti-semitic obsessions still lay just beneath the surface, Verrall provided the material for a more sophisticated presentation of racial nationalism. He combined arguments indicating the 'fraudulent' use of material by Jewish social scientists with a totally uncritical acceptance of the findings of 'true' racial scientists to prove an alleged Negro inferiority.[37] However, this case did not depend on the traditional superior-inferior dichotomy of the fascist racial nationalist tradition. Verrall now used the findings of socio-biology to indicate that genetic factors and not environment were responsible for differences in performance between racial groups in society and that it was a natural instinct to be racially prejudiced. This argument came perilously close to genetic determinism and implied a belief in the crudest form of Social Darwinism:[38] man was a pre-programmed bundle of instincts and reactions with little volition or control over his behaviour. This truly dismal creed was made even more gloomy by its racist assumptions: according to such a view, racial degeneration would be the inevitable outcome of ethnic cross-breeding, despite the obvious contradictions with the basic principles of Darwinian and Mendelian thought.

It is also interesting to note the fundamental difference between Mosleyite and NF views on race, culture and evolution. Mosley was a neo-Lamarckian with his views firmly grounded in Shaw's critique of Darwinism and, like Spengler, of the opinion that culture was more important than race. However, the essential difference was not in the supposed inferiority of non-European

---

[36] M. Billig, *Psychology, Racism and Fascism* (Birmingham, 1979).
[37] R. Verrall, 'The reality of Race', *Spearhead*, Apr. 1976.
[38] Idem, 'Sociobiology; the instincts in our genes', *Spearhead*, Mar. 1979; idem, 'Science is championing our creed of social nationalism', *New Nation*, 1 (Summer 1980).

cultures or races: Mosley, like Spengler, believed in pseudo-morphosis – that you could not impose different values on another culture without internal decomposition and decay. Other cultures, to the European, were not superior or inferior but different, and this led him to an apartheid perspective. To Mosley, European (Faustian) man through action and striving could achieve a qualitative leap in evolutionary form.[39] The quest for Superman had parallels with the more optimistic side of nazi ideas in the thought of Houston Stewart Chamberlain; while that of the NF was firmly rooted in the pessimistic degeneration hypothesis of Gobineau.[40]

The lowest level of propaganda in the NF was indistinguishable from the racialist tone of much of the neo-fascist press prior to its formation. Martin Webster, responsible for *National Front News*, kept up a dreary repetitive output of reports of murder, lootings, muggings and rapes in which race was seen as the key to behaviour and the New Commonwealth immigrant was made the scapegoat for the increase in crime;[41] compulsory repatriation of all immigrants was seen as the only response to the developing crisis of Britain's inner city areas.

With the split between Webster and Tyndall in 1980 and the retirement of Verrall, the NF went into a steep decline. There were severe financial problems and a drop in publishing activity. Webster tried to revive the movement through his copying of the tactics of the British Movement. However, the most interesting feature of the period after 1980 was the rise of a third generation of British fascists who led the NF on a new path. Self-styled 'Strasserites', they deliberately followed the policies of the main opposition to Hitler in the nazi party. After an internal row which finally led to the dismissal of Webster from the movement and the retirement of Brons, the long period of the ex-GBM dominance in the NF finally came to an end.

Strasserism, although represented quite improbably as 'national bolshevism' by John Tyndall, was an attempt to merge economic radicalism with populist policies. In its original German form it

---

[39] R. C. Thurlow, 'Some more peculiarities of the English', 'fascist views of evolution, race and national character', International Conference on History and Ideology of Anglo-Saxon Racial Attitudes, 1870–1970 (1982).

[40] G. C. Field, *Evangelist of Race* (New York, 1981), p. 223; M. Biddiss, *Father of Racist Ideology* (London, 1970), p. 244.

[41] 'Multi-racialism is murder', *National Front News*, 34.

was against finance capitalism, for the break-up of agricultural estates, and demanded the decentralization of political power and the replacement of parliamentary democracy by a corporate system. It represented a utopian radical dream which had more in common with the traditional and medieval forms of economic organization in Germany than modern industrial capitalism.[42] Its latter-day exponents tried to locate English tradition within which to place the new ideas. They found this in the national socialism of Robert Blatchford and the ideas of the Chesterbelloc circle, and they again, somewhat implausibly, tried to relate their views to those of the first NF Chairman of the Directorate, A. K. Chesterton.[43] The back-to-the-land, national syndicalism ideas sounded somewhat incongruous, particularly as they seemed to have connections with individuals who held distinctly un-Strasserite views. Otto Strasser (who spent much of his life after 1933 denouncing nazi murder squads and political violence) would have been less than happy seeing his new British protegés providing safe houses for alleged Italian fascist terrorists. The third generation of British fascists appears to seek a convergence of the political and underground tradition in a new guise.

[42] A. J. Lane, 'Nazi ideology: some unfinished business', *Central European History*, 7, 1 (Mar. 1974), p. 24.
[43] Baker, 'A. K. Chesterton, the Strasser brothers and the politics of the National Front'.

Conclusion:
The Sawdust Caesars

History always repeats itself. The first time as tragedy, the second as farce.

Karl Marx, *The Eighteenth Brumaire of Louis Napoleon*

Marx's view of the Bonapartist interludes in nineteenth-century French political history is distinctly appropriate for the history of British fascism. Whatever one may think of the highly controversial personality of Sir Oswald Mosley, there is little doubt that his involvement in British fascism proved the last straw for his prospects of a potentially highly successful career within the orbit of high politics. The self-destructive side of his personality, his inability to compromise on issues of policy and principle, his notorious short temper and failure to suffer fools gladly, and his poor judgement of men and events, represented the negative side of a brilliant but erratic man. The establishment rationalized these drawbacks in terms of the narrow Nonconformist puritanical moral ethos into which the great liberal tradition of British politics had sunk by the 1920s. As both Robert Skidelsky and Nicholas Mosley have pointed out, Mosley's revolt went beyond the refusal to play the game of party politics and was justified by him in terms of the need not only for a revolutionary transformation of the political system but in the nature of man himself.

Of course such views were utopian and unrealistic, given the straitjacket within which the British economy and political system operated within the inter-war period. Mosley's chosen vehicle to spearhead the assault on the establishment, the British Union of

Fascists, also failed to live up to such high expectations. It did motivate an interesting collection of talented idealists and political mavericks who were attracted by Mosley's dream in the drab Depression years; it also drew a motley crew of cranks, anti-semites, petty criminals, opportunists, thugs and literal social fascists who recognized an easy ride when they saw it. Mosley's organizational weaknesses, his personal flaws, his counter-productive obsession with secrecy and security-consciousness, and his failure to paper over the developing fissures within the movement after the collapse of membership in 1934, meant that the BUF increasingly attracted at all levels of the movement the deeply alienated or those who had chips on their shoulders. The original revolutionary economic and political programme of *The Greater Britain* increasingly came to play a secondary role to populist campaigns which appealed to local prejudices, of which the whipping up of anti-semitic sentiment in the East End of London was to become the most notorious.

Indeed, although there was a constant ideological core to the BUF in the 1930s, the move from emphasis on a revolutionary economic and political policy to anti-semitism and to preserving the peace of Europe, reflected both the changing sociological base of British fascism and the alteration in political emphasis from a pseudo-left-wing to a radical right organization. The supposed 'third way' in British politics in the 1930s was a shifting alliance of disparate groups and individuals in a movement which appeared to be in constant turmoil and crisis.

Mosley's failure in the 1930s was achieved partly by his own inadequacies, the lack of impact of the BUF, and astute political management by the National government. Mosley was a poor judge of events and had wretched luck in the 1930s. His much-vaunted economic expertise led him to misjudge the nature of the crisis; the mass unemployment of 1929–32 was not the final crisis of capitalism and the economy made a significant recovery in the 1930s. Only in regional blackspots too dependent on staple industries did recovery fail to occur. Even in these areas, apart from the cotton campaign in Lancashire in 1934 the BUF cut little ice. Mosley failed to accept that the British public had deep conservative instincts; that they preferred a slow economic decline to radical reform which would revolutionize the social fabric of the nation.

The Home Office, worried by increased conflict between communists and a rapidly growing fascist movement, began a policy of surveillance of the BUF in 1934. MI5 and Special Branch reported on developments, although their sources of information proved to be not as useful as elsewhere from the fascist political fringe. Mosley's counter-subversion strategy, which compromised the organizational efficiency of the BUF, was specifically designed to minimize damage caused by infiltration by the security service. The available evidence suggests that MI5 had a cosy view of Mosley and his activities in the 1930s; unlike the Communist party the BUF was seen as patriotic and by 1935 they were no longer seen as a threat. Renewed conflict between fascists and communists and Jews in 1936 did lead the government to act to maintain public order and political uniforms were banned. However, only in the special circumstances of spring 1940 did MI5's attitude to Mosley change overnight in the aftermath of the Tyler Kent affair.

The other major aspect of government management of the BUF was the publicity boycott. After the withdrawal of Rothermere's support in 1934 the BUF was given little coverage in the media and that only of a negative kind, associating it with political violence. From then until the publication of his autobiography in 1968, Mosley was kept beyond the pale, a political unperson. He was carefully shunted into a siding of British politics, and the BUF and later political movements associated with him became a dead end. Internment in the war meant that a general attitude of indifference to him was turned into a deep suspicion of his motives and activities; the always hostile view of the political left became an accepted view of society as a whole.

After 1968, however, Mosley's political reputation began to stage a recovery. Members of the establishment praised his autobiography and academics began to portray him as a visionary seer and prophet of Britain's decline, a trend which reached its peak in Robert Skidelsky's biography. The critical reception of Skidelsky's work was most interesting, however; some reviewers castigated the author for whitewashing the most controversial aspects of Mosley's career, most particularly the political violence and anti-semitism associated with fascism. Little was said about Skidelsky's stimulating and often brilliant exposition of Mosley's economic ideas and the interesting development of his thought after 1945. Nicholas Mosley's volumes, too, represented a fascinating account of his attempt to come to terms with the mind of his father, from a more critical perspective than that of Skidelsky. Both authors emphasized that Sir Oswald Mosley possessed a powerful intellect as well as brilliant oratorical skills. I suggest that such ability was woefully misused in British fascism; not only did Mosley talk a lot of nonsense in the 1930s but his self-imposed political isolation meant that the cause of economic and political radicalism was seriously weakened as a result.

Thus Mosley, the deeply flawed hero, was both the tragic victim and incomparably the most significant figure in the tradition. Indeed, without him British fascism would never have been even of minor significance in the politics of the inter-war period. Of all the sawdust caesars and tinpot Führers of the British fascist political tradition, only Mosley had the requisite political ability to look the part as a credible leader or the author of an alternative economic and political vision for Britain. He was also the most important political sugar-daddy of the tradition, who poured more money down the political drain of British fascism than any other single individual either before or since the Second World War.

Yet doubts still persist about Mosley. These centre around the obsessive secrecy with which he disguised his fascist activities. Mosley's strategy of releasing as little information as possible about the BUF was aided both by the accident of fire damage and by the fact that most of the documentation on the BUF disappeared into the innermost recesses of police files or the Security Service in 1940. Only now can part of this material be consulted in the Home Office Papers. Almost certainly the fact that Mosley's memory about the BUF seemed so selective had laudable motives. He wished to protect many who were true patriots from the negative perceptions which state and society held of the BUF even many years after the war.

However, such an attitude also meant that much which was embarrassing could be covered up. Recent discoveries have shown that much of the early growth and collapse of the BUF was underwritten by subventions from Mussolini, that Mosley had audacious plans based on the profits of commercial radio to fund the BUF, including a potentially highly controversial agreement with Hitler, and that the decision to intern British fascists was connected, however improbably, with the Tyler Kent affair. The present volume adds significantly to the internment saga by bringing together information and plausible arguments to show that this political decision derived chiefly from essentially accurate intelligence linking Mosley to Ramsay and much of the rest of the pro-German, anti-semitic and neo-fascist fringe. However, I feel that although this was the case MI5 misinterpreted the significance of this information in the hysterical atmosphere of spring 1940. British fascism was crushed in 1940 as a result of a number of factors: as a by product of Hitler's conquest of much of the rest of Europe, of Maule Ramsay's stupidity, and Mosley's obsession with secrecy. British fascists may have been politically naive, but the vast majority of them, like Mosley, were patriots not potential traitors.

If the BUF can be seen as part of a political tragedy, then the most important post-war variant on the fascist political tradition, the National Front, is deserving of the more negative side of Marx's aphorism. Although not all aspects of the NF can be considered fascist (indeed, much of the political shambles of the organization has derived from internal arguments about the significance of past blatant nazi associations of ex-GBM members), it nevertheless can be seen as directly connected to the tradition. In essence the NF represented a synthesis of three separate British fascist traditions: Mosley's BUF economic and political programme, the rationally expressed conspiracy theory mentality of conservative fascism, and the virulent racism of Arnold Leese's racial nationalism.

For much of its history after 1970 the NF was effectively controlled by a clique who derived their inspiration from the Leese tradition but who had learned to express their ideas in the more rational language of conservative fascism. To the fore now were the supposedly respectable ideas of A. K. Chesterton, whom many – although not all – among the second generation had derided when he was alive, which were used as a form of code to mask more extremist sentiments. However, faction fights with ex-Tories, racial populists and Strasserites, and the total lack of discipline of the ex-nazis, gave an often farcical aspect to the internal politics of the NF. The surprising thing about the NF is the fact that it made such an impact, given such blatant internal contradictions.

The history of British fascism can be traced back in those three separate traditions which failed to synthesize harmoniously in the NF. To most observers this somewhat seedy and dark underside in recent British history has now nearly collapsed, at least in organizational terms, although the NF and BNP continue to exist with much reduced numbers compared to the 1970s. State and left-wing opposition have effectively neutralized the open political threat posed by neo-fascist mass movements in racial populist clothing. However, some of the more militant and hard-line of the individuals associated with the revival of nazism in the 1960s appear to have organized a basically illegal underground tradition which has been implicated in racial violence and paramilitary training, and there are also connections with political terrorism and European movements. Although only of minor interest to the Security Service, compared to the more obvious terrorists and guerilla warfare problems posed by the IRA and various left-wing international organizations, the known presence in London of wanted Italian fascists suspected of terrorism, who have connections to most of the contemporary organizations on the neo-fascist fringe, is a worrying development.

British fascism then was small beer. At no stage could it be considered a credible political threat. In terms of numbers it reached its peak in 1934 when it had the backing of the Rothermere press and was alleged to have had 50,000 members. After 1945, it was only in the early 1970s that a movement which had some fascist associations approached half that size. The actual hard core membership probably never numbered more than a few thousand at any stage. During the 1930s single-issue populist campaigns, of which the two most significant were anti-semitism and anti-war, boosted membership and kept up flagging morale. After 1945 racial populism and anti-New Commonwealth immigration policies fulfilled the same function.

In terms of its impact on society and politics, British fascism has been over-rated. The BUF failed to put forward a slate of candidates in the 1935 election; and it polled disastrously in the three phoney war elections it fought. Only in the East End of London was there success of a kind; they polled respectably in three boroughs in both local and GLC elections in 1937, although no seats were won. Elsewhere local election results in 1938 and 1939 were abysmal. In spite of the reams of analysis of NF election results their performance, although better, has hardly been anything to crow about. Only a couple of councillors have ever been elected and only once, in 1973 at West Bromwich, did an NF candidate ever save his deposit in a parliamentary election.

The impact on government was also not of enormous significance. The street conflict between Jews, communists and fascists in 1936 explains the timing of the Public Order Act of 1936, although its terms were explicitly designed for wider significance than just keeping fascists under control. The long delay in providing legislation against racial incitement, despite the obvious and persistent use of loopholes in the existing law by fascists, did highlight an interesting aspect of domestic policy. Throughout the inter-war period and from 1945 to 1965 the Home Office was more concerned with safeguarding freedom of speech than with protecting ethnic minorities from racial abuse. Only where public order was threatened, as in 1936, or grave external threats intervened, as in 1940, or the situation was in danger of getting out of hand as during the 1960s, were stronger measures contemplated.

A kind of ethnocentric liberalism has generally been the norm in such matters, although the mouse that was British fascism was rapidly crushed in 1940 when the usual practice was swept away, habeas corpus effectively suspended and DR 18b (1a) was used to intern without trial many fascists. In a sense this represented the final irony for British fascism in the inter-war years. The BUF, whose principal *raison d'être* was to close down all other political parties if it ever got the chance, had its own activities terminated by its enemies in a summary fashion. Once the security of the political system appeared to be threatened, British fascism became one of the scapegoats as the traditional liberalism of the Home Office broke down for the duration of the war.

Bibliographical Note

There is already extensive bibliographical coverage of most aspects of British fascism and it is unnecessary to duplicate such material here. The purpose of this note is to guide readers to this information, to describe the new or little-used sources which have been important in the writing of this book and to comment briefly on the most valuable secondary literature.

PRIMARY MATERIAL

The new or little-used primary material to which the author would like to draw attention is as follows:

The PRO at Kew

Cabinet Papers: material relating to the internment of British fascists is to be found in Cab. 65, 66, 98, 128 and 129 series (for details see footnotes to chapters 9 and 10).

The 'Mosley Papers': intelligence and Home Office papers relating to the BUF and other fascist organizations between 1918 and 1948 are to be found in the HO 45, 144 and 283 series (for details see footnotes to chapters 3–10). Much of this material is available on microfilm.

Board of Deputies of British Jews

There are extensive collections relating to fascism, anti-semitism and Jewish defence organizations between 1918 and the present day, much of it held in the archive. The material is particularly good on lunatic fringe organizations like the IFL and NL. Infiltration of the BUF was less successful, although the Board of Deputies did receive weekly information of future fascist activities.

National Council for Civil Liberties Archive, University of Hull

A useful source of mainly anti-fascist responses from the 1930s to 1970s. See Boxes 40–42, 144, 172.

The Domvile Diaries, National Maritime Museum

See DOM 56 for the crucial lists of names and fragmentary gossip relating to the attempts to form an anti-war alliance of fascist, anti-semite and pro-nazi elements during the phoney war period.

Searchlight

This is the most interesting intelligence source for post-1945 British fascism. Gerry Gable is particularly keen that more academics should be made aware of his resources.

SECONDARY MATERIAL

For those who wish to study further the nature of British fascism, P. Rees, *Fascism in Britain: An Annotated Bibliography* (Hassocks, 1979), is the indispensable source reference book; see also his essay, 'Changing interpretations of British fascism', in K. Lunn and R. Thurlow (eds), *British Fascism* (London, 1980). The best bibliographies in the secondary literature are to be found in the books listed below.

G. Anderson, *Fascists, Communists, and the National Government* (London, 1983). A useful summary of the political violence associated with British fascism, but unfortunately needs to be supplemented by the material in the third release of Mosley papers which appeared within a few months of its publication.

D. Baker, 'A. K. Chesterton. The making of a British fascist', PhD thesis, University of Sheffield, 1982. A pioneering biography of a key fascist which successfully shows that political extremism may have roots in social and cultural factors and, in this case, is not due to personality disorder.

R Benewick, *The Fascist Movement in Britain* (London, 1972). Still useful on political violence but has been superseded by more recent work.

M. Billig, *Fascists* (London, 1978). More attention should have been given to the history and rather less to the ideology of the NF. This book, despite its dry over-academic presentation, is seminal to understanding that fascism emerges from normal cognitive processes and is not only the product of mental derangement or abnormal psychology.

H. Blume, 'Anti-semitic groups in Britain 1918–40', MPhil, University of Sussex, 1971. An extensive survey of political anti-semitism with an excellent bibliography.

J. Brewer, *Mosley's Men* (London, 1984). Although more readable and less tautological than the thesis from which it derives, the minute and unrepresentative sample of members should be treated with a great deal of caution. The discussion of ideology is insubstantial and for a study reputedly based on Birmingham the author fails to explain why Mosley was so successful in the city in the 1920s and such an abysmal failure in the 1930s. The sections on 'Fascism in Evesham' and the Hamm election campaign in 1966 in Handsworth fail to connect with the argument in the rest of the book.

C. Cross, *The Fascists in Britain* (London, 1961). Still valuable after twenty-five years, this well written and sensible analysis by a journalist is an excellent introduction to the subject.

N. Fielding, *The National Front* (London, 1981). An interesting study of racial violence but a rather mundane and long-winded treatment of the ideology and organization of the NF.

R. Griffiths, *Fellow Travellers of the Right* (London, 1983). A stimulating account of the Hitler appreciation society in the 1930s. The discussion of the 'extremists' needs to be supplemented with the material presented in the present work.

C. Holmes, *Anti-semitism in British Society 1876–1939* (London, 1979). The definitive study of the subject. The most substantial criticism of this work is that, like all other published surveys of anti-semitism, the important activities of Maule Ramsay in 1939–40 are not analysed.

C. Husbands, *Racial Exclusionism and the City* (London, 1983). A good survey of urban racialism and a useful and thought-provoking antidote to those who would apply uncritically simplistic fascist or nazi labels to the NF.

G. Lebzelter, *Political Anti-Semitism in England 1918–1939* (London, 1979). As with Holmes, it would have been more logical to have the terminal date at 1940 rather than 1939. The activities of the NL and RC and their significance are not assessed and the interesting thesis which attempts to apply the nazi genocide model to practically all forms of British anti-semitism is questionable.

K. Lunn and R. Thurlow (eds), *British Fascism* (London, 1980). A useful compendium of views on many aspects of British fascism prior to the release of the PRO material. See in particular the essays by Holmes, Rawnsley and Skidelsky.

W. Mandle, *Anti-Semitism and the British Union of Fascists* (London, 1965). Now superseded by Holmes's essay 'Anti-semitism and the BUF', in Lunn and Thurlow, *British Fascism*.

N. Mosley, *Beyond the Pale* (London, 1983). Although not as good as the first volume, *Rules of the Game*, about his relationship with his father, this is a useful and frank discussion of Oswald Mosley's fascism. There is an interesting account of two of the more dubious aspects of the cover-up of fascist activities, Mussolini's funding and the air-time project.

S. Rawnsley, 'Fascism and fascists in Britain in the 1930s', PhD thesis, University of Bradford, 1983. Much better than Brewer's attempt to study 'Mosley's men', although the regional bias of his sample means that not too many general conclusions should be drawn. Although interesting, the discussion of fascist ideology is somewhat misleading and attempts to apply Billig's model for the NF to the BUF is questionable.

R. Skidelsky, *Oswald Mosley* (London, 1975). Although not as good as the brilliant first volume of his biography of Keynes, this is far more than a whitewash of a Blackshirt. It is excellent on Mosley's political career and the historical development of his ideas but rather more debateable and controversial on anti-semitism and political violence in the BUF. On this latter topic, see his modified views in Lunn and Thurlow, *British Fascism*. While admirably putting the case for Mosley, Skidelsky has not been critical enough of his subject and his undoubted weaknesses to give an entirely objective picture.

S. Taylor, *The National Front in English Politics* (London, 1982). A solid, if somewhat pedestrian, study of the political impact of the NF.

M. Walker, *The National Front* (London, 1977). A good and lively account of the first ten years of the NF by a journalist with a sound historical training and perspective. Needs bringing up to date.

P. Wilkinson, *The New Fascists* (London, 1981). Stimulating but thin on empirical material.

Readers should also be aware of the important article by Gerry Webber on 'Patterns of membership and support for the British Union of Fascists', *Journal of Contemporary History*, 19 (1984), pp. 575–606, and several forthcoming publications by him on this theme and the British Right between 1918 and 1940.

Index